C000161890

Bicycle History

A Chronological Cycling History of People, Races, and Technology

1860-2015

James L. Witherell, M.S. Ed

McGann Publishing
McMinnville, Oregon

Published by McGann Publishing
P.O. Box 864
McMinnville, OR 97128
USA

McGann
Publishing

ISBN: 978-0-9859636-5-1
Printed in the United States of America

To Sue, whose support and faith in me made this book possible.

and

To my wonderful mother, who is always there.

"Get a bicycle. You will not regret it if you live."
                                                    —Mark Twain

Table of Contents

Introduction

Several years ago I began collecting random cycling-related facts as part of another project. Before long, I'd accumulated hundreds of these little tidbits and they kind of took on a life of their own. Before I knew it, I had enough of them to justify their own book. I basically collected anything that I thought was interesting, hoping that other people would find it interesting too.

Gradually I came to realize that the contents of this book reflect my own interests, which tend to be in the area of road cycling and racing. Still that doesn't mean it's easy to describe its contents. While there's a lot about Europe's three grand tours—especially the Tour de France—I've also tried to include information about as many English-speaking riders as possible. And major American races. And advances in technology. And bicycles during times of war, and people who can best be described as "characters." You get the idea.

Including cycling trivia that ranges from outrageous to obituaries, this book is meant to be both entertaining and informative. While the "entertaining" part hopefully speaks for itself, I'd like to elaborate a bit on the "informative" part. Any undertaking of this magnitude is bound to be haunted by any number of random errors, and while I had tried round them all up and correct them, some inevitably got away. And then there are the "facts" that keep changing: the spelling of a Belgian rider's name or the "official" length of a race or one of its stages, for example. For an excellent discussion of "official" distances, see pages 302 and 303 of Matt Rendell's *Blazing Saddles: The Cruel and Unusual History of the Tour de France.*

Even though I have made every effort to ensure the accuracy of my entries, I recommend that this book be used for entertainment purposes, and maybe to settle the occasional bar bet. Those doing any type of scholarly research should verify the enclosed information elsewhere—always a good idea in any undertaking of this nature. Suggestions and corrections supported by sufficient information will be welcomed. Nitpickers and the hypercorrect will be ignored.

The title says this book is a chronological look at cycling history, and it is. Sort of. Probably a more accurate description of this book's contents would have been "year-by-year," since the entries contained within a particular year are arranged randomly.

Last but certainly not least, I'd like to thank Bill McGann for making this little book possible. I recently had the distinct pleasure of collaborating with Bill and his wife, Carol, on their wonderful book, *The Story of the Tour de France*, and he sensed that I may have been sitting on something worth publishing. We'll see. I hope you like it.

Chapter 1

1860–1899
Off and Rolling

1860 • Ignaz Schwinn is born in Hardheim, Germany.

1865 • Henri Desgrange, future organizer of the Tour de France, and his twin brother Georges are born in Paris on January 31.

1866 • In April, 23-year-old Pierre Lallement files for a United States patent for a two-wheeler with cranks affixed to the front hub, an idea he'd come up with four years earlier while working in Nancy in eastern France. Frustrated with his lack of success, Lallement returns to France in 1868 and soon opens a bike shop in Paris.

1868 • What is generally believed to have been the world's first bicycle race is run in a park in western Paris, held on May 31, 1868 in the Parc de St.-Cloud. The 1,200-meter "track" race is won by James Moore, a British veterinary student residing in Paris. Moore, riding a machine built by the event's sponsor, Michaux et Compagnie, completes the event in 3 minutes 50 seconds, outsprinting the favorite named Drouet, and eight other racers, to take home the 600-franc first prize.
 • In November Miss Julie nips Miss Louise in the first women's bicycle race. The race's four contestants, all of whom wear "unusually short skirts" for the event, compete in Bordeaux, France.
 • Thomas R. Pickering of New York substitutes an iron tube for the solid iron backbone on the Pickering and Davis "American velocipede."
 • The Hanlon Brothers acrobatic troupe performs riding tricks on bicycles. On July 7 the Hanlons are granted a patent for their invention of solid rubber rings that go around the wheels to quiet them and prevent slippage. The group also claims credit for improvements such as an adjustable crank and seat.

1869 • On November 7 the first bicycle road race, which takes the riders from the Arc de Triomphe in Paris to Rouen, 134 kilometers (83 miles) to the northwest, is sponsored by the newspaper *Paris Vélocipède Illustré*, with James Moore again the clear winner over more than 200 other racers, including 4 women. His velocipede has been constructed by the governor of St. Pelagis prison, and features ball bearing hubs (the bearings had been made by the inmates) and solid rubber tires. His victory is not an easy one however. Several times the Englishman was said to have collapsed due to lack of food. "Spectators revived him with food and wine,"[1] and he made his way back up through the remaining 32 riders to win the race and its 100-franc purse. Again riding a machine with a front wheel more than one meter in diameter, Moore finishes the event in 10 hours 25 minutes. Miss America, a small woman from Lyon who was married to English racer Rowley B. Turner, and herself probably of English descent, also competes in the event.[2] She comes in 29th out of the event's 33 finishers.

- An acrobat known as Dr. Jenkins rides a bicycle across Niagara Falls on a high wire.

1870 • Not far behind the French in their passion for cycle racing are the Italians. On February 2, the newly-formed Veloce Club Fiorentino puts on Italy's first road race which is run from Florence to Pistoia, a distance of roughly 32 kilometers (20 miles). This race is also won by a foreigner, but this time it's a young American named Rynner Van Neste, aboard a Compagnie Parisienne velocipede, who captures the victory,[1] undoubtedly making the 17-year-old the first American to win a European bicycle race. For his win, which he accomplishes in 2 hours 12 minutes, Van Neste is awarded a gold medal and a revolver.

- The Starley Ariel high wheeler, with its radially spoked front wheel, becomes England's first mass-produced all-steel bicycle.

- W. H. J. Grout patents the radially spoked, nipple-adjusted bicycle wheel. The previous year France's Eugene Meyer was said to have built the first bicycle wheel to use tensioned wire spokes.

1871 • Future Tour de France winner Maurice Garin is born on March 23.

1872 • Friedrich Fischer begins producing steel ball bearings. By 1883 Fischer will have perfected a process for milling ball bearings of uniform sizes.

1873 • Dr. James Moore sets what may be the first ever hour record, covering 23.331 kilometers (14.465 miles) on a pennyfarthing.

1877 • In the spring, "A.D. Chandler, Frank W. Weston, and several other men from Boston imported and rode English machines. These men were enthusiasts, but Weston was the greatest enthusiast of them all. He organized the firm of Cunningham, Heath & Co., the first bicycle dealers, and installed the late 'Happy Days' Pitman as the first instructor in the art of bicycle riding. He started the first bicycle paper in the United States and was the prime mover in the organization of the Boston Bicycle Club, the first club in America."[1]

1878 • The first American bicycle race takes place in Boston's Beacon Park (now the Beacon Park Freight Yard) on May 24. It is won by Harvard student C.A. Parker.

1879 • The Bicyclette, the first bicycle to feature a chain-driven rear wheel, is introduced by Henry J. Lawson. By powering the rear wheel, the rider enjoys much smoother steering since the front wheel is unaffected by pedaling.
  • On July 5, the *New York Times* runs a short, front-page piece about Wentworth Rollins who is in the first days of a week-long bicycle trip. Rollins plans to ride north along the Hudson River to Saratoga 175 miles away, making stops at Tarrytown, Sing Sing, Poughkeepsie, Hyde Park, Hudson, Albany, and Troy.

1880 • The League of American Wheelmen is formed on May 31 in Newport, R.I., as cycling is becoming hugely popular, both as a means of recreation and as a sport. On September 19 the organization meets at the Metropolitan Hotel in Boston where representatives of 14 bicycle clubs adopt a crucial rule defining an amateur rider:

> An amateur is a person who has never competed in an open competition, or for a stake, or for public money or for gate money, or under a false name, or with a professional for a prize, or where gate money is charged, or has never professionally taught or pursued bicycling or other athletic exercises as a means of livelihood.[1]

1881 • In Europe, it's the French who are leading the way in competitive cycling. The *Union Vélocipédique de France* (UVF) is formed and holds the first French national championship on a dirt track in the Place du Carrousel in Paris.
  • The freewheel and "rim acting brake" appear.
  • Future Tour de France winner Louis Trousselier is born on June 29.

1882 • Sixteen-year-old George M. Hendee wins the League of American Wheelmen's first national championship, which covers a mile, at the LAW's second annual convention in Boston. The well-to-do Hendee, who passed up college at Yale to pursue bike racing, would repeat as national champion for the next four years. In 1902 he and former bike racer Carl O. Hedstrom would start the Indian Motorcycle Company in Springfield Massachusetts.
  • Future Tour de France winner Lucien Mazan is born on October 18. He would adopt the surname Petit-Breton to keep his watchmaker father from learning of the profession he'd chosen.

1883 • "A. H. Overman came into the market with his Victor tricycle, the first American three-wheeler. The tricycle was then a very popular machine and formed an important link in bicycle development. It was made in many different shapes and sizes. There were front, rear, and side steerers, sociables, on which the riders sat side by side, tandems, the woman occupying the front seat, and a few machines for three or four riders or more."[1]

1884 • Thomas Stevens is the first person to ride (and push, pull and carry) a bicycle across the United States. It takes Stevens 103½ days to get his 75-pound, high-wheel "ordinary" from Oakland, Calif., to Boston.
  • Future Tour de France winner Henri Cornet is born on August 4.
  • Future Tour de France winner Gustave Garrigou is born on September 24.
  • "The first distinctly American innovation in bicycle design was the American Star, brought out in 1884. It was called a safety, but had the big wheel of the 'ordinary,' with a little wheel in front, which gave immunity from 'headers.' Instead of cranks, the machine was driven by lever and clutch action."[1]

1885 • Henri and Ernest Peugeot's "*Les Fils de Peugeot Frères*"—which had been making wire hoops for women's clothing—begins mass-producing bicycles in the Beaulieu area of France's Le Doubs region. Cycles Peugeot quickly flourishes and would later dominate the Tour de France during its early years.
  • Back in Paris, the Avenue de la Grande Armée is known as l'Avenue du Cycle, as it sports no fewer than 30 bike shops.
  • In May American Champion John S. Prince of Washington, D.C., defeats four trotting horses in Charlotte, N.C. For beating his world record by covering a mile and four yards in 2:35½, Prince is awarded "a beautiful medal."
  • Eugène Christophe, the first man to officially wear the Tour de France's yellow leader's jersey, is born on January 22.
  • John Kemp Starley debuts his Rover "safety" bicycle; it is similar to the Bicyclette, but features a diamond frame, which remains the basis of virtually all bicycles to this day. The machine is manufactured by Starley & Sutton of Coventry, England.

1886 • "But the 'ordinary' maintained its supremacy until 1886 or later, when it had reached its highest state of perfection. Into it had been incorporated all possible grace and refinement. The weight of the racer had been cut down to twenty, and even sixteen pounds, for the fifty-five-inch machine. The Rover was placed upon the American market in 1886 and caused no little excitement among the cycling fraternity. As soon as it was tried out it found many adherents, although many experienced riders refused to come down from their perch on the high bicycle until long after the safety had been firmly established."[1]
  • Future Tour de France winner Firmin Lambot is born on March 14.
  • On June 6 riders Brooks and Woodside defeat a "long distance rider" named Anderson 957 miles to 953 miles in a 72-hour race at Madison Square Garden.
  • S. P. Hollingsworth sets the amateur 24-hour record for America and Great Britain at 281.9 miles. Hollingsworth's lap times on the 17.8-mile circuit in Indianapolis range from 1 hour 3 minutes to 1 hour 35 minutes. The previous American record had been 259½ miles, the British record, 266 miles. During

his ride the 25-year-old rider loses six pounds. His actual riding time during the 24-hour period is 21 hours 23 minutes.

1887 • Future Tour de France winner François Faber is born on January 26.
   • Future Tour de France winner Octave Lapize is born on October 24.

1888 • An innovation that rivals even chain drive is the first pneumatic tire to gain widespread acceptance. The invention of John Boyd Dunlop (1840–1921) features a one-way valve that permits only inflation of the tubular tire, which is stuck to a wooden rim with glue. The new tire is expensive and prone to punctures, but it is light, lively and very fast. Dunlop would partner with Irishman Harvey Du Cros to start the Pneumatic Tyre Company, and French bicycle manufacturer Gustave Adolphe Clément would purchase exclusive sales rights to the invention.
   • In late summer, the world championship bicycle tournament is held in Buffalo, N.Y., at the International Fair. H. C. Crocker of Newton, Mass., wins the one-mile professional handicap in 2:43⅖, and the first heat of the three-mile professional race. William A. Rowe of Lynn, Mass., wins the two-mile professional handicap in 5:54⅗, and the one-mile professional final in 2:52⅗. Englishman F. W. Allard of Coventry wins the two-mile professional rovers' handicap, with his countryman Jack Lee of Nottingham second. Allard and Lee also win the one-mile professional tandem free-for-all in 3:16⅗. During the three-mile amateur race, the seat of W. E. McCune of Worcester, Mass., breaks causing him to crash headfirst, collecting Van Sicklen of Chicago and Kingsland of Baltimore. All three are "badly, but not dangerously, hurt." The race is won by Will Mindle of Millsbury, Mass., in 9:27. Jules Dubois of Paris, France, wins the one-mile professional rovers' race in 2:51⅗.
   • Future Tour de France winner Leon Scieur is born on March 19.
   • On April 28 English cyclist Richard Howell defeats America's William A. Rowe by 20 yards in the world championship one mile race at Wolverhampton's Molineux Grounds. Two weeks earlier Howell had won the five-mile event. The 10-mile race was scheduled for May 12.
   • Future Tour de France winner Odile Defraye is born on July 14.

1889 • Future Tour de France winner Henri Pélissier is born on January 22.
   • Lottie Stanley protests that she is offered $50 in prize money—the same as the non-winning riders—for winning a women's six-day bicycle race at Madison Square Garden in February. She settles for the $50 plus an IOU for $100 and a bicycle.
   • Ellis B. Freatman of Rochester, N.Y., dies three weeks after competing in a bike race between Buffalo and Rochester. Three days before the race, he'd complained of a cold, and during the event the racers got caught in a snowstorm for ten miles. Freatman "finished eleventh in the race and was the fourth man of the Genesee Club to cross to cross the line, making the distance of seventy-four miles in 6:27:00. He never recovered from the effects of the race."[1]

1890 • Future Tour de France winner Philippe Thys is born on October 8.
- The first rudimentary derailleurs appear around this time, even though professionals in the Tour de France wouldn't be allowed to use them for nearly another 50 years.
- William Bartlett of the North British Rubber Company invents the clincher tire. The edges of the tire fit under the edges of the rim and do not contain wire.
- Edward Checkley, a Long Island, N.Y., medical student, rides from New York to Chicago in 14 days 6 hours 25 minutes, breaking the record of "Nelson" by more than 17 hours. It should be noted that Checkley "traveled a much greater distance and over much harder roads than Nelson took."[1]

1891 • The Disc Wheel Company of London begins producing (what else?) disc bicycle wheels.
- On August 14, Frenchman Charles Terront (Michelin) aboard a 21-kilogram (46-pound) British Humber bicycle, wins the initial edition of Paris–Brest–Paris (sponsored by *Le Petit Journal*) averaging 10 mph, and beating Dunlop's Joseph Laval (who calls himself Jiel-Laval), the first of the other 205 participants, by more than nine hours. Frenchmen Édouard and André Michelin use the race and Terront's machine to introduce their inflatable wire-bead bicycle tire. It's said that the pair began running ads touting the benefits of their pneumatic tire even before the race was over. Within five years, inflatable tires would be on almost every bicycle sold.
- A race from Bordeaux to Paris is organized by *Veloce-Sport*. It's won by British amateur Georges-Pilkington Mills. Not to be outdone by the French, in 1892 the Italians and *La Bicicletta* put on the 513-kilometer (318-mile) Milan–Turin bicycle race, which is won by Enrico Sauli in 26½ hours.
- With the first Tour de France still 12 years away, managers at the Raleigh bicycle company of Nottingham, England realize that having racers on their cycles being first across the finish line is a good way to promote their product. They sign American ace August Zimmerman, who'd win 100 races in 1894, earning him an unheard of $40,000. "The prestige this brought to the firm," said one writer, "was incalculable." Its eventual squad of well-supported top riders would make Raleigh the first successful international sponsor in cycle racing.
- In July the Right Reverend A. Cleveland Coxe of Buffalo, N.Y., writes a letter to the editor of the *New York Times* claiming that his words in an earlier piece had been taken out of context when he was quoted as saying, "Women on bicycles look like witches on broomsticks." Reverend Coxe chastised the paper, saying "that to pick out a word or two from a deeply serious and well-studied lecture, and to treat them apart from time, place and circumstance, with no reference to the argument in which they were embedded, is not fair to any speaker." The reverend does note in his letter, however, that he is "still of the opinion that bicycling is grossly immodest as well as ridiculous for women."[1]
- Three months later the Ladies' Cycling Club of New York votes unanimously to adopt a riding uniform which includes: "a yachting cap, a tailor-made waist, tight-fitting, and a straight skirt of walking length. The color throughout is

dark blue, and the material serge." During their rides, the ladies will be followed by a gentleman who will "be on hand to assist in case of accident…," and to "…distribute professional pointers as he sees fit."[2]

1892 • The wired-on tire is invented by New Yorkers T. A. Brown and G.F. Stillman. The wires in the tire bead fit in the shoulders of the rim.
  • In Italy, Giovanni Battista Pirelli introduces the Milan Pneumatic Tire, his version of the wire-bead tire.
  • In France and neighboring Belgium long races between major cities become hugely popular. In eastern Belgium, a race which continues to this day, takes the racers south from Liège to the city of Bastogne and then back to Liège. The first three editions of this race, now nicknamed *La Doyenne* (The Old One), are held between 1892 and 1894 and are all won by Belgium's Leon Houra.
  • English cyclist R. L. Edge rides from Land's End, Cornwall to John O'Groat's House in northeastern Scotland in 4 days 40 minutes, beating the old record by more than 10½ hours.
  • A certain Judge Morehouse acquits Jeremiah B. Osborne of riding in Fairfield, Connecticut, on Sunday, saying that the current law does not prohibit a person from riding on the Sabbath. Osborne had been charged with "indulging in the vain sport and recreation of riding a bicycle on Sunday."

1893 • Future Tour de France winner Lucien Buysse is born on February 22.
  • The International Cyclists Association is formed to regulate the sport. One of the first orders of business at the ICA—which is the forerunner to the *Union Cycliste Internationale* (UCI)—is to hold the world championship competition that year in Chicago. Scheduled to coincide with the World's Columbian Exposition, the competition is open only to amateur men and features races of one mile and ten miles. Both events are won by Arthur "August" Zimmerman of Asbury Park, N.J., making him the first undisputed world champion.[1]
  • The League of American Wheelmen suspends Charles M. Murphy, saying that he violated his amateur status by asking for, and receiving, cash instead of accepting a medal for winning a trainer race in Philadelphia.
  • On May 11, 28-year-old Henri Desgrange officially attempts an unpaced hour record. Most sources say that Desgrange was the first bicycle racer to attempt the hour record, but one account has him breaking the mark of 35.110 kilometers (21.82 miles) set by 1890 Italian champion Carlo Braida. It should also be noted that another source has a pair of Englishmen setting hour records well before Desgrange made his mark: James Moore covered 23.33 kilometers (14.47 miles) in 1873 and Herbert Lidell Costis rode 32.46 kilometers (20.17 miles) in 1882. One thing is certain about Henri Desgrange's 60 minutes of suffering in Neuilly at the month-old Buffalo track (named after the popular American Wild West shows which had recently been put on at the site): they were rewarded with a total distance of 35.325 kilometers (21.937 miles).
    "I reached into the depths of my willpower," said Desgrange of his effort. Later, he would write:

> When I got off my machine at the end of the 60 minutes, I wasn't only the world recordman for the hour on a bicycle, I was an object of horror to the people who took care of me after my 35.325 km. I was filthy, streaked with oil and snot, covered with dust; in short, nobody would touch me with a pair of tongs. My director bought me lunch at la Porte Maillot, a sumptuous meal, 2.50 francs a head; he also offered me several bank notes which I could cash for gold Louis; because of my amateur status I refused instantly. But my God! How happy I was.[2]

Desgrange said that he did not expect his record to stand for long and that he had set the mark for the sake of the sport—to give others something to shoot for. During the ride he carried a bottle of milk on his handlebars in case he bonked.

- Riding on horseback, Captain "Buffalo Bill" Cody loses a race against two cyclists at the Velodrome de la Seine in Paris. Mr. Gaby and Mr. Fournier, riding a tandem bicyclette, cover 178 kilometers, compared to 173 for Capt. Cody. During the race, which runs for two hours the first day and four hours the second, Cody rides six different horses.
- In October Frenchman Charles Terront cycles from St. Petersburg, Russia to Paris, where he's cheered upon his arrival at the Buffalo Velodrome. Terront covered 2,000 miles in 12 days, and was shot at by a drunken German peasant during his ride.
- Frederick T. Bidlake (GBR) sets the 24-hour tricycle record at 410 miles (660 kilometers) at the Herne Hill Velodrome in South London. Bidlake's record would still stand when he dies in 1933.
- In the fall Mrs. Angeline Allen of Newark, New Jersey, rides "her safety bicycle wearing a 'natty uniform as near like that worn by men as possible.' Her lower limbs were all but exposed, covered only by 'knee high leggings.'" During the summer Mrs. Allen had appeared at an "Asbury Park resort wearing a shockingly skimpy costume that one journalist branded an 'apology for a bathing suit.'" She was promptly escorted back to the bathing house by the police.[3]

1894 • The Saint Louis Refrigerator Company claims to have produced the first all-aluminum bicycle frame called the LU-MI-NUM.
- Frenchman Jules Dubois covers 38.220 kilometers (23.75 miles) on the Buffalo track, beating Henri Desgrange's hour mark by nearly 3 kilometers (1.9 miles). Dubois would win the French national championship the following year.
- Louis Callahan of the Press Cycling Club sets a world record for 25 miles during the Martin road race in Buffalo, N.Y. Callahan's new standard of 1:10:37 betters the previous mark of 1:11:28½ set by Nat Butler less than a month earlier.
- In his book *La Tête et les Jambes* (*The Head and the Legs*; Paris; L. Pochy, 1894), which is written in the form of letters to a fictitious young rider, Henri Desgrange stresses that the racer is best served by not only by being in top physical condition but also by thinking through each situation in which he finds

himself. Saying that a certain rider "will never win the Tour because he is rid-ing with his legs and not with his head" would become one of Desgrange's frequently-heard refrains as the Tour de France matured and grew in stature during the early 1900s. That one racer or another "will never win the Tour because he is not willing to suffer," would become another of his famous barbs. As a former racer, Henri Desgrange would certainly have little sympathy for other racers. A few years later Desgrange would write a novel, *Alphonse Mar-caux* (Paris; L. Pochy, 1899), about racers competing on the area's velodromes.

- Future Tour de France winner Ottavio Bottecchia is born on August 1.
- Shozaburo Shimano is born in Sakai, Japan.
- The Spalding Bicycle Company of 126-130 Nassau Street in New York offers an installment plan for the purchase of its $125 machines: $30.00 down and $10.00 a month.
- The Velo Dog Revolver is offered as one solution to being chased by man's best friend.

1895 • In his book about the 1904 Tour de France[1] Jacques Seray relates the tale of how Théophile Joyeux became the first Frenchman to ride around his beloved six-sided country. It seems that by the mid-1890s Charles Terront and another Frenchman named Jean Corre had developed a fierce rivalry (in 1893 Terront had beaten Corre by 9 kilometers in a 1,000 kilometer track race which lasted 41 hours), so Corre had planned to outdo Terront and establish a name for himself by being the first rider to cycle around France. When Corre was forced to postpone his Tour of France because of fatigue from the Bordeaux–Paris race, Joyeux seized the opportunity. On May 11, 1895, Théophile Joyeux, rid-ing a shaft-driven Metropole Acatene, began his clockwise trek around the six sides of France. Slowed by rain in the early part of his trip, Joyeux completed his 4,429-kilometer (2,750-mile) odyssey in 19 days. Four months later, Jean Corre rode his Tour of France, covering 5,102 kilometers (3,170 miles) in 25 days.

- Ignaz Schwinn, with the financial backing of meat packer Adolph Arnold, be-gins producing bicycles in his new factory on the corner of Lake and Peoria Streets in Chicago, Ill. The Schwinn Bicycle Company would officially remain "Arnold, Schwinn and Company" until 1967 even though Schwinn would buy out Arnold in 1908.
- The United States has two patent offices, one just for advances in bicycle tech-nology.
- On November 26, Charles M. Hanson of Peace Dale, R.I., receives patent num-ber 550,409 for his "attachment for bicycle pedal" invention. The device con-sists of a four-arm clip that mounts to the pedal and engages a corresponding cleat attached to the sole of a special shoe.
- All of the recent advancements in technology have made the bicycle very fast, indeed—too fast for the likes of some people, and Britain bans road racing in order to keep "fast-moving vehicles" from startling horses. The ruling causes great numbers of British racers to get up early on Sunday mornings, dress in

black and meet on quiet country roads to compete in the local time trial. The road racing ban wouldn't be lifted until several years after the second world war, about the time that Great Britain fielded its first major effort in the Tour de France. In October, the North Road Cycling Club puts on the first time trial in England where the discipline remains a very popular type of competition to this day.

- Schweinfurter Praezisions Kugellagerwerke Fichtel und Sachs, which special-izes in bicycle hubs and ball bearings, is founded in Schweinfurt, Germany.
- Canadian Albert Weaver invents and patents a side-by-side tandem bicycle. The sociable machine, which costs $150, is made by the Punnett Cycle Manu-facturing Co. of Rochester, N.Y.
- Col. Albert A. Pope of Boston, one of America's pioneer bicycle manufacturers, believes that having riders set long-distance riding records on his machines is the way to sell bicycles. One of his advertisements notes that Charles Terront, the French distance ace, rode one of Pope's Columbia bicycles "363 miles in 26 consecutive hours."
- More than 10,000 people turn out for the opening of the new velodrome at Manhattan Beach in New York City. The track, which is three laps to the mile, is made of cement and has banked turns that are fully six feet high. It is located directly behind the Manhattan Beach Hotel.
- In Paris Gaston Rivierre rides 523 miles 1,044 yards to break the 24-hour mark of 514 miles 750 yards set by Constant Huret a month earlier.
- Eddie C. "the Cannon" Bald of Buffalo, N.Y., lowers his own one-mile world record to 2:04 riding a 21½-pound road bike in San Jose, Calif. He also lowers the two-mile record to 4:15⅕ and, in doing so, lowers the mark for the flying mile to 1:59⅖ along the way. In August 1893 he had won all nine races he en-tered at a meet in Troy, N.Y. Bald was born on January 27, 1874 and weighs 170 pounds (77 kilograms).
- Charles Morel of France begins the manufacture and marketing of a folding bicycle.
- Just before Christmas, Tiffany & Co. takes "one of the latest standard models [Columbia] for men" and heavily silver plates its "handle bars, pedal bars and pedals, the bars holding the seat, and the rivets and bolt heads." Not stopping there, the *New York Times* adds that "the handles are of carved ivory, partly encased in chased silver. All the joints of the frame are encased in solid silver, etched and chased in repoussé style. On the saddle are dainty silver ornaments, with shell scrollwork in the style of Louis Quinze. To go with this is a search-light lantern which will be ornamented with chased silver. The entire silver work was done by hand." And the coming year promises even more: "A ladies wheel is now being prepared. It will be much more elaborate. The frame will be entirely covered with chased silver, while the lantern will probably be fur-ther decorated with precious stones." The brief article concludes with, "Tiffany & Co. announces that these wheels are merely the forerunners of very costly bicycles that will be finished before the next season begins. Designs are now being prepared for the ornamentation of wheels with gold and precious stones.

These are all for the benefit of the smart set, who have long been desirous of having something better than the standard products."[2]

• Diamond Jim Brady buys one of the later machines for singer and actress Lillian Russell. The gold-plated machine, which comes in a plush-lined leather case, has handlebars inlaid with mother-of-pearl and rubies, diamonds, and sapphires in the spokes and hubs. It costs more than $3,000.00.

• Manufacturers display some interesting products at the January bicycle show in Madison Square Garden. One is the Crawford Manufacturing Company of Hagerstown, Md., which is displaying its bicycle with either Crescent steel rims or Plymouth interlocked joint wood rims. The Meyers Company of New York offers a machine with a frame made of polished bamboo which is connected by Johnwhit fittings. The wooden bikes come with Simplex rims which are trued by making adjustments at the hub.

• Interest in the puncture-proof tire heats up. Three entries in this area come from Boston mechanical engineer John Mariani, the Puncture-Proof Tire Company of Quincy, Ill., and the (unnamed) mayor of Brooklyn.

1896 • The Tonk Manufacturing Company of Chicago introduces the Old Hickory, a bike made of 16-ply laminated hickory. The machine's frame, fork, rims, handlebar, fenders and chain guard are all made of hickory. The 17.5-pound bike is joined by nickel-plated lugs and costs $100.00.

• Early in the year Théo Vienne and Maurice Perez, two mill owners in the city of Roubaix, write a letter to Paul Rousseau, director of Le Vélo newspaper, asking him to consider putting on a race between Paris and their northern-France city. The new race, the pair explains in their letter, could be used as a training run for the much longer Bordeaux–Paris event which would be held four weeks later, adding that Paris–Roubaix, at "roughly 280 kilometers…would be child's play for the future participants of Bordeaux–Paris,"[1] and the "Queen of the Classics" was born. The first Paris–Roubaix is held on April 19, 1896—Easter Sunday—and is won by German rider Josef Fischer. Of the 100 riders who sign up for the race, about half—including future Tour de France founder Henri Desgrange—fail to show up for the start.

• On August 9, Evan E. Anderson rides a mile in 1:03 drafting a locomotive and one car on the St. Louis, Chicago, and St. Paul Railroad.

• "Let me tell you what I think of bicycling. It has done more to emancipate women than anything else in the world. It gives a woman a feeling of freedom and self-reliance. I stand and rejoice every time I see a woman ride by on a wheel…the picture of free, untrammeled womanhood."[2]—Susan B. Anthony

• Future Tour de France winner Maurice DeWaele is born on December 27.

1897 • Henri Desgrange may have skipped Paris–Roubaix because he was busy doing other things: in 1897 he and other investors open the Parc des Princes velodrome in the countryside west of Paris.

• The hour record is again broken in Paris when Belgian rider Oscar van den Eynde manages to extend Dubois' distance by a kilometer to 39.24 (24.382

miles). This mark stands for a year before being bettered by an American rider.
- The Eagle Bicycle Company of Torrington, Conn., manufactures aluminum wheel rims.
- On Monday June 12, Lieutenant James A. Moss leads 20 black volunteers of the 25th Infantry Bicycle Corps out of Fort Missoula, Mont., in hopes of reaching Jefferson Barracks, near St. Louis, Mo., in about six weeks. Averaging better than 40 miles a day on their specially built Spalding bikes, Lt. Moss and most of his charges arrive in St. Louis 41 days later. Besides various cooking utensils, each soldier carries a blanket and a shelter tent as they plan to ride from one supply point to the next. Ten of the men carry Krag-Jorgensen rifles slung under their bike's top tubes, while the others carry pistols. Each soldier has 50 rounds of ammunition. They would return to Montana by train.
- "Bike" brand athletic supporters are introduced for men riding over the rough roads of the era.
- In England the Princess of Wales has given up her bicycle in favor of the tricycle. Many of the society ladies there are following suit, and it is predicted that the same thing may soon happen in the United States: Mrs. Frederick Vanderbilt and several other fashionable New York women have already taken up "triking."
- Eighteen-year-old Ernest Thurman, an African-American living in Bowling Green, Ky., rides his bike everywhere in spite of the fact that he lost one arm and one leg when he jumped from a fast-moving train. "When he made his first appearance, he attracted as much attention as a circus parade, but after the novelty wore off only strangers paid any attention to the strange sight."[1]
- Let's call it grease. The *New York Times* reports that "[a] solid lubricant for bicycle bearings is rapidly growing in favor. Bearings packed with it run fully 3,000 miles without attention." The piece goes on to note that "[f]ew riders have heard of its merits, although many factories use it now to a limited extent. If its use should become general it would do away with oil cups and destroy the market for tool-bag oil cans."[2]
- Charles Murphy rides a paced mile in 1:00⅘. He was paced by a sextet on 22nd Avenue in Brooklyn between 60th and 80th Streets.
- Mrs. A. M. C. Allen of Worcester, Mass., rides 21,026 miles during the year, including 117 centuries. According to the *New York Times*:

> Mrs. Allen was in the saddle 266 days of the year. Her longest ride was 153 miles, and in returning home a ferocious dog fastened its teeth in her ankle. She drew a revolver and shot the animal, and then pedaled sixteen miles before receiving medical attention. Four years ago she was an invalid, barely able to move about. During her riding she gained in weight from 118 to 125 pounds.[3]

1898 • Willie Hamilton becomes the first and only American to hold the unpaced hour record. On a wooden velodrome in Denver, Colo., Hamilton rides at night so he can follow a spotlight which is set to keep his lap times at exactly

36 seconds. This device helps him become the first rider to exceed 40 kilometers (25 miles) when he rides 40.781 kilometers (25.28 miles) in an hour's time. While his mark would endure for seven years, Hamilton's name does not appear on the UCI's list of hour record holders because he did it two years before the sport's current governing body was formed. As for his use of the spotlight, the "Europeans protested. The international officials disagreed, deciding the spotlight wasn't a pacer. Even so, a rule was later added to ban such practices."[1]

- Henry Sturmey of Coventry, England, secretary of the International Cyclist's Union, suggests that the governing organization of each country send him their cycling records on or before January of each year so he can compile a list of genuine world records. Along with James Archer, Sturmey would develop the venerable Sturmey-Archer three-speed hub to be introduced in 1902.
- Based on the tube butting process he'd developed in 1887, Alfred Milward Reynolds founds the Patented Butted Tube Company in Birmingham, England, where he produces high-quality tubing for bicycle frames.
- In Germany Ernst Sachs introduces the first commercially successful freewheel.
- When the New York State legislature passes the Collins Law forbidding track racers at Madison Square Garden from riding more that twelve hours a day, the riders form two-man teams. Races featuring these teams become known as Madisons.

1899 • When the International Cyclists Association holds the last world championship of the 1800s in front of 18,000 people on a dirt track in Queen's Park in Montreal, it is Major Taylor of the United States who wins the one-mile and two-mile races, and is awarded second place in the half-mile event which finishes in a three way dead heat.
- December 4–9, the first sanctioned six-day race to be held in North America under the Collins Law takes place in New York City with The Flying Dutchmen (Chicago's Charles W. Miller and Frank Waller of New York City) riding 2,733 miles plus 4 laps to defeat The Unpaced Champions (Otto Maya of Erie, Penn., and Archie McEachern of Toronto), who complete 2,733 miles plus 2 laps. After his partner drops out, Georgia's Bobby Walthour completes 1,402 miles plus 8 laps to take home a $500 prize.
- Future Tour de France winner Nicolas Frantz is born on November 4.
- French racer Albert Champion wins the fourth edition of Paris–Roubaix. The following year, Champion would emigrate to the United States where he would begin manufacturing spark plugs for the fledgling automobile industry five years later.
- John C. Bean receives patent no. 638,861 for a tether designed to limit a cyclist's upward movement, allowing him or her to apply more downward force on the pedals. The tether, which attaches to the handlebars and behind the saddle, goes over the rider's shoulders and crosses in the back, like a pair of suspenders.

- When fifty-year-old William Reardon of Brooklyn takes it upon himself to tell Miss S. V. Schenck of 7th Avenue, "You are not a respectable woman to ride a man's wheel. You should go home and get a wheel made for your own sex," the young lady disagrees and has him arrested. Later in court Judge Worth fines Reardon five dollars and tells him to mind his own business from now on.
- On June 30, Brooklyn's Charles Minthorne "Mile-a-Minute" Murphy (born 1872), of the King's County Wheelmen, covers a mile in $57\frac{4}{5}$ seconds while drafting a train in Long Island, New York. His times, taken every quarter mile, are: 15 seconds, $29\frac{2}{5}$ seconds, 44 seconds, and $57\frac{4}{5}$ seconds. To set the mark, Murphy rides between Maywood and Babylon on a track two and three-eighths miles long, which is constructed of five white pine boards, each ten inches wide. The section of track on which he rides rises three feet in every hundred and does not curve. Murphy wears blue tights and a thin, light-blue jersey with long sleeves as he drafts Long Island Railway engine number 74, which pulls one car and is driven by engineer Sam Booth. The fireman is Ed Howell. To the rear of the rail car has been added an enclosure which is five feet long, and runs from the car's roof to six inches above the track to shelter Murphy from the wind. After Murphy sets the record, the engine slows so suddenly that he hits the back of the train car and avoids crashing when he grabs the car's railing and is hauled onto the speeding train by L.I.R.R. employees Hal B. Fullerton and J.H. Cummings. "Whew, what a relief at the signal of the American flag, signifying the finish. The joy in my heart of success and a moment more of suspense. I was riding faster than the train itself, as I was making up lost ground. Head still over the handlebars, pedaling more fiercely than I ever did before, it seemed like an endless task." As the train slowed suddenly at the end of the run, "I came and crashed head-on into the rear of the train. The front wheel recoiled, while the back wheel rebounded and continued to revolve in the air. I pitched forward as a yell of despair went up from the officials on the rear platform. They expected me to be dashed to pieces and sure death. The men on the back of the platform reached out in sheer nervousness and gradually drew me close. The pleasure and glory of my long-cherished idea was not to be taken from me by death. I reached forward, grabbed an upright on the rear of the car as Hal Fullerton, then special agent for the railroad, caught me by the arms...."[1] A third man grabs Murphy's Tribune bicycle, which is still strapped to his feet. It would be another four years before a car—a souped-up Ford "999" driven by former bicycle racer Barney Oldfield—would exceed 60 mph. Oldfield would take $59\frac{3}{5}$ seconds to cover a mile at Indianapolis.

Chapter 2

1900–1909
Picking Up Speed

1900 • Following his record-breaking ride Murphy briefly tours the vaudeville circuit competing against other riders—including Major Taylor—in stationary trainer races. Murphy was said to have ridden a mile in 37 seconds, or 97 miles an hour, on his home trainer while preparing for his mile-a-minute record attempt.[1] Afterward Murphy retires from bicycle racing to join the New York City Police Department, where he becomes a motorcycle cop.

• With the new century comes a change in cycling's international governing body when the *Union Cycliste Internationale* (UCI) is formed on April 14, 1900, supplanting the International Cyclists Association. Attending the organization's inaugural meeting in Paris are representatives from the national cycling federations of France, Italy, Switzerland, Belgium and the United States. Holland and Germany would join two months later, with Britain coming onboard in 1901.

• In April some Paris policemen begin patrolling on bicycles in order to respond more quickly to trouble in the city's problem areas.

• On October 25 Will Stinson of Cambridge, Mass., sets the world record for the paced hour, covering 40 miles 330 yards at the Shoe City oval in Brockton.

1901 • At Paris' Parc des Princes velodrome, which frequently holds contests featuring big-name riders, the great African-American rider Marshall "Major" Taylor rides against French world champion Edmund Jacquelin in a best-of-three matchup. Taylor wins the first race by four lengths. Before the start of the second race twenty minutes later, the American extends his hand to Jacquelin, getting him to shake it, showing the Frenchman, said Taylor, "that I was so positive that I could defeat him again that this was going to be the last heat." It was. "His triumph was so upsetting to race director Henri Desgrange, creator of the Tour de France, that Desgrange paid Taylor in ten-centime pieces—coins like dimes—and Taylor needed a wheelbarrow to carry his winnings away."[1]

1902 • Raleigh Bicycle Company owner Frank Bowden helps Henry Sturmey and James Archer refine and produce the Sturmey-Archer 3-speed hub.

• Italian cycling great Alfredo Binda is born on August 11.

- Even following the win of a rider on a bike with a 3-speed derailleur over French champion Edouard Fischer, who rode a single-speed machine, in a 150-mile race with 1,200 feet of climbing, future Tour de France founder Henri Desgrange stands firm in his opposition to variable gears, writing in his newspaper, which was still called *L'Auto-Vélo* at the time:

  > I applaud this test. But I still feel that variable gears are only for people over forty-five. Isn't it better to triumph by the strength of your muscles rather than by the artifice of a derailleur? We are getting soft. Come on, fellows. Let's say that the test was a fine demonstration—for our grandparents! As for me, give me a fixed gear![1]

- On June 12 Harry Elkes sets the world record for the paced hour, covering 41 miles 250 yards at the Charles River Park bicycle track in Boston, Mass.

1903 • On July 11 former Paris–Roubaix bicycle race winner Albert Champion rides a four-cylinder, fourteen-horsepower motorcycle a mile in 0:58⅘ on the Charles River Park bicycle track in Boston, Mass.

In the Tour de France:
- Maurice Garin (La Française) leads the Tour de France from start to finish. Garin's winning margin of 2 hours 49 minutes 21 seconds remains the largest ever.
- By winning the race's fourth leg between Toulouse and Bordeaux, Switzerland's Charles Laeser becomes the first non-French rider to win a stage in the Tour de France.
- The event's starting field of 60 ties the 1903 Tour with the 1905 and 1934 events for the smallest number of starters.
- The leader of the race is awarded a green armband, while the stage winner receives a yellow one.

1904 • American cyclists turn in impressive performances on the grounds of London's Crystal Palace, site of the 1904 world championship races, with Bobby Walthour, Sr. taking the win in the 100-km (62-mi.) motorpace event over riders from 17 other countries. Also, Iver Lawson wins the professional sprint championship, and Marcus Hurley takes the amateur sprint title.[1]
- Cyclist Burton Downing wins two gold medals, three silvers and a bronze at the 1904 Olympics in St. Louis. The IOC does not recognize the results because "only Americans competed."[2]
- Future Tour de France winner Antonin Magne is born on February 15.
- Future Tour de France winner André Leducq is born on February 27.

In the Tour de France:
- France's Henri Cornet (Cycles J.C.; 19 years 11 months 20 days) becomes the Tour's youngest winner four months after the race when a dozen riders are disqualified for cheating.
- Following the UVF's disqualifications, Swiss rider Michel Frederick retroactively becomes the first foreigner to lead the Tour de France.
- A time limit is added so slower riders are disqualified after each stage.

- The race's fourth stage is the first leg of the Tour to be run completely during the day.
- Camille Fily (did not finish), who'd recently turned 17, competes in the race. He would die in Belgium on May 11, 1918—two days before his 31st birthday.
- Also in the race is 50-year-old Henri Paret, who finishes eleventh overall.
- The 1904 race is generally considered to be the shortest Tour de France—although there is much disagreement on this point.
- By running two finishing laps at the Parc des Princes velodrome, the Tour de France begins its tradition of finishing at the Paris track.

1905 • France's Lucien Petit-Breton rides 41.110 kilometers (25.546 miles) to break the 1898 unpaced hour record of Willie Hamilton. Petit-Breton's mark is the first unpaced hour record to be recognized by the UCI.

In the Tour de France:
- France's Louis Trousselier (Peugeot) wins the third Tour de France.
- A knee injury forces René Pottier to quit while leading the race.
- The race is scored on points instead of time (and will continue to be through the 1912 event).
- The Tour de France passes through the Alps, Normandy and Brittany for the first time.
- The number of stages is increased from 6 to 11, all of which are run during the day.
- The race has its fewest starters, 60, tying it with the 1903 and 1934 events.

1906 • The Dreyfus Affair, which had spurred the founding of the newspaper *L'Auto*, which in turn started the Tour de France, finally comes to a conclusion. In a third trial, Capt. Dreyfus is exonerated of all spying charges. He is restored to the army, promoted to major, and awarded the Legion of Honor. This marks the end of the "Dreyfus Affair" which had shaken the Third Republic, resulting in the discrediting of the military and the political right and increasing the influence of the socialists and the Radicals.
- France's Fernand Vast wins the men's cycling road race in an unusual off-year Olympiad which is held in Athens, Greece.

In the Tour de France:
- The fourth Tour de France is won by René Pottier who wins 5 of the race's 13 stages, including 4 in a row.
- A red flag is introduced to signify the final kilometer of each stage.
- Between the first and second stages, the Tour's first transfer takes the riders from Lille to Douai, 30 kilometers (19 miles) to the south. The event's next transfer will be in 1955.
- The race makes its first excursion out of France by passing through Metz in the German-occupied Alsace-Lorraine region.

1907 • France's Marcel Berthet sets a new hour record of 41.520 km (25.8 miles) in Paris.

- First-year professional Gustave Garrigou becomes the first professional champion of France.
- Future Tour de France winner Georges Speicher is born on June 8.
- Lucien Petit-Breton wins the inaugural running of Milan–San Remo, the *Primavera*.
- United Parcel Service personnel use bicycles to make their deliveries.

In the Tour de France:
- France's Lucien Petit-Breton (Peugeot) wins the fifth Tour de France on a hallmarked bicycle (parts cannot be replaced).
- René Pottier, winner of the 1906 Tour, commits suicide on January 25, 1907. A memorial to him is constructed at the top of the Ballon d'Alsace climb.
- The number of stages is increased to 14.
- The increased number of reporters following the race, including some from Italy's *La Gazzetta dello Sport* newspaper, requires the use of two press cars.
- The tour's fifth stage takes the race out of France and into Switzerland.
- Following four leisurely stages "Baron" Henri Pépin and his small entourage of support riders abandon during the fifth stage.
- After the ninth leg, race leader Émile Georget (Peugeot) is relegated to last place in the stage for an illegal bike change. Alcyon manager Edmond Gentil pulls his squad out of the race to protest of the fact that Georget wasn't disqualified from the event.
- Using a freewheel on his bike, Émile Georget wins six stages.

1908 • The first Tour of Belgium is held. It's won by Lucien Petit-Breton, whose only major win after the 1908 season would be the fifth stage of the third Giro d'Italia in 1911.
- Great Britain wins the gold medal in the men's team pursuit at the IVth Olympiad in London.
- No medals are awarded in the men's match sprint because the time limit is exceeded.
- Two-time Tour winner Lucien Petit-Breton writes a book about his racing experiences, *How I Ride the Route*.
- "Lee Welch of Lewiston [Maine], said to be the fastest roller skater in this vicinity, won the race with Fred St. Onge, a celebrated bicycle rider, at the Lake Grove Rollerway Wednesday evening—Welch being on rollers and St. Onge on a wheel. St. Onge was not satisfied with the result. He believes he can beat Welch or any other skater. He is so confident that he will race Welch again this Thursday evening for a purse of $100."[1]

In the Tour de France:
- France's Lucien Petit-Breton (Peugeot) wins the sixth Tour de France becoming the race's first two-time winner.
- François Faber becomes the first racer from Luxembourg to win a stage of the Tour.
- The race follows the same route as 1907.
- The Tour makes its first visit to the Champs Élysées where its first stage starts at 3 A.M.

- Wolber announces "*le Prix Wolber*" in which it awards 3,500 francs to the best-placed of the tour's 36 finishers using removable tires. The prize is won by runner-up François Faber.
- A "mountain prize" is offered by Labor and Hutchinson. *Le Prix Labor-Hutchinson* is won by Lucien Petit-Breton.
- According to one account, beginning in 1908 "all riders must use sealed [hall-marked] bicycles" assembled from frames provided by the race's organizers.
- Riders of the Peugeot team win all of the race's 14 stages.

1909 • The first *Giro d'Italia* (Tour of Italy), which starts and finishes in Milan, is won by Italian Luigi Ganna. The race was originally dreamed up by the newspaper *Il Corriere della Sera*, but when Armando Cougnet, the editor of rival *La Gazzetta dello Sport*, and his partners Emilio Costamagna and Tullio Morgagni learned from the Atala bicycle company what *Il Corriere* and Bianchi bicycles were planning, they acted first. Beaten to the punch, *Il Corriere della Sera* quickly decided to sign on as a major sponsor of the event. The 127 starters of the 2,369-kilometer (1,469-mile) race were scored on points, supposedly because the race's organizers couldn't afford to clock them. The points system would remain in effect through 1913, with the 1912 Giro run as a points-based team rather than individual event. The first Giro to be claimed by a non-Italian would be the 33rd Giro won by Swiss rider Hugo Koblet in 1950.
- In July four spectators in Berlin, Germany, are killed when a motorcycle pacing riders in an endurance event blows a tire and flies into the crowd. "Two women were instantly killed, and their bodies, saturated with flaming benzine, were burned to cinders." Two men also die at the track "and the hospital surgeons say that several of the injured are in hopeless condition."[1] Four more people would succumb to their injuries the following day. Six days after the crash the German government bans the use of motorcycle pacers.
- Future Tour de France winner Sylvère Maes is born on August 27.

In the Tour de France:
- François Faber (Alcyon) of Luxembourg wins the seventh Tour de France, becoming first non-French winner of the event.
- Faber wins five consecutive Tour de France stages. His five straight victories in the event's "most demanding" stages are still a record.
- The organizers provide a single car in which all the teams' mechanics can follow the race.
- To keep riders from urinating in public, the organizers install bathrooms at the race's checkpoints.
- Alcyon breaks Peugeot's stranglehold on the Tour de France. Peugeot organizes a "Tour de France" for independents and stays away from the real Tour de France until 1912.
- *L'Auto* rejects a female reader's suggestion that the Tour's organizers put on a race for women (the first Tour de France Féminin would be held in 1984).

1910 • "Rudolph Perrot, 17 years old, is confined to his home [in Clinton, N.J.] with a swollen head, the result of being thrown headforemost from his bicycle into a beehive to-day. His head was wedged in the hive for several minutes, and the bees, suddenly aroused from their Winter lethargy, attacked him viciously." Perrot had been speeding down Caldwell Hill, "bent over the handlebars" and failed to see Jacob Trautwein's wagon, which was hauling the hive, until it was too late. After the crash Trautwein quickly threw a blanket over the hive and rushed to the rider's aid. "Perrot hastened to his home, where he received medical treatment. The beehive was badly wrecked."[1]

• Italy's Carlo Galetti wins the second Giro d'Italia.

• Bobby Walthour of the U.S. wins the silver medal in the motorpace event at the worlds in Brussels. The U.S. Cycling Federation incorrectly lists it as a bronze.[2]

• René Guénot (J.B. Louvet-Continental) wins a 3,000-kilometer (1,865-mile), 14-stage *Tour de France independants*. Leon Vallotton finishes second and Henri Pélissier, who'd win the Tour de France in 1923, comes in third.

• "George Wiley of Syracuse defeated Elmer Collins, the American pace-following bicycle champion, by two laps in a thrilling one-hour match race at the Clifton Stadium [in Passaic, N.J.] to-day. Wiley rode 41 miles 3 laps, breaking the former world record behind the small motor cycles, held by Collins, by three laps."[3]

• Amateur bike racer Maurice Ven Den Dries of Manhattan is killed in a training accident at the Newark Velodrome. While practicing sprinting at the end of his training session, Van den Dries loses control of his bicycle and crashes into a pole in front of the grandstand. The County Physician said Van den Dries died of a ruptured heart.

• East Orange, New Jersey's Frank L. Kramer sets a world record by riding 25 miles in 54:13. Kramer, who bettered the old record by more than two minutes, set the mark in New Haven, Conn.

• Forty New York bicycle policemen are threatened with transfer to foot patrol unless they reveal to Deputy Commissioner Clement J. Driscoll who damaged fifteen cots set up at the West 30th Street Station to accommodate extra officers there.

In the Tour de France:

• An ailing Henri Desgrange appoints his deputy, cycling journalist and promoter Victor Breyer, to fill in as race director.

• The number of stages in the race is increased to 15.

• "The Circle of Death" climbs in the Pyrenees (the Peyresourde, Aspin, Tourmalet, and Aubisque) are introduced.

• The *voiture balai* (broom wagon) is introduced.

• Adolphe Hélière drowns after being stung by a jellyfish during a rest day in Nice, becoming the first rider to die during the Tour de France.

• Ernesto Azzini wins the 15th stage, becoming the first Italian to win a stage in the Tour de France.

1911 • Forty year-old Maurice Garin, who'd won the first Tour de France in 1903, comes out of retirement to place tenth in Paris–Brest–Paris, beating his winning 1901 time by six hours.
  • Italy's Carlo Galetti wins the third Tour of Italy, becoming the first rider to win two Giri d'Italia.
  • Future Tour de France winner Roger Lapébie is born on January 16.
  • The son of Jewish shopkeepers, future Tour de France director Félix Levitan is born in Paris.

  In the Tour de France:
  • France's Gustave Garrigou (Alcyon) wins his only Tour de France.
  • The Col du Télégraphe and Col du Galibier Alpine climbs are added to the route.
  • The riders begin to use various type of gearing systems to climb the newly-added mountains. For example, Petit-Breton uses a 3-speed SA hub, and Henri Alavoine uses a P. d'A. derailleur.
  • Race organizer Henri Desgrange first applies the term *domestique* to Tour de France rider Maurice Brocco. It is not meant as a compliment.

1912 • Swiss rider Oscar Egg sets the unpaced hour record at 42.360 kilometers (26.322 miles) in Paris.
  • In October, Australia's Alfred Goullet sets the world record for the mile at 1:47³⁄₅ in Salt Lake City.
  • In France, a rider named Lavalade tries to prove he has created a flying bicycle by jumping his "aviatte" a distance of three feet, seven inches over a cord stretched eight inches above the ground. Lavalade had rigged his machine with a wing in hopes of winning the following day's prize equal to $2,000 for the first person to fly thirty-three feet under his own power.
  • The fourth Giro d'Italia is the only edition of the event to have no individual classification. It's won by the Atala team of Carlo Galetti, winner of the 1910 and 1911 Giri. The Peugeot and Gerbi squads finish second and third.
  • Shikanosuke Maeda starts manufacturing freewheels in Sakai, Japan. His company will eventually be called SunTour.
  • Rudolph "Okey" Lewis of South Africa wins the men's road race at the Vth Olympiad in Stockholm, Sweden. Lewis finishes nine minutes ahead of silver medalist Frederick-Henry Grubb (GBR), who finishes a minute in front of Kansas City, Mo.'s Carl O. Schutte. Great Britain and the United States also finish second and third in the four-man team race, which follows the same 230-kilometer (143-mile) course around Lake Malmar.
  • The world championships are held in Newark, N.J. The professional sprint title is won by Indiana's Frank Kramer whose annual earnings are said to be $20,000—twice that of baseball great Ty Cobb.[1] "In 1915, the manager of the Newark velodrome signed Kramer to a long-term contract. Although he would not reveal the details, he crowed: 'Kramer's earnings for the next three years will make Ty Cobb and his yearly stipend look like a jitney bus alongside a limousine.'"[2]

- President-elect Woodrow Wilson goes "on a relaxing cycle tour of Bermuda, where he reportedly did 'a lot of thinking in the saddle.'"[3]
- Louis M. Fisher, former secretary of the Associated Cycle Clubs of New York, predicts in a letter to the editor of the *New York Times* that the bicycle will once again have its day on American roads. He concludes his missive with the following reasoning: "The bicycle superseded by the automobile, the automobile compelling attention to the necessity for good roads, and with good roads throughout the country we may again see the bicycle coming into its own. Who will make the first move among the big manufacturers?"[4]

In the Tour de France:

- Odile Defraye (Alcyon) becomes the first Belgian to win the Tour de France.
- For the first time, the Tour departs from Luna Park, Port Maillot in Paris.
- Octave Lapize and his La Française team quit in protest over the Belgian riders' tactics.
- Eugène Christophe logs one of the Tour's longest breakaway wins by riding 315 kilometers (195 miles) alone to Grenoble.
- Vincenzo Borgarello becomes the first Italian to lead the Tour de France.
- Bicycle manufacturers are allowed to sponsor entire teams consisting of 10 riders instead of individuals and smaller groups in order to discourage their subsidiary companies from sponsoring small teams which then work together.
- Cycles Peugeot returns to the Tour following a three-year absence.
- This is the final year the race is scored on a points system.
- Several riders (such as Lucien Petit-Breton, Maurice Brocco, Henri Cornet, and Jean Alavoine) use gear-changing mechanisms.

1913 • The Michelin Tire Company publishes its first road maps.
- Marcel Berthet (FRA) takes the hour record away from Switzerland's Oscar Egg on August 7 by riding 42.741 kilometers (26.559 miles). Egg retaliates on August 21 by covering 43.525 kilometers (27.046 miles), before Berthet increases the mark to 43.775 kilometers (27.201 miles) on September 20. All the records are set in Paris.
- In France Berthet rides Etienne Bunau Varilla's torpedo-shaped *Vélo-Torpille* 32.5 mph (52.3 km/h) for 5 kilometers (3.1 miles), or about two miles per hour faster than a regular bicycle. The UCI promptly bans streamlined bicycles.
- The fifth Giro d'Italia is won by Italy's Carlo Oriani. It's the final time that the race is scored on the basis of points. The 1912 Giro was also run on points even though it was a team event.
- Future Tour de France winner Romain Maes is born on August 18.
- In mid-April, World Champion Frank Kramer returns to America from two months in Europe "during which time he did not lose a single match race." He had raced in Paris and Charleroi, Belgium.
- Leon Meredith (GBR) wins his seventh world title in the amateur 100-kilometer (62-mile) paced event. He had also won the title in 1904-05-07-08-09-11.
- New York's Joe Fogler (1884–1930) and Aussie Alf Goulet (1891–1995) win

the first six-day race to be held at the *Vélodrome d'Hiver* (Winter Velodrome) in Paris.

- Washington bicycle messenger Robert Crawford collides with the car in which President Woodrow Wilson is riding. "So concerned was he for Crawford's health, he assigned his personal physician to oversee his recovery. A few days later, Wilson paid a visit to the hospital and presented the stunned lad with a new bicycle. 'I didn't know it was the President's car I ran into,' stammered the boy from his bed. A smiling Wilson replied, 'I rather thought it was the President's car that ran into you.'"[1]
- On July 17, Newark, N.J.'s Mayor Haussling directs "Acting Chief of Police Ryan to prevent the running of auto-paced bicycle races scheduled for Saturday night at the Stadium Motordrome."[2]

In the Tour de France:
- Race winner Philippe Thys (Peugeot) *may have been* the first rider to wear the race leader's yellow jersey after the tenth stage, but no newspaper articles that support his claim can be found.
- The Tour de France follows a counterclockwise route around France for the first time.
- The scoring system is changed from points back to time.
- Belgian rider Marcel Buysse wins six stages.
- Gustave Garrigou finishes on the final podium for the sixth time, his record won't be tied until 1964 when it's equaled by the great French rider Jacques Anquetil.
- A Tour stage concludes in Switzerland for the first time. The race's 11th stage finishes in Geneva.
- Christian Christensen becomes the first Danish rider to compete in the Tour de France. He is disqualified on time after getting lost and losing several hours during the 13th stage to Longwy, but continues in the race all the way to Paris, where he's not classified in the official rankings.[3]
- France's Lucien Petit-Breton uses a Sturmey-Archer 3-speed internal hub gear system on some of the race's mountain stages (even though freewheels were reportedly banned early in the race). Maurice Brocco utilizes a 2-speed Cornet hub.
- Winners of the team category and the first independent rider, eighth-place finisher Camillo Bertarelli of Italy, are awarded "a superb sash with a silver cartouche" thanks to four supporters at the firm Coeur.
- Wearing a red fez, Henri Pélissier's "discovery" Ali Neffati (1895–1974) of Tunisia becomes the first African rider to compete in the Tour de France after having bought a bicycle the previous afternoon. Before long, the eighteen-year-old Neffati (who did not finish the 1913 and 1914 Tours) is hired to work as a driver for *L'Auto,* and would still be working for its successor *L'Équipe* in the 1950s, 10 years after the death of Henri Desgrange.[4]
- French writer Colette (Sidonie Gabrielle Claudine Colette, 1873–1954) becomes the first woman to write about the Tour de France after watching its final stage in Paris.

1914 • Swiss rider Oscar Egg covers 44.247 kilometers (27.495 miles) to reclaim the hour record from France's Marcel Berthet. Egg's record would stand for 20 years. Berthet and Egg would be the only riders to hold the hour record three times until Britain's Chris Boardman reestablishes the "non-aero" mark 86 years later.

• The sixth Giro d'Italia, the first to be scored on the basis of overall time, is won by Alfonso Calzolari.

• Cycling great Gino Bartali is born on July 18.

• Velodrome riders who follow pacers begin riding a new type of bicycle which is much faster but also more dangerous. The new machine "that looks like a freak" alongside the era's ordinary lightweight safety bicycles, "is constructed with a large rear wheel and a small front wheel, which throws the rider's weight forward and nearer to the pacing machine. The front forks of the bicycle are turned backward, and the rider is sitting nearly over the front wheel."[1] The danger comes from the bike's design which has its front wheel revolving between the circling pedals, making accident-avoiding quick turns very difficult to execute.

• On September 2, Bobby Walthour sets a new record for the paced fifty miles, covering the distance in 1:02:49⅖. Walthour's feat is witnessed by 6,000 spectators at the Brighton Beach Velodrome. Walthour laps the entire field, except for Clarence Carman, by the fifth mile.

• In the Six Days of New York, Australians Alf Goulet and Alfred Grenda ride 2,759 miles plus one lap, which is still a record.

In the Tour de France:
• Belgian rider Philippe Thys (Alcyon) leads the race start to finish, and becomes the first foreigner to win two Tours de France.

• The racers' numbers are affixed to the frames of their bicycles.

• L'Auto's average circulation jumps to 320,000 readers during the Tour de France.

• Nearly all the riders use the Eadie two-speed hub gear and freewheel.

• Thys' margin of victory (1:40) is the race's smallest prior to 1956.

• The riders climb the Ballon d'Alsace twice in 24 hours.

• Two Australian riders, Don Kirkham and Iddo "Snowy" Munro, complete the Tour in 17th and 20th places respectively.

• The Peugeot-Wolber team wins 12 of the race's 15 stages.

• All living Tour winners from 1905 through 1923 (Louis Trousselier, Lucien Petit-Breton, François Faber, Octave Lapize, Gustave Garrigou, Odile Defray, Philippe Thys, Firmin Lambot, Leon Scieur and Henri Pélissier) start the 1914 Tour de France as well as 1926 winner Lucien Buysse.

During The Great War:
• On August 3, 1914, Germany declares war on France. Nothing if not patriotic, Tour boss Henri Desgrange prints an impassioned plea (in red ink) in L'Auto imploring the country's cyclists and other good Frenchmen to become Poilus (hairy, tough soldiers) in La Grande Guerre and go into battle for the defense of France. He wrote in part:

For 14 years, *L'Auto* has appeared every day. It has never let you down. So listen up my dear fellows, my dear Frenchmen. There can be no question that a Frenchman succumbs to a German. Go! Go without pity!

And his patriotism doesn't stop at merely calling his countrymen to arms. Now nearly fifty years old, the feisty Desgrange shows up at the conscription station in Autan and offers himself for service. He's accepted as a foot soldier, and will win the Croix de Guerre, and be made an officer shortly before his discharge. All the while he continues to write for *L'Auto* under the pseudonym "Desgrenier."

- One of the first Tour riders to be lost in the war is France's Emile Engel (killed September 14 at Maurupt-le-Montois) who'd finished tenth in 1913 and won the third stage of the 1914 Tour.

1915 • Luxembourger François Faber, winner of the 1909 Tour de France, serving in the French Foreign Legion, is shot in the back on the Carancy (Pas-de-Calais) battlefield on May 9, while carrying a wounded comrade to safety on his shoulders. He is unarmed. The "Giant of Colombes" was 28.

- "King of the Pacers," Marius Thé dies in 1915. Before he'd started driving the motorbike, Thé had competed in six-day races as a rider, including the 1899 event at Madison Square Garden where he and M. Pastaire raced as the Marseille Pair.

- Australia's Reggie McNamara defeats 40 other racers and lowers the 25-mile record to 53:38⅖ at the Newark, N.J., Velodrome.

- Most of the *New York Times* brief article about the National Motor Cycle, Bicycle, and Accessory Show focuses on motorcycles, with the only mention of bicycles being: "There is a plentiful supply of bicycles, and they too partake of the atmosphere of the motor cycle, for there are equipments which may be attached to them so that they may be temporarily turned into power-driven wheels."[1]

- Amateur bicycle racer Louis Kuehl is killed instantly when he flies over the north rail at a Chicago velodrome. Kuehl, who had gone high to avoid another rider, plunged 30 feet to the concrete floor.

1916 • Five-time French track champion and 1910 world track champion Emile Friol is killed in combat in a motorcycle accident in Dury in 1916.

- Australia's Reggie McNamara betters the world record for the mile by 2⅗ seconds. McNamara's time of 1:45 eclipses the four-year-old mark set by his countryman Alf Goulet in Salt Lake City.

- The 1916 Olympic games, scheduled for Berlin, are canceled because of the war.

- Promoter Dave MacKay announces plans to construct a five-lap (to the mile) velodrome in Belleville, N. J. MacKay said he expects the $45,000 track to be completed in three weeks, in time for an April 2 opening.

- Octave Lapize, winner of the 1910 Tour, a *sergent pilote* (a fighter pilot), is killed on July 14, Bastille Day, when his plane is shot down during aerial combat south of Metz over Pont-a-Mousson, which just happens to be the hometown of Pierre Lallement, who'd taken out the first American bicycle patent in 1866.

1917 • Petit-Breton, the first two-time winner of the Tour (in 1907 and 1908) is killed on the night of December 20 near Troyes during a "special mission" when his car hits a farmer's wagon.
   • Major Taylor wins an old-timers' race on the track at Newark. Taylor defeated Arthur Ross, John Chapman, and Howard Freeman in a one-mile race.
   • The 11th annual Boston six-day race (10 hours a day) begins on November 5. The event is considered good preparation for the international race to be held at Madison Square Garden in a month.

1918 • Camille Fily, who'd competed in the 1904 Tour de France at the age of 17, and finished 14th a year later, also loses his life in the war. He's killed in May at Millekruis, Belgium, two days before his 32nd birthday.
   • Four French war heroes (Gilbert Cassagneau, Georges Copearux, Albert Greisser, and Andrew Lamenchic—who finish in that order) calling themselves the Blue Devils compete in a half-mile bicycle race before 16,000 fans at the Newark velodrome. "There was a spill in the race, but the French war heroes got up laughing. After Cassagneau won the bike race he rode around the track waving his blue velvet hat."[1]
   Also During the War:
   • Alfred Dreyfus serves as a Lieutenant Colonel in the French army.
   • In Italy, Bianchi gets an 80-year head start on other cycle manufacturers when it begins producing full-suspension military bikes.
   • A.L. Columbo of Milan starts producing steel tubing for the war effort. Twelve years later, Columbus would begin making high-quality tubing for racing cycles.

1919 • Italy's Costante Girardengo wins seven of the seventh Giro d'Italia's 10 stages to defeat runner-up Gaetano Belloni by nearly 51 minutes.
   • On September 15, cycling great Fausto Coppi is born in Castellania, Italy.
   • Future Tour de France winner Ferdi Kübler is born on July 24.
   • World champions are first awarded a white jersey with horizontal blue, red, black, yellow and green "rainbow" stripes. The first world championship road race wouldn't be held until 1927.
   • A Parisian journalist, appalled by "the many craters, ruined houses and charred trees" he sees after inspecting the postwar route of the Paris–Roubaix race, writes "that the race was going across 'the Hell of the North.'"[1] Just 5 of the 40 automobiles following the race are able to make it to the finish.
   • Arthur Spencer pleads guilty to disorderly conduct in the Third Criminal Court of Newark, admitting that he assaulted national champion Frank Kramer at the local velodrome. At the start of the quarter-mile semifinal, Spencer's toe strap broke and he requested that the race be restarted. When the official told Kramer to keep riding, Spencer waited for him and knocked him off his bike

at the beginning of the second lap. Kramer landed on his head and remained unconscious for about 15 minutes. For his actions, Spencer was fined $200, placed under $500 bail and suspended from racing at the velodrome.

- "Tony Pizzo, a young sailor, who on a wager crossed the continent from Los Angeles, chained to a bicycle, was received yesterday [October 30] by [New York city] Mayor [John F.] Hylan. He had his bicycle with him. It had taken Pizzo since May 18, to make the trip and he declared yesterday, as he regarded his bicycle with dislike, that he would not do it again for a million dollars."[2]

In the Tour de France:

- Despite the ravages of war, the 13th Tour de France begins on June 29, 1919, the day after the peace treaty is signed in the Hall of Mirrors at the Palace of Versailles.
- Race winner Firmin Lambot (La Sportive) is the first Belgian to officially wear the yellow jersey (see 1913).
- The 1919 event is the slowest Tour de France ever—24.06 km/h (14.95 mph), 3 km/h (nearly 2 mph) slower than the 1914 event, which had followed a very similar route.
- The 1919 Tour also has the fewest finishers: 11 out of 69 starters, an attrition rate of 84 percent. In August, the number of finishers drops to 10 when Paul Duboc is disqualified for taking a car to get his pedal repaired during the race.
- The first feeding areas are introduced, they consist of tables piled with food provided by the race's organizers.
- Trade teams are virtually eliminated when most of the pros ride for the La Sportive collaborative.
- The Tour's longest stage is introduced; it runs 482 kilometers (299.5 miles) from Les Sables d'Olonne to Bayonne.
- The yellow jersey introduced after the tenth stage. France's hard-luck favorite Eugène Christophe is the first to wear it.
- The professional riders become known as the "A" category, the independents as "B"s.

Chapter 3

1920–1929
Roaring 'Round the Track

1920 • The Amateur Bicycle League of America is formed because of "the poor state of Amateur racing" in the United States. In 1976, the ABLA would become the United States Cycling Federation (USCF).

• Italy's Gaetano Belloni wins the eighth Giro d'Italia.

• After the four minutes he'd waited at railroad crossings are deducted from his time, Belgium's Harry Stenqvist wins the men's road race at the VIIth Olympiad in Antwerp. South Africa's Henry Kallenbrun, who initially thought he'd won the race, finishes second @ 1:25. The Olympic flag, with its five interlocking rings, is flown over the games for the first time. The flag had been designed seven years earlier by Olympic founder Pierre de Coubertin.

• The Bicycle Trades of America, Inc. launches its "Ride a Bicycle" promotional campaign in hopes of persuading commuters to bike to work instead of riding the trolley. "Make your trips to and from work a pleasure," urged one of the program's posters, "instead of a mean ride on a hot, crowded car. Ride a bicycle. Enjoy to the fullest the exhilarating tonic of fresh air and the open country."

• In March, the New York Velodrome Company announces plans to construct a 30,000-seat, six-lap (to the mile) track on the upper end of Manhattan at 225th Street and Broadway. Work on the $250,000 complex is to begin immediately.

In the Tour de France:

• Belgian rider Philippe Thys (La Sportive) becomes the first three-time winner of the Tour de France.

• Each rider is required to give the organizers a suit he can wear in case his luggage is lost.

• The yellow jersey is not awarded until after the ninth stage in Nice, where it goes to Philippe Thys. Evidently Henri Desgrange had forgotten to order the jerseys.

• Half the riders quit the Tour after the fourth stage at Les Sables d'Olonne to protest Henri Desgrange's dictatorial style of running the event.

• Organizers hold the first annual Miss Tour de France beauty pageant. (With rare exceptions, female reporters wouldn't be allowed to cover the race until the early 1980s.)

- Belgian riders take the Tour's top 7 places and win 12 of its 15 stages.

1921 • In January a receiver is appointed against the receipts of a six-day bike race at the Chicago Coliseum put on by the New York Velodrome Company. The NYVC "has just gone into the hands of a receiver, appointed here by Federal Judge Julian Mack, to take care of its half completed track and building at 225th Street and Broadway."[1]

- Shozaburo Shimano founds the Shimano Iron Works in Sakai, Japan. Shimano begins manufacturing 24-tooth freewheels, which it backs by telling customers, "If it breaks, we'll replace it with two." Within a year, the company is producing 3,000 of its "333" freewheels a month at a cost of 0.30 yen each.

- Italy's Giovanni Brunero wins the ninth Giro d'Italia.

- Hans Ohrt, a track sprinter from Beverly Hills, California, has a bootmaker in Nice, France, construct two leather helmets for him following the lingering effects of a pair of serious crashes. Ohrt first wore one of the helmets on Christmas day at the *Vélodrome d'Hiver* in Paris.[2]

- Ernest Hemingway makes what may be the first mention of a rider-carried hydration system when he writes of his days spent watching bicycle races at, among other tracks, the "big banked five-hundred meter bowl of the Stade Buffalo, the outdoor stadium at Montrouge…" There, he observed riders like multiple Belgian and world champion Victor Linart, who would "suck up cherry brandy from a rubber tube that connected with a hot water bottle under his racing shirt when he needed it toward the end as he increased his savage speed."[3]

- A proposed ordinance introduced by New York Alderman John F. McCourt aims to limit racers competing within the city limits from riding more than six hours in any twenty-four-hour period. The Commissioner of Health shall also appoint, says the ordinance, an inspector to the races "for the purpose of better enforcement of such statutes bearing upon the question of the unlawful use of drugs which in such event may be employed for the continuation or success of such undertaking." Six-day manager John Chapman "flatly refuted the intimation that drugs played any part in the conduct of the races or the riders participating therein." "To the best of my knowledge," he said, "the only stimulant used is brandy, which is given to the foreign riders in the latter stages of the race."[4]

- Future Tour de France winner Jean Robic is born on June 10.

- Officials in Amsterdam agree to let the 1924 Olympics be moved to Paris to honor the founder of the modern games, Pierre de Coubertin, who's retiring.

- The UCI holds its first world road championship for amateur men in Copenhagen (a race for professionals won't be held until 1927). The 190-kilometer (118-mile) event is won by Sweden's Gunnar Skold.

In the Tour de France:

- With the victory of Leon Scieur (La Sportive) added to those of Firmin Lambot in 1919 and 1922, the Belgian village of Florennes becomes the only city to be the hometown of two Tour de France winners.

- Feeling that the riders aren't trying hard enough, Henri Desgrange imposes a separate-start format—which is sort of like a team time trial—for the race's eleventh stage.
- Lucien Pothier, 38, rides in his eighth and final Tour de France, finishing 32nd. He had finished second overall in the first Tour de France in 1903.
- Fourth place Luigi Lucotti (Ancora) is the highest-placed Italian in the race's final standings so far.

1922
- Giovanni Brunero wins the 10th Giro d'Italia, it's his second consecutive victory in the race.
- Also in Italy, Regina produces its first bicycle chain.
- In February the UCI says it plans to readmit Germany on January 1, 1923, if it reapplies. Germany had applied for admission the previous summer, but apparently had withdrawn its request in a recent letter.
- "LOS ANGELES, July 14. Clarence Wagner, 22-year-old amateur bicycle rider, completed the last lap of a transcontinental ride here yesterday. His time from New York was 28 days 4 hours and 15 minutes, which clips more than six days from the previous record of 35 days."[1]
- Mr. H. M. Huffman, President of the Cycle Tradesmen of Dayton, Ohio, told those attending the sixteenth annual Cycle Trades Association convention in Atlantic City that a 40-percent price reduction will bring a fivefold increase in bicycle sales over the previous year. "This organization," he said, "is looking forward to a great reduction in prices in bicycles and accessories and that will bring about a greater demand for the stock."[2] Also planned for the convention is a parade of 2,000 school children on bicycles on the Atlantic City Boardwalk.

In the Tour de France:
- At 36, Belgium's Firmin Lambot (Peugeot) becomes the oldest rider to win the Tour de France. Lambot also becomes the first rider to win the Tour de France without winning a stage.
- In order to increase the Tour's publicity, the organizers allow an additional 10 press cars to follow the race, bringing the total to 15.
- The Col de Vars and Col d'Izoard climbs are included for the first time.
- A stage of the race finishes in the high-altitude city of Briançon for the first time.
- The scheduled ascent of the Col du Tourmalet is canceled because of snow.
- Eugène Christophe breaks a fork for the third time (this had also happened in 1913 and 1919).
- Riders on the Peugeot team win 11 of the race's 15 stages.
- Georges Goffin starts the Tour de France for the third time. As he'd done on his two previous attempts, he abandons during the first stage. The 39-year-old Goffin, who also went by "Nemo," had previously tried the Tour in 1909 and 1911.

1923
- The Patented Butted Tube Company Changes its name to Reynolds Tube Company, Ltd. It continues to produce 'HM' (high manganese-content) tubing for bicycles.

- Paris gets its first traffic light.
- Italy's Costante Girardengo wins the 11th Giro d'Italia.
- Pierre Giffard dies. Giffard had been the editor of the rival newspaper *Le Vélo* in 1900 when Henri Desgrange founded *L'Auto-Vélo* (whose name was changed to *L'Auto* following a court battle with *Le Vélo*). By 1904 *L'Auto*'s new Tour de France had driven *Le Vélo* out of business and Giffard was hired to work for Henri Desgrange, who offers a glowing eulogy at his funeral.
- In order to stimulate the sales of juvenile bikes in America, the Cycle Trades of America trade association releases a short film entitled "How Dreams Come True," which shows the lengths to which a boy would go to get the bicycle he desperately wants.
- Mid February's National Motorcycle, Bicycle and Accessory Show at New York's 69th Regiment Armory features more than just the latest equipment for two-wheeling; also on the schedule are the bicycle roller championship races. "The bicycle roller championship races, which are being held under the auspices of the Amateur Bicycle League of America, providing [*sic*] an interesting feature. No circular length of track is necessary for the holding of these cycle contests. The rider merely sits on his machine and pedals. The frame of the cycle remains stationary while the rear wheel revolves, and, as it does so, sets in motion two steel rollers upon which it rests. These two rollers are connected by a system of shafts and gears to a tiny model cyclist that moves around a small circular track as fast or as slow as the human cyclist pedals."[1] Each lap completed by the tiny cyclist indicates that the large one has pedaled one tenth of a mile. Bert Marquard of the Century Road Club posts the best time in the contest.
- Ettore Bugatti of Italy, holder of many of his country's bicycle and tricycle records, is given the title of Chevalier of the Legion of Honor by the government of France. "For more than 55 years his name has stood in the record books of Italy and more than one paragraph in the section devoted to noteworthy performances discusses his feats. In recent years he has devoted much time to perfecting racing automobiles and has achieved no little success in this line of endeavor."[2]

In the Tour de France:

- Henri Pélissier (Automoto) gives France its first Tour de France victory since 1911.
- Riders are allowed to swap parts with teammates or get a spare bike from their team director in the event of a mechanical problem.
- Each stage winner is awarded a two-minute time bonus.
- A month after Jean Alavoine had crashed out of the Tour during the eleventh stage, a fund set up for him at *L'Auto* had received 8,200 francs in donations.
- After the race, *L'Auto* publishes a special edition which sells a million copies.
- Ottavio Bottecchia is the first Italian rider to wear the yellow jersey, and is also the first Italian to finish on the podium.

1924 • On November 4, Tullio Campagnolo is unable to unscrew his wheel nuts to turn his rear wheel around for the ascent of the Croce d'Aune Pass during the

Gran Premio della Vittoria (Great Prize of the Victory) because his fingers are numb from the cold. Soon he would begin development of the quick-release hub.

- Gerard Debaets claims the first of his two Tour of Flanders victories. "In the early 1930s, he felt ill after winning the Chicago international six-day and checked into a hospital for tests that revealed he had a congenitally bad heart—his aorta valve leaked with each beat."[1]
- Giuseppi Enrici of Italy wins the 12th Giro d'Italia.
- Arnaud Blanchonnet of France wins the men's road race at the VIIIth Olympiad in Paris.
- In France Albert Raimond markets Le Cyclo, the first commercially successful derailleur.
- During the month of October, former world champion Leon Vanderstuyft (1890–1964) of Belgium goes on a tear at the newly opened auto racing circuit in Monthléry, France. On the first day of the month Vanderstuyft establishes a new mark for an hour behind a heavy motorcycle by pedaling 107.710 kilometers (66.930 miles). Eleven days later he sets the motor-paced (small motorbike) marks for 20 kilometers (12.43 miles) at 13:46⅖ and for 25 kilometers (15.53 miles) at 17:09⅖. On the 19th, the speedy Belgian sets a motor-paced hour mark of 81.9 kilometers (50.9 miles). That same day, Vanderstuyft's hour mark behind the heavy motorcycle is broken by French cyclist "M. Brunier," (Jean Brunier, 1896–1981?) who traveled 112.44 kilometers (69.87 miles) in the allotted time.
- French sportswriters are concerned that a new, lighter bicycle, and improvements in track surfaces will enable "slightly better than average" riders to equal old cycling marks and allow "leading cyclists" to set new records with ease—even though the current crop of riders, they say, is not nearly as capable as those who had set the original marks.

In the Tour de France:
- Ottavio Bottecchia (Automoto) becomes the first Italian winner of the *Giro di Francia*, wearing the yellow jersey from start to finish (except when disguised in a purple jersey to protect himself during the 11th stage).
- Produits Gibbs soap company pays the Tour 45,000 francs to be divided among the stage winners and the race's top two overall riders.
- Eighteen-year-old Jacques Goddet goes to work for his father, Victor, at *L'Auto*.
- Time bonuses for stage winners are increased from two minutes to three minutes.
- The *Slaves of the Road* media coup staged by Henri and Francis Pélissier details treatment of the riders and their use of drugs.
- Jules Banino, a 51-year-old policeman from Nice, becomes the oldest rider to ever take part in the Tour de France. He abandons during the first stage.
- The Tour's 482-kilometer (300-mile) fifth stage from Les Sables d'Olonne to Bayonne is the race's longest day (by time) in Tour history, taking the winner 19 hours 40 minutes to complete.
- "Notwithstanding the rival attractions of Olympic swimming, tennis, and

gymnastics, 25,000 Parisians today [July 20] assembled in the Parc des Princes Stadium to see the end of the classic cycle race around France."[2]

1925 • Belgium's Leon Vanderstuyft recaptures the hour record behind a heavy motorcycle, riding 115.098 kilometers (71.521 miles).

• The 13th Giro d'Italia is won by Alfredo Binda, who also takes the first of his 41 Giro stage wins. It's the first of the great Italian rider's five overall victories in the Giro between 1925 and 1933.

• France's Félix Sellier, winner of the 1925 Paris–Roubaix has a 13-tooth cog made by a mechanic. "When he was on form he cautiously and discreetly took it out of the pocket of his jersey to screw it onto his rear hub."[1]

• Henri Pélissier, winner of the 1923 Tour de France organizes a riders union in order to protest Henri Desgrange's plan to issue the racers standardized provisions during the upcoming Paris–Tours race. The end of the union comes almost immediately when the Belgian riders, who never liked Pélissier to begin with, ignore his call to strike and are soon joined by many of the French riders.

• Future Tour de France winner Louison Bobet is born on March 12.

• Future Tour de France winner Hugo Koblet is born on March 21.

In the Tour de France:

• Ottavio Bottecchia (Automoto) becomes the third rider to win consecutive Tours de France.

• The number of stages increases from 15 to 18.

• In light of the Pélissier brothers' protest of the previous year, race organizer Henri Desgrange makes a rule stating that riders who protest the rules by quitting or getting other riders to quit will be banned from the following year's race.

• No French riders are among the top 10 finishers.

• Footage for *Le Roi de la Pedale* (*The King of the Pedal*), the first film based on the Tour de France, is shot during the race. Based on the Henri Decoin and Pierre Cartoux book of the same name, the film follows Fortune Richard, a young bellhop, who improves his social standing by entering—and doing well in—the Tour de France. The movie stars an actor named "Biscot."

1926 • Italy's Giovanni Brunero wins the 14th Giro d'Italia to become the event's first three-time winner. Brunero's Legnano teammate Alfredo Binda wins six stages.

• Victor Goddet dies. Goddet, father of eventual Tour de France director Jacques Goddet, was the treasurer of *L'Auto* in 1902 and gave Henri Desgrange the go-ahead to put on the first Tour, telling Desgrange that he could buy a bigger vault with the race's proceeds.

• As they're preparing to board the French liner *La Savoie*, eight foreign riders who'd recently competed in the March six-day race in New York are met by government agents looking to collect the taxes due on their winnings. When one of the riders, Harry Stockelynch, refuses to show the tax men his contract, they calculate that he owes Uncle Sam $99.19. This figure prompts the big

Belgian to talk "indignantly in three languages and [say] he would remain in America before he would pay the amount required. Just as the vessel was about to sail, a compromise was reached. He paid $30 and ran up the gangplank as it was about to be pulled in. The seven other riders paid an average of $17 to $25."[1]

- In France, a nation of 38 million people, there are 6.4 million bicycles, or one to every six persons. The country's production of about a million bicycles a year is accounted for by replacement needs, and sales to French colonies and the rest of Europe. There are about 650,000 automobiles in France.

- "The mania among women for weight reduction will result in the early return of the bicycle and the bloomer girl in the near future, said L. N. Southmayd of New York, President of the Cycle Trades of America [in Atlantic City, N. J.] today. He added that a special type of bicycle for the woman who wants to reduce was being perfected."[2]

- In Concord, N.H., Mr. F. E. Gale, the oldest bicycle dealer in continuous business in the country, is awarded a silver loving cup for his achievement. Gale, who's been in the retail bicycle business since 1880, is also elected president of the Old Timers' Club of America.

- French motor-paced champion Gustave Ganay (born 1892) is killed in a racing accident at the Parc des Princes veldrome in Paris.

- A $100,000, six-lap velodrome is planned for the Miami area in the fall. If the venture, proposed by John M. Chapman, General Manager of the Cycle Racing Association of New York, comes to fruition, riders wishing to compete during the winter won't have to go to the indoor tracks of Europe.

In the Tour de France:
- Lucien Buysse (Automoto) has the longest elapsed time by a Tour de France winner: 238:44:25.
- The 20th Tour de France is the longest ever: 5,745 kilometers (3,562 miles).
- With an average speed of just 18.9 km/h (11.7 mph), the race's 10th stage between Bayonne and Luchon remains the Tour's slowest ever.
- During the race, Buysse's daughter dies. He receives the news after the third stage and continues in the Tour only at the urging of his family.
- The Tour de France makes its first start outside of the Paris area when the riders are taken by special train to Evian.
- For the first time, there are no French stage winners.
- Kisso Kawamuro is the first Japanese rider to compete in the Tour de France. He abandons the race during the first stage.
- Jules and Lucien Buysse become the first brothers to lead the race in the same year.

1927 • After three years of development, Tullio Campagnolo introduces the quick-release hub.
- Shimano Iron Works closes its doors because of Japan's Showa Depression. The company would soon reopen and build a 25,000-square-meter (290,000-square-foot) factory.

- Albert Champion, winner of the 1899 edition of Paris–Roubaix, dies of a heart attack while attending a dinner in his honor at the Hotel Meurice in Paris. There are rumors that he had been beaten by his wife's lover. The 49-year-old Champion was being honored because he had made the AC spark plugs used in Charles Lindbergh's *Spirit of St. Louis*.
- "In a Boston hospital, the bicycle is used in the study of heart trouble and respiratory ailments, to determine the amount of oxygen consumed by the blood under given conditions of body work. By means of a tube connection, the rider receives air from outside, which when exhausted is diverted into a gasometer, where the oxygen and the carbonic acid can be measured. The amount of carbonic acid gas shows how much oxygen the body has consumed from the blood in doing a certain amount of work, and the work is measured by the speed of the bicycle and the amount of weight on the wheel."[1]
- Two-time Tour winner Ottavio Bottecchia dies mysteriously while on a training ride, leaving behind a wife and two children. It is widely believed that he was beaten up by Fascists.
- Italy's Alfredo Binda wins 12 of 15 stages to take the 15th Giro d'Italia. It's the second of his five wins in the event after winning six stages and finishing second the previous year. So far, the great Italian rider has won 19 stages in three Giri d'Italia.
- In Washington, D.C., 17-year-old Milton A. Smith rides 250.4 miles in 24 hours 15 minutes, setting a new record for the event. During his ride, Smith consumes a chicken sandwich, three and a half pints of ice cream, water, and "several" cups of coffee.
- Attacking with 20 miles to go, Alfredo Binda defeats countryman Costante Girardengo by 7:15 to win the UCI's first professional world championship road race. After six and a half hours of racing, only 18 of the 55 starters finish the event. Binda wins the race, which is held at the newly-opened Nürburgring auto racing circuit in Germany's Eifel Mountains, on a bicycle that does not have a derailleur. Between the 1968 Tour and the 1996 Olympics in Atlanta, the world championship would be the only road race in which professional riders would compete on national teams.
- Belgium's George Ronsse (Automoto) is awarded the victory in Paris–Roubaix over apparent winner Joseph Curtel (Peugeot) of France. Many observers suspect that Ronsse's team manager, Pierrard, is behind the matter. Plagued by financial troubles caused by ambitious expansion plans, Automoto had elected to skip the 1927 Tour and concentrate instead on classics. When Peugeot takes over bankrupt Automoto in 1929, managers find a receipt dated April 17, 1927 that is signed by Paris–Roubaix judge Andre Trialoux for a "substantial amount of money."

In the Tour de France:

- Race winner Nicolas Frantz (Alcyon) becomes the first rider from Luxembourg to wear the yellow jersey.
- Most of the flat stages are run by starting the professional teams at 15-minute intervals.

- The number of stages is increased to 24.
- For the first time since 1903, there are no former Tour winners entered in the race.
- Francis becomes the second of the three Pélissier brothers to wear the yellow jersey.
- During the sixth stage, Pélissier retires from the race while in the lead because of illness.
- Radio-Toulouse broadcasts a 15-minute Tour update every evening.

1928 • Richard "Happy Dick" Diamond of East 118th Street is locked up in the West 47th Street Police Station and charged with soliciting alms without a license and disorderly conduct for collecting "generous contributions" from New York's theatergoers. Diamond's backdrop in this endeavor was his bicycle, which was covered with posters detailing his many adventures. "Diamond told the police he had traveled more than 35,000 miles on his bicycle since 1922, when Los Angeles doctors told him that he would not live another six months because of tuberculosis. He said that his travels had been supported by public sympathy. Arraigned later in Night Court, Diamond told Magistrate Ewald that he had come to New York to publish a book. He admitted trying to sell pamphlets. The Court advised him to find another field of endeavor and suspended sentence."[1]
- Italian Alfredo Binda wins the 16th Giro d'Italia and brings his total number of stage victories in the event to 25. It's the third of Binda's five Giro victories.
- Georges Ronsse of Belgium wins world professional road race in Budapest, Hungary.
- Henry Hansen of Denmark wins the men's road race at the IXth Olympiad in Amsterdam. Great Britain's Frank Southall is second @ 7:48.
- Belgium's Leon Vanderstuyft increases the hour record behind a heavy motorcycle, riding 126.050 kilometers (78.327 miles).
- Future Tour de France winner Federico Bahamontes is born on July 9.

In the Tour de France:
- In the yellow jersey era, race winner Nicolas Frantz (Alcyon) is the second rider (after Bottecchia) to wear the *maillot jaune* from start to finish. Having won the 1927 Tour, Frantz starts the 1928 race in yellow, becoming the only rider to truly wear the yellow jersey from start to finish.
- The 1928 Tour is the second (and final) one to make extensive use of the separate-start format.
- Because of the format, each team is allowed to use five substitute riders.
- The race's 162 riders make up its largest starting field so far, a figure which wouldn't be exceeded until 1982.
- During the twelfth stage to Nice, two women cyclists follow the peloton for nearly 100 miles.
- Beginning with the 1928 Tour, the lengths of the stages are generally acknowledged to be *fairly* accurate. Previously, the distances had been estimated.
- Harry Watson is the first rider from New Zealand to compete in the Tour.

Watson, who rides on the Ravat-Wonder-Dunlop team with Australians Hubert Opperman, Perry Osborne, and Ernest Bainbridge, finishes 28th, 16:53:32 behind race winner Frantz.

1929 • James A. Armando of Hartford, Conn., may be the first racer to use a derailleur in an American road race. Jack Simes II, a spectator that day, recalls Armando using the three-speed gear changer during a race in New York: "Armando rode a Cyclo derailleur, made in England. It was a crude contraption that literally had a complete figure eight in the back to keep the chain tension, and it sounded like a coffee grinder. But the crowd loved it. They kept yelling at him, 'Throw it in high gear! Let's see what you've got! Throw it in high!'"[1]
- Italy's Alfredo Binda wins the 17th Giro d'Italia, claiming the fourth of his five Giro victories. By winning eight of the Giro's stages (which brings his total to 33), Binda dominates the event to such an extent that the following year the organizers would reportedly pay him more than 20,000 lire to skip the race.
- In late March, Bermudan officials report a shortage of women's bicycles caused by the large number of American coeds visiting the island for Easter break, and many ladies are having to ride men's bikes instead. Horses and bicycles are the only means of transportation on the island.
- Thirty-year-old Victor Seghetti, an Italian veteran of the Great War, arrives in New York in early December, concluding a 22-month-long bicycle trip from Buenos Aires, Brazil. During his trip, Seghetti, who was armed with a pistol and a rifle, slept in trees for safety from wild animals and swam across streams. He used 16 sets of tires.
- Georges Ronsse of Belgium wins the world road championship for the second consecutive year. The worlds are held in Zurich after the event was taken away from Newark, N.J., because the American organizers wanted to put on only the track events and not the road races.[2]
- Cycles Peugeot buys Automoto.
- French writer Jacques Chabannes publishes *Microbe*, a novel about a young man who becomes a national hero because of his racing success.

In the Tour de France:
- Ailing race leader Maurice DeWaele (Alcyon) of Belgium is helped to victory by his Alcyon team which controls the race.
- Seventeen-year-old Félix Levitan begins his sports-writing career by recounting stories of star riders at the *Vélodrome d'Hiver*. Levitan would become co-director of the Tour de France in 1947.
- Twenty-three-year-old Jacques Goddet begins following the Tour on its itinerary around France. He will follow the race every year until 1989 except for 1932, when he was covering the Los Angeles Olympics and 1981, when he was ill.
- France's Victor Fontan becomes the second leader of the Tour de France to abandon the race. Fontan's crash sparks calls for racers to have access to spare bicycles.
- The race organizers revert to having all the riders repair their own punctures.
- Factory worker Benoît "The Mouse" Fauré wins the *Touristes-Routiers* category

on a bike equipped with a derailleur designed by his boss, Joanny Pannel.

- Charles Pélissier becomes the third of the three Pélissier brothers to win a Tour stage.
- Alex Virot and Jean Antoine broadcast the race live on short-wave radio.
- The "separate start" format, which had been used in the previous two Tours, is dropped except for stages 12, 19 and 20 and "in the case of an average inferior of 30 km/h."
- For the race's first three stages, four riders are tied for the overall lead: Marcel Bidot of France (La Française), and three Belgian Alcyon Riders—Aimé Dossché, Aimé Deolet, and Maurice Dewaele.
- The riders are divided into two classes; A (Aces), and *Touristes-Routiers*.
- The race's official prize money totals 150,000 francs.

Chapter 4

1930–1939
A Tool of the Depression

1930 • In Italy, Angelo Luigi Columbo's aircraft tubing company begins making Columbus double butted tubing for bicycle frames.
  • On February 8 Tullio Campagnolo is granted a patent for his new quick release hub.
  • Three Harvard students, Austen T. Gray, Kenneth W. Pendar, and John S. Ames, are considering careers as six-day bicycle racers after completing a 242-mile trip from Boston to New York in 25 hours of riding time (35 hours total). The trio made the ride on a wager that they couldn't complete the trip in less than 48 hours. Gray believes their feat is a record.
  • Alfredo Binda wins the 1930 world professional road championship in Liège, Belgium.
  • A team of boys in Bloomfield, N.J., has taken turns riding a bicycle for 219 hours, so far, in an attempt to break the record of 384 hours set by Jimmy Dooley's original Hackensack Wheelers.
  • Italy's Luigi Marchisio wins the 18th Giro d'Italia.
  • The "business depression" is given for the reason that bicycling is gaining in popularity as the sales of automobiles slump. At the Cycle Trades of America's annual September convention in Atlantic City, treasurer J. P. Fogarty spoke of the plight of the average wage earner, "His car is worn out, and he has no money to replace it. More than that, the bicycle costs almost nothing for upkeep."[1]
  • Future cycling great Gastone Nencini is born on March 1.
  In the Tour de France:
  • France's André Leducq wins the first of his two Tours de France.
  • The Tour format is changed so the race is contested by national teams instead of trade teams.
  • All the riders compete on generic yellow bicycles provided by the organizers. Word soon gets out that they're made by Alcyon.
  • A rider suffering a mechanical difficulty can be assisted by his teammates or a following car.
  • The publicity caravan is introduced to help finance the race.

- Charles is the third Pélissier brother to lead the race. He wins eight stages including the last four.
- Riders on the French team win 12 of the race's 21 stages. France will also win 12 of 22 stages in 1957.
- Photos of the race are transmitted over telephone lines and are published in Paris within hours.

1931 • Italy's Francesco Camusso wins the 19th Giro d'Italia. During the race Learco Guerra becomes the first race leader to wear the event's new pink jersey.
- Italy's Learco Guerra dominates the 1931 world road championship in Copenhagen, which is the only world championship to be run as a "time race" (time trial).
- After being "Freed as a Beggar" in 1928, Richard Diamond is still going strong. The Canadian Press gives the following update: "Starting from Balboa, Panama Canal Zone, in February, 1922, at the age of 16 with a bicycle, a banjo and 50 cents in capital, 'Happy' Dick Diamond pedaled into [Quebec City] today after visiting thirty-three countries and covering 60,000 miles. Diamond, who is now 25 years old, is on his way to Halifax."[1]
- In September, Australia's Hubert Opperman (Alleluia-Wolber, Elvish-Wolber) wins the 1200-kilometer (745-mile) Paris–Brest–Paris.
- "Bicycle races of the tenth Olympic games will be held in the famed Rose Bowl, scene of the New Year's Day football games, under terms of a contract made public today. A special track will be installed next Spring with the approval of the International Cycling Federation. The Olympic Committee has agreed to pay [Pasadena, Calif.,] $217 a day for the use of the Bowl."[2]

In the Tour de France:
- France's Antonin Magne wins the first of his two Tours de France.
- The teams start separately in stages 2, 3, 4, 6, 7, and 12.
- Max Bulla is the first Austrian to ride the Tour. He's also the first Austrian to win a Tour stage, and to wear the yellow jersey.
- Switzerland and Australia field a Tour team made up of four riders from each country.
- After the race, the seating capacity of the Parc Des Princes Velodrome, the Tour's finishing venue from 1904 through 1967, is increased from 20,000 to 50,000. Following the '67 Tour, it will be torn down to make way for a road and a soccer stadium.
- French cartoonist Pellos (René Pellarin, 1900–98) draws his first Tour de France caricatures.

1932 • Professional racers are banned from Paris–Brest–Paris; most had already stopped competing in the race.
- Italian rider Antonio Pesenti wins the 20th Giro d'Italia.
- Italy's Alfredo Binda wins the world professional road championship in Rome. It's his third victory in the event in six years.
- Italy's Attilio Pavesi wins the men's road race at the Xth Olympiad in Los Angeles.

- In Bermuda, Robert Frederick Young is sentenced to two years' hard labor after pleading guilty to stealing a bicycle. Since cars are not allowed in Bermuda, bicycle theft is considered a serious crime by the island's Supreme Court.
- American cycling champion Major Taylor dies of an apparent heart attack. He was 53.
- Fighting a crosswind he estimated at 60 mph, 63-year-old Robert Morrison, of Jersey City, N.J., pedals a high-wheel bicycle across the George Washington Bridge (from New York to New Jersey) in 18 minutes 54 seconds. Thirty-five years ago Morrison, who wore "an ordinary golf suit" for his ride, had been the captain of the Harlem Wheelmen, an organization of 450 high-wheelers.
- Behind a pacer, Hubert Opperman of Australia rides 860 miles in 24 hours.
- The first Grand Prix des Nations time trial is held in La Haute Vallée de Chevreuse near Paris. The race, which is the brainchild of *Paris-Soir* editor Gaston Bénac and star reporter Albert Baker d'Isy, is modeled after the previous year's world championship race, which was run as a time trial. The race is won by France's Maurice Archambaud, who averages 37.13 km/h (23.07 mph) on the 142-kilometer (88-mile) course. The last G. P. des Nations would be held in 2004.
- Future Tour de France winner Charly Gaul is born on December 21.
- Journalist Jacques Goddet covers the Olympic games in Los Angeles. Goddet, who would replace Henri Desgrange as director of the Tour de France in 1937, would also cover the 1984 Los Angeles games at the age of 79.
- Albert Londres dies when the *George-Philipar*, the ship on board which he was returning from China, catches fire killing all on board. Londres was the French journalist who'd written the 1924 *Slaves of the Road* exposé detailing the conditions under which riders in the Tour de France toiled. A journalistic prize will be established in his name the following year. Albert Londres was 48.

In the Tour de France:
- France's André Leducq wins his second Tour de France in three years.
- Time bonuses of four, two, and one minute are awarded to the first three finishers of each flat stage. A rider winning a stage by at least three minutes would be awarded an additional three-minute bonus.
- Kurt Stoepel becomes the first German to wear the yellow jersey and the first to finish on the final podium.
- Switzerland enters a full national team for the first time.
- There is no Spanish team entered in the 1932 Tour de France.
- Radio Cité broadcasts Jean Antoine and Alex Virot's coverage of the riders crossing the Col d'Aubisque an hour after it happens.

1933 • A late selection to the French team when Paul Chocque falls ill, Georges Speicher wins the 1933 world professional road championship in Monthléry, France. Not sure of his form, Speicher, who was using a Huret derailleur on his machine, attacks early, riding away from teammates Antonin Magne and Roger Lapébie to win the event by five minutes. Speicher, who was notified of his selection to the team at the movies on the Friday before the race, becomes the first rider to win the Tour and the world championship in the same year.

- Tullio Campagnolo starts Campagnolo S.P.A. in Vicenza, Italy. On May 4, he receives a patent for his new rear derailleur mechanism.
- In Holland, a nation of 8,000,000 people, there are 2,858,569 bicycles—or thirty-five bicycles to every 100 persons. Ninety-nine percent of the machines are Dutch-made.
- "Joseph Sartorious of Garden City[, Kan.,] claims the one-bicycle championship of the United States. For twenty-six years he has pedaled the same bicycle to work at the sugar factory. In this time he has ridden 34,320 miles, never had a collision, worn out fifty pairs of tires and never been late to work."[1]
- On August 25, Jan van Hout of the Netherlands breaks Oscar Egg's 19-year-old hour record by riding 44.588 kilometers (27.707 miles) in Paris. Four days later, France's Maurice Richard extends the mark to 44.777 kilometers (27.824 miles) in St. Trond, Belgium.
- Frank Connell of Jersey City, N.J., breaks the 32-year-old record for 15 miles, motor paced, by more than two-and-a-half minutes. Paced by Tommy Grimm at the Nutley Velodrome, Connell covers the distance in 21 minutes 51 seconds.
- Charles Mochet's "Velocar" recumbent, ridden by Francis Faure, shows the value of aerodynamics by covering 45.055 kilometers (27.997 miles) in an hour.
- 31-year-old Alfredo Binda wins six stages (bringing his final total to 41) including the Giro's first time trial, and the event's first climbers' title on his way to victory the 21st Giro d'Italia. It's his fifth and final win of the event. Sprinter Mario Cipollini would win his 42nd Giro stage in 2003.
- On September 29, Georges Lemaire, who'd recently finished fourth in the Tour de France, is killed in a crash at the Belgian interclub championship. He was 28.
- The initial Tour of Switzerland is won by Austria's Max Bulla (Oscar Egg).
- The first edition of the Paris–Nice race is won by Belgium's Alfons Schepers (La Française).
- Schwinn introduces the Aerocycle, a bike equipped with two-inch-wide balloon tires, fenders, a headlight, a push button bell, and a "fuel tank."

In the Tour de France:

- France's Georges Speicher wins his only Tour de France.
- Time bonuses for stage winners are cut from four minutes to two.
- Independent Spanish rider Vicente Trueba wins the Tour's first *Grand Prix de la Montagne* title. Of the race's 21 major climbs, Trueba was first over 10 of them: the Ballon d'Alsace, Galibier, Lautaret, Vars, Braus, Port, Peyresourde, Aspin, Tourmalet, and Aubisque.
- "Martini-Rossi (are) the sponsors of the first official King of the Mountains competition."[2] Many sources state the race's 1933 climbing competition was unofficial.
- The Tour receives its first police escort. Since 1952 the race has been escorted by the elite *Garde Republicaine* motorcycle gendarmes.

- Independent Italian rider Giuseppe Martano finishes the Tour in third place.
- With the Tour's fourth consecutive French winner, the circulation of *L'Auto* climbs to a record 854,000 issues.
- The race follows a clockwise route around France for the first time since 1912.

1934 • The French company MAVIC (*Manufacture d'Articles Vélocipediques Idoux et Chanel,* or Idoux and Chanel's Manufactory of Articles for Cycling) patents the aluminum-alloy rim for bicycle wheels on January 5, two hours after Italy's Mario Longhi, who "allowed MAVIC to exploit the procedure under license until 1947."
- When French promoters decide that American professional champion Bill Honeman should wear a national champion's jersey in their races, they have one designed by a Parisian sporting goods store called Unis. "The jersey featured a blue field with white stars on the upper part and vertical stripes below. The design quickly became popular and soon was adopted as the official jersey of U.S. champions."[1]
- Belgium's Karel Kaers wins the world professional road championship in Leipzig, Germany at the age of 20 years 3 months, making him the youngest rider to win the worlds. Jean-Pierre Monseré and Lance Armstrong, respectively winners of the 1970 and 1993 worlds, are both 21 at the time of their victories.
- In Great Britain, an organized effort is being made to tax the country's estimated 10,000,000 cyclists there by imposing a license and registration system on riders and cycles. Not only are motorists peeved at the large number of bicyclists clogging the region's fine roads, British automobile manufacturers, who are already worried about shrinking exports due to depreciation of the American dollar, are concerned about what affect the two-wheelers will have on car sales.
- Italy's Learco Guerra wins the 22nd Giro d'Italia.
- "Frank Southall, English cyclist, today [October 5] set a new world's record for twenty-four hours of unpaced cycling, covering 457 miles. The previous record was 431½ miles established by Hubert Opperman of Australia. During his run Southall broke the record from Land's End to London by 1 hour 37 minutes."[2]
- Warner Brothers releases the movie *Six Day Bike Racer,* a comedy starring Joe E. Brown.
- Cycling great Jacques Anquetil is born on June 8 in Mont-St. Aignan, near Rouen.
- A relay team bicycles from Los Angeles to New York in 7 days 2 hours 51 minutes. The last leg of the trip is ridden by Howard Rupprecht, William Zeigiebel, and Harry Weinthal.
- Actors Joan Crawford and Douglas Fairbanks, Jr. start a small bicycle craze in California in the early 1930s when they take up cycling for exercise. A photo of Crawford riding a bike attached to rollers is featured on the cover of the July, 1934 issue of *Toy World and Bicycle World.*

In the Tour de France:

- The Tour's first individual time trial is won by final race winner Antonin Magne.
- French national champion Raymond Louviot wins the twenty-second stage. In 1990 his grandson Philippe Louviot would also win the French road championship.
- Two-time winner André Leducq is not selected by race director Henri Desgrange for the French Tour team at the request of Alcyon owner Edmond Gentil because Leducq had abandoned the strict Alcyon team for Emile Mercier's squad after Alcyon team director Ludovic Feuillet refused to increase his salary of 200 francs a month.
- Time bonuses are cut to 60 seconds for stage winners, :45 for runners-up and :30 for the third-place finishers, and are added for mountain stages.
- Stages 21A and 21B usher in the era of half-stages.
- René Vietto of France is the first *official* winner of the King of the Mountains competition (see 1933).
- The race has its fewest starters: 60 (also in 1903 and 1905).
- For the first time, the average speed of the race exceeds 30 km/h (18.6 mph).
- France's national team holds the yellow jersey from start to finish, wins 19 of the race's 23 stages, places three riders in the top five (Magne, Lapébie and Vietto) and wins the race's international challenge.
- During the Tour, race winner Antonin Magne successfully tests a pair of banned MAVIC aluminum-alloy rims, which are "painted in wood colors" to disguise them.
- The film *Le Facteur du Tour de France* is shot partially on location during the race.

1935 • French Army Colonel Alfred Dreyfus dies at the age of 76. It was the Dreyfus Affair that had led to the founding of *L'Auto-Vélo* (later *L'Auto*), whose editor, Henri Desgrange, started the Tour de France.
- Reynolds introduces 531 manganese-molybdenum tubing for bicycle frames.
- Italy's Giuseppe Olmo (1911–1992) extends the hour record to 45.090 kilometers (28.019 miles) at the newly completed Vigorelli Velodrome in Milan, Italy.
- French racer Julien Moineau (1903–1980) uses a 52-tooth chainring.
- "Replying to a question in the House of Commons today [February 28] regarding the attitude of bicyclists toward recent restrictions imposed upon their use of roads, Leslie Hore-Belisha, Minister of Transport, said that nearly one-fifth of those killed on the roads were bicyclists. The increase in the number of bicyclists killed in 1933, as compared with 1928, was 96 percent, whereas for pedestrians the increase was only 8 percent, he said."[1]
- Chicago's Joe Magnani, who is living in southeastern France, turns professional with the regional Urago team. Known as *"L'Américain,"* Magnani wins the Marseille–Nice race that year.
- In a race which only 12 of the 26 starters finish, Jean Aerts of Belgium wins the 1935 world road championship in Floeffe, Belgium. American rider Joe Magnani is one of the non-finishers.

- The first *Vuelta a España* (Tour of Spain) is held. The 14-stage, 3,411-kilometer (2,120-mile) race is won by Belgium's Gustaaf Deloor (Colin). For the race's first two years, its overall leader's jersey will be orange.
- "Chinese peasants use bicycles—most of them German, Japanese and British make—in going to and from their fields, and in the Shantung Province alone there are more than 10,000 of these vehicles licensed. Tiny donkeys, ridden by gowned men, shy at the tinkle of the little bells as the cycles pass in sunken roads that have been trodden down through the centuries, but the donkey is on his way out in the face of his new competition."[2]
- Twenty year-old Gino Bartali turns professional with the powerful Legnano team and wins the Italian national road championship.
- Oxford is the first town in England to provide parking for bicycles. The parking area can accommodate 150 bicycles in a specially shaped steel channel which is raised off the ground.
- Italy's Vasco Bergamaschi wins the 23rd Giro d'Italia. Gino Bartali wins one stage and the climbing title.
- On the evening of May 1, former Tour de France winner Henri Pélissier, deep in the throes of ever-worsening mental illness, is shot five times by his girlfriend Camille Tharault during an argument in Fourcherolles outside of Paris. Pélissier was shot with the same gun his wife, Léonie, had used to commit suicide two years earlier. Saying she'd acted in self-defense, Camille receives a one-year suspended sentence. Henri Pélissier was 46.

In the Tour de France:
- Romain Maes leads the Tour de France from start to finish.
- *Le Tour de France* is probably the first documentary made about the race.
- Spanish rider Francesco Cepeda dies three days after crashing on the Col du Galibier.
- Charles Pélissier enters as an individual and rides the Pélissier brothers' final Tour de France.
- The team time trial returns as the second part of three half-stages.
- The winner's share of the record 1.1 million francs in total prize money is listed as "0 francs" in order to thwart the tax collector.
- *L'Auto* rival *Paris-Soir* of Jean Prouvost begins printing an extra edition about the Tour every evening thanks to the team of 40 led by Gaston Bénac and their fleet of eight cars, five motorcycles, two airplanes and a bus. Photos for the paper are developed on site, and then flown to Paris for that evening's edition. *Paris-Soir* also begins publication of *Sprint*, a weekly sports magazine.

1936
- In the world road championship in Berne, Switzerland, France's Antonin Magne is the first of the race's 10 finishers (out of 39 starters). He beats Italy's Aldo Bini by nearly 10 minutes.
- Joe Magnani becomes the first U.S. rider to complete the worlds road race, finishing tied for last place. Magnani also finishes 18th in the Grand Prix des Nations time trial.[1]
- Simplex introduces a 5-speed freewheel with cogs 2 millimeters thick.

- "In an effort to revive what is virtually a lost art on Manhattan Island the Park Department will reserve the Center Drive in Central Park for bicycling every Saturday morning. The Center Drive is hardly a lengthy bicycle course—it extends only five blocks from Sixty-seventh to Seventy-second Streets—but park officials said it was all the space they could allot, at least until they could determine the popular demand."[2]
- In Milan, Maurice Richard rides 45.398 kilometers (28.201 miles) to reclaim the hour record from Giuseppe Olmo.
- In the 2nd Vuelta a España, Belgian Gustaaf Deloor repeats as champion. Because of the Spanish Civil War, the Vuelta will not be held again until 1941.
- In the 24th Giro d'Italia, Gino Bartali wins three stages and the race, beating Giuseppe Olmo who wins 10 stages. A week after the Giro, Bartali's brother Giulio is killed by a hit and run driver during a race.
- France's Robert Charpentier wins the men's road race at the XIth Olympiad in Berlin.
- "With one good leg, George Steutermann [of St. Louis, Mo.,] has pedaled his bicycle 60,000 miles. A sixth cyclometer soon will register its capacity of 9,999 miles. Steutermann started his riding in 1920, hoping the exercise would strengthen his right leg, impaired almost from birth."[3]
- Future hour record holder Roger Rivière is born on February 23.
- Capitalizing on the popularity of winter ski trains, the first bicycle train to leave New York's Grand Central Terminal makes the four-hour trip up to Canaan, Conn., in April carrying 222 cyclists, and two boxcars full of bikes. From Canaan the happy adventurers pedal the 26.6-mile round trip to Gibson's Grove in Lake Buel, Mass., where they enjoy a picnic. Sixteen similar trains were also scheduled to depart from Boston. Thirty-three years later, Dr. Roland C. Geist would recall the first trip to depart New York, (his recollection would be off by exactly one year):

> On April 26, 1935 [sic], the New Haven Railroad operated its first bicycle train. The destination was Falls Village in the Berkshire Hills in New England. More than 150 cyclists met at Grand Central Terminal to enjoy a new adventure. The fare was $2.50 round trip.
>
> The veteran riders of the Gay Nineties wore their knickers and fancy jerseys with club emblems; the novices came in tennis and golf outfits. Few knew what was correct for bicycling, then a new sport.
>
> About 11 A.M. the train pulled into a siding at Falls Village. Many natives came out to look at the city people who dared venture forth on their back-country roads astride bicycles. The 10-car train had three baggage cars, one filled with rental bicycles brought down from Boston by Ben Oken [sic] of the Bicycle Exchange, Cambridge.
>
> The riders had been given maps of the route on the train. The tour was about 20 miles to Lake Buel and return via back roads. There were markers with arrows: "Cyclists." An automobile also followed the riders with a big sign "Drive Carefully—Cyclists Ahead."[4]

- Future perennial Tour de France runner-up Raymond Poulidor is born on April 15.
- The first bicycle traffic court is held in Racine, Wisconsin.
- Italy's Gino Bartali (Legnano) wins the season-long competition of international races.

In the Tour de France:
- Belgium's Sylvère Maes takes the first of his two Tour de France victories.
- Suffering from ill health, Henri Desgrange turns over Tour directorship to Jacques Goddet after the race's second stage.
- Winner of the race's first stage, Paul Egli becomes the first Swiss rider to wear the yellow jersey.
- Before his retirement, Desgrange introduces the first three-part stage (19A, 19B, and 19C) to the Tour.
- He also reduces the number of time trials from six to five—but makes them all team time trials, and increases the number of rest days from four to six.
- French workers enjoy their first annual paid summer leave under the Popular Front government of Leon Blum.
- Under orders from Mussolini, the Italian national team boycotts the race.
- Holland, Yugoslavia and Romania send their first teams to the Tour de France.
- Holland's Theo Middelkamp wins that country's first Tour stage.
- Abdel-Kader Abbes is the first Algerian rider in the Tour de France. He finishes the race next-to-last, in 42nd position, nearly five hours behind the winner.

1937 - Gino Bartali (Legnano) wins the 25th Giro d'Italia. It's his second consecutive victory in the event. Bartali also wins the season-long international competition for the second straight year.
- Doris Kopsky of Jersey City, N.J., wins the first American Bicycle League women's championship. She is the daughter of 1912 Olympic bronze medalist Joe Kopsky.
- Belgium's Eloi Meulenberg wins the world road championship in Copenhagen.
- New York's Governor Lehman signs a bill requiring all bicycles to be equipped with adequate brakes, a horn or bell, a headlight, and front and rear reflectors. The bill was sponsored by Assemblyman Edward S. Moran, Democrat.
- On September 29, Franz Slaats of the Netherlands sets the hour record at 45.535 kilometers (28.295 miles) at the Vigorelli Velodrome in Milan. Four days later, France's Maurice Archambaud pushes the mark to 45.840 kilometers (28.485 miles) in Milan.
- Englishmen E. V. Mills and W. G. Paul set a world tandem record in Milan of more than 31 miles in an hour.
- Sidney H. Ferns (GBR) rides the 866 miles (1,393 kilometers) from Land's End to John O'Groats in 2 days 6 hours 33 minutes. He continues on to cover a total of 1000 miles (1,609 kilometers) in 2 days 22 hours 40 minutes.
- Future world champion Tom Simpson (GBR) is born on November 30.
- William C. Bailey, 84, of Underhill, Vt., rides his "girl's bicycle" 1,028 miles to

visit his granddaughter, Mrs. Ralph Griswald, in Chicago, making the trip in eighteen days. Bailey spends two weeks at Mrs. Griswald's before riding back to Vermont.

- At its December convention in Boston, the Amateur Athletic Union decides to terminate its alliance with the National Cycling Association and assume jurisdiction over all amateur cycling in the United States, effective immediately. The A.A.U. will appoint a cycling committee to supervise amateur cycling in each of its 39 districts.
- Outboard motor maker Evinrude debuts the Streamflow Imperial. In addition to its aluminum frame, the bike also sports a spring-supported seat that moves up and down with the bottom bracket. The bike also features a locking fork, speedometer and headlight.

In the Tour de France:
- Roger Lapébie is the last French rider to win the Tour de France before the war.
- *L'Auto* competitor *Paris-Soir* criticizes the Tour's organizers for running a trio of three-part stages to increase its profits and for imposing a minimum speed rule.
- 1937 is the final year that *Individuel* riders are allowed in the race.
- Italy's Mario Vicini wins the Tour's last *Individuel* category and finishes second overall.
- Professional riders are permitted to use derailleurs for the first time. Winner Roger Lapébie becomes the first Tour winner to ride every stage using a derailleur.
- Service cars are allowed to follow the racers for the first time.
- Bonuses which double the time gap of a solo stage winner are introduced.
- The first British team enters the Tour de France. America's Joe Magnani was supposed to be a member of the team along with Great Britain's Charlie Holland and Bill Burl, but reportedly got bumped off the squad when Canada's Pierre Gachon came up with more money.
- A light truck is placed at the disposal of each team to transport equipment and personnel.
- Third-place Leo Amberg is the first Swiss rider to finish on the final podium.
- La Vie Insurance Company donates the race's 200,000-franc winner's prize.
- *Le Petit Parisien* sends a female journalist to cover the race from a woman's point of view.
- The team of Belgian race leader Sylvère Maes quits to protest a time penalty and angry crowds. Belgian journalists also leave the race.
- Despite having abandoned the race, Belgium's Félicien Vervaecke wins his second climber's title.
- By winning the race's final leg in Paris, Edward "Ward" Vissers (BEL) finishes sixth overall and becomes the last *Individuel* rider to win a Tour de France stage.

1938 • American Joe Magnani wins the two-day Circuit of Lourdes in the Pyrenees riding for the Urago team. Magnani also improves the hour record for the Nice Velodrome to 42 kilometers (26.25 miles).

- James A. Armando of Hartford, Conn., rides his bicycle to the summit of Pikes Peak in 3 hours 25 minutes, shaving 35 minutes off the 1922 record set by Glen Howard of Colorado Springs, Colo.
- The Paramount line of bicycles debuts in Schwinn's 1938 catalog. Bikes with the Paramount name (built of British Accles & Pollack tubing by Emil Wastyn) had begun to appear late the previous year. Schwinn calls the machines "The best bikes on earth."
- "Sales of bicycle tires in 1938 will reach a total of about 5,000,000, a gain of about 10 percent over 1937 and a record for the industry, it was predicted today [January 7, 1938] by H. W. Brown, sundry sales manager of the Fisk Tire Company [of Springfield, Mass.] The increase would come mostly from replacement business for the 2,000,000 bicycles sold in 1936 and 1937 and the other 4,000,000 in use."[1]
- "A total of 1,130,736 bicycles was built last year—five times more than in 1909 and within 50,000 of the number in 1899, the banner year."[2]
- After two years of development, Roger Derny and Sons of Paris introduce the Derny, a heavy-duty bicycle with a small engine used for pacing riders in some velodrome and road events. The original type of Derny will remain in production through about 1957, and continue to be used through the mid 1970s.[3] In neighboring Italy, the popular Lambretta scooter often serves the same purpose.
- Cino Cinelli rides for the Frejus team in 1938 and 1939.
- Belgium's Marcel Kint wins the 1938 world road championship in Valkenburg, the Netherlands. Kint will remain world champion for eight years since the race won't be held again until 1946, when he would finish second. Kint (Mercier, F. Pélissier) also wins the season-long competition of international races.
- The UCI again bans the use of fairings and recumbents in hour record attempts.
- Italy's Giovanni Valetti wins the 26th Giro d'Italia. The Italian government orders Gino Bartali not to take part in the race so that he might properly prepare for the Tour de France.

In the Tour de France:

- Gino Bartali becomes the first rider to win the Tour and its climbing competition in the same year.
- For the first time in 32 Tours de France, independent riders are excluded from the race.
- Former race winners Antonin Magne and André Leducq ride toward retirement, winning the last stage of the race together.
- The 2,762-meter Col de l'Iseran is added to the Tour route and a live radio program produced there.
- The stage winner's time bonus is reduced to one minute. There is also a one-minute time bonus for the first rider at each mountain summit.
- Emile Masson, Jr. wins a stage 18 years after his father wore the race's yellow jersey.

1939 • 1905 Tour de France winner Louis Trousselier dies on April 24 at the age of 57.
• Giovanni Valetti repeats, winning the 27th Giro d'Italia.
• The outbreak of war in Europe cuts off the supply of foreign riders which signals the end of six-day racing in New York's Madison Square Garden. The last race, which is shortened to five days, is held in December before a half-full house. The May six-day race, which had been moved from its usual March date so the Garden Corporation could put on more ice shows, marks the twentieth year on the track for Belgium's Gerard Debaets, who's teamed with his countryman Fred Ottevaere.
• At the June 4 Tour of Piedmont, 20 year-old Fausto Coppi "arrived on the scene and scrambled [Gino] Bartali's orderly life"[1] by breaking away from the pack. He's caught when his chain starts slipping and eventually finishes third behind the victorious Bartali (Legnano). Alerted to the young rider's potential by his masseur Giuseppe "Biagio" Cavanna, Legnano's manager Eberardo Pavesi signs Coppi to ride as Bartali's *domestique* for the 1940 season.
• On August 16, *L'Auto* becomes *L'Auto-Soldat* and begins publishing war news until France capitulates. Once sporting events resume in France, the newspaper returns to using its old name.
• On August 24, the Circuit de L'Ouest in Lorient is canceled after five of eight stages. Race leader Briek Schotte (BEL) is declared the winner.
• During the 365 days of 1939, British cyclist Tommy Godwin rides 75,065 miles. He continues his riding streak, and reaches 100,000 miles in 500 days on May 14, 1940.
• France's "Robert Oubron [20th in the 1937 Tour de France, 41st in 1938] became a light infantryman, allowing him to capture, at the beginning of December, [Germany's] Kurt Stoepel, the runner-up behind Leducq in 1932!"[2]
• The UCI announces the dates (June 26–July 21) for the 1940 Tour de France. After Germany invades France, Henri Desgrange refuses to hold the event.
• "When [Buffalo, N.Y.,] police decided...to issue license plates for bicycles many applicants asked for low or unusual numbers. The problem of license No. 1 was disposed of last night [April 7], when it was made the prize in a drawing among members of a Boy Scout Troop. Kenneth Dierken, 14, won the plate."[3]
• Italy's Gino Bartali (Legnano) wins the season-long international competition for the third time in four years.
• The John Player & Sons branch of the Imperial Tobacco Company releases a set of 50 cycle collector cards in the United States. An "attractive album" in which to keep the 1½-inch by 2½-inch (38-mm by 64-mm) cards is available for one penny. Card number 28 depicts a female tourist in front of a youth hostel, highlighting how cycling has aided women's rights: "This modern girl cyclist is a picture of health and fitness and contrasts favourably with the narrow-waisted, over-clothed female riders of 40 years ago. The cycling girl has been one of the greatest influences in gaining freedom for women to act and travel independently, a right that was denied her grandmother."

In the Tour de France:

- Also having won the race in 1936, Sylvère Maes becomes the only rider to win the Tour de France both before and after professionals were allowed the use of derailleurs.
- Absent German, Italian and Spanish teams are replaced by four French regional teams and an extra Belgian squad.
- Because his fiancée keeps showing up on the route Victor Cosson of the French national team is fined 50 francs.
- The 1939 event is the tenth and final Tour to be contested on its generic yellow bikes after other manufacturers complained that word of who made the machines (Alcyon) had gotten out. There is strong evidence that the frame of Gino Bartali's winning 1938 machine was made by his regular bike sponsor, Legnano.
- The Tour's first mountain time trial (stage 16B) is held on the Col de l'Iseran.
- René Vietto uses a double chainring and welds two extra cogs to his five-speed freewheel.
- The Tour's average speed is its fastest so far, 31.98 kph (19.8 mph).
- After the first stage, the race's last rider overall was to have been eliminated each day, but the rule is suspended after the seventh stage when the year's first yellow jersey, Amédée Fournier, finishes last because of a crash.
- The Edacoto pen company awards prizes of up to 2,000 francs to the six racers whose penmanship is the best at the race's checkpoints.
- During the race, Jean Stelli films the "comedy/drama" *Pour le Maillot Jaune* (91 minutes), starring Albert Prejean and Meg Lemonnier, who's married to Jacques Goddet's brother Maurice.
- Robert Capa, (nee Andre Friedmann) who would become famous for his vivid images of the 1944 Normandy invasion, photographs the race for *Match* (later to become *Paris-Match)* from the back of a motorcycle.

Chapter 5

1940–1949
The Bicycle Goes to War

1940 • The ravages of age, illness and the Axis powers prove too much for the frail Henri Desgrange and on August 16, 1940 he dies peacefully at his villa "Beauvallon," in Cogolin on the Côte d'Azur, a few kilometers from St. Tropez. He would probably have preferred to be remembered as a journalist, and for his achievements as an amateur bicycle racer who'd used his head as well as his legs to establish an early hour record of 35.325 kilometers. Desgrange had often said that he didn't expect his record to survive for long; he'd only established the mark to give others something to shoot for. His plan worked: by the time of his death, Henri Desgrange's hour record of 35.325 kilometers (21.937 miles) had been increased by 10.5 kilometers (6.5 miles).

Henri Desgrange will forever be remembered as the creator of the single greatest sporting event in the world—the Tour de France—eventually devoting half his life to the bike race that started as a newspaper publicity stunt. Like a father raises his children, he nurtured, praised and punished the riders in his great race. He threw mountains, time trials and multiple stages at them to ensure that they were truly worthy of the title "Giants of the Road." Many years earlier, Géo Lefèvre, who'd given him the idea for what would become to the Tour de France, called Desgrange "a hard man, in the good sense of the word."

Henri Desgrange fought right up until the end. The story goes that in his final days he'd walk across his bedroom carrying a stopwatch, trying to beat his time of the previous day. "The Father of the Tour de France" was dead at 75, survived by his longtime companion, avant-garde artist Jeanne "Jane" Deley (1878–1949), whom he had met shortly after the Great War (he was divorced and had a daughter). He is buried in Commentry, near his parents, who were born there.

• The 28th Giro d'Italia begins as scheduled in mid-May. Even though the 1940 Giro is to be the last running of the event until 1946, Benito Mussolini is a fan of bicycle racing, and other cycling events will continue to be held in Italy until *Il Duce*'s dismissal by King Victor Emmanuel in late July of 1943. Before the start of the Giro, everyone had thought that Italian star Gino Bartali would ride to another easy victory in the event—especially with the help of his new, young Legnano teammate Fausto Coppi, who's been granted a 30-day deferment from the army so he could take part in the race.

But the Giro doesn't go according to plan for Bartali. During the second stage from Turin to Genoa he crashes on the descent of the Scoffera and Coppi takes second in the stage while the injured Bartali hobbles to the finish. A few days later Fausto Coppi is in second place overall, and the roles of the two riders are reversed with Bartali now working for Coppi. On the 11th stage to Modena, the team director gives Coppi permission to attack. He sails over the stage's three mountain passes to win the leg by four minutes and take the Giro's pink leader's jersey for good, going on to become the youngest rider (20 years 8 months) to win the event. An unhappy Gino Bartali finishes the race in ninth place, 45 minutes back. The foundation for the famous feud between the two racers is being laid and the *tifosi*, the famous Italian fans, are already beginning to take sides.

- State amateur champion Furman Kugler of Somerville, N.J., wins the 50-mile Tour of Somerville in a time of 2 hours 5 minutes 17 seconds. A crowd of 20,000 watches the race, and Mayor Freas L. Hess says that the contest will be an annual event. The race had been started by Furman's father, Fred "Pop" Kugler, so his son could sleep in his own bed the night before a race. Because New Jersey state law prohibited racing on state highways for money—Somerville's main street is State Highway 128—the event's organizers called it a tour.
- Until this year, all 20,000 Western Union messengers had delivered telegrams by bike.
- A wartime version of Paris–Roubaix (from Le Mans to Paris) is won by France's Joseph Sofietti (Helyett-Hutchinson).
- "Bicycles constitute the bulk of Paris traffic. Civilians who are still permitted to circulate in automobiles virtually all have a bicycle tied on the top or side to fall back on in case the car is requisitioned or they run out of gasoline far from home…A bicycle salesman on Paris' Avenue de la Grande Armée says that a week before the German occupation panicked Frenchmen rushed his shop and offered outlandish amounts, even for the smallest children's bike. Incidentally, during that black week the most rickety 'hunk of tin' fetched up to 2,000 francs; the day after the occupation one could buy good bicycles abandoned at the railway stations by refugees for as low as 25 francs."[1]
- In Germany people are also turning to the bicycle as a means of transportation with the curtailing of automobile traffic. It is reported that some couples in Berlin are even riding tandems to their own weddings while already dressed for the occasion. German troops seize the headquarters of the International Cycling Union in Paris and move it to Berlin.
- Tullio Campagnolo hires his first full-time employee, mechanic Enrico Piccolo.
- "Italian infantrymen were reported today [October 30] to be pedaling along Greek roads on folding bicycles built for two, which can be slung across the back where the terrain is bad. The man in the front saddle can sling his rifle

across the handlebars, while his colleague has a small stand in front of him on which to mount a light machine gun. The bicycles have three-speed gears."[2]

- Future Tour de France winner Jan Janssen is born on May 19.
- On November 4 the *Union Vélocipédique de France* (UVF) reorganizes its statutes to discontinue bicycle races lasting several days.
- Future Tour de France winner Roger Pingeon is born on August 28.
- Riding for the Martini team, American Joe Magnani wins the Grand Prix de la Côte d'Azur.
- Former Tour de France stage winner Julien Vervaecke, Félicien's older brother, is shot and killed by Polish soldiers serving in the British army when he refuses to let them commandeer his furniture. "An enquiry [*sic*] by a certain Jean-Paul Delcroix argued that Vervaecke was shot by soldiers of the Middlesex Regiment."[3]

1941 • The only major tour contested in 1941 is the third Vuelta a España. Returning after a five year absence caused by the Spanish Civil War, the race is revived in an effort to bolster the morale of the Spanish people. After wins by Belgium's Gustaaf Deloor in the '35 and '36 events, Julian Berrendero becomes the first Spaniard to win the event. For this year only, the race's leader's jersey will be white, before returning to orange for 1942.

- On September 23, General Charles de Gaulle, living in exile in London, forms the Free French National Council which declares war on Germany on December 8, the day after the Japanese attack the U.S. naval base at Pearl Harbor, Hawaii.
- Known both as "The Joker" for his sense of humor and "The Fake" for the way he won the 1904 Tour, 57 year-old Henri Cornet (born "Henri Jaudry" or "Jardy") dies following a heart attack in the little French village of Eure-et-Loire. At the age of 19 years 11 months 20 days, Cornet became the youngest Tour de France winner ever when he was awarded the victory following the controversial disqualification of race winner Maurice Garin and 11 others.
- The first Grand Prix des Nations time trial is held since 1938. Because of the war, two editions of the event are held: one in France's northern zone and one in the southern zone. The 1941 events are won by Jules Rossi of Italy in the north, and by French rider Louis Aimar in the south.
- The chief of police in Berlin, Germany prohibits Polish workers and civilians in the city from owning, possessing, or riding bicycles. Poles are also not allowed to drink in public places, but may do so at home.
- In August the Vichy government cuts rations of several items, including three dear to most Frenchmen: bicycle tires may not be purchased without special permission, also wine is limited to one liter a week, and tobacco rationing has spurred "a flourishing trade in cigarette butts."
- Jules Rossi (Alcyon, La Française) of Italy wins the 1941 version of "Paris–Roubaix," which is run between Paris and Rheims.
- In May, France's Alf Letourner sets a bicycle land speed record by riding 108.92

mph while drafting a race car in Bakersfield, California. His ride is timed by the American Automobile Association. Earlier in the month, Letourner had increased the mark of 87 miles per hour set by Albert Marquette of Los Angeles in 1933 to 90.91 mph. Letourner's Schwinn Paramount is fitted with a 252-inch (114 x 6) gear with every other tooth removed from the chainring.

- The second annual 50-mile Tour of Somerville is held. Furman Kugler of Somerville, N.J., repeats as the race's winner. Kugler would die in World War II.

1942 • Carl Anderson of Clifton, N.J., wins the third annual Tour of Somerville. Like Furman Kugler, who won the first two editions of the race, Anderson would be killed in World War II. When the race returns in 1947 it will be called the Kugler-Anderson Memorial Tour of Somerville.

- As in 1941, the Vuelta a España is the only grand tour to take place. Berrendero repeats as winner of the event, the last one to be held until it is the first of the three grand tours to reappear toward the end of the war, doing so in 1945. Organized by *Informaciones de Madrid*, the race is one of the first to feature *extra sportif* (non cycling-related) sponsors when the riders are sponsored by RCD La Coruña soccer club, which joins Real Club Deportivo Español and Fútbol Club Barcelona from the previous year. Riders on squads not sponsered by soccer teams rode for one of five other sponsors, including Michelin, Cinzano, and Byass Wine.

- In an attempt to appease Italy's vast legions of cycling fans, who'd done without a Giro in 1941, a makeshift Tour of Italy is held. This "Giro" consists of points garnered over an eight-race series beginning with Milan–San Remo in March and concluding with October's Tour of Lombardy (the other six races are: the Tours of Latium, Tuscany, Emilia, Venetia, Piedmont, and Campania). The series is won by Gino Bartali, but does little to placate the Giro-starved *tifosi*: "The Italians were scornful and felt cheated. These eight races would have been run anyway, and the addition of a few points meant very little."[1] While no further actual Giri d'Italia would be held until 1946, the Italian national championship race is run in Rome on the first day of summer. The race is won by Fausto Coppi in a sprint finish while his rival Gino Bartali finishes seven minutes back.

- "The first really serious race of the season in the unoccupied zone of France was the 'Four Days of the Road' (*Les Quatre Jours de la Route*), organized by the newspaper *Le Petit Dauphinois* over the last four days of May."[2] The race, which starts and finishes in Bourg-en-Bresse, is won by France's Victor Cosson with American expatriate Joe Magnani finishing second at 2:19, and Italy's Pierre Brambilla third.

- From September 28 through October 4, *La France Socialiste* puts on the six-stage, 1542-km (958-mile) Circuit de France. The race is plagued by bad weather and its organization is "chaotic." Its "socialist leanings were tainted by a reception with Pierre Laval, the Vichy prime minister later shot as a traitor,"[3] but it's said to offer very generous prize money. The event, whose route twice crosses the demarcation line between the occupied and unoccupied zones, is contested by 72 riders on 6 multinational teams and is won by Belgian rider François Neuville with an overall time of 45:32:09. The Circuit de France notwithstanding, very little cycle racing takes place in northern France until late in the year. Because of the lack of French resistance to the British and American landings in North Africa, the Germans, who feel they need more of a buffer between themselves and the Allies, take over southern France in November. With all of France now occupied, the tensions and travel restrictions between the northern and southern zones are relaxed.

• In Italy, Fausto Coppi finishes the season the way he had started it, with an impressive display of power and speed, this time on the Vigorelli velodrome in Milan. Riding in between air raid sirens, and still feeling the effects of the broken collarbone he'd suffered a week after the national championship, Coppi rides 45.871 kilometers (28.504 miles) in an hour, bettering the five year-old record of France's Maurice Archambaud by 31 meters (34 yards). Later Coppi would remark, "If only others could comprehend the meaning of sixty minutes of solitude to achieve the record." His mark would stand for 14 years.

• The middle of July 1942 sees what have to be the darkest days of the entire war for France: *La Rafle du Vel d'Hiv* [*Vélodrome d'Hiver*] or The Roundup of the Winter Velodrome. According to Michael Curtis' 2002 book *Verdict on Vichy*, the raids commence at 4 A.M. on July 16, and continue through the following day. More than 9,000 French policemen, gendarmes and groups of youths from the *Parti Populaire Français* round up 13,152 Jews in Paris and its suburbs. Another 15,000 escape the raid because of inaccurate lists of names and addresses and leaks from the police. The prisoners are taken to detention centers by 50 Metropolitan Company buses. Single adults and families without children, 4,992 people in all, are taken directly to the Drancy transit camp just north of Paris, the last stop before being shipped off to the Auschwitz concentration camp. Families with children between the ages of 2 and 16—8,160 people in all (1,129 men, 2,916 women and 4,115 children)—are held for several days at the *Vélodrome d'Hiver* in squalid conditions before eventually being sent to Drancy and then on to Auschwitz. Only a few hundred people survive the ordeal— none of them children. The *Vélodrome d'Hiver* would be torn down in 1959.

As unthinkable as the roundup is, it is made even worse was the fact that not one German soldier takes part in the raids; they're all carried out by the French police in the occupied zone on the orders of their director, Jean Leguay, who'd received the directive from René Bousquet, head of the National Police force in Vichy in the unoccupied zone. It would be more than 50 years before the French government would apologize for the atrocity. In the interim, French leaders such as Charles de Gaulle and François Mitterrand contended that the Vichy regime, and not the French government, had been responsible for the roundup. Although Mitterrand, acting under political pressure, declared July 16 a day of commemoration and had a plaque erected in 1993, it wouldn't be until 1995 that President Jacques Chirac would issue a public apology for France's crimes against humanity. He spoke of "the criminal insanity of the occupying power [which] was assisted by the French, by the French state... On that day France delivered those she was protecting to their executioners."[4]

- In May German authorities in Paris ban the use of bicycles after dark in much of occupied France. The ban is an attempt to limit acts of sabotage and attacks on Nazi soldiers by Frenchmen who then quickly escape by bike.
- France's Emile Idée wins the northern edition of the Grand Prix des Nations time trial. Jean-Marie Goasmat, also of France, prevails in the event's southern version.
- Emile Idée also wins "Paris–Roubaix," which is again run from Paris to Rheims.
- To aid the war effort, American bicycle manufacturers plan to produce 750,000 "Victory" bicycles. This new model "uses no copper or nickel, has smaller wheels than bicycles previously made, and uses tires made of 90 percent reclaimed rubber and scarcely thicker than a thumb. The maximum weight is 34 pounds compared with an average of 55 pounds for each of the 1,827,000 bicycles made last year. Built plainly, without bright metal work or fancy fixtures, the 'Victory' bike is expected to cost about 40 percent less than any of the lightweight models previously made. Last year, the bicycle industry used about 3,000,000 pounds of copper and nickel. This year none will be used and, by reducing the size and output of its one model, the industry further expects to save about 30,000 tons of steel."[5]
- The government also forbids the manufacture of children's bikes, but permits a 300 percent increase in the manufacture of bicycles for adults in preparation "for the day when war workers, owing to tire restrictions and gasoline rationing, may have to depend upon bicycles rather than automobiles to reach their jobs."[6] During 1941, about 85 percent of all bicycles produced had been juvenile models.
- Italian cycling great Felice Gimondi is born on September 29.

1943 • As the war rages on the continent cycle racing, like everything else, is in very short supply. Most news of the sport in 1943 centers around the capture of one Pvt. Fausto Coppi by the British Eighth Army almost as soon as he arrives for combat duty in Tunisia. During his internment, Coppi trains to be a truck driver. Another POW in Coppi's camp is the father of Claudio Chiappucci. The younger Chiappucci would finish second in the '90 and '92 Tours de France, third in '91, sixth in '93 and eleventh in '95.
- Coppi's adversary, Gino Bartali passes the war safely in the Vatican, where he works as a courier for the Catholic Party. After his death in 2000, it would be learned that "Gino the Pious" had enabled hundreds of Italian Jews to escape the fascists by smuggling false papers to them in the tubes of his bicycle.
- By August, Sicily has fallen to the British. With the handwriting on the wall, Italy's King Emmanuel strips Benito Mussolini of power on July 25 and, with Mussolini gone, cycle racing in Italy grinds to a halt. In early September, British and U.S. forces cross to the toe of the boot-shaped Italian peninsula, and by year's end hold most of the country south of Rome.

- "Detroit's factories produced another vehicle of war today and named it the Waac-cycle. Lieut. Col. Joseph M. Colby of the Army Ordnance Department revealed that the Waac-cycle is a lightweight, streamlined bicycle for the use of the Women's Army Auxiliary Corps. Military bicycles, he said, were too heavy for the Waacs to handle."[1]
- In England unescorted Italian prisoners of war are riding bicycles, which are difficult for civilian war workers to come by, to and from their jobs on a farm. The War Office explains that only the prisoners who work seven miles from their internment camps got to bike to work and that they are unescorted due to the shortage of manpower.
- American cyclist Joe Magnani is arrested by the Germans early in the year and sent to a concentration camp in northern France. By the time he's freed in mid 1944 his weight will have dropped from 170 pounds to 98.[2]
- "...Paris–Roubaix returned [to its traditional route] and the Paris–Tours was run as normal."[3] Paris–Roubaix was won by Belgium's "Black Eagle," Marcel Kint (Mercier).
- For the first time since 1938, the Grand Prix des Nations time trial is run as a single, unified event. The race is won by Belgian time trial champion Joseph Somers (individual).
- One French racing series of note held in 1943 is the *L'Auto*-sponsored nine-race Grand Prix du Tour de France which is won by France's "Jo" Goutorbe (Helyett-Hutchinson), who wins the yellow jersey for his victory.
- On August 1, *L'Auto* sponsors the Grand Prix des Alpes. The one-day event, which includes climbs of the Télégraphe, Croix de Fer and Lautaret, is easily won by the naturalized French citizen Dante Gianello (France Sport-Dunlop).
- Paris–Roubaix winner Marcel Kint of Belgium claims the first of his three consecutive Flèche–Wallonne victories.
- Fifty-five-year-old Jean Alavoine dies after crashing during a race for former champions. Alavoine completed 8 of the 11 Tours de France he'd started between 1909 and 1925, winning a total of 12 stages and five times finishing in the top five.

1944
- French rider Eloi Tassen (Metropole-Dunlop) wins the Grand Prix des Nations time trial.
- The second Grand Prix du Tour de France is won by Belgium's Maurice de Simpelaere (Alcyon), who also wins the 1944 running of Paris–Roubaix.
- A patent has been granted for "a collapsible bicycle (No. 2,359,764), by William B. Johnson, Aberdeen Proving Ground, Md., featuring pivoting support bars and folding pedals for compact storage and shipment."[1]
- In Normandy in July: "The Germans are making much use of bicycles for troop movement to counteract the interference with the railways and the apparent shortage of motor transport or gasoline. Daily we see the highways from which fighting has been heard dotted with dead Germans lying near their bicycles. The French are gathering these cycles and we see them everywhere pedaling along the roads."[2]

- On August 25, the Allies liberate Paris, freeing it from four years of Nazi occupation.
- In early September: "The restoration of public transport is another urgent need in Paris. The Civil Affairs Section of the Army estimates that there are about 1,500,000 bicycles in use in the capital. They are the only form of transport available....However, [Colonel Howley] said, he though [sic] it might be possible to start the Metro operating again in from two to three weeks."[3]

1945
- As the war in Europe begins to wind down, Fausto Coppi, although still a POW, is transferred back to Naples.
- "Corp. Joseph G. Dannelly of North Charleston, S.C., a special service soldier attached to the Eighth Air Force in England, brought one of the most striking souvenirs, the first to be seen on the piers where returning soldiers land. It was a large, high-saddle English bicycle. Corporal Dannelly said he had overcome many obstacles to get it back, talking his way past one objecting officer after another."[1]
- By alternating between neutrality and support for the Axis powers during the war, Spain had spared itself the ravages of battle and emerges from the conflict relatively unscathed. As such Spain is the first country to renew its national tour, holding the event for the first time since 1942. The fifth Vuelta a España is won by Dello Rodriguez with '41 and '42 winner Julian Berrendero finishing second. This is the only time the race leader's jersey is red until the organizers choose the color again for 2010. The 1945 Vuelta is organized by the publishers of *YA*.
- In July and August, the Shimano and SunTour bicycle component plants (both of which had been converted to small-arms production) in Sakai, Japan are destroyed in B-29 raids. On August 16, Shimano holds a dissolution ceremony and pays its employees their retirement allowances. By November, a few workers return to sift through the rubble, searching for salvageable freewheels to sell. Both factories will be rebuilt after the war.
- The fourth issue of *Le Cycle* magazine is the first to feature the exquisite cycling-related line drawings of Daniel Rebour.
- Naturalized French citizen Dante Gianello (France Sport-Dunlop), winner of the 13th stage of the 1938 Tour de France loses a leg after being hit by a U.S. Army Jeep in Aubagne during the Grand Prix du Débarquement on August 15, which was being held to celebrate the first anniversary of the American landings at St. Tropez. Gianello's teammate Bruno Carini, also a naturalized Frenchman, is killed instantly. The Jeep's driver is never caught.[2]
- Robert Batot of France wins the Victory Marathon, predecessor to the Tour of Britain.
- France's Paul Maye (Alcyon-Dunlop) wins the 43rd Paris–Roubaix.
- Belgium's Lucien Storme, winner of the 1938 Paris–Roubaix and a stage of the '39 Tour, had been a POW since early in the war. "Interned in the camp of Siegburg in Germany he was inopportunely shot with the arrival of the Americans on 10th April 1945."[3] He was 28.
- Future Tour de France winner Luis Ocaña is born on June 9.
- Cycling great Eddy Merckx is born on June 17.

1946 • The war may have been over for nearly a year, but in Italy the hostilities between Gino Bartali and Fausto Coppi are just beginning. In late March, Coppi wins the season-opening Milan–San Remo by 15 minutes, embarrassing Bartali, who finishes a further 9 minutes back. The next skirmish between the Italian adversaries takes place six weeks later, on neutral ground at the Championship of Zurich in early May. A suffering Bartali, still the leader of the Legnano team, tells Coppi, who had signed with the rival Bianchi squad after the war, that if the two ride to the finish together, he'll let Coppi win the sprint. But at the crucial moment, just as Coppi reaches down to cinch up his toe straps, Gino Bartali takes off and steals the race. Thus begins the feud between Italy's greatest cycling champions. It would continue for years, bitterly dividing the passionate Italian *tifosi*.

• The two would soon meet again, this time in a truncated Giro d'Italia. The previous Giro, held in 1940, had become an easy victory for the young upstart Coppi after Bartali had been slowed by an early crash. This time the tables are turned with Coppi crashing during a descent in the race's fifth stage, fracturing his rib. Despite his injury, he goes on to win the stage, but his fall costs him in the long run and his best efforts fall 47 seconds short. Round two to Bartali.

• Also competing in the 1946 Giro d'Italia is Illinois native Joe Magnani who had moved to southeastern France as a youngster and is now riding for the Italian Olmo team. Although he crashes and retires from the race during the 13th stage with an injured knee, Joe Magnani will always have the distinction of being the first American rider to compete in a grand tour.

• The year also sees the Vuelta a España make another of its sporadic appearances. Dalmacio Langarica (Galindo) wins the sixth Vuelta to be held since its inception 12 years earlier. Julian Berrendero (Galindo, Cicles Tabay) who had won the race in '41 and '42 and finished second in 1945, finishes second once again. This year the race leader's jersey is white with a red horizontal stripe, a color combination it will retain through the 1950 event.

• The year's other important race is the 1316-kilometer (818-mile) La Course du Tour de France (also called "Monaco–Paris" or the "Little Tour de France"). It is organized by the Société du Parc des Princes and former freedom fighter Émilion Amaury's *Le Parisien Libéré* newspaper, which is edited by Félix Levitan, a Jew who'd hidden from the Germans during the war. The late-July race, which runs from Monaco to Paris via the Alps in five stages (as was then required by regulations), is billed as a "dry run" for the following year's full Tour and is won by Apôtre "Apo" Lazarides (FRA) in 44:31:42. Lazarides finishes ahead of his support rider, Tour regular René Vietto (FRA)—winner of the race's second stage—and future Tour winner Jean Robic (FRA)—who wins the event's third stage and its climbing title. The event's first stage is won by Italy's Aldo Baito (ITA), while the last two legs are claimed by his countryman Adolfo Leoni (ITA). Afterward, Vietto proclaimed, "We [the French] will be unbeatable next year. And if the Tour escapes us, I'll start pedaling a sewing machine." In an interesting footnote, Lazarides' bicycle is equipped with a Campagnolo "Corsa" gear changer, making this the first

"Tour" win (sort of) for "Campy."

- The staff of *L'Auto*, which had been shut down by the French government because it had continued to publish during the German occupation, moves across the street and starts a new newspaper called *L'Équipe*.
- The success of La Course du Tour de France along with the collaboration of Jacques Goddet and Émilion Amaury helps tip the French cycling federation's decision about who'll run the Tour de France in favor of the staff at *L'Équipe*, who probably figured that the Tour de France should have been theirs all along. Beginning with the first postwar Tour de France the following year, Félix Levitan and Jacques Goddet would run the race together, with Levitan coming to oversee the commercial and financial aspects of the race, and Goddet the sporting side.
- The world professional road championship race returns following a seven-year hiatus. Switzerland's Hans Knecht beats Belgian riders Marcel Kint and Rik Van Steenbergen in the sprint to win the rainbow jersey.
- Shimano resumes production of freewheels and hubs.
- Sir Harold Bowden of the National Committee on Cycling dedicates a plaque at Courthill Smithy Keir, Dumfriesshire, Scotland, to honor the centennial of Kirkpatrick MacMillan's inventing the pedal bicycle in 1839. The ceremony had been postponed from 1939 because of the war.
- Future Tour de France winner Lucien Van Impe is born on October 20.
- Future Tour de France winner Joop Zoetemelk is born on December 3.
- GS Rochet rider Georges Claes of Belgium wins the 44th Paris–Roubaix.
- "The Amateur Bicycle League of America [predecessor to today's USA Cycling], starts to make helmets mandatory in sanctioned races. The helmet requirement takes effect beginning with the ABL national championships that August in Franklin Park in Columbus, Ohio. Ironically, [18-year-old Louis C. Brill, Jr. of Buffalo, New York] died after…[h]e smashed headfirst, going at least 40 miles an hour, into a 350-pound Fox Movietone camera.… It was the first fatal accident at the nationals."[1]
- Mike Peers (Manchester) wins the Brighton–Glasgow race, another forerunner of the Tour of Britain.
- On February 25, France's René Le Grevès is killed in a skiing accident in Saint-Gervais. Le Grevès competed in 6 Tours de France between 1933 and 1939, winning 16 stages. He was 35.
- Italy's Fausto Coppi (Bianchi) wins the season-long competition of international races.
- On December 14, 1946, the International Cycling Union approves as a world record Fausto Coppi's unpaced hour mark of 45.871 kilometers (28.504 miles) set at the Vigorelli velodrome in Milan on November 7, 1942.

1947
- Edward Van Dijck (Garin-Wolber) of Belgium wins the seventh Vuelta a España.
- Fausto Coppi (Bianchi) defeats Gino Bartali (Legnano) by 1:43 to win the 30th Giro d'Italia.

- Theo Middelkamp of the Netherlands wins the 1947 world road championship in Reims, France.
- American Joe Magnani is the seventh (and last) finisher in the sweltering 275-kilometer (171-mile) world championship race. Magnani had finished 10th at the 1936 worlds.
- Cinelli Cino & C. which produces bicycle frames and lightweight alloy handlebars is founded by Cinelli and his wife Hedi.
- In order to gain priority for Japan's scarce raw materials, Shimano begins manufacturing bicycles, which it will continue to do through 1954.
- Belgium's Jeff Scherens wins his seventh professional sprint title. He had also won it in 1932-33-34-35-36-37.
- The Monarch Bicycle Company of Chicago introduces the Silver King, with a frame made of hexagonal aluminum tubing, and cast lugs. The machine also features a springer fork.
- Specialities TA (*Traction Avant*) introduces the *CycloTourist*, the first alloy crank.
- Riders start using double front chainrings for the first time. René Vietto (France Sport-Dunlop) and Fausto Coppi (Bianchi) are generally credited with bringing this innovation to the peloton.
- Paul Neri (France Sport-Dunlop) wins the French national championship. The result is annulled after it's discovered that Neri (who may also have raced under the name "Faldutto") is an Italian citizen. Neri, who had also won the French national amateur championship in 1942, would become a French citizen in 1955. The 1947 French championship would be run again three months later.
- George Kessock (Paris Cycles) wins the Brighton–Glasgow race.
- Newspaperman Georges Cazeneuve creates the five-stage Critérium du Dauphiné Libéré. The initial running of the event is won by Poland's Edouard Klabinski (Mercier).
- Italy's Gino Bartali (Legnano) wins the season-long competition of international races. He had also won the competition in 1936, 1937, and 1939.
- Illustrations for 1947 in *The Data Book* show a stem for a threadless headset and sealed bottom bracket bearings.[1]
- "By agreement with Cycles Peugeot, of France, the Indian Motorcycle Company will sell a quantity of French bicycles through its nationwide dealer organization, it was announced [in Springfield, Mass.] today [January 27]."[2]
- "The sixty British bicycle manufacturers who were reported in a London dispatch yesterday to have been balloting for the honor of presenting a bicycle to [avid cyclist] Lewis Douglas, United States ambassador, may find that American ingenuity has solved their dilemma. Otis L. Guernsey, president of Abercrombie and Fitch, sporting goods dealers, Madison Avenue and Forty-fifth Street, [New York] said last night he had stepped into the breach by sending to Mr. Douglas via air express, a new American bicycle. It is being preceded by this cable: 'British bicycle manufacturers' problem solved today [April 17]. American bicycle now on the way to you via air express.' Mr. Guernsey said he hoped the machine would reach Mr. Douglas in about a week."[3]

- Donald Sheldon of Nutley, N.J., wins the Kugler-Anderson Memorial Tour of Somerville.

In the Tour de France:

- Jean Robic (*Ouest*) is the first rider on a French regional team to win the Tour.
- Robic is the first rider to take the overall lead on the last day, and without wearing the yellow jersey.
- Robic becomes the only rider to take the lead on the final day when the stage is not a time trial.
- Robic is probably the first rider in the Tour de France to wear a helmet.
- *Le Parisien Libéré* joins *L'Équipe* as co-sponsor. The Parc des Princes velodrome is a co-sponsor this year only.
- *But et Club* and *Miroir-Sprint* begin printing pre-Tour souvenir issues of their magazines.
- The Judex Watch Company sponsors a Miss Tour de France pageant in which the young women who present the daily stage prizes compete for the overall title.
- Only sixteen riders in the '47 race had previously competed in the Tour de France.
- For the first time since 1927, there are no former winners in the race.
- Félix Levitan joins the Tour's staff as Jacques Goddet's assistant.
- Edouard Klabinski is the first Polish rider to compete in the Tour. He finishes 34th.
- The race visits Belgium and Luxembourg for the first time.
- The race crosses the Glandon and Croix de Fer cols for the first time.
- Raymond Impanis wins the Tour's longest time trial of 139 kilometers (86.4 miles) from Vannes to Brieuc. His time for the stage is 3:49:36.
- Albert Bourlon pulls off what is generally regarded as the Tour's longest solo breakaway: 253 kilometers (157 miles) in the 14th stage. However, the Tour's web site credits Eugène Christophe with a 315-kilometer (196-mile) breakaway in the 1912 Tour's fifth stage to Grenoble.
- The Tour's yellow bikes of the '30s are gone as racers return to riding their sponsors' machines.
- A small plane belonging to *L'Équipe* crashes on the Col du Tourmalet just before the arrival of the peloton. The plane's pilot, Georges de Seversky, is taken to the hospital.
- A *journaliste Américaine* named "Miss Collins" covers the race.
- France's René Vietto leads the race for 15 days, bringing his total number of days in the yellow jersey to 26, the most of any non-winner of the event.

1948 • Spain's Bernardo Ruiz (UD Sans Minaco) wins the eighth Vuelta a España.
- An illustration for 1948 in *The Data Book* shows what appears to be a shift lever mounted on a brake lever.[1]
- Future two-time Tour de France winner Bernard Thévenet is born on October 10.
- Fiorenzo Magni (Viscontea) wins the 31st Giro d'Italia by 11 seconds over Ezio

Cecchi (Welter)—the smallest margin ever. Fausto Coppi (Bianchi), who'd complained about the small penalties Magni had received for cheating, drops out after Magni takes the pink jersey with a "lucky" breakaway in the race's next to last stage. Gino Bartali (Legnano) finishes eighth and wins the climbing competition.

- In an attempt to shore up flagging British bicycle sales in the states, Arthur Chamberlain, managing director of a Birmingham bike factory, displays a new, lightweight machine intended for the U.S. market. This new English bicycle is said to weigh less than 26 pounds, or 21 pounds lighter than the average American machine and 8 pounds less than a typical British bike.
- American cyclist Joe Magnani returns to the United States from Europe and is signed by Schwinn to ride six-day races.[2]
- Tom Saunders (Dayton Cycles) wins Great Britain's Brighton–Glasgow race.
- Donald Sheldon of Nutley, N.J., repeats as winner of the Kugler-Anderson Memorial Tour of Somerville.
- Yugoslavia's August Prosinck wins the Warsaw–Prague leg of the first Peace Race. Yugoslavia's Alexander Zoric wins the Prague–Warsaw leg.
- "An initial shipment in quantity of Continental-type bicycles from occupied Japan arrived here early this week, and will be sold in the domestic market and for re-export to Latin America, it was announced yesterday [December 23] by L. N. White & Co., Inc., 24 Stone Street [New York]. Described as qualitatively competitive with similar imported bicycles, the price was said to be considerably lower."[3]
- Belgium's Alberic "Briek" Schotte wins the world professional road championship in Valkenburg, the Netherlands, after Bartali and Coppi again mark each other, falling 14 minutes behind before dropping out of the race. Schotte outsprints France's Apo Lazarides for the win after the pair break away on the hilly circuit which includes 26 climbs of the Cauberg hill. For their actions in the Giro and the worlds, Bartali and Coppi are reprimanded and suspended for two months by the Italian Cycling Union.
- France's Jose Bayaert wins the 195-kilometer (121-mile) men's road race at the XIVth Olympiad in London.
- Swiss rider Ferdi Kübler (Tebag, Peugeot) wins the 12th Tour of Switzerland. During the race, two-time Liége–Bastogne–Liége winner Richard Depoorter (Super, Garin & Mondia) of Belgium is killed when he crashes in a tunnel in Wassen and is run over by a following team car.
- Briek Schotte (Alcyon, Groene-Leeuw) wins the inaugural, season-long Desgrange-Colombo Challenge. The series, which consists of the year's most important races (the Tour de France, the Giro d'Italia, Milan–San Remo, the Tour of Flanders, the Tour of Lombardy, the Flèche Wallonne, Paris–Tours, Paris–Roubaix and Paris–Brussels; and later Liége–Bastogne–Liége and the Tour of Switzerland), comes about through the initiative of the major sports journals in France, Italy and Belgium (*L'Équipe, La Gazzetta dello Sport, Sportwereld* and *Les Sports*) and is named after Tour de France founder Henri Desgrange and Emilio Colombo.

- In the Netherlands, there are a reported 5 million bicycles in use, or one for every two people. In the United States, there are 19 million people who call themselves cyclists. This year, 2,761,000 bicycles will be manufactured in the U.S.

In the Tour de France:
- Winning the Tour after a 10-year interval, 34 year-old Gino Bartali becomes the race's oldest postwar winner. He wins seven stages including three in a row. He also wins all the mountain stages and takes the climbing title.
- French television broadcasts the Tour's finish in Paris live to the country's 5,000 TV sets.
- Bartali's win is the first victory for Campagnolo components in the Tour de France.
- The mountain climbs are divided into two categories ('A' and 'B') of difficulty.
- The race goes into Italy for the first time when the 11th stage finishes in San Remo.
- "...[A] points competition was held in 1948 and 1949, [but] it was not until 1953 that it became a permanent fixture in the tour."[4]
- Between the 3rd and 18th stages, the last rider overall is eliminated from the race, per article 41 of the rules.
- Wool manufacturer Les Laines Sofil awards a daily prize to the wearer of the *maillot jaune*.
- The news magazine *Le Miroir du Monde* prints a high-quality special edition devoted entirely to the Tour de France.

1949 • Faliero Masi establishes his frame shop below the Vigorelli Velodrome in Milan.
- Italian director Vittorio De Sica's movie *The Bicycle Thief* opens in New York on December 12 and is voted "Best Foreign Film" at the New York Film Critics Awards. It stars Lambreto Maggiorani and ten-year-old Enzo Staiola as the father and son who go searching around Rome for the father's Fides bicycle after it is stolen. The movie had been released as *Bicycle Thieves* the previous year in Great Britain where it won the British Academy Award for best picture.
- Fausto Coppi wins the 32nd Giro d'Italia as well as the race's climbing category. Gino Bartali (Legnano) is second, 23:47 back. "...(W)hen two flat tyres contributed to his defeat by Coppi in the Dolomites, a fan asked him the next day, 'Did you have two or three punctures yesterday?' Bartali's answer was sublime: 'Punctures? We never get punctures.'"[1]
- Coppi (Bianchi-Ursus) wins the second annual Desgrange-Colombo Challenge.
- The Vuelta a España is not held in 1949.
- Eugene McPherson of Columbus, Ohio, a 22-year-old senior at Ohio State, sets the official Amateur Bicycle League of America transcontinental record by riding the 3,054 miles between Santa Monica, California and New York in 20 days 4 hours 29 minutes.
- Belgium's Rik Van Steenbergen wins the 1949 world professional road cham-

pionship in Copenhagen by outsprinting Switzerland's Ferdi Kübler and Fausto Coppi of Italy.

- After being directed off the course at the entrance to the Roubaix velodrome, France's André Mahé (Stella-Dunlop) "wins" the Paris–Roubaix classic. Serse Coppi (Bianchi-Ursus), the first finisher to use the correct entrance to the track, protests the result (at the urging of his teammate and older brother, Fausto). Later in the year, after Fausto Coppi threatens to boycott future runnings of Paris–Roubaix, Serse Coppi and André Mahé are named co-winners of race.
- Great Britain's Geoff Clarke (ITP) wins the Brighton–Glasgow race.
- Chicago's Frank Brilando wins the Kugler-Anderson Memorial Tour of Somerville.
- Czechoslovakia's Jan Vesely wins the second annual Peace Race.
- France's Paul Choque (La Perle-Hutchinson) dies as the result of a crash on the Parc des Princes Velodrome on September 4. Choque, 39, had won Bordeaux–Paris in 1936 and had finished seventh in the 1937 Tour de France, in which he'd won stages 16 and 18B. He had also been the French cyclocross champion in 1936 and 1938.
- British cycle manufacturer Hercules introduces the "Herailleur," a rear derailleur with indexed shift levers.

In the Tour de France:

- Fausto Coppi becomes the first rider to win both the Tour de France and Giro d'Italia in the same year.
- Coppi defeats Gino Bartali by 7:02 in the 137-kilometer time trial between Colmar and Nancy. The mark still stands as the greatest margin of victory in a Tour de France time trial.
- Custodio Dos Reis is the first Moroccan to ride in the Tour de France.
- The initials "HD" are embroidered on the left breast of the yellow jersey in honor of the Tour's late founder, Henri Desgrange.
- Although the race's 17th stage skips the mighty Col du Galibier, a memorial to Henri Desgrange is dedicated on July 19 near the top of the mountain's south side. In 1911, Desgrange had penned "An Act of Adoration" to the awesome climb, saying that compared to it, the race's other cols were nothing "but pale and vulgar babies." For his design, the monument's creator, Bertola, is awarded the Grand Prix de Rome.
- The first Tour physician is assigned to follow the race.
- French television covers the finish of the race's final stage from Nancy to Paris, and begins a news broadcast five nights a week during the Tour.
- L'Équipe and Le Parisien Libéré produce 24 Jours de Course, "le film officiel" of the 1949 Tour de France.
- Tour de France "technician" Jean Garnault designs a route that takes the race to Spain for the first time.
- A third category of difficulty is added to the mountain ratings.
- The first riders to the top of the most difficult climbs receive a 60-second time bonus. Bonuses of 40 and 20 seconds are given to the first riders to the tops of the lesser climbs.

- Belgium's Norbert Callens leads the Tour after the third stage but never gets to wear his yellow jersey in the race because his *soigneur* had sent it ahead with the luggage.
- To honor Coppi's Tour win, Bianchi issues a "Tour de France" replica bicycle.
- France's Apo Lazarides uses a bike with a "Dural" aluminum frame.

Chapter 6

1950–1959
Cycling's Golden Age

1950 • Spain's Emilio Rodriguez (Sangalhos) wins the ninth Vuelta a España.
- Hugo Koblet (Cilo) of Switzerland wins the 33rd Giro d'Italia, the first *straniero* (foreign rider) to do so.
- Switzerland's Ferdi Kübler (Tebag) wins the third annual Desgrange-Colombo Challenge.
- Fausto Coppi (Bianchi-Ursus) wins Paris–Roubaix by 2:41. After the race runner-up Maurice Diot (Mercier-A.Magne) of France "made a remark which was to enter the annals of cycle sport: 'I won Paris–Roubaix, Coppi was supernatural.'"[1]
- France's Jean Robic (Thomann, Cilo) wins the first cyclocross world championship.
- Great Britain's Reg Harris (Raleigh Cycles) defends his world sprint title by defeating Holland's Arie Van Vliet (Butler Cycles) in consecutive races before 8,000 fans in Liège, Belgium.
- Great Britain's George Lander (Frejus Cycles) wins the Brighton–Glasgow race.
- Denmark's Willi Emborg wins the Peace Race.
- Richard Cortright of Buffalo, N.Y., wins the Kugler-Anderson Memorial Tour of Somerville.
- After having ridden his bike to the start from his home 20 kilometers (12 miles) away, Briek Schotte wins the 284-kilometer (177-mile) world professional road championship in Moorslede, Belgium in 7:49:54. With his one-minute victory over Dutchman Theo Middelkamp, Schotte reclaims the title from fellow Belgian Rik Van Steenbergen and is driven home in a limousine.
- American Ted Smith (individual) also takes part in the worlds, becoming the first U.S.-based rider to compete in the world championship race. Joe Magnani, an American living in France, had participated in the worlds in '35, '36 and '47. Smith punctures past the halfway point and fails to finish the race. When he climbs into the broom wagon, he notices that one of its passengers is Swiss star Hugo Koblet. "Smith knew Koblet from riding in track races with

him in the States. Smith asked what he was doing there and Koblet said he 'got tired.' The man who was to win the Tour de France by twenty-two minutes [in 1951] said he was tired. 'No excuses,' Smith says."[2]
- Tullio Campagnolo perfects the design of his new front derailleur.

In the Tour de France:
- Ferdi Kübler becomes the Tour de France's first Swiss winner.
- Les Laines Sofil provides 1,850,000 francs in total prize money.
- American actor Orson Welles is the starter of one of the last Tours de France to start in Paris.
- Reporter Hélène Parmelin covers the race "from a woman's point of view" for the communist paper *L'Humanité*.
- Gino Bartali and Fiorenzo Magni's Italian national team quits over unruly crowds while Magni is in the lead.
- Following the Italians' withdrawal, the 15th stage is shortened to avoid going into Italy.
- Ferdi Kübler refuses to wear the yellow jersey the day after Magni's retirement from the race.
- Algeria's Marcel Molines and Morocco's Custodio Dos Reis are the race's first stage winners from their countries and from the African continent. Dos Reis had become a French citizen in 1931 but still lived in the French colony of Morocco.
- Time limits for each stage are reduced to force the *domestiques* to make a more concerted effort.
- Daniel Rebour draws the Tour-winning bike for *Le Cycle* magazine from 1950 to 1976.
- The French TV news program *Journal Télévisé* follows the entire Tour in the race's media caravan.

1951 • Seventeen year-old Jacques Anquetil joins the A.C. Sotteville cycling team.
- Tullio Campagnolo introduces the Gran Sport, the first modern rear derailleur. All of Campy's subsequent derailleurs (Record, Nuovo Record and Super Record) will retain this same basic design until 1983. Cycling historian Frank Berto calls the Gran Sport "the most significant derailleur of this decade and it set the standard for quality and reliability."[1] He once remarked of the rugged units that "(t)hey would shift poorly forever."[2] Campagnolo also perfects his famous corkscrew in 1951.
- Giovanni Pinarello (Bottecchia-Ursus) wins the Tour of Italy's maglia nera (black jersey) of the race's last rider. He uses the 100,000 lire (about $160.00) he's paid not to ride in the next Giro to start his bike company.
- After previously finishing 2nd and 3rd in the event, Switzerland's Ferdi Kübler wins the world road championship in Varese, Italy. Coppi's woes continue when he misses the race because he is suffering from the flu.
- In February, the Federal Trade Commission orders the Cycle Jobbers Association of America, the Cycle Parts and Accessories Association, forty-six jobbers, and thirty-eight manufacturers to halt "unreasonable restraint of trade" prac-

tices in conspiring to "suppress and eliminate" competition. "The order against the jobbers association prohibits its members from restricting membership, compelling manufacturers to sell solely through association members, fixing prices, coercing retail dealers to buy only from association members, and preventing manufacturers from selling directly to chain stores at the same prices granted to jobbers. The parts association is forbidden to carry out any 'planned common course of action' with the jobbers organization."[3]

- "The United States is getting priority in the delivery of bicycles from Britain at the expense of other important markets in the world, it was said here [in Boston] today [October 9] by George H. B. Wilson, deputy chairman and managing director of Raleigh Industries, Ltd., Nottingham. Mr. Wilson is visiting the English company's assembly and servicing plant for the American market. The plant produces Raleigh, Rudge and Humber bicycles in the same manner as the Nottingham factory."[4]
- Italy's Fiorenzo Magni (Ganna) wins the 34th Giro d'Italia by 12 seconds over Belgium's Rik Van Steenbergen (Mercier).
- The Vuelta a España is not held between 1951 and 1954.
- Defending winner Ricardo Barcia of Mexico wins the opening stage of the 1,270-mile Tour of Central Mexico, covering the 40-mile leg from Mexico City to Toluca in 1:22:14.
- Great Britain's Ian Steele (Viking Cycles) wins the first Tour of Britain, another forerunner of the Milk Race.
- Denmark's Kay Allen Olsen wins the Peace Race.
- Serse Coppi (Bianchi-Pirelli), Fausto's younger brother, crashes near the finish of the Tour of Piedmont, hitting his head on the sidewalk. After finishing the race, he returns to his hotel but soon falls ill. He's rushed to the hospital where he's pronounced dead.
- Drafting a Talbot race car near Toulouse, France, José Meiffret achieves a bicycle speed record of 109.1 mph. Meiffret's M. Yvars bicycle features a small (about 22 inches in diameter) front wheel mounted on a rearward-facing fork and a huge 130-tooth TA chainwheel.
- Francis Mertens of New York City wins the Kugler-Anderson Memorial Tour of Somerville.
- France's Louison Bobet (Stella-Hutchinson) wins the fourth annual Desgrange-Colombo Challenge.

In the Tour de France:
- Switzerland's Hugo Koblet dominates the event in his only Tour de France victory.
- The organizers place a plaque at the site of the blacksmith's forge in Sainte-Marie-de-Campan, where Eugène Christophe lost four hours repairing his fork in 1913.
- The team classification is determined by the times of each squad's three best-placed riders.
- The race starts in Metz. It's the first time that the Tour has started outside the Paris area since its 1926 departure from Evian.

- France's Roger Lévêque wins the fourth stage in Paris. It's the only time a stage of the race that isn't the final one finishes in Paris.
- The race goes into the interior of France for the first time, visiting the Massif Central region, but skipping Puy de Dôme.
- The racers climb Mont Ventoux for the first time. Lucien Lazarides (FRA) is first over the top.
- Wim Van Est becomes the first Dutch rider to wear the yellow jersey. He crashes out of the race the following day.

1952 • Fausto Coppi (Bianchi) wins the 34th Giro d'Italia. It's Coppi's fourth Giro victory.
- Germany's Heinz Muller wins the 1952 world professional road championship in Luxembourg. France's Raphaël Géminiani is left off the team because French officials are afraid he'll work for his Bianchi teammate Coppi.
- In early March, Russia is admitted to the International Cycling Union. Spokesman Alexis Kouprianoff says his country will compete in all big international races, probably even the Olympics.
- Belgium's Andre Noyelle wins the 190-kilometer (118-mile) men's road race at the Helsinki Olympics.
- Schwinn introduces a road version of the Paramount 14 years after its introduction of the track edition. Former racer Joe Magnani, who had assembled many of the company's Paramount track bikes and tandems, will assemble all of the Paramount road bikes for many years.
- In late October, the United States government authorizes bicycle manufacturers to raise ceiling prices by 7 percent. The increase is authorized because the average earnings of the industry had fallen below 85 percent of its best three years between 1946 and 1949.
- 1929 Tour de France winner Maurice DeWaele dies on February 14. He was 55.
- Emmett Mueller of New York receives patent number 2,619,931 for an audible bicycle. The device works by having "a sound track...mounted to the front wheel, with a stylus fixed to the fork and controlled from the handlebars. The sound track may reproduce music, spoken words, or a warning..." Another version of Mueller's invention provides "keys on the handlebar to control a series of reeds attached to the fork."[1] By pressing the keys, the rider can play music as the reeds hit the spokes.
- Great Britain's Kenneth Russell (Ellis-Briggs) wins the Tour of Britain.
- Ernest Seubert of New York City wins the Kugler-Anderson Memorial Tour of Somerville.
- Riding for the England team, Scotland's Ian Steel wins the sixth annual Peace Race (*Freidensfahrt*) through Czechoslovakia, East Germany and Poland.
- Switzerland's Ferdi Kübler (Tebag) wins the fifth annual Desgrange-Colombo Challenge.

In the Tour de France:
- Fausto Coppi wins the 39th Tour de France by more than 28 minutes. Because of his domination of the event, the second and third-place prizes are doubled.

- Finding the pace of the of the race's 16th stage too slow for his liking, Tour director Jacques Goddet initially withholds the winner's prize money.
- A 100,000 franc prize is given to the winner of the new daily combativity award.
- Pierre Sabbaugh, commentator Georges de Caunes and cameraman Henri Persin bring television to the Tour. Shot from a motorbike, 16 mm film of each stage is sent by train to Paris where it's edited and aired the following day on French TV.
- Sales of television sets in France peak in July, when news coverage of the Tour is increased to three times a day.
- Mountaintop finishes (l'Alpe d'Huez, Sestriere, and le Puy de Dôme) are introduced to the race. Fausto Coppi wins all three stages.
- The event's two time trials are shortened to around 60 kilometers (37 miles) each.
- Dr. Pierre Dumas joins the race as its official physician, a position he would hold until 1977.
- Marcel Bidot becomes manager of the French national team, a position he'll hold until 1969.
- The race receives its first escort from the drivers and motorcycle gendarmes of the *Parisian Garde Républicaine*.

1953
- Nineteen year-old Jacques Anquetil turns professional with Hugo Koblet's La Perle team. He earns the first of his nine victories in the prestigious 140-kilometer (87-mile) Grand Prix des Nations time trial, beating time trial specialist Roger Creton (Stella-Dunlop) by nearly seven minutes.
- Fausto Coppi (Bianchi-Pirelli) drops Hugo Koblet (La Perle) on the Stelvio Pass on the next to last day to win the 36th Giro d'Italia by 1 minute 29 seconds.
- Coppi also wins the world professional road championship in Lugano, Switzerland, beating runner-up Germain Derijcke of Belgium by six and a half minutes. Belgium's Stan Ockers finished third, 10 minutes back.
- Coppi's world championship-winning Bianchi bicycle features an integrated headset, which would become popular nearly 50 years later.
- Great Britain's Gordon Thomas (BSA) wins the third Tour of Britain.
- The first "Tostal Tour" of Ireland is run, but no one seems to be sure who won it.
- Denmark's Christian Pedersen wins the Peace Race.
- On January 1, 1953, 19-year-old Ugo De Rosa opens Cicli De Rosa at 1 Via Franco della Pila in Milan, Italy.
- A seven-man Colombian amateur team headed by Ramon Hoyos and Ephraim Forero ("the Indomitable Zipa") and managed by France's Jose Beyaert sails to Europe and competes in the Route de France. After the others return to Colombia, Forero races in Europe for the rest of the season.
- Italy's Loretto Petrucci (Bianchi-Pirelli) wins the sixth annual Desgrange-Colombo Challenge.
- Twenty-two-year-old Richard Berg of Chicago, a Navy dental technician, shatters the existing transcontinental bike record by nearly six days, riding from Santa Monica, Calif., to New York in 14 days 16 hours 45 minutes.

- Cranford, N.J.'s Hugh Starrs wins the Kugler-Anderson Memorial Tour of Somerville.
- "Copies of the first handbook on group bicycle play to be published by the Bicycle Institute of America are available, the institute has announced. Titled *Bike Fun*, the booklet contains a hundred ideas for lively two-wheeler games, hikes, races, stunts, and similar activities for young enthusiasts."[1]
- In February, "H. Clyde Brokaw, president of the Bicycle Institute, returning here from last week's convention of the industry in Boca Raton, Fla., says 300 makers and dealers reported 2,000,000 two-wheelers made and sold in 1952 to give the country a record high of over 21,000,000 bicycles on the roads. He predicted that with the removal of metal restrictions the total for 1953 would be even higher."[2]
- Leon Henderson Associates is named exclusive distributor for the Travis Bike Motor. The motor, claims the manufacturer, will attach to the front wheel of any bike and propel it at speeds of up to 35 miles per hour while getting as much as 150 miles to the gallon. It sells for about $90. In 1942 Henderson, then administrator of the Office of Price Administration, had demonstrated the war's first Victory Bike for the press.

In the Tour de France:
- After emerging as the team leader, a victorious Louison Bobet begins the tradition of sharing his winnings with his teammates.
- The Tour celebrates 50 years with a gathering of past champions and a commemorative postage stamp.
- The sprinters' competition (called the *Grand Prix du Cinquentenaire* in 1953) is introduced. Its green jersey is initially sponsored by La Belle Jardinierem, a garden equipment company.
- A rift among top riders on the French team, which culminates with the stage-13 "Beziers Scandal," begins to raise questions about the race's national team concept.
- A new era begins when every rider to finish in the Tour's top 10 had turned professional after the war.
- The race's average speed is a then-record 34.6 km/h (21.5 mph).

1954
- Ernesto Colnago establishes *Particolari di Colnago* in Italy and begins making bicycle frames.
- Switzerland's Carlo Clerici (Condor & Guerra) wins the 37th Giro d'Italia because of the Bernina Strike during which the Italian riders refuse to race over the Bernina Pass. The strike is precipitated after the other riders stage a slowdown because they feel they aren't being paid enough by the organizers to race hard after Fausto Coppi (Bianchi-Pirelli), who'd received a sizable appearance fee, gets sick.
- By winning the world professional road championship in Solingen-Klingenring, Germany, over the likes of Coppi, Charly Gaul and Jacques Anquetil, France's Louison Bobet becomes the first rider the win the Tour de France and the world road championship in the same year since fellow Frenchman Georges Speicher in 1933.

- Future cycling great Bernard Hinault is born on November 14.
- France's Eugene Tamburlini (independent: Peugeot) wins the fourth Tour of Britain.
- The U.K.'s John Perks (Earlswood Cycling Club) wins the "Tostal Tour" of Ireland.
- Italy's Primo Volpi (Arbos) wins the 13-day, 2560-kilometer (1,591-mile) Tour of Europe in Strasbourg, France on October 3. Volpi's overall time for the race is 83 hours 51 minutes 59 seconds.
- An illustration in *The Data Book* shows a modern-type suspension fork which has a spring at the top of each leg.[1]
- Dutch trade groups ask their government to help prevent the United States from raising the tariff on imported bicycles. Last year Holland exported 16,000 units to America, this year it hopes to ship 35,000.
- Before the November 13 opening of London's International Cycle and Motorcycle Show, Hugh M. Palan, director of the British Cycle and Motorcycle Manufacturers' Union, tells reporters that he is disheartened to learn that American manufacturers had appealed to the Federal Tariff Commission for more protection from imports. Britain is the world's biggest exporter of bicycles, having shipped more than $53,000,000 worth in the first nine months of the year alone. In 1953 Britain had sold more than 400,000 bicycles in the United States.
- Fiorenzo Magni's Nivea-Fuchs squad ushers in the era of cycling's *extra sportif* sponsorship. Magni goes looking for other sponsors after 1909 Giro winner Luigi Ganna announces the dissolution of the Ganna team he'd first started in 1912. *Extra sportif* sponsors are companies that make products not directly related to cycling, such as Nivea skin cream.
- Denmark's Eluf Dalgaard wins the Peace Race.
- France's Jacques Anquetil (La Perle-Hutchinson) records the second of his nine victories in the Grand Prix des Nations time trial.
- Roy Richter begins making the "500" auto-racing helmet at Bell Auto Parts located at 3633 Gage Avenue in Bell, Calif., a suburb of Los Angeles. Two years later Richter would form the Bell Helmet Company as a division of Bell Auto Parts.
- John Chiselko of Somerville, N.J., wins the Kugler-Anderson Memorial Tour of Somerville.

In the Tour de France:
- France's Louison Bobet wins his second consecutive Tour de France.
- Jeeps are replaced by Peugeot 203 convertibles as the Tour's official vehicles.
- The Italians skip the Tour over a disagreement with the organizers over *extra sportif* sponsors, and the Giro's "Bernina Strike" rider slowdown.
- The race starts in Holland, marking the first time that the Tour has started outside of France.
- Bertram Seger (did not finish) becomes the first and only rider from Liechtenstein to compete in the Tour.
- Two-part stages return to the race for the first time since 1939.

- Also returning is the team time trial in its modern format in which the teams are timed.
- The Swiss national squad registers its only team victory in the Tour.
- During the race's 10th stage to Bayonne, journalist Antoine Blondin writes his first column for *L'Équipe*, entitled "Du Pin et des Jeux." In *An Intimate Portrait of the Tour de France*, Philippe Brunel writes that Blondin "...was always drunk 'with the joy of bicycle racing' they said euphemistically, and always prolific, 'he drank ink and peed copy,' as the argot had it."[2]

1955 • France's Jean Dotto (Terrot-Margnat-Debon) wins the 10th Vuelta a España, the first edition of the race to be held since 1950. Dotto is the first French winner of the event. The Vuelta, first run in 1935, has been held annually since 1955. Beginning this year the race leader's jersey is yellow, which it will remain through the 1997 Vuelta (except for the 1977 event, when it returns to its original orange). The 1955 Vuelta is also the first one in which the racers compete on regional and national teams.
- Italian national champion Fiorenzo Magni (Nivea-Fuchs) wins the 263-kilometer (163-mile) Tour of Romagna, beating Fausto Coppi (Bianchi-Pirelli) by half a wheel.
- Magni makes the 38th Giro d'Italia his third win in the event.
- Three riders, France's Raphaël Géminiani (St. Raphaël-Géminiani), Louis Caput (Arliguie, Vampire), and Spain's Bernardo Ruiz (La Perle-Hutchinson), complete all three major tours in the same year. "Gem" had ridden especially well in all three events, finishing third in the Vuelta, fourth in the Giro and sixth in the Tour.
- Stan Ockers of Belgium wins the 1955 world professional road championship in Frascati, Italy.
- Ockers (Elve-Peugeot) also wins the eighth annual Desgrange-Colombo Challenge.
- British amateur Anthony Hewson (Sheffield) wins the Tour of Britain.
- The UK's Brain Jolly (Kirkby Cycling Club) wins the Tour of Ireland.
- East Germany's Gustav-Adolf Schur wins the Peace Race.
- Raphaël Géminiani's St. Raphael-Géminiani squad brings *extra sportif* sponsors to the French peloton.
- Twenty-one-year-old Jacques Anquetil (La Perle-Hutchinson) is drafted into the French Army and sent to Joinville, where he continues his training for cycling.
- Princeton senior Peter T. "Marathon" McKinney, 21, from La Grange, Ill., hopes to ride 140 miles from Poughkeepsie, N.Y., to Princeton in order to raise the $75.75 he needs to pay his bill at the university store so he can graduate. Before McKinney even embarks on his ride, his fellow students have pledged $50 in support—in 25¢ increments—whether he completes his ride or not.
- Canada's Pat Murphy takes time out from his honeymoon to win the Kugler-Anderson Memorial Tour of Somerville.
- Soviet rider Tamara Novikova establishes the first women's hour record, riding

38.473 kilometers (23.907 miles) in Irkoutsk on July 7.

- The American Machine and Foundry Company (AMF) announces plans in May to build a $1.25-million factory in Little Rock, Ark., to manufacture Roadmaster, Shelby, and other models of bicycles. Currently AMF's bicycles are being produced by its Cleveland Welding subsidiary, which will shift its focus to "heavy mobile equipment and defense products."
- In August President Eisenhower increases duties on all imported bikes by 50 percent. "Under terms of the Presidential order, the new rates became effective immediately. The higher duties were imposed under the 'escape clause' of the Reciprocal Trade Agreement Act. The clause is intended to protect domestic manufacturers from intensive foreign competition that threatens serious injury to their industry."[1] The tariff increase means that the price of an imported bicycle will increase by about 10 percent.

In the Tour de France:
- Louison Bobet is the first French three-time Tour de France winner, and the first rider to win the race three times in a row.
- The Luxembourg-Mixte team includes two Australians (John Beasley and Russell Mockridge), and the first two Germans (Heinz Mueller and Gunther Pankoke) to compete in the Tour since 1938.
- Miguel Poblet becomes the first Spaniard to wear the yellow jersey.
- The 10-man British team is the first Tour squad from the U.K. since a 3-rider team in 1937.
- The 30-kilometer (18.6-mile) transfer between Poitiers and the start of the 21st stage in Châtellerault is the Tour's first since 1906.
- The 1955 Tour is the first to use photo-finish cameras.
- Film of the race is shown on French television only hours after the stage finishes.
- The organizers allow companies not involved in cycling to sponsor teams.

1956 • Shimano markets its first rear derailleur, the "333". The company would discontinue it after two years and not release another model until 1964.
- The first SunTour rear derailleur is made for Maeda by another Japanese company, Iwai Saisakusho.
- On April 29, "Stan Ockers [Elve-Peugeot] of Belgium, world cycling champion, today won the five-day, 1,145-kilometer [712-mile] Grand Prix of Nations [Rome–Naples–Rome] bicycle race. It was the 36-year-old Belgian's first triumph in the partly motorcycle-paced road race in which he twice finished second. He came in first in both of today's final laps from Naples to Rome on rain-splashed highways [Ockers won stages 1B, 3B, 4B, 5A and 5B]. Bruno Monti [Atala] of Italy, who won the race in 1954 and 1955, was second."[1]
- On August 26, Rik Van Steenbergen nips fellow Belgian Rik Van Looy in the world road championship in Ballerup, Denmark, beginning "The Battle of the Riks."
- On September 29, Belgian sprinter and former world road champion Stan Ockers crashes during a velodrome event in Antwerp, as he tries to avoid a fan who's too close to the track, and dies two days later. He was 36.

- During his military service, Pvt. Jacques Anquetil (Helyett-Potin) travels to Milan and sets the hour record at 46.159 kilometers (28.683 miles). He is promoted to corporal.
- In September, three months after Anquetil had set the record, Italian amateur Ercole Baldini increases the hour mark to 46.393 kilometers (28.829 miles) in Milan.
- Baldini also wins the 188-kilometer men's road race at the XVIth Olympiad in Melbourne by more than a mile (Great Britain's Alan Jackson is third @ 1:59). Baldini also takes the world championship in the 4,000 meter event.
- The Tour of Britain is not held.
- Poland's Stanislaw Krolak wins the Peace Race.
- Luxembourg's Charley Gaul (Faema-Guerra) wins the 39th Giro d'Italia, becoming the race's second foreign winner. Gaul secures his victory by erasing a 15-minute deficit on Monte Bondone in a blizzard, which forces 60 riders to abandon the race. During the stage, Gaul stops in a cafe to warm up.
- Italy's Angelo Conterno (Bianchi-Pirelli) wins the 11th Vuelta a España.
- Boston physician Paul Dudley White, who's a member of President Eisenhower's medical team, tells a New York audience in late February that the city should establish "safe bicycle paths so New York businessmen could pedal to work. Dr. White, a heart specialist, said that overeating and lack of exercise might be two of the most important contributing factors in the increasing number of heart attacks that physicians have encountered lately among their younger male patients."[2]
- Fitchberg, Mass., native Art Longsjo is the first American to compete in two Olympiads in the same year. A speed skater in the winter Olympics in Cortina d'Ampezzo, Italy, Longsjo also takes part in the Melbourne games as a cyclist. Two years later, he would be killed in an auto accident. Today the Fitchberg Longsjo Stage Race, one of the oldest and largest events in the eastern U.S., is held annually in his honor.
- Jack Heid of Westwood, N.J., wins the Kugler-Anderson Memorial Tour of Somerville.
- In July Nancy Neiman Baranet becomes the first American woman (and second American after Joe Magnani) to compete in a European stage race. She ends up 14th of 40 finishers in the 8-day French Criterium Cycliste Féminin Lyonnaise–Auvergne.[3]
- In Houston, Texas, the David Eisenhower Club holds a "Ride a Bike for Ike" rally for young Republicans. Local Eisenhower-Nixon campaign manager McLelland Wallace said kids participating in the event will receive an "IM4IKE2" license plate for their bikes.
- Future cycling great Sean Kelly is born on May 24.
- Belgium's Fred de Bruyne (Mercier) wins the ninth Desgrange-Colombo Challenge.
- Phillips Company displays a bicycle with a titanium frame at the London Cycle Show.
- May is designated National Bicycle Month.

In the Tour de France:
- Roger Walkowiak becomes the second rider on a French regional team (*Nord-Est-Centre*) to win the Tour since 1947.
- Walkowiak is also the second rider (after Firmin Lambot in 1922) to win the Tour without winning a stage.
- None of the top four overall finishers wins a stage. The best-placed rider to win a stage is Italy's Nino Defilippis, who finishes fifth.
- For the first time since 1947, there are no former winners in the field. There were also no former winners in the 1927 Tour de France.
- At the urging of the French Ministry of the Interior, much of the Tour de France is run on secondary roads resulting in many punctures for the racers and traffic problems for the publicity caravan.
- For the first time, a wheel change is allowed when a racer punctures, meaning riders no longer have to ride with a spare tire draped around their backs. During the race, team support staff listen to radio transmissions from the officials' car to learn which riders require mechanical assistance.
- The organizers offer a daily prize for the unluckiest rider who suffers the worst-timed puncture or crash.
- The average speed of the race is 36.2 km/h (22.5 mph), a new race record.
- Shay Elliot (Ile de France) is the first Irish rider to compete in the Tour de France. He abandons the race during stage 4B.
- Antonio Barbosa (Luxembourg/Mixte) is the first Portuguese rider to compete in the Tour de France, finishing 10th overall.
- The race visits the 1,262-meter Col du Luitel climb for the first time.
- By winning the eighth stage to La Rochelle, Spain's Miguel Poblet becomes the first rider to win at least one stage in each of the three major tours in the same year. He had won four stages of the Giro and three at the Vuelta.
- *Lanterne rouge* (the tour's last rider) Roger Chaussabel says, "I'm not a *rouleur*, I'm not a climber, I'm not a sprinter. I'm a complete racer. A man of the Tour." He also wins the race's *Prix de l'Humor du Peloton*.

1957
- Maurice Garin, winner of the first Tour de France, dies on February 18. While many sources say that he died still protesting his disqualification from the 1904 event, Les Woodland reports that when "it no longer mattered," Garin confessed to hopping a train during the second Tour. "He admitted it," said a friend (gravedigger Maurice Vernalde). "He was amused about it, certainly not embarrassed, not after all those years. There wasn't the same significance to the Tour then…"[1] Garin was 85.
- Italy's Gastone Nencini (Leo Chlorodont) wins the 40th Giro d'Italia by 19 seconds over Louison Bobet (L. Bobet-BP-Hutchinson). Nencini also completes the Tour de France (in sixth place) and the Vuelta (in ninth place) in 1957, to become the only rider to win a grand tour while finishing the other two in the same year.
- By winning Milan–San Remo, Miguel Poblet (Ignis-Doniselli) becomes the first Spaniard to win a classic.

- Spain's Jesus Loroño (Gamma) wins the 12th Vuelta a España.
- The Tour of Britain is not held.
- Poland's Nencho Khristov wins the Peace Race.
- For the third consecutive year, Spanish rider Bernardo Ruiz (Ignis-Doniselli) completes all three grand tours.
- Belgium's Rik Van Steenbergen repeats as the world professional road champion by outsprinting Frenchmen Louison Bobet and André Darrigade in Waregen, Belgium. Van Steenbergen joins Italy's Alfredo Binda as a three-time winner of the event.
- France's Roger Rivière (St. Raphaël-Géminiani-Dunlop) increases the hour record to 46.923 kilometers (29.158 miles) in Milan's Vigorelli velodrome.
- Brian Robinson becomes the first British rider to join a major continental team when he signs with St. Raphaël-Géminiani-Dunlop.
- France's Renée Vissac increases the two-year-old women's hour record to 38.569 kilometers (23.984 miles) on September 18 in Milan, Italy.
- Belgium's Fred de Bruyne (Carpano-Coppi) wins the tenth annual Desgrange-Colombo Challenge.
- "President Eisenhower's enthusiasm for the European bicycling habit promises happier United States-Dutch relations in 1957, at least in the realm of the two-wheeler. The Netherlands is to the bicycle what Texas is to oil. Not only do the people ride bicycles as do no others in any country in the world but they also make them and want to sell them, especially to the United States." The president's affinity for cycling should help to ease some of the tension created by America's recent increase of its tariff on imported bikes, reports the *New York Times*.
- Arnold Uhrlass of Yonkers, N.Y. wins the Kugler-Anderson Memorial Tour of Somerville.
- In Manhasset, Long Island, 290 of 549 third through eighth-graders fail to meet the standards to get their bicycles licensed. One-hundred-sixty-six kids fail either the written or riding skills test while the rest have bikes that fail the mechanical inspection. Those who flunk may not ride their bikes to school until they pass the part of the test they failed.
- A dozen Kansas City, Mo., mailmen are testing the idea of making their deliveries by bicycle. "According to George A. Lewis, General Superintendent of the Mails, the experiment is a part of the department's desire to mechanize. 'The department aims to get as many carriers as possible riding something,' he said. 'Bicycles, motor scooters, or otherwise. There's some thinking it will result in economies.' The bicycles are sturdy and are painted blue and red. The front wheel, smaller than the rear wheel, supports a wire basket big enough to hold a regulation leather satchel. On the handle bars are a thumb-operated warning bell and a mileage gauge."[2] Some downsides of the experiment are the maintenance of the bikes, local traffic laws, and dogs.

In the Tour de France:
- France's Jacques Anquetil takes the first of his five Tour de France victories.
- Television comes to the Tour with Robert Chapatte reporting directly from

the race's route. Unfortunately, a disagreement between the Tour's organizers and French television results in no live coverage of the race, only film of the previous day's stage.

- The Tour makes its first ascent of the Col de Portillon.
- Radio pioneer Alex Virot and his driver René Wagner are killed when their motorcycle plunges off a cliff in the Spanish Pyrenees.
- Members of the French team win 12 of the race's 22 stages. France had won 12 of 21 stages in 1930.
- Adolf Christian is the first Austrian rider to finish on the final podium.
- To accommodate the ever-increasing number of journalists covering the event, race director Jacques Goddet authorizes a mobile press room.

1958 • Italy's Ercole Baldini wins the 41st Giro d'Italia.
- Baldini also wins the 1958 world professional road championship in Reims-Gueux, France. The first world road championship for women is also held in Reims, France. The 59-kilometer (37-mile) race is won by Luxembourg's Elsy Jacobs.
- Italy's Adriano Rodoni is elected president of the International Cycling Union. He'll hold the position until 1981.
- Future French cycling great Jeannie Longo is born on October 31.
- The Tour of Britain returns as the Milk Marketing Board-sponsored Milk Race. It is won by Austrian amateur Richard Durlacher.
- Art Longsjo of Fitchburg, Mass., wins the Kugler-Anderson Memorial Tour of Somerville.
- The Netherlands' Piet Damen wins the Peace Race.
- France's Jean Stablinski (Essor-Leroux) wins the 13th Vuelta a España.
- On September 23, France's Roger Rivière (St. Raphaël-Géminiani-Dunlop) increases his own hour record to 47.346 kilometers (29.421 miles) at the Vigorelli velodrome in Milan. Three months after the death of Tom Simpson in 1967, Rivière would admit to the "massive use of amphetamines—a large injection and five pills for his hour record of 1959 [*sic*], for example."[1]
- France's Jacques Anquetil (Helyett-Potin) wins his sixth straight Grand Prix des Nations time trial, completing the 100-kilometer (62-mile) course in 2 hours 19 minutes, for a record average speed of 43.160 km/h (26.820 mph).
- Campagnolo introduces its first wood-boxed tool set.
- The end of the Asian bike boom causes four of Japan's six bicycle component companies to go bankrupt, leaving just Maeda (SunTour) and Shimano in business. With the closing of Iwai Saisakusho, Maeda begins manufacturing its own SunTour-brand derailleurs.
- Shimano founder Shozaburo Shimano dies on September 20 at the age of 64. Rumor has it that just before he died, Shimano had his wife free all his pets—from his "bell-ringing crickets to his paddy birds."
- In early July the United States government files "a civil antitrust suit charging price fixing and other illegal restrictions in the marketing of Schwinn Bicycles. The suit named Arnold, Schwinn & Co. of Chicago, the Schwinn Cycle

Distributors Association, and the B. F. Goodrich Company of Akron, Ohio. It was filed in Federal District Court in St. Louis. The department said Schwinn distributors and Goodrich sell respectively 80 percent and 15 percent of Schwinn's output of nearly $17 million a year. The complaint asked the court to enjoin the alleged practices and to void Schwinn's franchise and price mainte- nance agreements."[2] The case would drag on for six and a half years.

- Three judges at the United States Court of Customs unanimously reverse the 1955 tariff increase on imported bicycles, saying that the escape clause action used to implement the increase had not been taken within the legal time limits.
- Future novelist Robert Daley begins covering European sports, including pro- fessional bicycle racing, for the *New York Times*, a position he holds for six years. In 1961 he publishes *Cars at Speed*, a look at sports car and Grand Prix racing. Three of his books, including *Year of the Dragon* and *Prince of the City*, would eventually be made into movies.
- "Japan's first jet bicycle blew up today [May 10] and landed its inventor in a hospital. The student flier who made it for a cost of 5,000 yen (about $15) took it for a trial run in one of Tokyo's main streets. He had reached a speed of eight miles an hour when the mechanism exploded. He was slightly injured."[3]
- Belgium's Fred de Bruyne (Carpano) wins the 11th and final edition of the Des- grange-Colombo Challenge. It's his third consecutive win in the competition.
- Australia's Russell Mockridge (individual), who'd finished 64th in the 1955 Tour de France, is killed on September 13 when he's hit by a bus while compet- ing in the Tour of Gippsland in Clayton North, Victoria, Australia. He was 30.
- By completing the Vuelta, Spain's Bernardo Ruiz (Faema) finishes his twelfth consecutive grand tour, a streak that had begun with the 1054 Giro.
- France's Jean Forestier (Essor-Leroux) wins the inaugural Super Prestige Per- nod Trophy, which includes only French races through 1960.
- Great Britain's Mildred Robinson increases the women's hour record to 39.718 kilometers (24.681 miles) on September 25 in Milan.
- Elsy Jacobs of Luxembourg travels to Milan and bumps the women's hour re- cord to 41.347 kilometers (25.693 miles) on November 9.

In the Tour de France:
- Luxembourger Charly Gaul's victory aboard a bicycle made of Reynolds 531 tubing is the first of 27 Tour de France wins through 1988 for the British tub- ing manufacturer.
- The race features ten 12-man teams for the first time.
- There are no rest days during the race.
- The Tour begins in Belgium, its second foreign start.
- Thirty-year-old French singer and actress Line Renaud (née Jacqueline Ente) is the race's ceremonial starter. She would also wave the Tour's start flag 50 years later at the 2008 Tour de France.
- Parc des Princes Secretary General Constant Wouters dies following a collision with André Darrigade only 50 meters from the end of the race's final stage.
- Brian Robinson is the first rider from Great Britain to win a stage in the Tour de France.

- The race is led by a record eight different riders. This mark would be equaled in 1987.
- With his three stage wins, Italy's Pierino Baffi becomes the second rider in two years to score at least one stage victory in each of the year's three grand tours. Baffi had won one stage at the Giro and two in the Vuelta.
- Robert Chapatte covers the race live for French television from the summit of the Col d'Aubisque during the 13th stage. There is also live coverage of the leg's run-in to Luchon and of stage 18, the Mont Ventoux time trial.
- The Mont Ventoux time trial is the Tour's second-slowest individual time trial. The winner's average speed is 20.76 km/h (12.89 mph).
- Race organizers award a $250 prize to whichever foreign and domestic journalists write the best articles about the race.

1959 • English engineer Alex Moulton, Ph.D., begins working with the Dunlop Tire Company to develop 14- and 16-inch high pressure tires.
- Luxembourg's Charly Gaul (Emi) wins the 42nd Giro d'Italia.
- Antonio Suarez (Licor 43, St. Raphaël-Géminiani) of Spain wins the 14th Vuelta a España.
- "Pope John XXIII today [January 24] received one of Italy's most famous bicycle racing squads. The twenty-four-man Ignis squad was led by the world champion, Ercole Baldini of Italy and Spanish ace Miguel Poblet. The Pontiff said that although he knew little about sports, he considered them important 'in their Christian, human, and social aspects.'"[1]
- André Darrigade of France wins the 1959 world professional road championship in Zandvoort, the Netherlands.
- Great Britain's Bill Bradley (England) wins the Milk Race.
- East Germany's Gustav-Adolf Schur wins the Peace Race.
- Rupert Waitl of Brooklyn, N.Y., wins the Kugler-Anderson Memorial Tour of Somerville.
- France's Henry Anglade (Liberia-Hutchinson) wins the Super Prestige Pernod Trophy. Anglade also wins the Prestige Pernod Trophy (a series for only French riders) and the Sedis Challenge.
- After conflict between France and Italy leads to its cancellation, Henri "Rik" Van Looy (Faema) wins an unofficial version of the Desgrange-Colombo Challenge.
- Ireland's Shay Elliot (ACBB-Helyett-Leroux) wins Het Volk.
- Future cycling great Stephen Roche is born on November 28.
- Miguel Poblet (Ignis) wins Milan–San Remo for the second time in three years. It would be the last victory for a Spanish rider in a classic until Miguel Indurain (Banesto) wins the *Classica San Sebastian* in 1990.
- After being damaged by a fire (which probably was set), Paris' indoor *Vélodrome d'Hiver* (Winter Velodrome) is demolished in May to make way for a housing project.
- Francis Pélissier dies on February 22 and his younger brother Charles dies on May 28. Both brothers wore the Tour's yellow jersey, following in the footsteps

of their older brother Henri, who won the race in 1923. Charles won eight stages of the 1930 Tour de France. Francis was 64, Charles was 56.

In the Tour de France:

- Federico Bahamontes becomes the first Spanish rider to wear the yellow jersey and to win the Tour de France.
- Bahamontes wins the Tour's slowest-ever individual time trial, conquering the 12.5-kilometer (7.77-mile) climb of Puy de Dôme in 36:15 for an average speed of 20.69 km/h (12.85 mph).
- Spanish surrealist Salvador Dali (1904–89) and twenty-two other artists create a limited edition of one hundred 17 by 21-centimeter (6½ by 8-inch) commemorative post cards for the "Tour de France Cycliste 1959."
- André Darrigade wins the race's first stage for the fourth consecutive year.
- Louison Bobet, Jean Robic and Raphaël Géminiani each ride in their final Tour de France.
- Great Britain's Brian Robinson wins the race's 20th stage by more than 20 minutes.
- The Tour de France begins the regular use of transfers between the finish of one stage and the start of the next. The race had also utilized transfers in 1906 and 1955.
- The organizers give out the Tour's first overall Most Combative Rider award. It's won by France's Gérard Saint.

Chapter 7

1960–1969
Little Bikes and Big Wheels

1960 • Forty-year-old Fausto Coppi dies on the morning of January 2, 1960 from a misdiagnosed case of malaria or typhus. Coppi had been one of half a dozen cycling stars who'd traveled to French West Africa, where he finished second to Jacques Anquetil in a race at Ougadougou on December 12. The group returned home on December 18, and Coppi began feeling ill the day after Christmas. The only other member of the group to get sick was 35-year-old Raphaël Géminiani, all the other riders were in their 20s. When medication failed to help, Fausto Coppi was taken to the Hospital, where he died a few days later.

Former French champion André Leducq had once described Coppi's style on the bike: "His long legs extend to the pedals with the joints of a gazelle. At the end of each pedal stroke his ankles flex gracefully—all the moving parts turn in oil." Thirteen years earlier, during his feud with Gino Bartali, Coppi had declared, "…I will try right up to my last stroke of the pedal to be the best."[1] More than 50,000 people attend the *campionissimo*'s funeral. Afterward, Italy's *La Gazetta dello Sport* writes that "the great Heron has folded his wings."

Forty two years later, the Italian sports daily *Corriere dello Sport* would report that Brother Adrien, a 75 year-old monk in Burkina Faso (formerly Upper Volta) said that a man had confessed to poisoning Coppi as revenge for a racing accident which had claimed the life of a rider named "Canga" or "Kanga." According to the 2002 report, the murderer gave Coppi a drink containing a slow-acting potion derived from a local grass, to which he succumbed following his return to Italy. Coppi's physician and his son both "dismiss the report," and Adam Diallo, secretary of the Burkina Faso Cycling Federation, would respond to the news with, "We don't poison people."[2]

• Jacques Anquetil (ACBB-Leroux-Helyett) wins the 43rd Giro d'Italia. He uses his prowess in the time trial to defeat Gastone Nencini by 28 seconds and become the first French winner of the event.

• Irishman Shay Elliot (ACBB-Leroux-Helyett) wins the Giro's 10th stage.

• Belgium's Frans De Mulder (Groene Leeuw-Sas-Sinalco) wins the 15th Vuelta a España.

- The French Cycling Federation has a special touring bike made for President Eisenhower.
- Belgium's Rik Van Looy wins the 1960 world professional road championship in Hohenstein-Saschenring, East Germany. Runner-up André Darrigade of France finishes on the podium for a record fourth consecutive time (he had finished third in 1957 and 1958 and first in 1959).
- New York's Central Park is closed to vehicular traffic for the first time since its construction in 1857 so 250 amateur cyclists can compete for six spots on the Olympic cycling team. Saturday's tryouts for the two-man time trial have teams starting at three-minute intervals and riding ten circuits of a 6.2-mile loop around the park. The next day's road race is 18 laps (112 miles), with the top four finishers making the road team. The 1964 Olympic trials would also be held in Central Park.
- Harlem's Herb Francis is the United States' first African-American Olympic cyclist.
- After sprinting for the "win" one lap early, the Soviet Union's Viktor Kapitanov comes back on the next lap to win the 175-kilometer (108.5-mile) men's road race at the XVIIth Olympiad in Rome. It is the first year that the medals are hung around the contestant's necks. Knud Enemark Jensen, a rider on the Danish 100-kilometer team time trial squad, collapses in the heat and suffers a skull fracture. He later dies and an autopsy reveals traces of the blood circulation stimulant Ronicol in his system. "The doping of bike racers in Europe has been going on for years. It probably will continue. The only thing surprising about the case of the Danish Olympian, Kund Enemark Jensen, is that his coach, Oluf Jorsen, admitted dosing four Danish riders with a drug called roniacol [*sic*] before Friday's 100-kilometer race. Jensen died. Two other Danes [Jorgen C. Jorgensen and Vagn Bangsborg] collapsed. Usually in cases like this, all involved swear that no drugs were used. Illness or even the death of racers is then ascribed to 'food poisoning,'" French coach Robert Oubron said. "I'm not surprised to hear that Jensen had been drugged. A healthy young athlete does not die from sunstroke. Many pros are drugged, of course, but we don't drug amateurs."[3]
- Los Gatos, Calif.'s Mike Hiltner (Pedali Alpini) finishes 20th in a road race in Florence, Italy. "Hiltner won a hefty gold medal and made headlines in the local newspaper for being the first non-Italian finisher in an international race of more than 100 miles."[4] Hiltner would change his name to Victor Vincente of America in 1975.
- Hiltner also wins the Kugler-Anderson Memorial Tour of Somerville.
- France's Jean Graczyk (ACBB-Leroux-Helyett) wins the Super Prestige Pernod Trophy. It's the third and final year that the series consists of only French races.
- French cyclist Gérard Saint (Rapha-Gitane-Dunlop) is killed in an automobile accident on March 16. In the previous Tour de France, Saint had won the event's newly-created combativity award and finished on the podium five

times (stages 11, 14, 18, 19 and 21). He also finished second in the points competition and was third in the climbing competition. Gérard Saint was 24.

- The 1960 edition of Paris–Roubaix marks the first time that French television receives pictures directly from a camera in a helicopter. The race is won by the nearly 38-year-old Pino Cerami (Peugeot-BP), who'd become a Belgian citizen in 1956.
- Future Tour de France winner Pedro Delgado is born on April 15.
- Future Tour winner Laurent Fignon is born on August 12.
- Raymond Poulidor turns pro with Mercier-BP-Hutchinson. His career will largely coincide with those of Jacques Anquetil and Eddy Merckx.
- East Germany amateur Erich Hagen wins the Peace Race.
- When price cuts fail to stimulate sales of bicycles in the Soviet Union, production is cut 21 percent compared to the previous year's levels.
- T.I. Raleigh is formed when Raleigh merges with British Cycle Corporation which is owned by Tube Investments.
- English Amateur Bill Bradley wins the Milk Race for the second straight year.
- British engineer Benjamin Bowden has about 600 of his futuristic Spacelander fiberglass bicycles produced by Bomard Industries of Kansas City, Mo. The Spacelander, which Bowden had designed in 1956, retails for $89.50.

In the Tour de France:
- Italy's Gastone Nencini is the third rider to win the Tour de France without winning a stage.
- The size of the major national teams is increased from 12 riders to 14.
- Following the ninth stage, the Tour de France makes its first train transfer, taking the race from Bordeaux to Mont-de-Marsan.
- Germany sends a full team to the Tour for the first time since 1938.
- Goran Karlsson is the first Swedish rider to compete in the Tour. He abandons during the eighth stage.
- Hour record holder Roger Rivière is seriously injured in a crash on the descent of Mt. Aigoual's Perjuret pass in the Parc des Cévennes.
- French television uses a helicopter to cover parts of the race, and has cameraman François Magnen shooting the action from the back of a motorcycle during the 16th stage's descent of the Col d'Izoard.
- Radio-Television Français begins paying a small fee to broadcast more than nine hours of the Tour, four of them live.
- Alphonse Steinès dies. It was Steinès who was behind the introduction of the Tour's first major climbs, including those of the Col d'Aubisque and the Col du Tourmalet, over which he slogged through waist-deep snow in 1910 and reported them passable. Alphonse Steinès was 87.
- The yellow jersey loses its shirt collar (but will retain its two front pockets until 1970).

1961 - Géo Lefèvre dies. Lefèvre is generally credited with proposing the idea of a six stage "Tour de France" to *L'Auto* editor Henri Desgrange in November of 1902.

- Spain's Angelino Soler (Faema) wins the 16th Vuelta a España.
- Italy's Arnaldo Pambianco (Fides) wins the 44th Giro d'Italia. The race retraces the route Garibaldi and his army had taken (from Turin to Sardinia, Sicily, and then to Naples) to drive out invaders 100 years earlier.
- Belgium's Rik Van Looy repeats as world road champion, winning the event in Bern-Bremgarten, Switzerland.
- On July 17, Eddy Merckx rides his first "official" race in Laken, Belgium. He finishes sixth in the "*debutants*" category. He records his first victory on October 1 in Lettelingen, Belgium.[1]
- Great Britain's Tom Simpson (Gitane-Leroux) wins the Tour of Flanders.
- Great Britain's Brian Robinson (Rapha-Gitane) wins the Dauphiné Libéré.
- Peter Rich mimeographs the first eight-page issue of *Velo-Sport Newsletter* at his bicycle shop in Berkeley, Calif. After it undergoes several name changes, Harley M. Leete purchases the magazine and changes the name to *Bicycling*.
- Future American cycling great Greg LeMond is born on June 26.
- France's Jacques Anquetil (Helyett-Fynsec-Hutchinson) wins the Super Prestige Pernod Trophy.
- The Tour de l'Avenir (Tour of the Future) for riders under 26 is founded by *L'Équipe*'s chief cycling correspondent, Jacques Marchand. Through 1967 the race will be held on shortened stages ahead of the professionals during the last two weeks of the Tour de France. The first winner of the Tour de l'Avenir is Italian amateur Guido de Rosso.
- On July 22, police and agents of the Institute for Forensic Medicine and officers of the Cantonal Chemists Authority raid a locker room at the Swiss national championships and confiscate "substantial stores" of pep pills and other stimulants. One-hundred-ninety-two units are found in one locker alone.
- The Soviet Union's Yuri Melikhov wins the Peace Race. The first leg of the two-week race is watched by 70,000 fans who sit for four hours in Warsaw Stadium to see the racers go by four times during the 88-mile stage.
- English amateur Billy Holmes wins the Milk Race.
- Robert McKnown of Malden, Mass., wins the Kugler-Anderson Memorial Tour of Somerville.
- Cyclists and motorcyclists account for 45 percent of Europe's 60,000 annual traffic fatalities. In Europe the number of accidents per mile traveled is triple that of the United States.

In the Tour de France:
- Jacques Anquetil wins the Tour in the last year it's contested by national teams (except for a brief return in '67 and '68).
- A 12-man British team takes part in the Tour. Shay Elliot is its best finisher in 47th position.
- France's André Darrigade wins the Tour's opening stage for the fifth time in six years.
- Jacques Anquetil wears the yellow jersey from the race's first day until the finish.

- Guido Carlesi takes second place from Charly Gaul by two seconds on the race's final day.
- For the first time, a Tour stage finishes atop Superbagnères.

1962 • After being injured in an automobile accident late the previous year, three-time Tour winner Louison Bobet (Margnat-Paloma) retires in April after spending five months in a cast.

- Campagnolo replaces its Gran Sport derailleur with the Record model, giving the component maker its first complete gruppo. By 1965, Record will have become the equipment of choice for professional teams; they would use Huret or Simplex only if subsidized.[1] Cycles Peugeot would remain loyal to fellow French company Simplex for many years. At this time, Tullio Campagnolo manufactures neither handlebars and stems nor chains and freewheels so as not to compete with his friends at Cinelli and Regina.
- British engineer Alex Moulton (moultonbicycles.co.uk), who designs suspensions for British Motor Corporation, develops an adult bicycle with 16-inch wheels and rubber suspension. The bike's main frame is a single large-diameter tube. Two years later Moulton's creation would be featured in the *New York Times*, which says, "New bicycles with midget wheels that remind one of a gadget that talented bears ride in circuses are turning up everywhere in Britain. They are expected to go into production in the United States next year. The inventor Alex Moulton, describes the development as the first successful change in bicycle design in 60 years. A certain snob appeal appears to attach to the little bicycle, and this may account for its popularity. Riders are well-dressed, middle-age business types."[2] In 1967 Moulton will sell his company, Moulton Bicycles Limited, to TI-Raleigh, which had introduced its own version of his bike in 1965.
- Franco Balmamion (Carpano) of Italy wins the 45th Giro d'Italia.
- West Germany's Rudi Altig (ACBB-St. Raphaël-Helyett-Hutchinson) wins the 17th Vuelta a España, becoming the first German to win a grand tour. Altig secures his win during the rainy 51-mile time trial when he takes all risks to protect his four-minute lead instead of laying down so his team captain, Jacques Anquetil, can take the overall lead. Rather than finish second, Anquetil abandons on the morning of the last stage.
- Ireland's Shay Elliot (ACBB-St. Raphaël-Géminiani) wins the fourth stage of the Vuelta and finishes third overall.
- France's Jean Stablinski wins the 1962 world road championship in Salo, Italy. Ireland's Shay Elliot—who doesn't attack "Stab" because the two are normally teammates on the St. Raphaël team, and brothers-in-law—finishes second. Stablinski wins the first televised worlds on a bicycle he borrows from a spectator after puncturing.
- Future Giro d'Italia winner Andy Hampsten is born on April 7.
- On July 16, 49-year-old Frenchman Jose Meiffret (1913–83) increases his own 11-year-old bicycle land speed record to 127.243 mph, drafting a Mercedes 300SL sports car on the Autobahn in Friedburg, Germany. His 20-kilogram

(44-pound) bike is fitted with a 130-tooth chainring and wooden rims. During his ride, Meiffret carries in his pocket a note which reads:

> In case of fatal accident, I beg of the spectators not to feel sorry for me. I am a poor man, an orphan since the age of eleven, and I have suffered much. Death holds no terror for me. The record attempt is my way of expressing myself. If the doctors can do no more for me, please bury me by the side of the road where I have fallen.

- The Netherlands' Johannes "Jo" De Roo (St. Raphaël-Helyett) wins the Super Prestige Pernod Trophy.
- Spain's Antonio Gomez Del Moral (Faema) wins the Tour de l'Avenir.
- The Soviet Union's Gainan Saydkhushin wins the Peace Race.
- Polish amateur Eugen Pokorny wins the Milk Race.
- Richard Centore of the Bronx, N.Y., wins the Kugler-Anderson Memorial Tour of Somerville.
- Stuyvesant Town, N.Y., bans bicycles from its walks and service roads because they pose "a distinct hazard" to children and the elderly. Stuyvesant Town joins Peter Cooper Village in banning bicycles. Both communities are owned and operated by the Metropolitan Life Insurance Company, whose management offers to store the bicycles for free.

In the Tour de France:
- Jacques Anquetil (ACBB-St. Raphaël-Helyett-Hutchinson) becomes the third rider to win three Tours de France.
- Anquetil is the only rider to win the race riding both on national teams and a trade team.
- A fourth category of difficulty is added to the race's mountain climbs.
- Trade teams return to the race, replacing national teams.
- The Tour retains its publicity caravan, which had been created to help fund the race when it switched to national teams in 1930.
- West Germany's Rudi Altig (ACBB-St. Raphaël-Helyett-Hutchinson) is the first German rider to win a Tour stage since WWII.
- There are no rest days during the race.
- The race makes its first visit to the 2,802-meter (9,192-foot) Col du Restefond, the highest point in the Tour's history.
- French television airs live daily reports of the last 30 kilometers (18.6 miles) of each stage.
- The team time trial (stage 2B) returns after a four-year absence, but it has no effect on the General Classification; its results are used only calculate team standings.
- Great Britain's Tom Simpson (VC XII°-Leroux-Gitane-Dunlop) is the first British rider to wear the yellow jersey. He wears the *maillot jaune* for one day and finishes sixth.
- Émilion Amaury, owner of *Le Parisien Libéré*, signs a sponsorship deal with the Tour de France and promotes Félix Levitan, the paper's chief editor, from Jacques Goddet's assistant to deputy director.

- French director Louis Malle shoots the 18-minute short film *Vive le Tour* during the race. The film focuses on the race's spectators and its customs of the time, which include riders stopping to raid cafes along the route. Malle would later marry American actress Candice Bergen.
- During the race's 14th stage, 20 riders become ill in what will become known as "The Weil's Affair," probably as the result of morphine doping.

1963
- Jacques Anquetil (St. Raphaël-Géminiani-Dunlop) wins the 18th Vuelta a España. With the victory, the Frenchman becomes the first rider to win each of the three grand tours. He's also the only rider to win the Vuelta and the Tour in the same year until Bernard Hinault (Renault-Gitane) claims both events in 1978.
- In the 46th Giro d'Italia, Franco Balmamion (Carpano) repeats as winner. Vito Taccone (1940–2007) of the Lygie team wins five stages, including four in a row (stages 10 through 13).
- With more and more bike races being televised, Peugeot-BP adopts a black and white checkerboard design on its jerseys so its riders will be easier to see on black and white television.
- In an incident that would become know as "the Renaix Affair," Belgium's Benoni Beheyt wins the 1963 world professional road championship in Renaix-Ronse, Belgium. Beheyt pulls off his victory by pretending to be suffering from cramps and then pushing and sprinting past Rik Van Looy, his countryman and pre-race favorite, who is going for his third world's title in four years. Though "Emperor Rik" would soon force Beheyt "into early retirement...by systematically blocking him from riding in races," nearly three decades later he'd admit that he was dying in the sprint and that his countryman's "reaching out to push me back was completely normal. It was his right because I had shut the door on him."[1]
- Gustave Garrigou, winner of the 1911 Tour de France, dies on January 28. He was 81.
- Also dead is 1934 Giro winner and two-time Tour runner up (1930 and 1933) Learco Guerra. In 1931, Guerra won the world road championship and became the first rider to wear the Giro d'Italia's pink leader's jersey. He was 61.
- Future *VeloNews* Editorial Director John Wilcockson covers his first Tour de France—by averaging 200 kilometers (124 miles) a day on his bicycle.
- The Kissena Park velodrome is constructed in Flushing, Queens, for the 1964 Olympic trials. The quarter-mile track (formerly known as the Siegfried Stern Velodrome after a local promoter) is located at the intersection of Booth Memorial Avenue and Parsons Boulevard.
- The Park Tool Company introduces its Model PRS-1 repair stand, the first in a long line of bicycle tools.
- Schwinn introduces the Sting-Ray youth bike, which comes with 20-inch wheels, high-rise handlebars and a "banana" seat.
- French independent rider André Zimmermann wins the Tour de l'Avenir.
- East Germany's Klaus Ampler wins the Peace Race.

- English amateur Pete Chisman wins the Milk Race.
- Olaf Moetus of Indianapolis wins the Kugler-Anderson Memorial Tour of Somerville.
- Great Britain's Tom Simpson (Peugeot-BP) wins the 560-kilometer (348-mile) Bordeaux–Paris race. For the second half of the race Simpson is paced by a derny driven by Fernand Wambst, who would be killed in a 1969 Blois Velodrome crash involving Eddy Merckx.
- France's Jacques Anquetil (St. Raphaël-Géminiani-Dunlop) wins the Super Prestige Pernod Trophy. Great Britain's Tom Simpson finishes second in the season-long competition.

In the Tour de France:
- Jacques Anquetil wins a record (at the time) fourth Tour de France.
- To celebrate the 50th running of the event, the Tour makes its final 20th-century start from Paris.
- For his victory, Anquetil receives a special 50th anniversary trophy.
- Shay Elliot (St. Raphaël-Géminiani-Dunlop) becomes the first Irishman to win a stage—the third—and to wear the yellow jersey.
- Anquetil's victory is the first for Campagnolo components on a French bicycle.
- Spain's Federico Bahamontes (Margnat-Paloma-Motul-Dunlop) wins his fifth King of the Mountains competition.
- I.B.A.C. and Molteni each contribute five riders to form a Tour team. The squad is led by Molteni's Guido Carlesi, who'd finished second in the 1961 Tour. This time he'd abandon during stage 14.

1964 • Jacques Anquetil (St. Raphaël-Géminiani-Campagnolo) of France wins the 47th Giro d'Italia, becoming only the second rider after Fausto Coppi (1949 and 1952) to win both the Giro and the Tour in the same year. During the race, Pope Paul VI asks the Giro's fans and 116 remaining riders to control their emotions and avoid incidents such as the one that had recently killed more than 300 soccer fans in Lima, Peru. Sports "must be without passion in athletes and the public," says the Pontiff.
- France's Raymond Poulidor (Mercier-BP-Hutchinson) wins the 19th Vuelta a España. For the first two weeks of the race, the nonchalant Frenchman predicts that he will take the leader's golden jersey after the 15th stage, a 45-mile individual time trial from Lean to Valladolid. When the day arrived, "Poupou" "overpowered his opponents," just like he said he'd do.
- Poulidor also wins the Super Prestige Pernod Trophy.
- Barry Hoban (Mercier-BP-Hutchinson) becomes the first British rider to win a stage in the Tour of Spain (stage 12). He also wins the 13th stage and finishes 29th overall.
- Italy's amateur national champion Mario Zanin wins the 195-kilometer (121-mile) road race at the XVIIIth Olympiad in Tokyo. Eddy Merckx crashes on the last lap. During the Olympics, engineers from Japanese manufacturers study the components on the bikes of Americans and Europeans.
- Holland's Jan Janssen wins the 1964 world professional road championship in

Sallenches, France.

- Italy's Antonio Maspes wins his seventh professional sprint tile. He had also won it in 1955-56-59-60-61-62.
- Great Britain's Tom Simpson (Peugeot-BP-Englebert) wins Milan–San Remo.
- Great Britain's Vin ("Vic") Denson (Solo-Superia) wins Brussels–Verviers.
- 1951 Tour de France winner Hugo Koblet of Switzerland is killed in Zurich when his car hits a pear tree on the road to Esslingen. Koblet was 39.
- Firmin Lambot, 77, winner of the Tour de France in 1919 and 1922 dies on January 19.
- Future Tour de France winner Bjarne Riis is born on April 3.
- Future five-time Tour de France winner Miguel Indurain is born on July 16.
- At the end of December, Federal Judge Joseph Sam Perry rules that Arnold, Schwinn & Co. and B. F. Goodrich had conspired to suppress competition "by boycott and other means" in the antitrust suit brought against the companies by the United States Government. Judge Perry also finds that the companies had not conspired to fix prices. B. F. Goodrich had agreed to sell Schwinn bikes on the open market before the case went to trial. The Feds had filed the suit against Schwinn and Goodrich in June, 1958.
- Nobuo Ozaki of Maeda (SunTour) develops the "Grand Prix" slant parallelogram rear derailleur.
- Shimano's "Archery", its first derailleur in six years, is an inexpensive copy of the Campagnolo Gran Sport.[1]
- Italian amateur Felice Gimondi wins the Tour de l'Avenir.
- Czechoslovakia's Jan Smolik wins the Peace Race.
- English amateur Arthur Metcalf wins the Milk Race.
- Hans Wolfe of Ozone Park, N.Y., wins the Kugler-Anderson Memorial Tour of Somerville.
- In Washington, the Republicans defeat the Democrats in a bicycle race around the Capitol Ellipse. Senator Claiborne Pell (Democrat, R.I.) is the individual winner by a bike length, but the Republicans, led by Representatives Robert T. Stafford (Vt.), Donald Rumsfeld (Ill.), and Silvio O. Conte (Mass.) win the race based on points. The event is put on by Washington's Olympic Committee to promote physical fitness and the Tokyo Olympics. For his win, Senator Pell receives a laurel wreath and a bouquet of gladiolas.
- Marshall Dodge leads a group of 150 riders from New York's Columbus circle to the World's Fair. The ride is organized to call attention to the group's campaign for laws allowing cyclists to ride across borough bridges and for bike lanes in Manhattan. "Cyclists need safety lanes in the city and exit routes from New York," says Dodge. "Convince the city to provide for cyclists as it does for motorists and pedestrians."[2] The group has special permission, and a police escort, for the ride. Dodge is a 28-year-old philosophy student at New York University. In 1958 he and Bob Bryan had recorded the "down-east" comedy album "Bert and I." In 1973 Dodge would move to Maine where he would become a well-known humorist and storyteller. He would be killed on January 28, 1982 by a hit-and-run driver while riding his bike in Hawaii. At

the time of his death Marshall Dodge was 45.

In the Tour de France:

- Jacques Anquetil (St. Raphaël-Gitane-Campagnolo) wins his fifth Tour de France. It's his sixth time on the final podium.
- Spain's Federico Bahamontes (Margnat-Paloma-Dunlop) wins his sixth King of the Mountains title.
- For the first time, the Tour's final stage is an individual time trial.
- French television covers the entire race for the first time.
- France's André Darrigade (Margnat-Paloma-Dunlop) wins his last two Tour stages, bringing his career total to 22, the most of any non-winner.
- During the 19th stage to Brive, a police helicopter fuel truck goes off a crowded bridge at Port-de-Couze, killing eight people. The truck's driver, a gendarme named Guicheney, is beaten by the crowd and nearly lynched.
- Riders are no longer restricted to changing bicycles only when they have mechanical problems.
- The Tour de France visits Andorra for the first time.
- Though it had been 12 years since the Tour de France had visited L'Alpe d'Huez—and would be another 12 before the race would visit it again—Georges Rajon puts up markers numbering (in descending order) the 21 hairpin turns leading to his Hotel Christina at the top.

1965
- Tom Simpson (GBR) wins the 1965 world road championship in Losarte, Spain by outsprinting Germany's Rudi Altig. Simpson also wins the Tour of Lombardy.
- The 48th Giro d'Italia is won by Vittorio Adorni (Salvarani) of Italy.
- West Germany's Rolf Wolfshohl (Mercier-BP) wins the 20th Vuelta a España. He's the last German rider to win a grand tour until Jan Ullrich wins the Tour de France in 1997.
- Jacques Anquetil (Ford France-Gitane) finishes the Dauphiné Libéré on May 29 and starts the 557-kilometer Bordeaux–Paris event eight hours later. He wins both events.
- Anquetil also wins the Super Prestige Pernod Trophy. Great Britain's Tom Simpson (Peugeot-BP-Michelin) finishes second.
- British rider Vin Denson (Ford France-Gitane) wins the Tour of Luxembourg.
- Spanish amateur Mariano Diaz wins the Tour de l'Avenir.
- The Soviet Union's Gennady Lebedev wins the Peace Race.
- Great Britain's Leslie West (Midlands) wins the Milk Race.
- Germany's Eckhard Viehover wins the Kugler-Anderson Memorial Tour of Somerville.
- Eddy Merckx (Solo-Superia) fails to finish his first professional race, the Flèche Wallonne in April, because of a flat. His first professional victory comes three weeks later in Vilvoorde, Belgium.
- At the request of the International Olympic Committee (IOC), the *Union Cycliste Internationale* (UCI) establishes the *Fédération Internationale du Cyclisme Professionnel* (FICP) and the *Fédération Internationale Amateur de*

Cyclisme (FIAC) for the purposes of approving world records, licensing of riders and certifying *commissaires*.

- 1912 Tour de France winner Odile Defraye dies on August 20. He was 77.
- Cycle manufacturers from the United States and abroad display their goods at the National Bicycle Show in New York's Commodore Hotel.
- About 1,350 production workers at the Murray Ohio bicycle plant in Lawrenceburg, Tenn., cross picket lines set up by Teamsters Local 327 of Nashville, ending a five-week strike there. The union had lost a National Labor Relations Board bargaining election a few months earlier and has no contract with the company.
- Alex Moulton's recent creation, the small-wheel bicycle, is a big success. "The Moulton Company says it is exporting 300 small-wheel cycles a week to the United States. In a few months the Huffman Manufacturing Company of Dayton, Ohio, will be making the Moulton cycles under license. Raleigh is now trying to persuade its American distributors to carry the new line."[1]
- France's *la loi Herzog* goes into effect on June 1. The Herzog law (number 65-412), which had passed in the French assembly 356 votes to 0 late in 1964, makes *le dopage* in sports a crime punishable by a fine or a year in prison. While the new law doesn't specifically target cycling, its intent is clear since most French youngsters look up to the racers. The law's four articles say that: 1) individuals found guilty of using performance-enhancing drugs could spend up to a year in prison or pay up to a 5000-franc fine; 2) this penalty could be doubled if the drugs cause injury or death; 3) athletes suspected of drug use must submit samples and undergo testing; and, 4) if found guilty, face a ban from racing from three months to five years. The hastily written law is said to be full of loopholes.

In the Tour de France:

- At 22 years 9 months 15 days Italy's Felice Gimondi (Salvarani) becomes the Tour de France's youngest postwar winner, winning his only Tour on his first try.
- In May, Émilion Amaury purchases *L'Équipe* and the Tour de France.
- Departing from Cologne, the Tour starts in West Germany for the first time.
- Race leader Bernard Van de Kerkhove (Solo-Superia) and nine others abandon during the ninth stage, again giving rise to rumors of drug use.
- Spain's José Perez-Frances (Ferry's) solos 223 kilometers (138.5 miles) to win the 11th stage to Barcelona.
- Molteni and Ignis each contribute five riders toward a combined Tour team. The mostly Italian squad is led by Molteni's Gianni Motta.
- Great Britain's Michael Wright (Wiel's-Groene Leeuw) wins the 20th stage, the race's longest at 294 kilometers. Wright was born in Great Britain but moved with his parents to Belgium at a very young age, and speaks almost no English.
- The start ramp is introduced for the individual time trials.
- *L'Équipe* administrator Robert Thominet estimates that the race costs $540,000 to run, with the money coming from the following sources: $400,000 from the caravan advertisers ($6,000 to $8,000 apiece), $120,000 from cities in which

the race stops, and the rest from newspapers which see their circulation jump during the race.
- French director Claude Lelouch films *Pour un Maillot Jaune*, a 30-minute documentary of the Tour.
- Raymond Poulidor's (Mercier-BP) two stage wins (5B and 14) are the only individual French victories in the race.
- French rider François Mahé (Pelforth-Sauvage-Lejeune) rides in his 13th consecutive Tour de France, finishing 43rd. Mahé had finished fifth in 1959 and 10th in 1953 and 1955.

1966 • Italy's Gianni Motta (Molteni) wins the 49th Giro d'Italia.
- Great Britain's Vin Denson (Ford France-Gitane) wins the Giro's ninth stage.
- Spaniard Francisco Gabica (Kas-Kaskol) wins the 21st Vuelta a España.
- Germany's Rudi Altig wins the world road championship over Frenchmen Jacques Anquetil and Raymond Poulidor at the German Nürburgring racing circuit. After the race, in which France's Lucien Aimar repaid Altig for helping him win the Tour de France, fallout from the Tour's drug testing controversy continues when Altig, runner-up Anquetil, Gianni Motta, Raymond Poulidor, Italo Zilioli and Jean Stablinski refuse to submit to the post-race drug test. After 10 days, and the threat of a lawsuit by Altig's trade team, Molteni, the International Cycling Union lets the race's results stand.
- France's Jacques Anquetil (Ford France-Gitane) wins his ninth Grand Prix des Nations time trial title in 14 years.
- Anquetil wins his fourth Super Prestige Pernod Trophy in six years.
- Eddy Merckx signs with the Peugeot-BP team, for which he'll ride in 1966 and 1967.
- Italian amateur Mino Denti wins the sixth Tour de l'Avenir. He will join the Salvarani team in October.
- France's Bernard Guyot wins the Peace Race.
- Polish amateur Josef Gawliczec wins the Milk Race.
- The Bronx's John Aschen wins the Kugler-Anderson Memorial Tour of Somerville.
- Sylvère Maes dies on December 5. Maes, who was 57, won the Tour in 1936 and 1939.
- The UCI drops the "independent" class for semi-professional riders because not enough of them were moving up the pro ranks.
- Belgium's Yvonne Reynders wins her seventh world title. She won the pursuit title in 1961-64-65 and the road title in 1959-61-63-66.
- Speedwell Gear Case Co., Ltd., of Birmingham, England introduces the Titalite, the first mass-produced titanium bicycle. Speedwell's 4.1-pound frame (including the headset and titanium fork) is made of pure unalloyed titanium and is said to be welded by Lamborghini of Italy at a "staggering" cost. In spite of its "jewel-like" welds, the frame is very flexible. Production of the Titalite would continue until about 1978.
- Around this time, Fritz Fleck of Mannheim, West Germany produces the

Flema (the name comes from *Fle*ck and *Ma*nnheim), a four-pound titanium frame which features drilled-out gussets at the junctions of the top tube, head tube and down tube, and where the down tube meets the bottom bracket. Fleck also reportedly makes track bikes and track tandems for the German Olympic team.

- In August, Félix Levitan, the Tour's deputy director, announces that the 1967 event would be open to amateurs as well as professionals. "In 1960 the tour [*sic*] was split into two races run over almost identical routes: a race for commercially backed professional teams not representing countries; and the Tour de l'Avenir over a slightly shorter distance for national teams of amateurs. The organizers say they would invite 12 to 15 national teams for the 1967 race in which amateurs and professionals would compete side by side."[1] Levitan scraps the idea when the French riders union threatens to boycott the event.

- The New York City subway strike pushes people to pedal. "New Yorkers who hadn't ridden bicycles since they were wheel-high to a cross-town bus were busy trying to rent them yesterday. Frank Arroyo, the manager of Stan's Bicycle Shop at 353 East 10th Street, estimated that he had rented 75 bikes in the previous 24 hours, many of them to people who had not ridden in years. 'People say, "I've been meaning to get some exercise,"' said Mr. Arroyo, 'and then they rent bikes.'"[2]

In the Tour de France:

- France's Lucien Aimar (Ford France-Hutchinson) becomes the fourth rider to win the Tour without winning any of its stages.
- Aimar is said to have experimented with 55 x 13 gearing during the event.
- Jan Janssen (Pelforth-Sauvage-Lejeune-Wolber), who finishes in second place, is the first Dutch rider to finish on the final podium.
- During the ninth stage, Jacques Anquetil (Ford France-Hutchinson) leads a brief rider protest against drug testing and nighttime drug raids.
- Anquetil abandons during the 19th stage, announcing that this was his last Tour de France.
- Anquetil's wife, Janine, provides a nightly commentary on the race for Radio Luxembourg.
- Female reporter Huguette Debaisieux covers the race for *Le Figaro*.
- There are no time bonuses for the top three finishers of each stage.

1967 • Great Britain's Tom Simpson (Peugeot-BP-Michelin) wins Paris–Nice.
- On September 27 France's Jacques Anquetil (Bic) rides 47.495 kilometers (29.513 miles) in an hour on the velodrome in Milan, Italy. The mark would have been a new record for the hour except that the Frenchman goes to his hotel room instead of producing the required urine sample for the Italian doctor at the track. On October 13 the International Cycling Union would vote 6 to 1 (with 2 abstentions and 1 absence) to not accept Anquetil's hour mark "because he had failed to undergo an anti-drug test after his effort."
- On October 30, Ferdinand Bracke (Peugeot-BP-Michelin) of Belgium increases the hour record to 48.093 kilometers (29.885 miles) at the Olympic track in

Rome. Rumors that the track was inaccurately measured would prove untrue.

- Lucien Aimar (Bic) becomes France's national champion after apparent winner Désiré Letort (Peugeot-BP-Michelin) is disqualified for doping. Aimar refuses to wear the champion's jersey in races that season.
- Italy's Felice Gimondi (Salvarani) wins the 50th edition of the Giro d'Italia.
- The Netherlands' Jan Janssen (Pelforth-Sauvage-Lejeune) wins the 22nd Vuelta a España.
- Belgium's Eddy Merckx wins his first world professional road championship, beating Jan Janssen in Heerlen, the Netherlands.
- After 12 years as a first-category amateur racer, Phil Liggett begins his career in journalism.
- The United States Supreme Court rules 5 to 2 that Schwinn "violated Section 1 of the Sherman Act by allocating exclusive territories to wholesalers and jobbers and confining merchandise to franchised dealers."[1] In essence, the Court holds "that the legality of a manufacturer's allocating exclusive territories to distributors turns on whether or not the manufacturer actually sells his product to the distributor. If an outright sale is made by the manufacturer, the court said, territorial restrictions and limitations on the subsequent customers to whom the distributors may sell are both illegal."[2] Schwinn would respond to this ruling by building four large regional warehouses, a move which causes the company to begin losing touch with its customers.
- New York painter and illustrator Arthur Lidov receives U.S. Patent number 3,329,444 for a plastic bicycle with no hubs or spokes. The solid tires of the bike roll on bearings set into fender-like portions of the frame, and power is applied to the rear wheel either through a belt that runs through a groove in the perimeter of the wheel or through gears to teeth on the wheel.
- Following France's lead, the International Cycling Union drafts its own list of banned substances.
- The Netherlands' Jan Janssen (Pelforth-Sauvage-Lejeune) wins the Super Prestige Pernod Trophy. Belgium's Eddy Merckx (Peugeot-BP) finishes second.
- French amateur Christian Robini wins the seventh Tour de l'Avenir.
- Great Britain's Leslie West wins the Milk Race for the second time in three years.
- The UK's Nigel Dean wins the Tour of Ireland.
- Jackie Simes of Closter, N. J., wins the Kugler-Anderson Memorial Tour of Somerville.
- Belgian amateur Marcel Maes (1944–97) wins the Peace Race. He would turn professional with the Willem II team on September 10.
- While setting the women's 12-hour time trial record of 277.25 miles, Britain's Beryl Burton (1937–96) catches Mike McNamara, who is in the process of setting the men's record of 276.52 miles. As Burton is passing McNamara, she reportedly hands him a piece of licorice allsort, which he takes and eats. Burton's 12-hour mark wouldn't be bettered by a man until 1969.
- Burton wins her seventh world title. She won the pursuit title in 1959-60-62-63-66 and the road title in 1960 and 1967.

- Burton is invited to compete in the Grand Prix des Nations time trial where she finishes only a few minutes behind the male professionals. The event is won by Italy's Felice Gimondi (Salvarani).
- "The best present you can get for your girlfriend in Hanoi [North Vietnam] is not a box of candy or even a diamond ring. It's a new chain for her bicycle. The bicycle is just as essential to the North Vietnamese as the auto is in Los Angeles. Without the bicycle, Hanoi's life would come to a halt. If by some magic weapon all the bikes in North Vietnam could be immobilized, the war would be over in a twinkling. Hanoi citizens, according to foreign residents, are notably honest and theft is almost unknown. Diplomats say there is only one thing that sometimes disappears—a bicycle."[3]

In the Tour de France:

- France's Roger Pingeon wins his only Tour de France.
- The Tour is once again contested by national teams (and again in 1968). Of the race's thirteen teams, three are French, while Belgium, Spain, and Italy have two each.
- Great Britain's Tom Simpson dies on the sweltering slopes of Mont Ventoux. An autopsy confirms that amphetamines played a role in his death.
- The first "prologue" time trial is held.
- The race makes its last finish at the Parc des Princes velodrome, which is demolished beginning the next day. The site is now occupied by a soccer stadium.
- The logo of clothing company Le Coq Sportif appears on the left breast of the *maillot jaune*.
- During the race, several French riders begin using a new six-speed Italian freewheel.
- "Broadcasting officials [protested] in 1967 when the respected commentator Robert Chapatte was excluded from television in a row. Unhappy with his stand-in, they transmitted French TV to the sound of Belgian TV's commentators."[4]

1968 • Belgian Eddy Merckx signs with Faema. He'll ride for Faema and Faemino-Faema through 1970.
- The 12-year-old daughter of Merckx's former Peugeot-BP teammate Christian Raymond refers to Merckx as "The Cannibal."
- At 22 years 10 months, Merckx (Faema) becomes the youngest rider to win Paris–Roubaix.
- The 51st Giro d'Italia is won by Merckx. It's the first edition of the event to have a prologue.
- Campagnolo introduces its Nuovo Record components, which would remain largely unchanged for the next 15 years.
- The 23rd Vuelta a España is won by Italy's Felice Gimondi (Salvarani), making him the second rider (after Jacques Anquetil in 1963) to win each of the three grand tours at least once.
- Italy's Pierfranco Vianelli wins the 196-kilometer (122-mile) road race at the XIXth Olympiad in Mexico City, where the Olympics conducts its first drug tests.

- French amateur Jean-Pierre Boulard wins the Tour de l'Avenir.
- Swedish amateur Gosta Petterson wins the Milk Race.
- Ireland's Peter Doyle (Bray Wheelers) wins the Tour of Ireland.
- East Germany's Alex Peschel wins the Peace Race.
- Chicago's Siegi Koch wins the Kugler-Anderson Memorial Tour of Somerville.
- Great Britain's Beryl Burton rides a 100-mile (161-kilometer) time trial in 3:55:05.
- In October, Denmark's Ole Ritter (Germanvox-Wega) improves the hour record in Mexico City by riding his Benotto bicycle 48.653 kilometers (30.233 miles).
- Italy's Vittorio Adorni wins the 1968 world professional road championship in Imola, Italy.
- 35-year-old Rik Van Looy (Willem II-Gazelle) wins Flèche Wallonne. With the victory, "the Emperor of Herentals" becomes the only rider to have won every major classic.
- Georges Briquet, the radio voice of French cycling during its golden age of the '30s through the '50s, dies at the age of 70.
- Belgium's Herman Van Springel (Mann-Grundig) wins the Super Prestige Pernod Trophy.
- "[T]he master and the chief officer of the new 1,010-foot British tanker Esso Mercia have been furnished with bicycles to make it easier for them to patrol the 166,820-ton vessel's decks."[1] A spokesman for Standard Oil said that bikes put deck officers on par with the ship's engineers, who for decades have had small elevators to take them from their quarters to the engine room. "You might call the bicycles horizontal elevators," he said. The bicycles are safer than roller skates for getting around the deck of an oil tanker because their rubber tires don't give off sparks.
- The Vienna Convention on Road Traffic classifies a bicycle to be a vehicle and the person controlling it to be a driver.
- Schwinn introduces the Krate version of its Sting-Ray bike. The dragster-inspired machine features a 20-inch rear slick, a 16-inch front wheel with a drum brake, and a springer fork.

In the Tour de France:
- The Netherlands' Jan Janssen defeats Belgium's Herman Van Springel in the time trial to take the overall lead on the last day. Janssen's win gives the Tour four consecutive one-time winners for the first time since 1912.
- *Commissaires* begin following the race on motorcycles.
- The logo of jersey maker Le Coq Sportif moves from the left breast to just below the yellow jersey's zipper.
- Janssen is the first Dutch rider to win the race. His 38-second margin of victory is the smallest until Greg LeMond's 8-second victory in 1989. Janssen is also the second rider to win on the race's last day and without having worn the yellow jersey, following Jean Robic (1947) in both categories. (LeMond would also win the race on the last day in 1989.)
- In the final year of national teams, the Spanish squad registers its only team victory.

- French team director Marcel Bidot, who rode in the Tour six times from 1926 through 1932, manages the French national team for the last time and says goodbye to the race after a 42-year association with the event. Since 1952, Bidot had directed six Tour winners with the French squad.
- The race's best climber is recognized by a red and white patch affixed to the left breast of his jersey.
- The organizers implement drug testing at the finish of each stage.
- Italy's Franco Bitossi wins the event's first white "combination" (general classification, points, climbing) jersey. The white jersey would be worn by the race's best young rider from 1975–1988 and from 2000 on.
- The organizers add two rest days to the race and allow riders to get food and water from their *directeurs sportifs* in team cars.
- The race makes its first finish in the Piste Municipale ("Cipale") Velodrome in Paris.
- Reporters "strike" by partially blocking the route during the race's ninth stage.
- For 1968, the color of the points jersey is changed from green to red at the sponsor's request.
- After the eighth stage French national team rider José Samyn is the first rider kicked out of the Tour for failing a drug test.

1969
- French rider José Samyn (Bic) dies on August 28, three days after a collision with a program seller at the Prix de Zingem, an exhibition race in Belgium. Samyn had won the 11th stage of the 1967 Tour de France.
- On September 9, Eddy Merckx (Faema) and his derny driver Fernand Wambst crash when the lights go out in the velodrome at Blois, France. The 56-year-old Wambst, a former six-day racer who'd paced Tom Simpson to victory in the 1963 edition of Bordeaux–Paris, is killed in the accident and Merckx sustains a displaced pelvis, a cracked vertebra and trapped nerves in his back. He is flown back to Belgium in a military cargo plane. During his three-month recuperation, he suffers bouts of severe depression. Even after his "recovery," he's never the same; "I was still able to dominate, but no longer in the same emphatic way," he'd say later. "Before then, climbing had almost been a pleasure. Now it had become almost a source of torment. Sometimes I sat on my bike weeping with pain."[1]
- Merckx wins the Super Prestige Pernod Trophy.
- Italy's Felice Gimondi (Salvarani) wins the 52nd Giro d'Italia following Merckx's disqualification because of a "positive" drug test.
- Five-time Tour de France winner Jacques Anquetil (Bic) retires from riding on December 27 at the Wambrechies cyclocross event and becomes a commentator for French television.
- France's Roger Pingeon (Peugeot-BP-Michelin) wins the 24th Vuelta a España.
- Dutch rider Harm Ottenbros wins the 1969 world professional road championship in Zolder, Belgium.
- 1921 Tour de France winner Leon Scieur dies on October 7 at the age of 81.
- Audrey Phleger McElmury of La Jolla, California wins the world road championship on a rainy course in Brno, Czechoslovakia by more than a minute in

spite of crashing on her left side during the fourth of the 43.71-mile (70.33-ki-
lometer) race's five laps. She quickly remounts and catches up to the leaders
on a long hill. With her victory, McElmury becomes the first American rider
to win world road title. She has to wait on the podium for half an hour while
officials track down a copy of "The Star Spangled Banner."

- Australia's Bill Lawrie (Falcon-Clement) wins the British national champion-
ship. Lawrie, who had been a member of the British national team in the 1967
Tour, is allowed to keep his victory because he holds a British racing license.
- Dutch amateur Joop Zoetemelk wins the ninth Tour de l'Avenir.
- France's Jean-Pierre Danguillaume wins the Peace Race.
- Dutch amateur Fedor den Hertog wins the Milk Race.
- The UK's Morris Foster wins the Tour of Ireland.
- Twenty-six-year-old Olympic rider Jack Simes III of Closter, N.J., wins the 26th
annual Tour of Somerville. Simes, who will be discharged from the army in
December, rides the 50-mile course in 2:01:40.
- Bronx, N.Y., rider John Aschen (Unione Sportiva Italiana) wins the 100-mile
German Bicycle Sports Club race in Central Park. Aschen's time for the race,
which uses the same course as the 1960 and 1964 Olympic trials, is 3:56:51.
Women's national champion Nancy Burghart of Jackson Heights finishes 20th
of 71 starters.
- SunTour introduces the Five-Speed Click, an indexed shift lever, freewheel,
and hub combination, as well as a combined freewheel plus rear hub called the
Unit-Hub.
- Garfield A. "Gar" Wood, Jr. of Miami, Florida, is issued U.S. Patent number
3,431,994 for an electric bicycle drive. The device uses five small motors in the
front hub and rechargeable batteries. The motor, which will be produced by
Stelber Industries of Elmhurst, Queens, N.Y., is projected to be capable of a top
speed of between 10 and 15 miles per hour.
- Goodyear adds colors to its line of bicycle tires. Called Crazy Wheels, the new
tires come in five colors: Wild Orange, Fab Yellow, Mod Green, Tough Red,
and Cool Blue. They will be advertised during kids' shows on ABC-TV and on
the three Goodyear blimps.
- When Mrs. Rita Thomas and Mrs. Rosemary Carrig of Richmond, England
can't agree on which of them is the rightful owner of a battered blue boy's
bicycle, Magistrate Charles Moody awards the machine's seat, bell, chain,
pump, and handlebar grips to Carrig's son Gary. Little Stephen Thomas gets
the frame, wheels, and handlebars. An undaunted Mrs. Thomas declares that
she is going to buy her son all the parts he needs to make a complete bike.
- In August, North Vietnam's Internal Trade Ministry announces that it is ending rationing of 22 consumer items, including spare parts for bicycles.

In the Tour de France:
- Race winner Eddy Merckx (Faema) wears race number 51 to publicize Pastis
51, an anise-flavored brand of Absinthe of Pernod, first produced in 1951.
- Eddy Merckx completely dominates the event by winning the race, the sprinters competition, the King of the Mountains competition and the combination

classification. His Faema team also wins the team classification.
- The Tour returns again to the trade team format.
- There are no rest days.
- Rudi Altig (Salvarani), Pierre Matignon (Frimatic-De Gribaldy-Viva-Wolber), and Bernard Guyot (Sonolor-Lejeune) each receive a 15-minute penalty for doping.
- The race's peculiar route takes it nowhere near France's bicycle-crazy regions of Normandy and Brittany.
- The Tour's yellow jersey undergoes changes when the initials of Tour founder Henri Desgrange are moved from its left breast to the top of both sleeves. In their place, the name of a sponsor, *Virlux* (which produces synthetic dairy products), appears on the *maillot jaune* for the first time.
- Great Britain's Barry Hoban (Mercier-BP-Hutchinson) wins two stages, including the last one to finish in the historic Bordeaux velodrome.
- Joaquim Agostinho (Frimatic-De Gribaldy-Viva-Wolber) is the first Portuguese rider to win a stage of the race.
- Raymond Delisle (Peugeot-BP-Michelin) becomes the only reigning French national champion to win a stage of the Tour de France on Bastille Day.
- At 11 kilometers (6.8 miles) the prologue of the '69 Tour is the race's longest ever.

In the Tour de France:
- Race winner Eddy Merckx (Faema) wears race number 51 to publicize Pastis 51, an anise-flavored brand of Absinthe of Pernod, first produced in 1951.
- Eddy Merckx completely dominates the event by winning the race, the sprinters competition, the King of the Mountains competition and the combination classification. His Faema team also wins the team classification.
- The Tour returns again to the trade team format.
- There are no rest days.
- Rudi Altig (Salvarani), Pierre Matignon (Frimatic-De Gribaldy-Viva-Wolber), and Bernard Guyot (Sonolor-Lejeune) each receive a 15-minute penalty for doping.
- The race's peculiar route takes it nowhere near France's bicycle-crazy regions of Normandy and Brittany.
- The Tour's yellow jersey undergoes changes when the initials of Tour founder Henri Desgrange are moved from its left breast to the top of both sleeves. In their place, the name of a sponsor, Virlux (which produces synthetic dairy products), appears on the *maillot jaune* for the first time.
- Great Britain's Barry Hoban (Mercier-BP-Hutchinson) wins two stages, including the last one to finish in the historic Bordeaux velodrome.
- Joaquim Agostinho (Frimatic-De Gribaldy-Viva-Wolber) is the first Portuguese rider to win a stage of the race.
- Raymond Delisle (Peugeot-BP-Michelin) becomes the only reigning French national champion to win a stage of the Tour de France on Bastille Day.
- At 11 kilometers (6.8 miles) the prologue of the '69 Tour is the race's longest ever.

Chapter 8

1970–1979
The Bicycle Goes High Tech

1970 • By winning the 53rd Giro d'Italia, Eddy Merckx (Faemino-Faema) becomes the third rider after Fausto Coppi and Jacques Anquetil to win the Giro and the Tour in the same year.

• Eddy Merckx also wins the Super Prestige Pernod Trophy.

• Spain's Luis Ocaña (Bic) wins the 25th Vuelta a España.

• Bui Hoang, a 27-year-old South Vietnamese soldier, wins the 290-mile (467-kilometer) Tour de Vietnam between Nhatrang and Vinhlong. During one stage of the race, the riders have to travel 40 miles (64 kilometers) by truck when teams clearing the road of mines come under attack from the Vietcong, killing one of the 2,200 soldiers guarding the race route. "The Government-sponsored race is intended to show that the country's roads are safe."[1]

• Belgium's Jean-Pierre Monseré (b. September 8, 1948) wins the 1970 world professional road championship in Mallory Park, England on August 16. At 21 years 11 months 8 days, he's the second-youngest rider to win the world road title after Karel Kaers (BEL) in 1934. America's Lance Armstrong (b. September 18, 1971) will be 21 years 11 months 11 days old when he wins the worlds on August 29, 1993.

• Because of the country's racist policies, South Africa is barred from membership in the International Amateur Cycling Federation and from August's world championships in England.

• Eugène Christophe dies on February 1. Robbed of more than one possible Tour de France victory by bad luck (frequently a broken fork) in the race's early years, the popular French racer will always be remembered as the first man to wear the yellow jersey upon its introduction during the 1919 event. "The Old Gaul" was 85.

• Future Tour de France and Giro d'Italia winner Marco Pantani is born on January 13.

• French amateur Marcel Duchemin wins the Prix de l'Avenir, which is what the Tour de l'Avenir is called when it's canceled after two stages for financial reasons.

• Poland's Ryszard Szurkowski takes the first of his four Peace Race victories.

• Czechoslovakia's Jiri Manus wins the Milk Race.

- Ireland's Paul Elliot (Bray Wheelers) wins the Raleigh Dunlop Tour of Ireland.
- Robert Farrell of New York City wins the Kugler-Anderson Memorial Tour of Somerville.
- The Snell Memorial Foundation institutes a standard for bicycle helmets that's so tough only motorcycle helmets can pass it. The standard would be revised in 1973.
- When police raid the Mak Transportation terminal at 144 King Street in Brooklyn, they find $60,000 worth of English bicycles recently stolen from a Brooklyn pier. Police also recover stolen cigarettes, liquor, television sets, and silks. They also believe the company's trucks are stolen.
- Maeda Iron Works changes its name to Maeda, Inc., and begins calling all its products SunTour.

In the Tour de France:
- Race winner Eddy Merckx (Faemino-Faema) is the first rider to win eight stages of the Tour since Charles Pélissier in 1930.
- Merckx uses a 51 x 11 gear to win stage 7A from Valenciennes, France to Forest, Belgium.
- The Tour returns to Mont Ventoux three years after the death of Tom Simpson. The stage is run later in the day when the temperature is cooler.
- Third-place finisher Gosta Pettersson (Ferretti) is the first Swedish rider on the final podium.
- Mogens Frey (Frimatic-De Gribaldy-Wolber) is the first Danish rider to win a stage in the Tour.
- The organizers ban advertising on team clothing, allowing only the names of the teams' primary sponsor(s).
- The Faemino-Faema team wins 11 of the race's 29 stages. T.I. Raleigh will win 11 of 25 stages in 1980.
- The second-place riders in the points and combination classifications—Merckx (Faema) and Wagtmans (GAN) respectively—are awarded a green and black jersey and a white and black jersey.

1971 • Eddy Merckx of Belgium wins the 1971 world professional road championship in Mendrisio, Switzerland. He's the third rider to win the Tour de France and the World Championship in the same year. Merckx (Molteni) also wins 45 percent of his races in 1971[1] as well as the Super Pernod Prestige Trophy, amassing twice as many points as the next four riders combined.
- Sweden's Gosta Pettersson (Ferretti) wins the 54th Giro d'Italia.
- Belgian rider Ferdinand Bracke (Peugeot) wins the 26th Vuelta a España.
- Cinelli introduces the M71 clipless pedal.
- Future Tour director Jean-Marie Leblanc retires from cycling to become a journalist.
- Under the headline "U.S. Cyclist Wins at Cali," the *New York Times* runs a story about American John Howard's victory in the men's road race at the Goodwill Games in Cali, Colombia. Howard took the lead with about 50 meters to go, and beat Brazil's Luis Carlos Florez by four lengths. Often given

as the article's headline, "U.S. Wins in Cycling Breakthrough" is actually the column heading on page 20, where the article is continued.

- On March 15, reigning world champion Jean-Pierre Monseré (Flandria-Mars) of Belgium is hit by a Mercedes-Benz and killed while competing in the Annual Fair Grand Prix in Retie near his Belgian home. He was 22.
- Distraught over the recent death of his father, pioneering Irish rider Seamus "Shay" Elliot commits suicide with a shotgun on May 4. Elliot, who had recently retired from racing, had worn the Tour's yellow jersey for three days in 1963. He was 36.
- Philippe Thys, 80, the first rider to win the Tour de France three times, dies on January 16.
- Schwinn sells out its entire 1,225,000-unit production run. When U.S. bike sales reach 8.5 million units in 1971, American bike companies announce plans for a 20 percent production increase in 1972.
- Alan Goldsmith establishes his Bikecology shop on Wilshire Blvd. in Santa Monica, Calif.
- Joe Montgomery starts his Cannondale company in Wilton, Conn. The company's first product is the Bugger, a bicycle-towed trailer.
- Huffman manufacturing announces plans to increase prices on all types and models of its bicycles.
- Mayor Lindsay opens a bicycle ramp to the Brooklyn Bridge's pedestrian level. The mayor said that if the experiment works out, it could be expanded to other city-owned bridges. A white stripe separates bicycle and pedestrian lanes.
- After taking a spin on the rear of a Schwinn tandem, Chicago Mayor Richard J. Daley hails cycling as one answer to the city's traffic problem, but did not say he'd give up his car.
- Oregon Governor Tom McCall signs into law a bill mandating that 1 percent of the state's highway budget go toward the construction of bicycle trails and footpaths.
- Lance Armstrong is born on September 18 in Plano, Texas.
- French amateur Régis Ovion wins the Tour de l'Avenir.
- Holland's Fedor den Hertog wins the Milk Race for the second time in three years.
- Ireland's Liam Horner (County Dublin Road Club) wins the Raleigh Dunlop Tour of Ireland.
- Poland's Ryszard Szurkowski wins his second consecutive Peace Race.
- Edward Parrot of New York City wins the Kugler-Anderson Memorial Tour of Somerville.
- Former racer Peter Rich, who owns Velo-Sport in Berkeley, Calif., puts on "the seven-day Tour of California stage race, the first major stage race in the country. The budget was $50,000. Regional U.S. teams competed against teams from Germany, Canada, and Mexico."[2]

In the Tour de France:
- Belgium's Eddy Merckx (Molteni) wins his third consecutive Tour de France.

- Miko ice cream replaces Virlux as the sponsor of the yellow jersey.
- The prologue is run as a team time trial.
- The race's intermediate sprints classification is introduced.
- During stage 1A, the riders stage a slowdown to force the organizers to pay more prize money to the winners of the race's split stages.
- The transfers from Le Touquet to Rungis (Paris) and Marseille to Albi are the Tour's first air transfers.
- The Eddy Merckx-led 251-kilometer (156-mile) 12th stage to Marseille averages 45.35 km/h (28.1 mph) and finishes two hours ahead of schedule.
- Stage 15 (Luchon to Superbagnères) is the Tour's shortest road stage at just 19.6 kilometers (12.2 miles).
- Race leader Luis Ocaña (Bic) crashes out during the 14th stage while holding a huge lead over Merckx.

1972 • AlAn (*Al*uminum *An*odized) of Padua, Italy, produces the first modern aluminum bicycle frame.
- *VeloNews* is born. On March 13, 1972, Bob and Barbara George publish the first issue of *Northeast Bicycle News* in Brattleboro, Vermont. After two years as *Cyclenews*, the name is changed to *Velo-news*.
- Because of the "bike boom" in the U.S., Japanese component makers SunTour and Shimano make inroads into the American market when European manufacturers Simplex, Huret and Campagnolo are unable to meet the demand.[1]
- The Bendix Corporation announces plans to shift the production of its bicycle coaster brake from its Elmira Heights plant to one under construction in San Luis Potosí, Mexico. About 200 of the New York plant's 1,000 workers will lose their jobs.
- "Deere & Co. announced today [August 15] that it would re-enter the bicycle manufacturing business after more than 80 years. Officials said that adding bicycles to the John Deere line represented continued expansion in the field of recreational products. The expansion began last fall with snowmobiles."[2]
- The children's hazard division of the Food and Drug Administration says it plans to issue strict safety regulations for bicycles sold in the United States. The new rules, which are more stringent than the "BMA/6" standards currently in effect, especially target perceived shortcomings in children's high-rise bikes, which come with 20-inch wheels and banana seats. All major American bike makers except Schwinn adhere to the BMA/6 standards. Schwinn says that its own standards (which the company won't divulge) are tougher than those used by the other bike companies.
- Five Washington policemen give a ticket to Orville Jackson, who is recovering at George Washington University Hospital after President Nixon's $500,000 armor-plated Lincoln limousine and Jackson's $197, 10-speed Peugeot bicycle collide (the president was not in the car at the time of the accident). Jackson, a 32-year-old student, said, "I think it is very unusual for a man to receive a ticket when he is riding a bicycle and a car hits him." Damage to the limo is estimated at about $100.

- Mary Jane Reoch wins the road race and the time trial at the U.S. nationals. "Miji" Reoch would accumulate 11 national titles in all as well as dozens of national medals and state titles. She would be killed by a hit-and-run driver near Dallas, Texas, in September 1993 at the age of 47.
- Senator Ted Stevens (R-Alaska) proposes indoor bicycle parking, more visible bike racks, or a claim ticket system for the 100 or so employees of the old Senate Office Building who bike to work. Seven bikes have been stolen from the building recently.
- "The Massachusetts Institute of Technology has announced the development by two undergraduates of a 'thief-proof' bicycle lock made from a steel alloy similar to ship's armor. The single-jointed, pear-shaped loop resisted all attempts at cutting, filing or smashing made by the M.I.T. campus patrol. It weighs three pounds."[3]
- Italy's Marino Basso wins the 1972 world professional road championship in Gap, France, by taking the sprint over fellow Italian Franco Bitossi and France's Cyrille Guimard.
- Spain's José-Manuel Fuente (Kas-Kaskol) wins the 27th Vuelta a España.
- Holland's Hennie Kuiper wins the 182-kilometer (113-mile) road race at the XXth Olympiad in Munich. John Howard of the United States finishes 61st. During the games, members of the PLO terrorist group Black September kill 11 Israeli athletes.
- French racer François Le Bihan (formerly with Mercier) dies after competing for six years as an independent and *hors-catégorie* amateur. Newspaper accounts of his death imply that drugs were involved. Le Bihan was 37.
- Belgium's Eddy Merckx (Molteni) wins the 55th Giro d'Italia.
- Merckx also wins the Super Prestige Pernod Trophy.
- Merckx increases the hour record to 49.431 kilometers (30.716 miles) on October 25 in Mexico City. "I was still fresh coming out of the Tour," Merckx would later explain of his decision to travel to the high-altitude wooden track for his record attempt. Mexican company ACER-MEX may have pressured Merckx into turning his Colnago into a "Windsor" by getting officials to withhold use of the track until Windsor decals were affixed to his machine. Beginning the following year—and continuing for the rest of his racing career—Merckx would ride time trial and track bicycles built by Ugo De Rosa, and stage-racing bikes by Kessels. The hour bike, which weighs less than 15 pounds (6.8 kilos), uses wheels whose rims had been shaved between the spokes for increased lightness. Riding a conventional track bike, with its drop bars, a diamond frame and spoked wheels, the Cannibal sets a mark that no one would come within a kilometer of for 12 years. The record would finally be bettered in 1984 by Italy's Francesco Moser who benefited from many advances in the area of aerodynamics, and some advice from Dr. Conconi. After establishing the mark, Merckx would be unable to sit for four days and would later say that setting the hour record took two years off his career. "In Mexico, the only thing I knew was that one attempt at it was quite enough."[4] In September, 2000, the UCI would reinstate Merckx's 1972 record, reclassifying the 1996 aero-aided

mark of 56.375 kilometers (35.031 miles) by Great Britain's Chris Boardman as the "world best performance." Just prior to his retirement in late October 2000, Boardman would challenge the Cannibal's "conventional" hour record. The day before he attacked Merckx's retro record on a steel Look bicycle in Manchester, England, Boardman remarked, "If nothing else, tomorrow will prove how good Eddy Merckx was."[5] In the hour, Boardman would ride 49.441 kilometers (30.722 miles), beating Merckx's 28 year-old record by 10 meters (10.93 yards).

- Axel Merckx is born on August 8.
- Dutch amateur Fedor Den Hertog wins the Tour de l'Avenir.
- Holland's Hennie Kuiper wins the Milk Race.
- Czechoslovakia's Vlastimil Moravec wins the Peace Race.
- Detroit's Roger Young wins the Kugler-Anderson Memorial Tour of Somerville.
- On November 25, Italy's Maria Cressari increases the 14-year-old women's hour record to 41.471 kilometers (25.770 miles) in Mexico City.

In the Tour de France:
- Eddy Merckx (Molteni) caps his fourth straight Tour victory with six stage wins.
- After a crash, Bernard Thévenet (Peugeot-BP) rides much of the seventh stage suffering from amnesia.
- A lung infection forces Luis Ocaña (Bic) to withdraw following the 14th stage.
- After having led the race, Cyrille Guimard (GAN-Mercier-Hutchinson) is forced to retire with tendinitis in his knees. At the finish in Paris, Merckx gives Guimard the green sprinter's jersey, telling him, "you deserve it."
- The initials of Tour founder Henri Desgrange are removed from the sleeves of the yellow jersey and returned to its breast, this time on the right side with "Miko" on the left. The logo of jersey maker Le Coq Sportif moves from just below the zipper to the sleeves.
- Dr. Pierre Dumas, the Tour's official physician for the past 20 years is joined by Dr. Gerard Porte, who would become the Tour's medical chief in 1982.

1973 • Belgium's Eddy Merckx (Molteni) wins the 56th Giro d'Italia, wearing the race leader's pink jersey from start to finish. The race starts in Verviers, Belgium, marking the first time that the Giro has started outside of Italy. The race also passes through the Netherlands, West Germany, Luxembourg, France, and Switzerland before arriving in Italy.
- Eddy Merckx wins the 28th Vuelta a España, making him only the third rider (after Jacques Anquetil and Felice Gimondi) to win all three major tours. Merckx's win of the Vuelta's points competition makes him the first rider to win the sprint titles of all three grand tours.
- Merckx wins his fifth consecutive Super Prestige Pernod Trophy.
- Director Jorgen Leth shoots the classic cycling film *Stars and Watercarriers* at the '73 Giro.
- Italy's Felice Gimondi wins the 1973 world professional road championship at

Montjuich Park in Barcelona, Spain. Of the controversial finish, Eddy Merckx claims that fellow Belgian Freddy Maertens chased him down in the race's closing kilometers, helping Gimondi win. Maertens says that once caught, Merckx sat up so Gimondi, who was also sponsored by Campagnolo components, could win over the Shimano-sponsored Maertens, and Zeus-sponsored Luis Ocaña.[1] Maertens finishes second, Tour winner Ocaña third.

- Ralph Hurne's novel *The Yellow Jersey* is published by Simon and Schuster. The book centers around recently retired cyclist Terry Davenport, his protégé Romain Hendrickx and how they deal with the women in their lives and, of course, the Tour de France. Attempts to turn the book into a movie would ultimately fail.
- Steve Tesich writes *The Eagle of Naptown*, about cyclist Dave Blase. Five years later, the story will become the basis for Tesich's Oscar-winning screenplay *Breaking Away*.[2]
- The Century Road Club of America-Raleigh becomes America's first national trade team. "CRC of A-Raleigh" takes part in the Tour of Ireland, where John Howard wins a stage and finishes third overall.
- American Jonathan Boyer joins the ACBB (Athletic Club Boulogne-Billancourt) amateur cycling team in Paris.
- Bernard Thevenet (Peugeot-BP) wins the French road championship, covering the 249-kilometer (155-mile) course in 6:26:25.
- "Perfected" 22 years earlier, the Campagnolo corkscrew (*cavatappi*) is introduced in catalogue #17. It is referred to as "The Martian" in Italy because of its strange appearance.
- American Alan Abbott, M.D., 29, sets the bicycle land speed record of 138.674 mph for the measured mile while drafting a 650-horsepower '55 Chevy on the Bonneville Salt Flats. Abbott's 35-pound bike has 18-inch wheels and a 230-tooth chainring. The bike's gearing is so high that Dr. Abbott has to be towed to 60 mph before he can start pedaling. His cadence at 140 mph is 135 rpm.[3]
- NASA astronaut Allen Bean rides around the world in 80 minutes: the amount of time it takes the Skylab space station, in which he's pedaling a stationary bike, to orbit the earth. Bean breaks the 110-minute mark of Pete Conrad, who'd set his record in a different orbit.
- Dr. Paul Dudley White, the father of preventive cardiology, dies in Boston at the age of 87. Dr. White was a firm believer that proper diet and regular exercise play a big role in preventing heart attacks, even saying in a 1956 *New York Times* article that men should bike to work for the good of their health. He was an avid walker and cyclist. Five weeks after his death, Boston's Metropolitan District Commission announces plans to expand the bicycle paths along the Charles River and name them after Dr. White.
- "From 1922 to December 25, 1973, Tommy Chambers (b. 1903) of Glasgow, Scotland, had ridden a verified total of 799,405 miles. On Christmas Day he was badly injured and has not ridden since."[4]
- Future Tour de France winner Jan Ullrich is born on December 2.

- At Paris–Nice, MAVIC begins providing neutral support services, *service des courses*, to racers under the leadership of Bruno Gormand.
- Italian amateur Giambattista Baronchelli wins the Tour de l'Avenir.
- Holland's Piet van Katwijk wins the Milk Race.
- Poland's Ryszard Szurkowski wins his third Peace Race in four years.
- Ron Skarin of North Hollywood, Calif., wins the Kugler-Anderson Memorial Tour of Somerville.
- Great Britain's Beryl Burton rides a 10-mile time trial in 21:25.
- Michelin introduces the Fifty Chevron, the first high-performance clincher bicycle tire.
- Aerospace tubing assembly manufacturer Teledyne Linair Engineering of Gardena, Calif., introduces the "Teledyne Titan" titanium bicycle. Based on a bicycle originally built by Albert Eisentraut for Barry Harvey, approximately 2,000 Titans will be constructed of MIG-welded, CP (commercially pure), Grade 3, large-diameter (1.125- top tubes and 1.250 down tubes), thin-wall titanium tubing between December 1973 and December 1976. The tubing is not up to the standards of later aircraft-quality versions of the material, and the two necked-down portions of the down tube (where the shift levers and bottom-bracket cable guides clamp on) create stress risers where many of the frames eventually fail. The price of the 3.2-pound, 23-inch (58.4-centimeter) frame is $400, and includes a 1.2-pound titanium fork, Dura-Ace headset, and three oversized Shimano brake cable clamps for the top tube.[5] The frame is available in four sizes, from 21 inches (53.3 centimeters) to 24 inches (61 centimeters).
- In November the International Cycling Union strips Eddy Merckx (Molteni) of his October victory in the Tour of Lombardy after he tests positive for a banned substance contained in some cold syrup he took. The UCI awards the race win to Italy's Felice Gimondi (Bianchi-Campagnolo). "Maybe I'll quit racing," says Merckx. "It's not possible for me to keep riding. It's too serious."

In the Tour de France:

- Spain's Luis Ocaña (Bic) takes the 60th Tour de France by nearly 16 minutes and wins six stages of the race. After consulting with an engineer at Sud-Aviation in Toulouse, he's also the first to use titanium bicycle parts (a headset and a bottom bracket) in the race. On the Tour's 10 "most hilly" stages Ocaña also reportedly swaps his orange Motobecane for a polished Titalite titanium bicycle made by the British Speedwell Gear Case Company and delivered to him during the earlier Dauphiné Libéré.
- Saying that the French people are tiring of his domination of the event, Eddy Merckx (Molteni) skips the Tour de France.
- The Italians skip the event saying that it's too mountainous for them to do well in.
- During the 13th stage, the race skips the Pyrenean Col de Peguere, because it's too steep and the descent is deemed unsafe.
- Victories by Flandria-Shimano's Walter Godefroot and Wilfried David give Shimano its first Tour de France stage wins. According to gearing expert Frank Berto "the [short cage DB-100] rear derailleur was still called 'Crane.' Everything else was called Dura-Ac.e." Of the Tour's other 11 teams, 9 use

Campagnolo components, and the other 2 use components of French manufacture.

- Belgium's Herman Van Springel (Rokado) wins the green jersey at the age of 37.
- Protesting cattle farmers briefly disrupt the start of stage 18.
- Phil Liggett covers his first Tour de France as a journalist and driver for British television commentator David Saunders. "I reported all the Tours afterwards for national newspapers in GB and did radio for BBC until I started TV in 1978," recalls Liggett. "I did continue my other positions too, and to date still report for the *Daily Telegraph,* as well as for TV in various countries, not least OLN [Outdoor Life Network, now NBC Sports Network] in the States [beginning in 2001]."

1974 • In early April the UCI rules that Eddy Merckx (Molteni) did not intentionally dope before taking part in the 1973 Tour of Lombardy.
- Merckx (Molteni) takes the 57th Giro d'Italia over Giambattista "Gibi" Baronchelli (SCIC) by 12 seconds. The race becomes the subject of the epic documentary film *The Greatest Show on Earth* (75 minutes). It's Merckx's fifth Giro win (and third in a row) making him the only rider to capture three Giro/Tour doubles.
- Ten days after winning his fifth Tour de France, Merckx is made an officer in the Order of Leopold II in Brussels in honor of his achievement.
- Merckx also wins his sixth consecutive Super Prestige Pernod Trophy.
- Jorgen Leth films *The Impossible Hour* in Mexico City. The documentary is about the unsuccessful attempt of Danish rider Ole Ritter (Filotex) to retake the hour record from Eddy Merckx.
- Joel Santori makes *La Course en Tête* (*The Head of the Field*) about Merckx at the height of his career. The movie is produced by Vincent Malle, the brother of Louis Malle, who'd made the 1962 film *Vive le Tour.*
- Merckx wins the 262.5-kilometer (163-mile) world professional road championship ahead of France's Raymond Poulidor in Montreal, Canada. At the time, the victory makes Merckx only the third rider (along with Italy's Alfredo Binda and Belgium's Rik Van Steenbergen) to win the professional road title three times. Only 18 of the race's 66 starters finish the event. With his win at the worlds, Merckx becomes the first rider to win the Giro, the Tour and the worlds in the same year. Irishman Stephen Roche would also win all three events in 1987. Merckx is also the only rider to twice win the Tour de France and the Worlds in the same year.
- Spain's Jose-Manuel Fuente (Kas-Kaskol) wins the 29th Vuelta a España.
- Campagnolo introduces the Super Record gruppo. Similar in design to Nuovo Record, Super Record uses titanium parts for lightness. Customers can soon purchase a "Super Record reduced" gruppo, which substitutes a steel bottom bracket spindle for the titanium one. Campagnolo would cease production of Super Record in 1987, but would resurrect the name along with the unveiling of it's 11-speed drive train in 2008—the company's 75th anniversary year.

- In Morgan Hill California, 24-year-old Mike Sinyard starts Specialized Bicycle Components after selling his VW Microbus. Specialized imports bicycles, parts and accessories from Campagnolo and Cinelli.
- New Middletown, Ohio, advertising executive Arni Nashbar establishes the Bike Warehouse mail order company in his home with about $1,000 in startup money.
- During the gas shortage, the Sun Oil Company begins selling Suncrest bicycles and servicing all makes in 50 of the company's 15,000 service stations. Sunoco charges the participating stations, which are located in college towns and resort areas, a $500 franchise fee plus $5 a month for advertising and training. Suncrest bicycles are built for Sun Oil's Suncrest division by Stelber Industries.
- The Original Plastic Bicycle is a fraud. New York State Attorney General Louis J. Lefkowitz says that after the Toms River company took an untold number of orders for the new bike—at $125 apiece—it never made any bikes, and never intended to. A year and a half earlier the maker had said that the new machine would cost less that a hundred dollars and include amazing innovations such as a 17-pound weight, six fade-resistant colors, self-lubricating parts, reflectorized tires and a lifetime guarantee. Assistant Attorney General Earl S. Roberts said the AG's office is suing the Original Plastic Bike Company to get the customers' money back.
- Spanish amateur Enrique Martinez Heredia wins the Tour de l'Avenir.
- Holland's Roy Schuiten wins Britain's Milk Race. American John Howard finishes 31st.
- Poland's Stanislaw Szozda wins the Peace Race.
- The Amateur Bicycle League of America divides riders into three racing categories.
- British rider Barry Hoban (GAN-Mercier) wins Ghent–Wevelgem, beating Eddy Merckx (Molteni) and Roger de Vlaeminck (Brooklyn) in the sprint.
- Ron Skarin (North Hollywood Wheelmen) wins the Kugler-Anderson Memorial Tour of Somerville on a Teledyne Titan.

In the Tour de France:
- Eddy Merckx (Molteni) wins his fifth Tour de France in five tries.
- The Tour makes its first sea transfer and first trip off the European Continent when it visits England for the first time, spending a day in Plymouth. The riders and officials fly to England.
- The riders climb the Col du Tourmalet twice in 24 hours. France's Jean-Pierre Danguillaume wins both stages. The first of these stages, the race's 17th, marks the only time that a stage of the Tour finishes at the top of the Tourmalet until 2010, when the riders will again climb the mountain twice.
- Merckx's eight stage wins equal his own 1970 effort and the 1930 mark of Charles Pélissier. Belgium's Freddy Maertens will also win eight stages during the 1976 Tour.
- Merckx's total of 32 stage wins surpasses André Leducq's 1938 mark of 25.
- Merckx's average speed of 48 km/h (30 mph) in the 21st stage still ranks among the Tour's fastest road stages.

- Thirty eight year-old Raymond Poulidor (GAN-Mercier) finishes second.
- Awarded since 1968, the white jersey is given to the winner of the combination classification (Eddy Merckx) for the final time. Starting in 1975, the white jersey will be awarded to the race's Best Young Rider.
- The race makes its final finish in Paris' Municipal ("La Cipale") Velodrome. Beginning in 1975, the Tour de France will finish on the Champs Élysées.
- Daniel Mangeas begins his career as the Tour's official announcer when he takes over for Pierre Schori on short notice at Saint-Lary-Soulan (stage 17). Mangeas who hails from de Saint-Martin-de-Landelles in Normandy, has an encyclopedic knowledge of the riders which enables him to talk about all of them, without notes, often for an hour before and after each stage. He would continue as the event's announcer well into the 21st century.
- The initials of Tour founder Henri Desgrange move back to the left side of the yellow jersey, switching places with the jersey's sponsor, Miko.
- The leader of each team wears a racing number ending in 1 (Merckx, 1; Agostinho, 11; Thévenet, 21, etc.).
- The anti-Franco terrorist group the Internationalist Revolutionary Action Group, blows up six official Tour vehicles after the Tour's 16th stage in the Pyrenees.
- Farmers protesting low wages delay the riders for 14 minutes during the 19th stage and force them to take a 3-mile detour during the 20th stage. The detour is probably the first one taken by the race since the last stage of the 1904 Tour de France when the riders went around a checkpoint in Orleans to avoid troublemakers.

1975
- In February Pope Paul VI accepts from Eddy Merckx (Molteni) the bike on which he won the world championship in Montreal. The occasion is the blessing of all the riders in the Tour of Sardinia.
- Dutch rider Hennie Kuiper wins the world professional road championship in Yvoir, Belgium. Kuiper, who won the Olympic road race in 1972, becomes the only rider besides Ercole Baldini to win both the Olympics and the worlds. Baldini won the 1956 Olympics and the 1958 worlds.
- Avocet introduces the first modern bicycle saddle. It uses closed-cell foam over a "ThicThin" plastic shell, and leather or vinyl cover.
- Gary Klein begins producing the first modern American aluminum bicycle.
- Italy's Roberto Visentini wins the UCI's inaugural junior worlds road race in Lausanne, Switzerland.
- Italy's Fausto Bertoglio (Jolli Ceramica) wins the 58th Giro d'Italia. Belgian rider Roger De Vlaeminck (Brooklyn) wins seven stages.
- Agustin Tamames Iglesias (Super Ser) wins the 30th Vuelta a España, defeating fellow Spaniard Domingo Perurena (Kas-Kaskol) on the last day.
- Graftek Division of Exxon Enterprises, Inc., of Del Mar, Calif., introduces the 4.5-pound (with steel headset and Reynolds 531 fork) Graftek G-1 frame. Constructed of carbon fiber-wrapped aluminum tubes that are bonded with epoxy into investment cast, stainless steel lugs, the Graftek frameset is available in

five sizes. The frame's lack of stiffness earns it the nicknames "Flexxon" and "Graflex."

- Shortly before the Graftek frame comes out, Composite Development Corporation of San Diego, Calif, briefly markets its 2.5-pound Graphite USA frame.
- John Howard (Indy-Cool Gear-Exxon) wins the inaugural Red Zinger Classic in Boulder Colo., riding an Exxon Graftek bicycle. On the first day of the race, which is launched by Celestial Seasonings president Mo Siegel, Howard wins the road race and the time trial. The following day he finishes fourth in the criterium.
- Motorcycle daredevil Evel Knievel rides a 10-speed bike in Central Park to promote safety. Knievel does the ride in a leisure suit with bellbottom pants and no helmet. At the end of the ride another participant rear-ends Knievel's bike.
- Reynolds Tube Co., Ltd. introduces its 753 tubing, which it says is 30 percent lighter than standard 531 tubing but 50 percent stronger.
- O.F. Mosberg and Sons of North Haven, Conn., introduce their "X1000" road bike. Made of 100,000 psi carbon fiber tubes joined into steel lugs with an "aircraft adhesive," the 18.5-pound bike sells for $1,200. A 14-pound track version costs $1,300. A 3.1-pound frame costs $600.[1]
- After two years of research and development, Bell Helmets of Los Angeles introduces the Bell Biker, the first bicycle helmet to feature an expanded polystyrene liner. The $30 helmet, which features a Lexan shell and D-ring strap connection, weights 20.5 oz. (580 gm).
- "Tokyo gave a big boost to bicycle enthusiasts recently by opening an 11-foot-wide, 4.6-mile-long bicycle path along the rim of the Imperial Palace Grounds. The Japan Cycle Industry Association provided the public with 500 bicycles free of charge."[2]
- Eddy Merckx (Molteni) wins his seventh consecutive Super Prestige Pernod Trophy.
- The Tour de l'Avenir is not held.
- Sweden's Bernt Johansson wins Great Britain's Milk Race. Dave Chauner, 26, becomes the first American to win a stage of the event when he takes the 145-kilometer (90-mile) final stage by seven seconds.
- Future UCI president Pat McQuaid (Irish National Team) wins the Tour of Ireland.
- Poland's Ryszard Szurkowski wins the Peace Race for the fourth time in six years.
- California's Rory O'Reilly wins the Kugler-Anderson Memorial Tour of Somerville.
- France's Daniel Morelon wins his seventh amateur sprint title. He also won the event in 1966-67-69-70-71-73.
- Joe Magnani, who raced professionally in Europe from 1935 to 1948, dies in Chicago on November 30 at the age of 63. Magnani had become the first U.S. citizen to compete in a major European tour when he rode in the 1946 Giro d'Italia. He had finished 10th in the 1936 world championship road race in Berne, Switzerland, and was the seventh and final finisher in the sweltering

1947 world road championship in Reims, France.

- In November, a French court in Clermont-Ferrand orders Nello Breton to pay Eddy Merckx one French franc in damages for the Puy-de-Dôme punching incident in the Tour de France.
- The December issue *of Bicycling!* (as it was then punctuated) includes "a full-page ad for independent presidential candidate Eugene McCarthy, who said, 'We already have too many highways. We need more bike trails.'"[3]

In the Tour de France:

- France's Bernard Thévenet (Peugeot) hands Eddy Merckx (Molteni) his first loss in a grand tour in eight years.
- Prior to the prologue in Charleroi, Merckx is presented with one of France's highest honors, the *Croix de Chevalier de la Légion d'Honneur.*
- Belgium's Lucien Van Impe (Gitane) is the overall winner of the first *maillot blanc a pois rouges*, the Tour's polka-dot climber's jersey. The Poulain Chocolate Company will sponsor the jersey for seven of its first ten years (1975–78, and 1982–84).
- Holland's Joop Zoetemelk (GAN-Mercier) is the first rider to wear the polka-dot jersey early in the race.
- During the race, Van Impe experiments with a carbon fiber bicycle from Gitane.
- The white jersey is awarded to the Best Young Rider for the first time, Italy's Francesco Moser (Filotex).
- The Tour de France begins its tradition of finishing on the Champs Élysées in Paris.
- The Tour de France is shown in the United States on ABC's *Wide World of Sports.*
- Journalist Owen Mulholland is the first American to follow the race in the press caravan.
- For the first time since 1966, there are no time bonuses for the winners of the flat stages.
- The 1975 Tour is the only one held between 1962 and 1995 not to include a team time trial.
- Knut Knudsen (Jolli Ceramica) is the first Norwegian rider in the Tour. He does not finish.
- Martin "Cochise" Rodriguez (Bianchi) is the race's first Colombian rider. He finishes 27th in what will be his only Tour.
- Filmmaker Jacques Ertaud shoots the documentary film *Autour du Tour* (*About the Tour*), which airs on TF1 on January 2, 1976. In the film, racer Régis Delépine (Flandria-Carpenter) describes the Tour's riders as "itinerant cadavers" whom people might mistake for "survivors of Buchenwald."
- Great Britain's Barry Hoban (GAN-Mercier) wins his eighth and final Tour de France stage.

1976 • Eddy Merckx (Molteni) wins his seventh Milan–San Remo, beating the record of six set by Italy's Costante Girardengo (Maino & Opel-Torpedo) in 1928.

- Director Jorgen Leth films *A Sunday in Hell* about Belgian rider Marc De Meyer (Velda-Flandria) taking the victory in Paris–Roubaix.
- For the second consecutive year, the winner of the Vuelta a España is determined on the race's last day. This time, Spain's Jose Pesarrodona (Kas-Campagnolo) defeats Hennie Kuiper (T.I. Raleigh) to win the 31st edition of the event.
- Italy's Felice Gimondi (Bianchi-Campagnolo) wins the 59th Giro d'Italia by 19 seconds over Johan De Muynck (Brooklyn). Gimondi's victory marks the record ninth time he has finished on the podium at the Giro: he was first in 1967, '69, and '76, second in 1970 and '73, and third in 1965, '68, '74, and '75. It's Gimondi's last major win.
- Thirty-one-year-old Spanish rider Juan-Manuel Santisteban (Kas-Kaskol) is killed in an accident near the city of Catania during the Giro's first stage.
- Belgium's Freddy Maertens wins the 1976 world professional road championship in Ostuni, Italy. Mike Neel, of Berkeley CA, who joined the small Italian Magniflex-Torpado team following the Olympics, finishes 10th in the 288-kilometer race. Neel is generally credited with being the first American to compete in the worlds road race, but note should be made of the participation of Joe Magnani, who finished 10th in the 1936 worlds at Berne, Switzerland and seventh—and last—in the sweltering 1947 event in Reims, France.
- Freddy Maertens (Flandria-Velda) wins the Super Prestige Pernod Trophy.
- Sweden's Bernt Johansson wins the road race at the XXIst Olympiad in Montreal, Canada on a hilly 175-kilometer course. Twenty year-old George Mount is in the winning breakaway and finishes sixth, then the best ever finish for an American.
- Great Britain's Beryl Burton rides a 25-mile time trial in 53:21, and a 50-mile time trial in 1:51:30.
- For its second running, the Red Zinger Classic is expanded to three days and includes teams from Mexico and the Commonwealth. John Howard of the United States is the repeat winner.
- On January 1, the Amateur Bicycle League of America (ABLA), which was founded in 1920, changes its name to the United States Cycling Federation (USCF), saying that "amateur" is too negative, "league" is too archaic and "America" is wrong. Cycling historian Peter Nye notes that the change is also made to "resolve long-standing friction with Latin American cycling organizations that complained the United States was not all of America."[1]
- Trek Bicycle Company begins producing high-end bikes in Waterloo, Wisc. The frames are low-temperature brazed Columbus, Reynolds or Ishiwata tubing painted with DuPont Imron or Centari catalyzed urethane enamel. During the first year, Dick Burke, Bevil Hogg and their five employees produce 900 of the $200 frames.
- Craig Mitchell builds the first custom "klunker" (mountain bike) frame for Charlie Kelly because Joe Breeze is too busy.
- The Consumer Product Safety Commission (CPSC) introduces safety regulations for production bicycles sold in the United States.

- Denmark's Karl Krogshave builds a 72-foot bicycle that seats 35 riders. Construction of the machine requires 130 meters of pipe, 70 sprockets, 50 meters of chain, 3 automobile tires, and parts from 78 old bicycles.
- "The longest cycle tour on record is the more than 402,000 miles amassed by Walter Solle (b. Sunderland [England], 1926), an itinerant lecturer. From January 24, 1959, to December 12, 1976, he covered 159 countries, had 5 bicycles stolen and suffered 231 other robberies, along with over 1,000 flat tires."[2]
- The first mountain bike race is held on October 21 when seven riders compete in the inaugural Repack Downhill in Marin County, California. Organized by Fred Wolf and Charlie Kelly, the race is run on the Pine Mountain Fire Road on Mount Tamalpais. The winner is Alan Brooks, the only rider who doesn't crash.[3]
- Shimano introduces the Positron indexed shifting system for low-end bikes. Buyers in this price category don't want to pay extra for it, and Shimano would drop Positron after 1982.
- Massachusetts resident Joel Evett files a patent application for a "shift lever and integrated handbrake apparatus" for a drop-bar bicycle. He receives his patent on July 18, 1978.
- AlAn of Italy is the first company to offer a production carbon fiber bike frame for sale.
- Cycles Gitane is fully annexed into the Renault Factory Group. (Renault will sell Micmo-Gitane in 1985.)
- Radical Left Party Mayor Michel Crepeau puts 250 bright yellow bicycles on the streets of La Rochelle, France, for the public to use free of charge. "When people use the automobile for necessary transportation, that is one thing," he says. "But when a man uses it as a sign of social status, that is something else. Then there are also those people who become swine when they get in their cars." Even though 30 of the bicycles have already been stolen, and dozens more damaged, Crepeau says that, with the help of the government, he will purchase 250 sturdier bikes.
- Swedish amateur Sven Ake Nilsson wins the Tour de l'Avenir.
- Britain's Bill Nickson wins the Milk Race.
- Ireland's Pat McQuaid repeats as winner of the Tour of Ireland.
- East Germany's Hans-Joachim Hartnick wins the Peace Race.
- Dave Boll of Stanford, California, wins the Kugler-Anderson Memorial Tour of Somerville.
- Philadelphia's Mary Jane Reoch wins the inaugural Mildred Kugler Women's Open in Somerville.
- Disabled in a crash during the 1960 Tour de France, Roger Rivière dies of throat cancer on April 1. He was 40.

In the Tour de France:
- Belgian race winner Lucien Van Impe (Gitane-Campagnolo) receives a 100,000-franc apartment in the seaside resort of Merlin Plage as one of his prizes. The winner would continue to receive an apartment, and sometimes other prizes, through 1988.

- Belgian rider Freddy Maertens (Velda-Flandria) wins eight Tour stages, tying him with Charles Pélissier (1930) and Eddy Merckx (1970 and 1974).
- Maertens' 17-second defeat of prologue specialist Jesus Manzaneque (Super Ser) is the largest margin of victory in the Tour's prologue.
- Forty year-old Raymond Poulidor (GAN-Mercier) finishes on the final podium for a record eighth time, making him the oldest rider to finish on the race's final podium. He never wore the Tour's yellow jersey.
- After having sketched the winning machine since 1950, Daniel Rebour draws his final Tour de France-winning bike.
- Daniel Mangeas becomes the official announcer of the Tour de France, providing commentary on every stage of the race.
- Spanish rider Jose-Luis Viejo (Super Ser) caps a 160-kilometer breakaway by winning the 224-kilometer (139-mile) 11th stage to Manosque by 22:50, the greatest margin of victory in the postwar era.
- Stages 9, 10, and 12 through 15 are all mountain stages. Stage 11 has three third-category climbs, but none of first or second category.
- The race's 18th leg in southern France is the Tour's final stage to have three separate starts.
- Tour organizers ask Georges Rajon to host the finish of the event's ninth stage atop L'Alpe d'Huez 24 years after the race last had a stage finish there, because nearby Grenoble had declined the race's request to be a stage city.

1977
- Sixteen year-old Greg LeMond survives two crashes to win the national junior road championship, but he's too young to compete in the junior world championship.
- LeMond receives special permission to compete in the three-day Tour of Fresno for category-1 men and finishes second, six seconds behind John Howard.
- Following a successful early season, American rider Jonathan Boyer signs with the French Lejeune-BP team. He misses the Tour de France because of a crash just before the start of the event.
- Belgium's Freddy Maertens (Flandria-Velda) wins 13 stages en route to victory in the 32nd Vuelta a España.
- American Mike Neel (Magniflex-Torpado) competes in the Vuelta a España, finishing in the top four in a pair of stages before abandoning due to illness during the 13th stage.[1] Neel is the first American to compete in the Vuelta and the second to take part in a grand tour after Chicago's Joe Magnani (Olmo), who'd raced in the 1946 Giro d'Italia. Magnani crashed out during the 13th stage.
- Freddy Maertens wins 7 of the 60th Giro d'Italia's first 11 stages before crashing out. His teammate Michel Pollentier wins the race.
- In May, six of the world's top professional cyclists are suspended for a month and fined the equivalent of $300. Reportedly the six used a prescription medicine that contains pemoline, which is on the UCI's list of banned substances. Five of the suspended riders are Belgian, including Eddy Merckx (Fiat) and current world champion Freddy Maertens.

- Freddy Maertens wins his second consecutive Super Prestige Pernod Trophy.
- Italy's Francesco Moser wins the sprint from West Germany's Didi Thurau to claim the world professional road championship in San Cristobal, Venezuela. There Jonathan Boyer contracts an intestinal virus which would keep him from returning to racing in Europe until 1980.
- Wayne Stetina wins the third annual Red Zinger Classic.
- Belgian amateur Eddy Scheppers wins the Tour de l'Avenir.
- Soviet amateur Said Gusseinov wins the Milk Race.
- The USSR's Aavo Pikkuus wins the Peace Race.
- Dave Ware of Miami, Fla., wins the Kugler-Anderson Memorial Tour of Somerville.
- Ontario, Canada's Karen Strong wins the Mildred Kugler Women's Open.
- Reynolds Tube Co., Ltd. becomes T.I. Reynolds.
- Early in the year Raleigh Industries of England announces it is closing its only American plant. Raleigh Industries of America President Norman Langefeld says that the Oklahoma City factory is being shut down because bicycle sales in America are around 7 million units a year, about half of what they'd been just four or five years earlier.
- More than 3,000 cyclists take part in the *Des Moines Register*'s fifth Annual Great Bicycle Ride Across Iowa (RAGBRAI). The weeklong event covers about 400 miles.
- David Steed of Tucson, Arizona, does a trackstand for 9 hours 15 minutes.
- Businessman Percy Ross, 61, gives away 1,050 new bicycles at a $180,000 Christmas party for needy children, ages 7 to 11, in the Minneapolis-St. Paul, Minn., area. Too poor to afford a decent bike as a kid, Ross was once on the verge of bankruptcy. In 1969 he'd sold his company, Poly-Tech for $8 million.
- Belgium's Roger De Vlaeminck (Brooklyn Chewing Gum) becomes the only rider to win Paris–Roubaix four times. In his 13 starts, De Vlaeminck finished first or second eight times, and never finished worse than seventh.
- In August, 13 Chinese acrobats ride a single-seat bicycle in Peking (Beijing), China.
- Between March 17 and April 2, a Frenchman identified as M. Lotito (a.k.a. "Monsieur Mangetout") eats an entire bicycle after it's been reduced to a pile of filings.
- Bryan Allen pedals Dr. Paul MacCready's human-powered Gossamer Condor aircraft around a one-mile figure-eight course to collect the £25,000 ($54,000) Kremer Prize.

In the Tour de France:
- France's Bernard Thévenet (Peugeot-Esso) wins his second Tour de France in three years.
- Eddy Merckx (Fiat) rides in his last Tour de France. He finishes sixth, 12:38 back.
- France's Bernard Quilfin (Gitane-Campagnolo) caps a 222-kilometer (138-mile) solo breakaway with a win at Thonon-les-Bains.

- The win by Hennie Kuiper (T.I. Raleigh) at L'Alpe d'Huez popularizes the climb with Dutch cycling fans.
- Nearly half the field is eliminated on time at L'Alpe d'Huez.
- British photographer Graham Watson watches the Tour's final two days. A picture he takes of Eddy Merckx in Paris would be published early the following year.
- Only 10 teams start the Tour de France.
- Publishing magnate Émilion Amaury, who had purchased *L'Équipe* in 1965, is killed when he falls off his horse at his estate in Compiègne. Amaury was so disliked by some of the publishers of rival papers that one, *Liberation*, ran the story of his death below the headline, "Riding Accident: Horse is Safe."

1978 • "The barrel's empty," said Eddy Merckx (C&A), and "after a final run out on May 17, I decided to call it a day. The following day, I announced my retirement in public. I'd had enough."[1]

"The decision is final," announced the Cannibal, "and extremely painful. I have a very important decision to give you in connection with my career as a racing cyclist. I have decided, after consulting with my doctor, not to race any more." With that announcement, Eddy Merckx brought to a close a list of results of which other cyclists could only dream: five Giri d'Italia, three professional world championships, one Vuelta win and the hour record, which would endure for another six years (23 years, if aero-aided records are not counted). He'd won Milan–San Remo seven times, five Liège–Bastogne–Lièges and three Paris–Roubaixs. And in the Tour de France, the toughest cycling competition of them all, he'd twice won eight stages of the race, to bring his total number of stage victories to 34. He'd also spent 96 days (111 "days," if you count multiple stages) in the event's yellow jersey, twice that of his nearest rival at the time.

And those are only the highlights. In all, between 1969 and 1975, Eddy Merckx had won 250 races—nearly one a week for six years. During his career, he'd competed in 1,800 races and recorded 525 wins. He once figured that he'd covered enough miles to circle the globe 12 times![2] Of all those miles ridden in all kinds of conditions, Merckx had a surprisingly simple philosophy; just before his retirement, he noted that "No one has to continue, whatever the cost, and I have continued. One has to know how to suffer,"[3] adding, "If you really enjoy doing something, you are only too happy to put up with the suffering.

"Merckx had escaped again, but this time for good and no one would ever catch him or equal him."[5]

- Two months after finishing 73rd in his first Tour, Jean-Jacques Fussien (Fiat) is hit by a truck and killed during a training ride, leaving behind a wife and two children. He was 26.
- Newspaper and BBC Radio journalist Phil Liggett does his first live show on weekend television in London. His big break comes "when the regular cycling commentator, David Saunders, was killed in a car crash," recalls Liggett. "I was offered his job without an interview."

- The Netherlands' Gerrie Knetemann wins the world road championship in West Germany.
- Belgium's Johan De Muynck (Bianchi-Faema) wins the 61st Giro d'Italia.
- The 33rd Vuelta a España is won by Bernard Hinault (Renault-Gitane), making him the second rider after Jacques Anquetil to win the Vuelta and the Tour in the same year.
- George Mount wins the fourth Red Zinger Classic by 5:28 over Bob Cook. The race features a $30,000 purse. Michael Aisner is hired as the race's full-time, year-round promoter.
- The International Olympic Committee rules that amateur bicycle racers can accept unlimited expense money from their sponsors and as much as $200 in prize money per race, with any surplus prize money going the rider's club treasury.
- Philadelphia Phillies baseball players Tug McGraw and Steve Carlton want to ride their bicycles from Philadelphia to spring training in Clearwater, Fla., to help fight muscular dystrophy. "If they can ride on interstate highways, the trip, starting February 6, should take 17 days. If they can't, McGraw and Carlton may miss the exhibition season."[6]
- Italy's Francesco Moser (Sanson-Columbus-Campagnolo) wins the Super Prestige Pernod Trophy.
- DuPont and Swiss clothing maker Assos collaborate to introduce jerseys and shorts made of Lycra. The new material would quickly replace wool as cyclists' fabric of choice.
- Switzerland's Daniel Gisiger (Lejeune-BP) wears a skinsuit in the Tour of Romandie, starting the aero era.
- Georges Speicher, who won the Tour de France and the world road championship in 1933, dies on January 24, at the age of 70.
- Shimano introduces the Dura-Ace rear derailleur. Although the company celebrated the 25th anniversary of Dura-Ace in 1999 (which would make 1974 the gruppo's official year of introduction), gearing expert Frank Berto writes, "…Shimano set up the Dura-Ace division and introduced the Dura-Ace Road Ensemble in 1972. This consisted of front and rear derailleurs, down tube and bar-end shift levers, crankset, freewheel, hubs and brakes. Shimano called the rear derailleurs 'Crane' [through]…1977. The 1978 Shimano catalog introduced the Dura-Ace EX gruppo and the DA-200 rear derailleur was now called Dura-Ace."[7]
- Shimano introduces the freehub and six-speed cassette combination in its Dura-Ace EX and 600 EX gruppos.
- John Marino rides the 2,956 miles (4,756 kilometers) from Long Beach, Calif., to New York in 13 days 1 hour 20 minutes.
- Specialized introduces its Turbo line of road bike tires.
- Soviet amateur Serguei Soukhoroutchenkov wins the Tour de l'Avenir.
- Polish amateur Jan Brzezny wins the Milk Race.
- The Soviet Union's Alexander Averin wins the Peace Race.
- Canada's Jocelyn Lovell wins the Kugler-Anderson Memorial Tour of Somerville.

- Sue Novara of Flint, Mich., wins the Mildred Kugler Women's Open.
- On September 16 the Netherlands' Cornelia Van Oosten-Hage increases the women's hour record to 43.082 kilometers (26.771 miles) in Munich.

In the Tour de France:

- French national champion Bernard Hinault (Renault-Gitane) wins the Tour de France on his first try.
- Félix Levitan, "deputy director" since 1962 is made "co-director," Jacques Goddet's equal.
- No Italian riders take part in the ultra-mountainous race.
- Three teams—T.I. Raleigh, Renault-Gitane, and Fiat-La France—institute anti-doping policies which allow for the dismissal of any rider caught using illegal drugs.
- The Tour de France celebrates its Diamond Jubilee (75 years), with its 65th race.
- The results of the rainy 5-kilometer prologue time trial in Leiden are nullified.
- The French military has to clear the Tourmalet pass of snow so the 11th stage can be run.
- The first part of the 12th stage is canceled when the racers walk across the finish line to protest the organizers' putting the Tour's business interests ahead of their concern for the riders.
- To appease the riders, the race's 15th stage is shortened by 44 kilometers (27 miles).
- Michel Pollentier (Velda-Lano-Flandria) is kicked out of the race following the 16th stage for trying to cheat dope control after taking the yellow jersey atop L'Alpe d'Huez. He is the first race leader to be kicked out of the Tour de France for a doping-related infraction.
- The Team Points Competition is introduced. Members of the team leading the points classification wear green caps, while members of the team leading on time wear yellow caps. T.I. Raleigh-McGregor wins the former, Miko-Mercier the latter.
- During the 17th stage, the racers climb the Col de Joux-Plane for the first time.
- The 1978 event is the final Tour de France for British rider Barry Hoban (Miko-Mercier-Hutchinson). His 12 Tours de France in 15 years make him the only rider to have competed against Jacques Anquetil, Eddy Merckx and Bernard Hinault.

1979 • *Breaking Away* opens in American theaters. The Twentieth Century-Fox film, starring Dennis Christopher, wins the National Society of Film Critics "Best Picture" award in 1979. Writer Steve Tesich wins an Oscar for Best Screenplay. The part of one of the Italian Cinzano riders is played by John Vande Velde, father of future US Postal/Discovery/Garmin rider Christian Vande Velde. The rider Christopher's character beats in the movie is played Indiana student Bill Brissman (Delta Chi), whose team would win the real Little 500 for the third consecutive time in 1981.
- After Jonathan Boyer (Grab On) is penalized five minutes, Dale Stetina wins the fifth Red Zinger Classic without winning any of its eight stages. Wayne

Stetina is third and junior rider Greg LeMond, who received special permission to compete in the race, finishes fourth.

- America's George Mount wins the French Tour de l'Auvergne stage race.
- On June 12, 26-year-old biologist and cyclist Bryan Allen pedals Dr. Paul MacCready's Du Pont-sponsored Gossamer Albatross to the first successful human-powered flight across the English Channel in a time of 2 hours 49 minutes. The 70-pound aircraft has a wingspan of 96 feet and requires one-third horsepower to run. For their feat, the pair are awarded the £100,000 ($213,000) prize put up by British industrialist Henry Kremer.
- Eighteen year-old Greg LeMond wins the road race at the junior worlds in Buenos Aires when Belgium's Kenny De Marteleire is demoted to second for dangerous riding in the sprint. LeMond also wins the silver in the individual pursuit and the bronze in the team time trial. He tells *Velo-news*, "I want to be the first American to do really well in the Tour de France."[1]
- France's Bernard Hinault (Renault-Gitane) wins the Super Prestige Pernod Trophy.
- Soviet rider Serguei Soukhoroutchenkov wins his second consecutive Tour de l'Avenir.
- Soukhoroutchenkov also wins the Peace Race.
- The Soviet Union's Yuri Kashirin wins the Milk Race.
- Canada's Ron Hayman (Archer Road Club) wins the Tour of Ireland.
- William Martin of Bradford Woods, Pa., wins the Kugler-Anderson Memorial Tour of Somerville.
- Karen Strong wins her second Mildred Kugler Women's Open in three years.
- Vivekananda Selva Kumar Anandan of Sri Lanka cycles nonstop for 187 hours 28 minutes.
- Holland's Jan Raas wins the world professional road championship in Valkenburg, the Netherlands.
- Holland's Joop Zoetemelk (Miko-Mercier) wins the 34th Vuelta a España. Unipublic comes on board as a co-organizer of the race. It will become the Vuelta's sole organizer beginning in 1982. The race also begins its tradition of finishing in Madrid. Between 1979 and 2009, 28 of the race's 31 finishes will have been in the Spanish capital. The Vuelta also finished in Madrid in 1935-50, 1963 and '64, and 1971.
- Twenty-one year-old Giuseppe Saronni (SCIC-Bottecchia) of Italy wins the 62nd Giro d'Italia.
- At the national time trial championships in Wautoma, Wisc., America's Beth Heiden becomes the first female rider to break the 25-mile-per-hour barrier.
- MAVIC introduces a "nearly complete" bicycle component gruppo,[2] but it is rarely seen outside of France.
- On July 24, only 60 miles from the end of his cross-country record attempt, 30-year-old John Marino is unable to keep his balance and is forced to abandon. He is rushed to Lennox Hill Hospital, where he is expected to remain overnight. Marino was trying to break his own cross-country record of 13 days 1 hour 20 minutes.

In the Tour de France:

- Race winner Bernard Hinault (Renault-Gitane) wins seven stages, including all four time trials.
- Hinault is the only rider besides Eddy Merckx to win the yellow and green jerseys in the same Tour de France.
- Members of the Renault-Gitane team use aerodynamic Gitane bicycles for the time trial stages.
- The race features no fewer than 16 challenges and classifications for which the riders are awarded daily and overall prizes.
- Portugal's Joaquim Agostinho (Flandria-Ca Va Seul) finishes third at age 37.
- For the second year in a row, the same three riders finish on the podium, in the same order—Hinault, Holland's Joop Zoetemelk (Miko-Mercier), and Agostinho.
- The racers climb L'Alpe d'Huez on consecutive stages.
- L'Alpe d'Huez and the Col du Galibier are the first climbs to receive the Tour's *Hors Catégorie* (Beyond Category), or HC difficulty rating.
- Paul Jesson (Splendor) is the first New Zealander to ride in the Tour de France since 1928.
- Holland's Gerrie Knetemann (T.I. Raleigh) is the first rider to average better than 50 km/h in a Tour stage when he rides the 5-kilometer (3.1-mile) prologue in 5:59.
- During the event, former winner Luis Ocaña, covering the race as a radio commentator, is injured in a car crash.
- The polka-dot jersey is sponsored by A Form Sport.
- Joop Zoetemelk and his Miko-Mercier teammate Sven Ake Nilsson use freewheels with seven cogs instead of the more normal six.

Chapter 9

1980–1989
Americans in Paris

1980 • John Marino rides from California to New York in 12 days 3 hours 31 minutes, breaking his own record of 13 days 1 hour 20 minutes. During his ride, Marino uses three Peugeot PY10CP bicycles.

• American rider Jonathan Boyer returns to racing in Europe with the Puch-Campagnolo team.

• American George Mount signs with the Italian San Giacomo-Benotto team.

• 18 year-old Greg LeMond wins the springtime Circuit de la Sarthe race in France. In July, he agrees to ride with Bernard Hinault on the Renault-Gitane team in 1981. LeMond signs his contract on November 21 at New York's United Nations Plaza Hotel with Bernard Hinault as a witness. "[W]hen Hinault, the current world road champ, pedaled down Park Avenue that afternoon in his bright yellow Renault/Gitane jersey, no one gave him a second look."[1]

• America's Beth Heiden wins the women's road race at the world championships in Sallanches, France.

• Celestial Seasonings turns over sponsorship of the five-year-old Red Zinger Classic to the Adolph Coors Brewery because Coors has the finances to make the event "bigger and better." Michael Aisner stays on as the race's promoter. America's Jonathan Boyer (Puch-Sem-Campagnolo, Sidi-Grab On) makes an amazing comeback when he joins a breakaway that laps the field four times in the Boulder Mountain criterium to win the nine-day Coors International Bicycle Classic, which includes 80 riders from 13 countries.

• To commemorate the 100th anniversary of the League of American Wheelmen, the United States Postal Service issues a stamped envelope honoring the bicycle. A white old-fashioned high-wheel "ordinary" is embossed in a maroon circle next to "15¢, USA" in the envelope's upper right corner, and in the lower left corner is a silhouette of "modern" blue bicycle. The new envelope is issued on May 16 in Baltimore, Md., where the headquarters of LAW is located.

• Bike Warehouse catalogue No. 19 offers a Columbus SP frame kit for $135. A Gios Torino frame and fork made with Columbus SL tubing goes for $570.

Dura-Ace EX and SunTour Superbe rear derailleurs cost less than $29 each. Campagnolo Nuovo Record and Super Record gear changers cost $55 and $80 respectively. The price difference between the Italian components and their Japanese counterparts is called the "Campagnolo tax," or "the price of beauty"—not to mention the extra cost of the Super Record's titanium bits. A Shimano Link Lock master chain link costs $3.50. After years of specifying special Hyperglide pins to connect its derailleur chains, Shimano would reintroduce a master link, the SM-CN79 Quicklink, with the 2008 revision of its flagship Dura-Ace gruppo.

- Tom Doughty, a 27-year-old accountant from Hobart, Ind., wins the 100-kilometer (62-mile) Tour of Nutly ahead of Dale Stetina. Former Olympic speed skater Eric Heiden "finished a distant 19th." "Eric is still developing," said Doughty. "The day will come when he'll be a world-class racer if he keeps at it. But he still has to pick up a lot of savvy. Still, he has a lot of talent."[2]
- Leonard Harvey Nitz wins the 100-kilometer "Grand Prix" race in New York's Central Park ahead of Steve Bauer of Fenwick, Ontario, Jim Ochowicz of Lake Placid, N.Y., and Wayne Stetina of Indianapolis.
- Olympic medalist Beth Heiden beats Heidi Hopkins by five lengths in the 35-mile USCF national championships in Bisbee, Ariz. Heiden also wins the time trial.
- The USSR's Serguei Soukhoroutchenkov wins the 189-kilometer men's road race at the American-boycotted XXIInd Olympiad in Moscow.
- Bernard Hinault (Renault-Gitane) wins the Super Prestige Pernod Trophy.
- France's Bernard Hinault wins the world professional road championship in Sallenches, France. America's Jonathan Boyer finishes fifth on the difficult course, 4:25 behind Hinault, and is signed by Cyrille Guimard to ride with Hinault on the Renault-Gitane team in 1981. By being the best-placed American rider at the worlds, Boyer also becomes the American professional road champion. He would wear his stars-and-stripes jersey while riding in the '81 Tour de France.
- Bernard Hinault wins Liège–Bastogne–Liège in a blizzard. At the Stockeu Wall, with 80 kilometers (50 miles) to go, Hinault trails Rudy Pevenage (Ijsboerke-Warncke) by more than two minutes. He attacks on the climb, soon catching and dropping Pevenage. As he continues to pick his way along the race's frozen roads, the Badger tells himself "The other riders must be in the same state and if they could stand it so could I." Bernard Hinault wins La Doyenne by 9:24 over Hennie Kuiper. It takes half an hour for the next 21 riders (out of 171 starters) to trickle in, and three weeks for the feeling to return to Hinault's index and middle fingers.
- After dropping race leader Wladimiro Panizza (Gis Gelati) on the Passo dello Stelvio, Bernard Hinault wins the 63rd Giro d'Italia by almost six minutes, becoming the fourth rider (along with Jacques Anquetil, Felice Gimondi and Eddy Merckx) to win each of the three grand tours at least once. Guiseppe Saronni (Gis Gelati), who'd won the race in 1979, wins seven stages.
- Faustino Ruperez (Fosforena-Vereco) of Spain wins the 35th Vuelta a España.

- André Leducq, 76, winner of the 1930 and 1932 Tours, dies in an auto accident on June 18.
- Recently retired Spanish racer Vicente Lopez-Carril dies of a heart attack on March 29. Lopez-Carril recorded three stage wins in the Tour de France and finished in the top ten six times, including a third-place finish in 1974. He was 37.
- Lucien Buysse, winner of the 1926 Tour de France, dies on January 3. He was 86.
- Gastone Nencini, winner of the 1960 Tour de France, dies on February 1. He had suffered a career-ending crash near his home during the Menton–Rome race in 1965. A heavy smoker, Nencini died of cancer. He was 49.
- Jean Robic, winner of the 1947 Tour de France, dies on October 6. Robic was on his way home from an old timer's reunion when his car hit a tree at 2:00 A.M. He was 59.
- Five-time Tour winner Eddy Merckx establishes his bicycle company with the help of his friend Ugo De Rosa.
- Colombian amateur Alfonso Florez wins the Tour de l'Avenir.
- Soviet rider Ivan Mitchenko wins the Milk Race.
- The USSR's Yuriy Barinov wins the Peace Race.
- Canada's Steve Bauer wins the Kugler-Anderson Memorial Tour of Somerville.
- Fellow Canadian Karen Strong wins her third Mildred Kugler Women's Open in four years.

In the Tour de France:

- "Honorary Frenchman" Joop Zoetemelk wins the Tour de France after finishing second five times. He declines the yellow jersey for a day when two-time winner Bernard Hinault abandons with knee problems just before the Pyrenees.
- All of the race's top five finishers are at least 31 years old.
- The race is now put on by the Amaury-owned *la Société du Tour de France*. Amaury also owns *L'Équipe*.
- A French television network sponsors the "GP TF1" combination award (general classification, climbing, and sprinting) through 1982.
- On the race's last weekend, CBS Sports devotes a segment to the Tour de France.
- Between stages 14 and 20, the last rider in the general classification is eliminated from the race.
- Austria's Gerhard Schonbacher (Marc-IWC-VRD) finishes as the *lanterne rouge* for the second year in a row. He is the first Tour rider to accomplish the feat since France's Daniel Masson did it in 1922 and 1923.

1981 • On May 17, Greg LeMond (Renault-Elf-Gitane) beats Phil Anderson in the 61-mile first stage of the Tour de l'Oise to pick up his first professional victory.
- In early July, 20-year-old LeMond wins the Coors Classic by 4:47 over members of the powerful Soviet national team, who take the next three positions.

- After three crashes—including one with a standard poodle—and seven falls, Bernard Hinault (Renault-Elf-Gitane) wins Paris–Roubaix. A year earlier, he'd criticized the event, exclaiming, "It's not a race, it's a cyclocross." After his victory, the Badger says that he will never again race the "steeplechase."
- Bernard Hinault wins his third consecutive Super Prestige Pernod Trophy.
- Spain's Luis Puig becomes president of the UCI, a position he'd hold until his death in 1991.
- Italy' Giovanni Battaglin (Inoxpran) wins the 64th Giro d'Italia. George Mount (San Giacomo-Benotto) is the first American to compete in the event since Joe Magnani in 1946. Mount finishes 39 minutes back in the 25th position.
- Battaglin also wins the 36th Vuelta a España.
- Belgium's Freddy Maertens caps off a remarkable comeback season when he beats France's Bernard Hinault and Giuseppe Saronni of Italy in the sprint to win the world championship race in Prague, Czechoslovakia.
- Readers of *Bicycling* magazine can order one of 2,500 sets of three silver and gold Campagnolo belt buckles from Brown & Koby of Houston, Texas. The steel dies for the buckles are designed by sculptor Klaus Marschel. Each set costs $295. Other Campagnolo collectibles of the day include; the nutcracker ($100), plastic corkscrew ($70), bronze or aluminum corkscrew ($100 each), and the gold corkscrew ($500).
- Campagnolo's alloy freewheel, the last project with which Tullio Campagnolo is directly involved before his death, comes to market. The price of the 13-28 tooth six- (and later seven-) speed freewheel is about $200. The 12-tooth version, which has two titanium cogs, costs $300, while the hardwood-boxed tool kit required to service it costs $500. Development of the freewheel took almost six years.
- Huffy sells a $250 "Aero" bike that's equipped with Shimano's $300 Dura-Ace AX gruppo. Equipment expert Frank Berto would later write, "Smart buyers bought the bike, took out the AX gruppo and threw the rest in the dumpster."[1]
- Specialized Bicycle Imports of San Jose, Calif., introduces the $750 Stumpjumper, the first mass-produced mountain bike.
- Yamaha International Corporation recalls 30,000 model GPM, PRC, and PRT 10-speed bicycles after the Consumer Product Safety Commission receives complaints of 30 failures of the bikes' aluminum forks.
- Yoplait Yogurt donates 20 bike racks to the Department of Transportation office in Washington, D.C. The secure racks can accommodate 40 bicycles.
- A year after its Chicago workers vote to affiliate with the United Auto Workers, Schwinn moves most of its manufacturing operations to Greenville, Miss., and constructs a factory for its Paramount Design Group in Waterford, Wisc.
- Held in the brand new $3 million Bill Armstrong stadium, the 31st running of Indiana University's Little 500 bicycle race is watched by an overflow crowd of 27,412 people. The team from Delta Chi wins the race with the Willkie Quadrangle squad second.
- Bob Cook dies on March 11 from a brain tumor at the age of 23. Cook, who maintained a 3.9 grade point average as an engineering major at the Univer-

sity of Arizona, finished second to George Mount in 1978 Red Zinger Classic. On March 10 Cook's parents receive a letter from a woman in France who'd heard of Cook's illness. She had included an autographed photo of Eddy Merckx, Bob's childhood idol. "Cook's parents wanted to show the letter to their son, who was in a semi-coma in the hospital. During their evening visit, Cook came out of the coma briefly. Ellen Cook showed him the picture, he smiled and touched it. Three hours later Cook died." At the time of his death, Bob Cook held the record for the 28-mile climb of 14,264-foot Mount Evans at 1:54:27. "'From 10,000 to 14,000 is like a no man's zone,' said Alexi Grewal, a 20-year-old member of the United States national team from Aspen, Colo. 'Bob owned that territory.'" Bob Cook had won the race the last six times it was held.[2]

- Fichtel & Sachs buys majority ownership of the Huret Derailleur Company.
- Beginning in 1981, the Tour de l'Avenir is open to professional riders. It is won by France's Pascal Simon (Peugeot-Esso).
- Soviet amateur Sergueï Krivosheev wins the Milk Race.
- Ireland's Bill Kerr wins the Tour of Ireland.
- The Soviet Union's Shakhid Zagretdinov wins the Peace Race.
- Wayne Stetina of Indianapolis wins the Kugler-Anderson Memorial Tour of Somerville.
- Canada's Karen Strong wins the Mildred Kugler Women's Open for the fourth time in five years.
- Distance specialist Lon Haldeman of Harvard, Ill., rides across the country from west to east and back again in less than 25 days.

In the Tour de France:
- Race winner Bernard Hinault (Renault-Elf-Gitane) and Belgium's Freddy Maertens (Sunair-Sport 80-Colnago) each win five stages.
- Jonathan Boyer (Renault-Elf-Gitane) is the first American to ride in the Tour. He rides in his American champion's jersey, and finishes 32nd at 59:21.
- Phil Anderson (Peugeot-Esso-Michelin) becomes the first Australian rider to wear the yellow jersey.
- British photographer Graham Watson receives his first official Tour media credentials.
- Future yellow jersey sponsor Banania issues a series of eight yellow postcards featuring caricatures of the tour's great riders by the French artist Pellos.
- The organizers restore time bonuses for the finishes of the flat stages.
- Race director Jacques Goddet is too ill to follow the Tour. Except for when he had covered the Los Angeles Olympics in 1932, it is the first time Goddet has missed going with the race since 1928.
- Belgium's Lucien Van Impe (Boston-MAVIC) finishes his 13th consecutive Tour de France. Van Impe's mark ties him with the number of finishes by France's André Darrigade between 1953 and 1966 (Darrigade did not finish in 1963).
- At the race's presentation the previous October the Tour's organizers said that, because of the race's financial situation, commercialization is necessary to keep it out of the hands of the French government.

1982 • Bernard Hinault (Renault-Elf-Gitane) wins the 65th Giro d'Italia, making him the fourth rider (after Fausto Coppi, Jacques Anquetil, and Eddy Merckx) to win the Tour and the Giro in the same year.

• Bernard Hinault wins his fourth consecutive Super Prestige Pernod Trophy.

• A co-organizer of the event since 1979, Unipublic takes over as sole organizer of the Vuelta.

• Two days after the conclusion of the event, Spain's Marino Lejarreta (Teka) is declared the winner of the 37th Vuelta a España when Angel Arroyo (Reynolds-Galli) is disqualified because of a positive urinalysis.

• Italy's Giuseppe Saronni wins the world professional road championship in Goodwood, England when he outsprints Greg LeMond and eight others, including Jonathan Boyer, who had been caught by the group on the race's final climb. Boyer later claimed that the LeMond-led group hunted him down, while LeMond said that his fellow American was fading fast and "misjudged how quickly he was going to get gobbled up by the pack behind."[1] Although disappointed at the outcome of the race, the 10th-place Boyer is pleased with his performance and says he may reconsider his earlier decision not to ride the Tour again. "Boyer knew from the start," said LeMond, "that we weren't friends and that we were both riding for ourselves. I wore the American jersey but there really wasn't an American team and I certainly didn't belong to one. I paid for my trip to England, my hotel bills, and everything myself. If I was riding for a team it was Renault." Dutch sociologist Benjo Masso notes that LeMond's closing chase was probably motivated by the fact that "Cycle racing was still so underdeveloped in the United States that there was room for *one* star at most....Were Boyer to become world champion, *he* would be the one to whom American sponsors would give all their attention."[2]

• Ivyland, Penn.'s John Eustice (Sem-France Loire, Assos) wins the $100,000 U.S. professional championship, a criterium around the harbor in Baltimore. The race ends up being run as a pro-am event because there aren't enough American professionals to fill out the field.

• Over the winter LeMond (Renault-Elf-Gitane) and his wife Kathy move from Nantes, France to the more Anglicized city of Kortrijk, Belgium.

• Huffy Corp. enters into a long-term agreement with T.I. Raleigh of England which allows Huffy to make and sell Raleigh bicycles and related items in the United States. Two months later Huffy says it expects a fourth-quarter operating loss and will close its Azusa, Calif., factory, the smallest of the company's three facilities. Soon thereafter, Huffy also closes its Ponca City, Okla., plant, leaving just the company's 19-acre plant in Celina, Ohio. Together, Huffy and Murray Ohio Manufacturing Company of Brentwood, Tenn., account for about 55 percent of all bicycles sold in the United States.

• Mike Burrows designs the Lotus Sport superbike. It would remain largely unknown until a change in the UCI rules would allow its use a decade later.

• Belgium's Marc Demeyer, winner of the 1976 Paris–Roubaix, dies of a heart attack on January 19. Demeyer, who had also won two stages of the Tour de France, had missed much of 1981 with an injury. "His planned comeback", remembers former teammate Freddy Maertens, "which was due to take place with the Splendor team in 1982, was never to happen as, shortly before the team presentation, he died suddenly. The peloton had lost its locomotive forever."[3] Marc Demeyer was 31.

- Greg LeMond (Renault-Elf-Gitane) dominates the Tour de l'Avenir, winning three stages of the 11-stage race and finishing 10:18 ahead of runner-up Robert Millar (Peugeot-Shell) of Scotland.
- Colombian amateur Jose Patrocinio "Patro" Jimenez wins the Coors Classic by 4:24 over his countryman Martin Ramires.
- Connie Carpenter (Puch) of Boulder, Colorado, wins the Coor's International Bicycle Classic by 2:37 over France's Jeannie Longo. Nineteen-year-old Rebecca Twigg of Seattle is third, eight minutes back. Carpenter wins five of the race's nine stages.
- East Germany's Olaf Ludwig wins the Peace Race.
- Soviet amateur Yuri Kashirin wins the Milk Race.
- Gary Tevisiol of Ontario, Canada wins the Kugler-Anderson Memorial Tour of Somerville.
- Sue Novara-Reber of Flint, Mich., wins the Mildred Kugler Women's Open.
- The ABC television network produces an award-winning 90-minute documentary about the Great American Bicycle Race. The GABR, in which riders race across the country, is won by Lon Haldeman of Harvard, Ill., who completes the 2,976-mile trek in 9 days 20 hours 2 minutes. "'All I thought about in the last six days was going to sleep,' Haldeman said. He averaged 300 miles and 14,000 calories a day. To train for the event, Haldeman said he commuted the 84-mile distance to work by bicycle. 'I have a paper route too,' he said."[4] The event will be renamed the Race Across America (RAAM) the following year.
- "Eddy Merckx...was recently offered a contract by a Spanish team that tops the money he made in his best years with Molteni. But Merckx didn't hesitate in turning the offer down, saying, 'I'm happy to live on my memories. I'm several kilos overweight and I have no wish to go on a Cassius Clay-type farewell tour.'"[5]
- "In our 'Fiddling While Rome Burns' department: during an emotional debate on congressional tax breaks for those living in Washington, tax deduction defender Senator Ted Stevens (R-Alaska) heatedly denounced the capital city for its poor air, poor schools, and high crime. After the debate, Stevens' chief aid went outside the Capitol to find that his bicycle had been stolen."[6]
- Faliero Masi introduces the Volumetrica, a bike frame with oversize steel main tubes and internal lugs.
- Police in Beijing, China ban roller skating on city streets because it disrupts the flow of bicycle traffic.

In the Tour de France:
- Bernard Hinault (Renault-Elf-Gitane) wins his fourth Tour de France in five years.
- To help finance the race, there are more than 50 official corporate sponsors.
- In response to co-director Félix Levitan's plan to make the race an "Open Tour" which would pit national squads against the established trade teams, Jacques

Goddet proposes a "World Tour" to be held every four years in which only national teams from around the world would compete. Goddet's plan would have "new" cycling nations such as Canada, the United States, Colombia, Portugal, Eastern European nations and African Countries competing against the established cycling powers of Europe and the British Empire.

- Joop Zoetemelk's (Coop-Mercier-MAVIC) seventh appearance on the podium puts him second to Raymond Poulidor, who leads with eight podium finishes. Eddy Merckx, Jacques Anquetil and Gustave Garrigou each have six podium finishes. Lance Armstrong's seven podium appearances between 1999 and 2005 will all be victories. His record-tying eighth podium appearance in 2009 would be for third place.
- The '82 Tour is the third and final year for the GP TF1 combination award. It is won by Bernard Hinault.
- The fifth stage, a team time trial between Orchies and Fontaine-au-Pire, is canceled when steelworkers block the road in Denain. The leg is rescheduled and run as part of the ninth stage.
- Phil Anderson finishes fifth, the best finish yet for an English-speaking rider.
- The Tour de France makes its first start in Switzerland.
- Dr. Gerard Porte, who has worked with the Tour since 1972, becomes head of the race's medical service.
- In the U.S., Tour fans can make a toll call to a *Velo-news* (as it was then spelled) number for a daily two-minute update on the race.
- Only 9 of the Tour's 21 stages start in the city where the previous stage had finished.

1983 • T.I. Raleigh's Bert Oosterbosch (NED) wins the $100,000 Tour of America, beating Australia's Phil Anderson by 33 seconds. Seventy-five racers take part in the four-stage, 271-mile (437-kilometer) race, which is held in the District of Columbia and Virginia during the Cherry Blossom Festival.
- In October, Félix Levitan announces plans for a 15-stage women's race to be called the Tour de France Féminin. Its stages would be run two hours prior to the men's race, and would cover the last part of the day's route, being no more than 55 kilometers (35 miles) long.
- Italy's Giuseppe Saronni (Del Tongo-Colnago) wins the 66th Giro d'Italia.
- France's Bernard Hinault (Renault-Elf-Gitane) wins the 38th Vuelta a España, to become the first rider to win each of the three grand tours at least twice. The victory of Hinault's teammate Laurent Fignon in the Tour de France also gives Renault-Elf two grand tour wins by two different riders in the same year. The US Postal/Discovery Channel team would match this mark in 2003 and 2005.
- Twenty-two year old American Greg LeMond wins the 1983 world professional road championship in Altenrhein, Switzerland, to become the third-youngest world champion, after 20-year-old Karel Kaers (BEL) in 1934, and the late Jean-Pierre Monseré, who was 21 in 1970. LeMond drops Spain's Faustino Ruperez on the final climb and rides most of the 169-mile race's final lap alone to beat Holland's Adri Van der Poel by 1:11.

- LeMond (Renault-Elf-Gitane) wins the Dauphiné Libéré when France's Pascal Simon is disqualified three days after the finish for taking Micoren to treat his hay fever. LeMond becomes "the first American to win a major all-professional stage race".[1]
- LeMond also captures the 1983 Super Prestige Pernod Trophy, becoming only the fourth rider (after Eddy Merckx, Freddy Maertens, and Bernard Hinault) to win the worlds and the SPPT in the same year.
- Greg LeMond comes the closest he'll ever get to winning a classic when he loses the Tour of Lombardy to Ireland's Sean Kelly (Sem) by three inches.
- American Dale Stetina wins the Coors Bicycle Classic without winning any of its stages. Davis Phinney wins four stages. Stetina also won the Red Zinger Classic in 1979.
- John Eustice (Gios-Torino) wins his second consecutive U.S. professional championship in Baltimore.
- The six-year old Cannondale company begins making aluminum bike frames in Stamford, Conn., debuting its TIG-welded ST500.
- Vitus of France introduces its carbon frame, the Plus Carbone, which is modeled after the company's 979 aluminum frame.
- La Prealpina is Europe's largest-selling rooftop car rack for bicycles.
- Campagnolo releases its 50th anniversary gruppo. Included with the gruppo, which comes in a special carrying case, is the "Blue Card," that guarantees the original purchaser "unique replacement parts at any time."
- Steve Tilford and Jacquie Phelen win the first NORBA mountain bike national titles.
- Lon Haldeman of Harvard, Ill., wins the 3,170-mile (5,101-kilometer) Race Across America (RAAM) in 10 days 16 hours 29 minutes, five hours ahead of the next rider.
- Avocet introduces its first bicycle computer, the $35 "Avocet 20."
- Bell introduces the $43, 434-gram, V1 Pro. The helmet, which has eight vents, is designed specifically for bicycle racing.
- Alex Moulton introduces his AM series of bicycles which feature a "space frame" constructed of Reynolds 531 tubing, and 17-inch wheels.
- Oakley introduces the Factory Pilot Eyeshade, which uses an optically corrected lens from the company's line of motorcycle goggles. Oakley was the name of company founder Jim Jannard's dog.
- PowerFood founders Brian and Jennifer Maxwell bake the first batch of PowerBars in their oven.
- Shortly after Campagnolo releases its 50th anniversary gruppo, Tullio Campagnolo dies of heart failure in Monselice, Italy. He was 81.
- Three-time Tour de France winner Louison Bobet dies of cancer on March 13, the day after his 58th birthday.
- Romain Maes, winner of the 1935 Tour de France, dies on February 22. He was 69.
- Antonin Magne, winner of the 1931 and 1934 Tours de France dies on September 8 at the age of 79.

- East German amateur Olaf Ludwig wins the 22nd Tour de l'Avenir.
- Matt Eaton becomes the first American to win Great Britain's Milk Race, defeating Sweden's Stefan Brykt by 16 seconds in the two-week, 1,057-mile event.
- East Germany's Falk Boden wins the Peace race.
- Canada's Steve Bauer wins the Kugler-Anderson Memorial Tour of Somerville.
- Sue Novara-Reber wins the Mildred Kugler Women's Open.

In the Tour de France:

- At just 22 years 11 months 12 days, Laurent Fignon becomes the second-youngest Tour winner in the past 50 years. In 1965, Italy's Felice Gimondi won the race the age of at 22 years 9 months 15 days.
- Race leader Pascal Simon abandons six days after fracturing his collarbone in a crash.
- Scotland's Robert Millar becomes the first British rider to wear the polka-dot jersey.
- "Patro" Jimenez becomes the first Colombian—and first amateur—to wear the polka-dot jersey.
- Belgium's Lucien Van Impe (Metauromobili-Pinarello) wins his sixth King of the Mountains title, tying him with Spain's Federico Bahamontes.
- The initials of Tour de France founder Henri Desgrange appear on the yellow jersey for the last time until 2003.
- The Colombia-Varta amateur squad is the first non-European team to compete in the Tour.
- American rider Jonathan Boyer (Sem) finishes 12th, 19:57 back.
- During the 13th stage, the riders stage a slowdown until race boss Félix Levitan allows Patrick Clerc (Sem) to remain in the race following his positive drug test.
- The team time trial of the second stage concludes in Fontaine-au-Pire, the smallest community (population 1,217) to host the Tour.
- The team time trial is scored on a bonus system in which the Colombian team loses only about 3:30 to the winning Coop-Mercier squad after actually finishing more than 10:30 back.
- Michel Laurent (Coop-Mercier-MAVIC) is awarded the win in the sixteenth stage after being forced into the barriers and finishing seventh.
- Australia's Phil Anderson's (Peugeot-Shell-Michelin) Tour is the subject of the 50-minute film *23 Days in July*.
- Philippe Amaury ends a six-year court battle with his sister, Francine, over the publishing empire that their father had left to her (Philippe had detested his father, and, by association, Félix Levitan, the man he had hired to help run the Tour de France). The two finally agree that she will get the magazines (*Marie France* and *Point de Vue: Images Du Monde*) and he will get the newspapers (*L'Équipe* and *Le Parisien*).
- The German band Kraftwerk releases *Tour de France*. The minimalist single would be included on the band's *Tour de France Soundtracks* album 20 years later.

- Kim Andersen (Coop-Mercier-MAVIC) is the first rider from Denmark to wear the yellow jersey.
- From 1983 through 1986 the Tour's Best Young Rider jersey will be awarded to the best young rider making his first appearance in the race. This year's best young rider is race winner Laurent Fignon.

1984 • Forty-two year-old Joaquim Agostinho (Sporting Raposeira) dies from head injuries after crashing when a dog runs into the road during a finishing sprint at Portugal's Tour of the Algarve. After the fall, a friend would say of Agostinho, "If he had a brick for every fall, what a castle he could have built....As a tribute in *L'Équipe* pointed out, it was to be the last fall for a world champion faller. He was in a coma in Lisbon, clinically dead for nearly two weeks, until his life support system was turned off."[1] Joaquim Agostinho had finished in the top ten in the Tour de France eight times, including third overall in 1978 and 1979.
- Riding a special aerodynamic bicycle, Italy's Francesco Moser (Gis-Tuc-Lu) breaks Eddy Merckx's 12-year-old hour record of 49.431 kilometers (30.716 miles). On January 19, the 32-year-old Moser rides the Antonio dal Monte-designed bicycle 50.808 kilometers (31.572 miles) on the velodrome in Mexico City. Moser's machine, which relies on momentum (it is four kilos heavier the Merckx's bike) and aerodynamics for its sustained speed was the tenth version of the bike to be built. It also features upturned handlebars and two lenticular disc wheels, which reportedly weigh six pounds each. Moser rode wearing a skinsuit and an aero helmet after having fine-tuned his riding position in a wind tunnel in Turin, Italy. Four days later, he extends his new mark to 51.151 kilometers (31.785 miles). Moser's machine, and the fact that it receives "post-race technological approval" from the UCI, outrages the public and the press in Merckx's native Belgium. Later in the year, three Belgian journalists argue in a 90-page dossier that Moser's machine violated UCI regulation 49 which forbade streamlined bicycles, and claimed that on a similar machine, Eddy Merckx could have achieved a distance of 52 kilometers (32.3 miles). The UCI responds by establishing two hour records: one below 2000 feet (reinstating the 1967 mark of 48.093 kilometers (29.885 miles) set in Rome by Belgium's Ferdinand Bracke), and an altitude mark (Moser's). The issue of aerodynamics would remain unaddressed until September of 2000 when the UCI would announce that it would recognize only records set on traditional bicycles, thereby resurrecting Eddy Merckx's 28-year-old hour mark.
- Moser uses the same bike later in the year to defeat Laurent Fignon (Renault-Elf) in the 67th Giro d'Italia. Many feel that Moser stole the event from Fignon with the help of the race's organizers who "...canceled the highest mountain stage (because of snow), where Moser was certain to crack; they overlooked numerous pushes up hills by Moser fans and relatives and, in addition, prevented Guimard's car from approaching Fignon with advice....Still, Fignon held the lead into the final day, a time trial; but Moser used the aerodynamic

bicycle he took with him to Mexico City to break the record for the hour and picked up nearly four minutes, to win by a little over a minute."[2] Fignon would ride the prologue of the following Tour de France on an aerodynamic Gitane "Delta" bicycle.

- France's Eric Caritoux (Skil) wins the 39th Vuelta a España over Alberto Fernandez (Zor) by its smallest margin: six seconds. At 19, Spanish junior champion Miguel Indurain becomes the youngest rider to wear the race leader's jersey. Later that year, Indurain turns professional with Reynolds.
- Marianne Martin (USA) wins the inaugural Tour de France Féminin. She completes the 18-stage, 991-kilometer (616-mile) course in 29:39:02, putting her 3:17 ahead of the Netherlands' Heleen Hage. American rider Deborah Schumway is third.
- Doug Shapiro (G.S. Mengoni) wins the Coors Classic when Alexi Grewal is disqualified after testing positive for phenyethylamine, a drug that's later traced to an herbal tea called Chi Power. Grewal appeals the subsequent 30-day suspension and is allowed to compete in the Los Angeles Olympic games. During the Coors, scenes of the "Hell of the West" stage race are filmed for the up-coming Warner Brothers movie *American Flyer*.
- America's Alexi Grewal wins the 190-kilometer men's road race in Mission Viejo, Calif., over Canada's Steve Bauer at the Soviet-boycotted XXIIIrd Olympiad. Connie Carpenter wins the women's race ahead of fellow American Rebecca Twigg. Years later, Grewal would admit, "I took at least 100 milligrams of caffeine with just under two laps to go,"[3] before breaking away with Bauer.
- After finishing second in the Olympic road race, Bauer signs a professional contract with La Vie Claire and finishes third at the world championships in Barcelona.
- Seventy-nine-year-old journalist Jacques Goddet covers the 1984 Los Angeles Olympic games. Goddet had also covered the 1932 Los Angeles Olympics.
- Belgian Claude Criquielion wins the world professional road championship in Barcelona.
- Ireland's Sean Kelly (Skil-Reydel-Sem) wins the Super Prestige Pernod Trophy.
- Greg LeMond signs a three-year, $785,000 contract with the La Vie Claire team.
- Jean-Marie Leblanc, a journalist with the French cycling magazine *Vélo*, conceives the world computer ranking of professional riders. The system would be adopted by the FICP (*Fédération Internationale du Cyclisme Professional*) two years later.
- SunTour's 20-year-old patent on the slant parallelogram rear derailleur expires, giving Shimano access to the last key part it needs to introduce its Shimano Index Shifting (SIS) system.
- Look begins selling clipless pedals in bike shops in France.
- Bell Helmets develops the Pursuit, the first aerodynamic helmet fairing, for the United States Cycling Team.
- Tsuyama Manufacturing Company, Limited of Osaka, Japan introduces the

Cateye Solar bicycle computer, which has nine functions and is "99.9 percent" accurate.

- Plans for a U.S.-based, Skil-backed cycling team are canceled because of lack of funding. The plug is pulled on the squad, which would have been led by Jonathan Boyer and co-sponsored by Murray bicycles and Heuer Timing, when executives at Skil Power Tools decide that the $450,000 race budget isn't "enough money to do it big."[4]
- France's Charly Mottet (Renault-Elf) wins the 23rd Tour del'Avenir.
- The Soviet Union's Oleg Czougeda wins the Milk race.
- The UK's Bob Downs wins the Tour of Ireland.
- Soviet rider Sergueï Sukhoroutchenkov wins the Peace Race.
- Davis Phinney of Boulder, Co., wins the Kugler-Anderson Memorial Tour of Somerville.
- Sue Novara-Reber wins her fourth Mildred Kugler Women's Open.
- In June, 28-year-old Dave Kiefer of Smithville, Ohio rides across the country in less than 18 days. Years earlier, Kiefer had lost his left leg when his motorcycle was hit by a drunk driver.

In the Tour de France:

- France's Laurent Fignon (Renault-Elf) defeats fellow Frenchman Bernard Hinault (La Vie Claire-Terraillon) to win his second consecutive Tour de France.
- American racer Greg LeMond (Renault-Elf) is the first rider from the U.S. to finish on the podium. LeMond also wins the white jersey as the race's best young rider.
- Scotland's Robert Millar (Peugeot-Shell) places fourth, best yet for a rider from Great Britain (Tom Simpson had finished sixth in 1962). Millar also wins a stage and the polka-dot climber's jersey.
- Colombia's Luis "Lucho" Herrera is the first Colombian, the first non-European, and the first amateur, to win a stage in the Tour de France.
- Banania replaces Miko as the sponsor of the *maillot jaune*. The initials of Tour founder Henri Desgrange are removed from the jersey to make room for more advertisers' logos.
- The red jersey is introduced to designate the leader in the intermediate sprints competition, which had begun in 1971.
- Carrera-Inoxpran's Carlo Tonon (1955–96) of Italy lapses into a coma after crashing head-on into a bike-riding spectator during the 19th stage's descent to Morzine. He never races again.
- At the request of the riders, the 21st stage is shortened from 320 kilometers (198 miles) to 290 kilometers (180 miles).
- American actor Dustin Hoffman, director Michael Cimino (*The Deer Hunter*, and *Heaven's Gate*) and screenwriter Colin Welland (*Chariots of Fire*) follow the race for two days (from Bordeaux to Pau) to prepare for next year's filming of *The Yellow Jersey*, based on Ralph Hurne's 1973 novel. The movie would never be made.

1985 • Bernard Hinault (La Vie Claire) edges Francesco Moser (Gis Gelati-Trentino Vacanze) in the 68th Giro d'Italia. 7-Eleven competes in the race, becoming the first American team to take part in a grand tour. Ron Kiefel is the first American to win a stage of the Giro when he takes the event's 15th stage while Andy Hampsten wins the 20th. Greg LeMond (La Vie Claire) finishes third overall. 7-Eleven's Eric Heiden wins the Hot Points sprint competition.

• French cycling superstar Jeannie Longo marries her coach Patrice Ciprelli.

• Italy's Wladimiro Panizza (1945–2002; Ariostea-Benotto), age 39, starts his 18th Giro d'Italia, finishing in 28th place. He completes the race 16 times, including 11 top-12 finishes. His best finish was second to Bernard Hinault in 1980.

• Pedro Delgado (Orbea-MG-Gin) wins the 40th Vuelta a España over Scotland's Robert Millar (Peugeot-Shell) after Spanish riders, led by the Zor team, thwart the Scot's attempts to chase Delgado during the 18th stage to the Spaniard's hometown of Segovia. Millar finishes second, 36 seconds back.

• Ireland's Sean Kelly (Skil-Sem-Kas-Miko) wins his second consecutive Super Prestige Pernod Trophy. Phil Anderson (Panasonic) is second, Greg LeMond (La Vie Claire) third.

• Eric Heiden (7-Eleven) wins the inaugural CoreStates USPRO road race in Philadelphia. The event is held on a 156-mile (251-kilometer) course designed by Dave Chauner and Jack Simes III.

• Greg LeMond of La Vie Claire (which is called "Red Zinger-Celestial Seasonings" while racing in the U.S.) wins the Coors Classic over countryman Andy Hampsten of Levi's-Raleigh.

• Thurlow Rogers wins the first Redlands Bicycle Classic.

• Thirty-eight year-old Joop Zoetemelk breaks away from Greg LeMond and Moreno Argentin in Montello, Italy to become the oldest winner of the world professional road championship.

• European professional Jonathan Boyer (USA) wins the 3,120-mile (5,020-kilometer) Race Across America in 9 days 2 hours 6 minutes, beating runner-up Michael Secrest by four hours.

• At the worlds, FICP head Hein Verbruggen floats the idea of a World Cup competition. To make his plan work, he suggests shortening major stage races in order to open up more dates for one-day races, an idea Tour de France co-director Félix Levitan calls a "complete waste of time." Eventually the organizers of all three grand tours will oppose the World Cup idea as well as the UCI's later ProTour concept.

• Technological advances include the introduction of Campagnolo's new Record components (popularly referred to as "C-Record"), a complete gruppo from Mavic (the *Special Service du Course 1000*), Shimano's "SIS" indexed shifting system, disc wheels, Wolber's "Profil" aero rims, and, in Europe, Look pedals. Riders such as Greg LeMond and Steve Bauer also popularize Oakley Factory Pilot Eyeshade sunglasses.

• To celebrate the 50th anniversary of its 531 tube set, TI Reynolds of Birmingham, England, offers a special commemorative tube transfer to owners of 531 frames for the price of postage and one British pound (about $1.16). Reynolds claims that more than 20 million frames have been built with its 531 tubing over the past half century.

- True Temper Cycle Products of Memphis, Tenn., begins producing two types of bicycle tubing. The company's Custom Performance series T1 tubing is made of aircraft-grade chrome-moly steel and is available in four different sets. T2 Aluminum tubing is also available from True Temper.
- Phil Wood introduces his now-famous Tenacious Oil. A four-ounce bottle of the no-splatter oil costs $2.50, or $6.50 with stainless steel bottle holder.
- The Lynskey brothers form Litespeed in Tennessee and begin producing bike frames from 3Al/2.5V titanium.
- *Rolling Stone* reports that some American track riders benefited from illegal "blood boosting" in the 1984 Olympics, forcing the resignation of USCF president Rob Lea. The U.S. Cycling Federation bans blood doping but notes that it "does not violate International Olympic Committee rules." Of the three cycling federation staff members involved in the incident, "Eddy Borysewicz, the national and Olympic cycling coach, and Ed Burke, the federation's Elite Athlete Program director, are suspended without pay for 30 days and are given a letter of reprimand. Mike Fraysse, a former president of the federation, is demoted from first vice president to third vice president."[1]
- A Gallup poll shows that bicycling (33 percent) is the second most popular outdoor activity among Americans, ending up between swimming (41 percent), and fishing (30 percent).
- Utah becomes the 50th state to recognize bicycles as vehicles, giving cyclists the same rights and responsibilities as cars, trucks and buses.
- On July 20, 31-year-old American John Howard (Pepsi-Campagnolo) sets a bicycle land speed record of 152.284 mph (245.025 km/h) while drafting the "444," a 350-cubic-inch Chevy-powered streamliner race car, driven by Rick Vesco on the Bonneville Salt Flats. Howard's 46-pound Skip Hujsak bicycle is fitted with a 390-inch gear.
- Two of the products being demonstrated at the bicycle show in the New York Coliseum are Henry and David Hon's 28-pound folding bike, and the $595 Schwinn Air-Dyne stationary exercise bike.
- Bell introduces the L'il Bell Shell helmet for kids. It fits children's head sizes 5½ to 6½ is made of expanded polystyrene, and passes the ANSI Z90.4 bicycle helmet impact test.
- Sean Kelly (Skil-Sem-Kas-Miko) wins the first Nissan International Classic in Ireland.
- The Renault Factory Group, which had fully annexed Cycles Gitane in 1976, sells off its Micmo-Gitane division.
- Poland's Lech Piasecki wins the Peace Race.
- Colombia's Martin Ramirez (Varta-Cafe de Colombia) wins the 24th Tour de l'Avenir.
- The Milk Race switches from an amateur event to a pro-am format. It is won by Belgium's Eric van Lancker (Fangio-Ecoturbo).

- Matt Eaton of Renfrew, Pa., wins the Kugler-Anderson Memorial Tour of Somerville.
- Eaton's sister, Sophie, wins the Mildred Kugler Women's Open.
- Italy's Maria Canins wins the second Tour de France Féminin, finishing nearly nine minutes ahead of France's Jeannie Longo-Ciprelli. To get around the new UCI rule that limits women's races to 12 stages, the racers take a day off after the 12-stage "Tour National," before competing in the 5-stage "Champs Élysées" event. Of the race's 72 starters, 65 finish the 748-mile (1,204-kilometer) race. The best-placed American is Janelle Parks in seventh. The American women's B team is coached by New York headwaiter Richard Lavelot, who's a native of Brittany. Before the race, he recalls another team he'd coached a few years earlier: "I brought a United States men's team to France in 1980 and one of our riders was Greg LeMond."
- America's Rebecca Twigg wins the world championship in the 3,000-meter individual pursuit in a time of 3:52.75. Twigg's victory, which comes in Bassano del Grappa, Italy, is her second consecutive world title and third since 1982. Jeannie Longo is second in 3:53.83.
- American Shelley Verses becomes the first female *soigneur* in professional cycling when her 7-Eleven team turns professional and begins competing in Europe.
- The UCI allows sponsor's logos to appear "nearly anywhere on a rider's uniform."[2]
- Nicolas Frantz, who won the Tour de France in 1927 and then led the entire 1928 event (becoming the only rider to wear the yellow jersey literally from start to finish), dies on November 8. He was 86.
- After ten years of trying, frame builder Gary Klein of Chehalis, Wash., is granted a patent covering a bare frame of less than five pounds that exceeds certain minimums for torsional and bending stiffness, regardless of material. "Every frame [Cannondale is] putting out the door, they're going to pay me royalties for,"[3] he says. A few months later Klein sues Cannondale Corporation in Federal District Court in Bridgeport, Conn., seeking a permanent injunction preventing Cannondale from selling "infringing products in the future."

In the Tour de France:
- Bernard Hinault (La Vie Claire-Wonder-Radar) wins his fifth Tour de France, equaling the marks of France's Jacques Anquetil and Eddy Merckx of Belgium.
- Greg LeMond (La Vie Claire-Wonder-Radar) is the first American rider to win a Tour stage, an individual time trial.
- Third-place finisher Stephen Roche (La Redoute) is the first Irishman to finish on the Tour's podium.
- Race co-director Jacques Goddet is honored at a June dinner for his involvement with 50 Tours de France since 1929.
- Jacques Goddet and Félix Levitan want to ban disc wheels from the race in order to level the playing field. They are overruled by the UCI's technical commission.
- Doug Shapiro (Kwantum) is the third American to ride in the Tour. He finishes 74th.

- Tenth-place Steve Bauer (La Vie Claire-Wonder-Radar) is the first Canadian to ride the Tour since Pierre Gachon in 1937.
- Previous winners Joop Zoetemelk (Kwantum) and Lucien Van Impe (Santini-Selle Italia) each finish their 15th Tour de France.
- The sportswriters of *L'Équipe* can no longer get rooms at the same hotel as the race directors when they're replaced by employees of France 2 TV, which bought the race's television rights.
- "Lucho" Herrera (Cafe de Colombia) is the first Colombian rider to win the King of the Mountains competition.
- Cafe de Colombia becomes the sponsor of the race's polka-dot jersey.
- Greg LeMond wins the race's first patchwork jersey for the *Classement Combine de la Présence* award, which combines general classification, sprint points, climbing points, and intermediate sprint points.
- Tour organizers sign a 12-year contract with Coca Cola to replace Perrier bottled water—which had been a Tour sponsor for 50 years—as the race's official drink.
- When the Renault Factory Group sells Micmo-Gitane to a small bike company shortly after the Tour, team director Cyrille Guimard and Laurent Fignon form a corporation and shop for a sponsor, eventually settling on Système U. Initially the supermarket chain agrees to sponsor the team through 1988 for 15 million francs (about $2 million) a year.
- Spain's Miguel Indurain (Reynolds) competes in his first Tour. He finishes the prologue in 100th place and abandons the race during the fourth stage.

1986 • Beginning on January 1, hard-shell helmets become mandatory at all USCF-sanctioned events.
- Jim Gentes' company, Giro, introduces the Prolight bicycle helmet.
- Look starts selling three models of "toe clipless" pedals in the United States: the black Competition model ($110), the white Sport model ($80), and the black and yellow plastic Leisure model ($55), which is later renamed ATB after it becomes popular with mountain bikers.
- Pacemaker designer Ulrich Schoberer starts Schoberer Rad Messtechnik (SRM) and begins perfecting a power measuring device for cyclists.
- Italy's Roberto Visentini (Carrera) wins the 69th Giro d'Italia. Greg LeMond (La Vie Claire-Wonder-Radar) wins the fifth stage and finishes fourth overall.
- The 41st Vuelta a España is won by Spain's Álvaro Pino (Zor-BH). Scotland's Robert Millar (Panasonic) is second, and Ireland's Sean Kelly (Kas-MAVIC) finishes third.
- Kelly wins his third consecutive Super Prestige Pernod Trophy.
- Bernard Hinault (La Vie Claire) and Greg LeMond help teammate Andy Hampsten defeat Robert Millar in the Tour of Switzerland.
- Bernard Hinault wins the Coors Bicycle Classic. His Red Zinger teammate Greg LeMond is second, 1:26 back. Levi's Pro riders Phil Anderson and Andy Hampsten finish third and fourth.
- Jeannie Longo-Ciprelli wins the Women's Coors Classic.

- A sparse crowd watches Italy's Moreno Argentin win the world professional road championship in rainy Colorado Springs. The event, which is held at the Air Force Academy, is the first world championship to be held in the United States in 75 years.
- Thomas Prehn (Schwinn-Icy Hot) beats Denmark's 36-year-old Jorgen Marcussen (Pinarello) in the sprint to win the CoreStates USPRO race in Philadelphia.
- Tucson, Ariz.'s David Steed does a trackstand (both feet on the pedals and neither wheel making one complete revolution) for 24 hours 6 minutes.
- From 1986 through 1990, the Tour de l'Avenir is called the Tour of the European Community. The race is won by Spain's Miguel Indurain (Reynolds-Reynolon). America's Alexi Grewal (RMO) wins the hardest mountain stage, and finishes third overall. During the spring, Grewal (7-Eleven) stayed in Europe and rode with RMO while the rest of his team raced in the southwestern United States. He would reunite with 7-Eleven for the Tour de France and then return to RMO after being kicked off the 7-Eleven team for spitting at a CBS cameraman during the Tour de France.
- East Germany's Olaf Ludwig wins the Peace Race.
- Great Britain's Joey McLoughlin (ANC-Halfords) wins the Milk Race.
- Ireland's Sean Kelly (Guiness-Kas-MAVIC) repeats as winner of the Nissan International Classic.
- Belgium's Marc Maertens wins the Kugler-Anderson Memorial Tour of Somerville.
- Peggy Mass of Fort Worth, Texas, wins the Mildred Kugler Women's Open.
- On September 20, France's Jeannie Longo-Ciprelli increases the women's hour record to 44.770 kilometers (27.820 miles) in Colorado Springs.
- Italy's Maria Canins defeats Jeannie Longo-Ciprelli by 15 minutes 31 seconds to win the Tour de France Féminin for the second year in a row. Inga Thompson of the Paula Andros-coached American team is third.
- Bernard Hinault retires on November 14, his 32nd birthday.
- Five-time Giro d'Italia winner Alfredo Binda dies on July 19. He was 83.

In the Tour de France:

- Greg LeMond (La Vie Claire-Wonder-Radar) is the first American to win the Tour de France.
- Canada's Alex Stieda (7-Eleven) is the first North American to wear the yellow jersey, and subsequently LeMond is the first U.S. rider to wear it.
- 7-Eleven is the first American team to compete in the Tour de France.
- 7-Eleven's Davis Phinney is the first American rider on an American team to win a Tour de France stage, and the first American rider to win a Tour de France road stage.
- Phinney wins his stage on an American-made "Huffy," built by Ben Serotta.
- 7-Eleven's Shelley Verses is the first female *soigneur* at the Tour de France.
- A record 210 riders on 21 teams start the 73rd Tour de France.
- A record 10 American riders start the Tour de France.
- Four riders from La Vie Claire finish in the top 10, with LeMond, Hinault, Hampsten and Niki Rutimann placing first, second, fourth and seventh, respectively.

- The conclusion of the 17th leg to Serre Chevalier atop the 2,413-meter (7,915-foot) Col du Granon is the Tour's highest stage finish. It's won by Spain's Eduardo Chozas (Teka).
- Mexico's Raul Alcala (7-Eleven) and Brazilian Renan Ferraro (Malvor-Bottecchia-Vaporella) are the first Tour riders from their countries.
- Primoz Cerin (Malvor-Bottecchia-Vaporella) is the first Yugoslavian Tour rider since a four-man team took part in the 1936 event. He finishes 32nd.
- After having competed in the Tour de France since the beginning, Peugeot ends its sponsorship of its professional cycling team at the conclusion of the 1986 season. The team will become Z.
- Greg LeMond's "Look" (TVT) bicycle is the first machine with a carbon-fiber frame to win the Tour de France.
- Bernard Hinault (La Vie Claire-Wonder-Radar) is awarded the Legion of Honor by French President François Mitterrand.
- For the fourth time since 1983, the white jersey is awarded to the best young rider competing in his first Tour de France. Beginning in 1987, the race will again give the award to the best young rider under 26, as it had done previously.
- Paul Sherwen joins his countryman Phil Liggett as a cycling commentator.
- Joop Zoetemelk (Kwantum-Yoko) finishes his record 16th Tour de France.
- Hinault's seventh podium finish ties him for second-most podium appearances with Holland's Joop Zoetemelk. France's Raymond Poulidor leads with eight. It's the eighth Tour de France in which Hinault has worn the yellow jersey (1978–1982 and 1984–1986). Lance Armstrong would win seven Tours de France between 1999 and 2005, and finish third in 2009.
- By winning the polka-dot jersey, Hinault becomes the first rider since Eddy Merckx (in 1969 and 1970) to win both the green jersey (in 1979) and the climbing competition.
- Belgium's Eric Vanderaerden (Panasonic) finishes second in three stages and third in three more to claim the green jersey without winning a stage.
- Spain's Pedro Delgado (PDM) abandons during the L'Alpe d'Huez stage because of the death of his mother.

1987 • Five-time Tour de France winner Jacques Anquetil dies on November 18. For the past decade, suffering from bouts of pulmonary congestion "...he passed his nights observing the wild boars racing about in the Volgboel woods near his home. He was so afraid to sleep fearing that he would not wake up, that he practically never slept, revealed a close friend."[1] In May of 1987, Anquetil was diagnosed with stomach cancer. In August, doctors in Rouen removed his stomach and put him on a strict diet, which he ignored. Shortly before his death on November 18, in an oft-told but disputed story, Anquetil summoned former rival Raymond Poulidor (with whom he'd since become good friends) to his bedside and told him, "Sorry Raymond...but once again you will finish second." Among those attending his funeral are Eddy Merckx and Bernard Hinault, the Tour's other two five-time winners. The French cycling magazine

Vélo publishes a special issue dedicated to Anquetil which includes a statement from French President François Mitterrand. Raphaël Géminiani said that Anquetil "did for cycling what Mozart did for music."

"If the Tour were a person, it would be Jacques Anquetil," remembered former teammate Lucien Aimar. "Someone who is refined and serious, mysterious and enigmatic, disconcerting and indefinable." Aimar added that "For me, he was like a big brother, essential to my life. I had a lot of trouble continuing without him. He was beautiful from every point of view. If I could, I'd tell him how much I miss him."[2] Eight thousand mourners pack his funeral at the cathedral in Rouen. Jacques Anquetil was 53.

- Greg LeMond is shot in a hunting accident and spends six days in the hospital. In September, he returns to racing in Europe and soon signs a letter of intent to ride with PDM in 1988.
- American Andy Hampsten (7-Eleven) wins his second consecutive Tour of Switzerland beating Holland's Peter Winnen (Panasonic) by one second.
- Ireland's Stephen Roche (Carrera-Inoxpran) scores a controversial victory in the 70th Giro d'Italia, taking the lead from teammate Roberto Visentini. Scotland's Robert Millar (Panasonic) is second.
- While the sprinters are watching his fellow Irishman Sean Kelly, Stephen Roche accelerates away from a 12-man group in the final kilometer to win the world professional road championship in Villach, Austria, becoming only the second rider to win cycling's "Triple Crown" after Eddy Merckx in 1974. When his informed of this fact, Roche replies, "Merckx wasn't so bad a rider." Roche's time for the 276-km (172-mi.) race is 6:50:02. The members of the winning Italian team time trial squad fasten themselves to their bikes with guy wires.
- Stephen Roche (Carrera) wins the Super Prestige Pernod Trophy. Sean Kelly (Kas) is second.
- France's Catherine Marsal wins the UCI's inaugural junior women's road race in Bergamo, Italy.
- Colombia's Luis "Lucho" Herrera (Cafe de Colombia) wins the 42nd Vuelta a España after race leader Sean Kelly (Kas-Miko) quits with two days remaining because of an infected saddle sore. Herrera is the first Colombian rider to win a grand tour.
- Mexican rider Raul Alcala (7-Eleven) wins the Coors Bicycle Classic. His teammates Jeff Pierce and Andy Hampsten are second and third, respectively.
- France's Jeannie Longo-Ciprelli improves her own hour record to 44.933 kilometers (27.921 miles) in Colorado Springs on September 23. She also wins her third Coors Classic and third road race world championship.
- While transitioning from the role of bicycle racer to the role of television commentator, Paul Sherwen (Raleigh-Banana) wins the British national road championship. Sherwen includes "at least being British Pro champ once before I retired," and, "Finishing the Tour—any time," as some of the best moments of his riding career.
- Tom Schuler (7-Eleven) wins the CoreStates USPRO championship race in Philadelphia by outsprinting Roy Knickman (Levi's-Raleigh) and Cesare Ci-

pollini (Pepsi Cola-Mirinda). Cipollini is the French-born older brother of Mario.

- French racer Pascal Jules (Caja Rural) is killed in an automobile accident on October 25. Jules, who won the eighth stage of the '84 Tour de France in Nantes, was a close friend of Laurent Fignon.
- Jeannie Longo-Ciprelli defeats Italy's Maria Canins to win the Tour de France Féminin.
- Gwyn Jones, Gary Helfrich and Mike Augspurger form Merlin Metalworks in Somerville, Mass. Their company is initially called Kestrel Metalworks until *Bicycling*'s John Kukoda tells them the name Kestrel is already taken.
- Campagnolo ceases production of the Super Record derailleur, marking the end of the basic design that had debuted in 1951.
- Campagnolo introduces its Chorus gruppo which includes the component maker's first slant-parallelogram rear derailleur.
- The Carlisle Tire and Rubber Company, the last American maker of bicycle tires, closes its doors. During its 38-year run the Pennsylvania-based company produced nearly 250 million tires and tubes.
- Shimano introduces a seven-speed Dura-Ace cog set.
- Bador produces its 100,000th Vitus 979 Duralinox aluminum frame in eight years.
- Trek displays its "5000" model monocoque bicycle at a trade show in October. The non-OCLV carbon fiber bicycle will become available to the public in early 1989. The Dura-Ace-equipped model will cost $2,495.
- After buying the rights to Boone Lennon's invention the previous year, Scott USA begins producing the DH clip-on aerodynamic handlebar extension.
- Stanley R. Day starts OLLO Bicycle Components, Inc., in Chicago. Two months later he changes the name of his company to SRAM, reportedly after the names of its principals: attorney Scott Ray King, Stanley R. Day, and Sam Patterson. The new company's first product is the DB Shifter, designed by Patterson.
- France's Marc Madiot (Systeme U) wins the Tour of the European Community.
- East Germany's Uwe Ampler wins the Peace Race.
- Ireland's Malcolm Elliot (ANC-Halfords) wins the Milk Race. Britain's Mark Walsham (Percy Bilton-Holdsworth) and Belgium's Willi Tackaert (ADR-Fangio) test positive for drugs. Each is fined the equivalent of $800 and suspended for a month.
- Great Britain's Joey McLoughlin (ANC-Halfords) wins the Kellogg's Tour of Britain.
- Sean Kelly (Castrol-Burnmah-Kas) wins his third consecutive Nissan International Classic.
- Paul Pearson of Allentown, Pa., wins the Kugler-Anderson Memorial Tour of Somerville.
- Holland's Henny Top wins the Mildred Kugler Women's Open.
- British professional sprint champion Dave LeGrys sets a world roller speed record of 126.6 mph (203.7 km/h). To set the mark, he pedals about 200 rpm

for six seconds in a 233-inch (95 x 11) gear.

- "The 1987 comeback of the year award goes to Chris Carmichael, the 7-Eleven pro who shattered his leg while cross-country skiing last winter. After doctors inserted a 2-pound steel rod in his leg they told him he wouldn't walk for at least a year and would never ride competitively again. But just 7 months after the accident, Carmichael finished a close second to Thurlow Rogers [ICN] at the Bud Light Grand Prix in La Jolla, California."[3]
- The good news: Tonga's King Taufaahau Topou IV loses 102 pounds (46 kilos) thanks to cycling. The bad news: he still weighs 360 pounds (164 kilos).

In the Tour de France:

- Stephen Roche (Carrera) becomes the first Irishman to win the Tour de France.
- Longtime Tour director Félix Levitan is fired amid accusations that he mishandled some of the *Société*'s funds. His replacement, Jean-François Naquet-Radiguet would leave after a year.
- Claiming that the race's VIP guests have more access to the riders than they do, the Tour's photographers protest by refusing to photograph the 23rd stage to Dijon.
- Graham Watson photographs the race from a motorcycle for the first time.
- The 1987 Tour de France's 25 stages are the most ever.
- A record 23 (nine-man) teams take part in the race.
- Eight different riders wear the race leader's yellow jersey, tying the 1987 Tour with the 1958 event for the most leaders ever.
- Credit Lyonnais replaces Banania as sponsor of the yellow jersey.
- Roche's 40-second victory margin is the smallest since Jan Janssen's 38-second win in 1968.
- CBS broadcasts Tour segments in the U.S., including same-day tape of the race's final stage.
- Guido Bontempi (Carrera) of Italy and West Germany's Dietrich Thurau (Roland) are caught using "illegal drugs" and are relegated to the bottom of the standings of stages 7 and 8, respectively. Each is also penalized 10 minutes.
- The Tour makes its most distant start from Paris in West Berlin, Germany.
- Lech Piasecki (Del Tongo-Colnago) is the first Polish rider to wear the yellow jersey.
- Kvetoslav Pavlov (ANC-Halfords), who finished 103rd, and Milan Jurco (Brianzoli-Chateau d'Ax), who did not finish, are the Tour's first Czechoslovakian riders.
- ANC-Halfords is the last British team to compete in the Tour de France in the 20th century.

1988 • Andy Hampsten (7-Eleven-Hoonved) wins the 71st Tour of Italy, becoming the first American to win the Giro. Hampsten also wins the event's 12th and 18th stages. Hampsten rides an American "Huffy" bicycle built by John Slawta of Land Shark.
- Pier Mattia "Pierino" Gavazzi (Fanini-7 Up) starts his 17th Giro d'Italia. He would finish the race 14 times.

- Ireland's Sean Kelly (Kas-Canal 10-MAVIC) wins the 43rd Vuelta a España.
- Kelly also wins his seventh consecutive Paris–Nice.
- East German rider Olaf Ludwig wins the road race at the XXIVth Olympiad in Seoul, Korea. Bob Mionske finishes fourth in the 197-kilometer race, 24 seconds back, the best-ever finish for an American rider at a non-boycotted Olympics.
- After Canada's Steve Bauer and Belgium's Claude Criquielion collide 75 meters from the finish, Italy's Maurizio Fondriest goes on to win the world road championship in Renaix, Belgium. Criquielion would end up suing Bauer for estimated lost earnings, beginning a lawsuit that would drag on for years before the Canadian is exonerated. "Crique" had won the Barcelona worlds in 1984.
- Chasing back after an earlier crash during Liège–Bastogne–Liège, Davis Phinney (7-Eleven) crashes through the back window of Isoglass's Peugeot station wagon. Surgeons spend more than two hours putting 150 stitches in the cuts to the left side of his face and both eyelids. In 7-Eleven's team photo for the following year, Phinney is in the front row, sitting on a small tricycle with a helmet hanging from the handlebars.
- Phinney wins the Tour of the Americas, taking three of the race's seven stages.
- Phinney wins the final edition of the Coors Classic in his hometown of Boulder, Colo. Phinney's victory gives him more Red Zinger/Coors Classic stages than anyone (22). Phinney also won the Coors points competition seven consecutive times (1981–'87). Coors soon pulls it sponsorship of the event because of its unwillingness to spend extra money on television coverage and because of the race's "local nature."
- America's Inga Benedict (7-Eleven) wins the women's edition of the Coors Classic.
- At the end of the year, real estate developer Donald Trump announces plans for a 10-day stage race from Albany, N.Y., to Atlantic City, N.J. The event, dreamed up by basketball analyst and entrepreneur Billy Packer, will be called the Tour de Trump, will feature $250,000 in prize money, and will be covered by NBC and ESPN.
- At the time, Coors organizer Michael Aisner says that plans are still on for a 1989 Coors Classic.
- Peter Joffre Nye's definitive history of American bicycle racing, *Hearts of Lions*, is published by W. W. Norton. In 1991 the book would be optioned for a PBS documentary with AT&T and Johnson & Johnson as possible sponsors.
- On March 1, bicycle shops in New York City begin applying stickers to the packaging of Kryptonite locks saying, "This Kryptonite lock is not guaranteed in New York City." The guarantee of up to $1,000 to customers whose bikes are stolen now applies only to Kryptonite's $50 motorcycle lock. As many as 100,000 bicycles are stolen in the city every year.
- Mountain biker John Tomac takes to the road and wins the mid-May Subaru Criterium in White Plains, New York.

- On December 31, Greg LeMond parts ways with PDM and signs a one-year, $500,000 contract with François Lambert's team which is sponsored by ADR, a Belgian truck-leasing firm. The deal allows LeMond's team to be sponsored by Coors Light in the U.S.
- Italy's Roberto Gaggioli (Pepsi-Fanini) becomes the first foreigner to win the CoreStates USPRO race in Philadelphia, beating Norway's Dag-Otto Lauritzen (7-Eleven). Lauritzen's teammate Ron Kiefel finishes third to become the U.S. professional champion.
- Jonathan Boyer, the first American to compete in the Tour de France, retires at age 33.
- General Mills distributes 10 million boxes of Wheaties which feature a likeness of 1986 U.S. Amateur Road Champion Doug Smith, who's now a professional with Wheaties-Schwinn. Nearly 20 years later the game show *Jeopardy!* would feature a clue that claimed Lance Armstrong was the first professional cyclist to be featured on the Wheaties box.
- *Niet van Horen Zeggen* (Not just Hearsay), the autobiography of recently-retired Belgian racer Freddy Maertens is published. The English version of Maertens' tell-all book is entitled *Fall From Grace*.
- Sachs/Huret debuts its ARIS (Advanced Rider Index System) components, which are available for two price points: New Success, for bicycles costing around $600, and Rival for bikes in the $300-$400 range. The components are designed to work with 6- or 7-speed Sachs/Maillard freewheels.
- Computing meets cycling when RacerMate develops the Model CAT 6000 CompuTrainer. The system's 8-bit microprocessor is able to instantly simulate different courses, hills, and headwinds while showing the route on a computer monitor.
- *Bicycling* magazine builds a ridable 15.1-pound bicycle around a $1,900 Merlin titanium frame. Components used on the bike include: Edco crankset, Aero-Lite titanium pedals, American Classic seatpost, Sachs/Huret Jubilee rear derailleur, CLB brake calipers, Regina SL hollow-pin chain and alloy freewheel, and Modolo shift levers, brake levers, handlebar and stem. The wheels consist of: Bullseye hubs, Wheelsmith spokes, Mistral M19A rims, and Continental 110B Olympic sew-ups.
- 7-Eleven and Toshiba-Look test prototype 8-speed Dura-Ace components—the Dura-Ace CS 7400 cassette and the FH 7402 freehub.
- Shimano releases its Rapid Fire dual control lever for mountain bikes.
- SRAM introduces its twisting Grip Shift gear shifter.
- René Vietto dies on October 14. Vietto, who raced in the Tour de France between 1934 and 1949, wore the race's *maillot jaune* for a total of 26 days—more than any other non-winner. He was 74.
- A change in French law banning the sports-related advertising of alcohol ends the season-long Super Prestige Pernod Trophy competition. France's Charly Mottet (Système U) is the series' final winner.
- Holland's Steven Rooks (PDM) wins the first season-long World Cup competition.
- France's Laurent Fignon (Système U) wins the Tour of the European Community.

- East Germany's Uwe Ampler repeats as winner of the Peace Race.
- The Soviet Union's Vasily Zhdanov wins the Milk Race.
- Ireland's Malcolm Elliot (Fagor) wins the Kellogg's Tour of Britain.
- Germany's Rolf Gölz (Superconfex-Yoko-Opel) wins the Nissan International Classic.
- Roberto Gaggioli (Pepsi-Fanini-Mirinda) of Italy and Philadelphia wins the Kugler-Anderson Memorial Tour of Somerville. George Hincapie of Farmingdale, Long Island wins the junior event.
- Susan Elias of Readfield, Maine, wins the Mildred Kugler Women's Open.
- Twenty-nine-year-old Jeannie Longo-Ciprelli, of Grenoble, France, wins her second Tour de France Féminin, again defeating Maria Canins, this time by 1 minute 20 seconds.
- Greek cycling champion Kanellos Kanellopoulos pedals the 70-pound (32-kilogram) aircraft Daedalus '88 from the island of Crete to the island of Santorini. The 74-mile (119-kilometer) trip, which takes just under four hours to complete, doubles the previous distance record for human-powered flight.

In the Tour de France:

- Race winner Pedro Delgado (Reynolds) tests positive for Probenecid, which can mask the use of steroids, but keeps his victory because the drug has not yet been added to the UCI's list of banned substances.
- The 1988 edition of the race marks the 75th running of the Tour de France.
- The organizers introduce the *Village-Départ*, a tent-covered area for sponsors at the start of every stage.
- The first stage has to be restarted after striking shipyard workers block the road.
- Dutch rider Gert-Jan Theunisse (PDM) tests positive for testosterone. After the other riders stage a short strike on his behalf, Theunisse is penalized 10 minutes, dropping him from 5th place overall to 11th.
- Fabio Parra (Kelme) finishes third, becoming the first Colombian on the podium in Paris.
- Canada's Steve Bauer (Weinmann-La Suisse) finishes fourth overall after winning the first stage and wearing the Tour's yellow jersey for a total of five days.
- With 193 points, America's Davis Phinney (7-Eleven) finishes second in the sprint competition to Belgium's Eddy Planckaert (ADR-Mini Flat), who has 278 points.
- Steven Rooks (PDM) becomes the first Dutch rider to win the polka-dot climbers' jersey.
- The UCI and the FICP agree to limit "…the major Tours to no more than 22 days, including three weekends…."[1]
- For the first time since its inception in 1967, no prologue is held (it was run as a team time trial in 1971). Instead, a six-kilometer (3.7-mile) "preface" is held which is won by the Weinmann team, with Carrera's Guido Bontempi posting the fastest individual time in the leg's final kilometer.
- Stage 16A/16B is the race's last two-part stage.
- Shipyard workers demanding higher wages delay the race caravan (but not the riders) at the Loire bridge.

- Before the start of the 19th stage, the riders stage a brief strike to protest the leaking to the press of some riders' positive drug tests.
- It is the 12th and final year that the Merlin Plage apartment is included among the winner's prizes. For his win, Delgado also receives a Peugeot automobile, money from Credit Lyonnais and an "art object."
- It is the final year that the team points competition—signified by green caps and won by PDM—is held. 1988 is also the last year that the white jersey is awarded to the best young rider, the Netherlands' Erik Breukink (Panasonic), until its return in 2000. Between 1989 and 1999, the best young rider classification would continue without a special jersey and would be renamed the "Souvenir Fabio Casartelli" in 1997.
- Jean-Pierre Courcol replaces Jean-François Naquet-Radiguet as director of the Tour de France. Courcol, himself, is replaced after the race's "Delgado affair." His successor is journalist and former rider Jean-Marie Leblanc.
- Tour director Xavier Louy revives a 1979 plan to hold a race from Paris to Moscow by combining the Tour of the European Community (Tour de l'Avenir) with the Peace Race. Originally the race had not been held because of the Cold War. This time, the idea is shot down by the professional riders' federation (FICP).
- For the first time since 1910, the race has no Belgian stage winners.

1989 • Amgen introduces the hematopoietic hormone Erythropoietin Alfa (EPO), which acts on the bone marrow to stimulate the production of red blood cells in order to treat anemia in AZT-treated, HIV-positive people and people on dialysis due to chronic kidney failure.
- France enacts the Bambuck Law, named after the minister of sports who tried to reduce doping by athletes. The law, which is stricter than the UCI and IOC guidelines, is adopted by the French Cycling Federation.[1]
- The UCI announces it will recommend that professional riders wear helmets in 1990 and that it will require them beginning in 1991.
- Dutch rider Bert Oosterbosch dies of a heart attack on August 18. Oosterbosch, who had recently retired, was a member of Tour winner Joop Zoetemelk's 1980 T.I. Raleigh-Creda team. He won a stage that year and two more in 1983. He was 32.
- Former Norwegian paratrooper Dag-Otto Lauritzen (7-Eleven) wins the inaugural, 10-stage Tour de Trump, after Belgium's Eric Vanderaerden (Panasonic) goes off course during the final time trial. The 10-stage, 837-mile (1,347-kilometer) race is co-sponsored by the NBC television network.
- ABC and ESPN sign a three-year deal worth about $1 million per year to cover the Tour de France and Paris–Roubaix, outbidding CBS, which had covered the Tour for six years.
- Greg Oravetz (Coors Light-ADR) outsprints Mike Engleman (Wheaties-Schwinn) to win the CoreStates USPRO championship in Philadelphia.
- Spain's Pedro Delgado (Reynolds-Banesto) wins the 44th Vuelta a España.
- Laurent Fignon (Super U) wins the 72nd Giro d'Italia. American Andy Hamp-

sten (7-Eleven) finishes third, in part because a landslide had forced the cancellation of the stage over the Gavia Pass where he had taken the race lead the previous year. Greg LeMond (ADR-Agrigel) finishes 39th, 54:23 back.

- Fignon also wins the Tour of Holland, defeating teammate Thierry Marie by one second.
- Canada's Steve Bauer (Helvetia-La Suisse) wins the Championship of Zurich.
- After Laurent Fignon helps to chase down his French teammate Thierry Claveyrolet and two other escapees, Greg LeMond wins the rain-soaked, 259-kilometer (161-mile) world professional road championship in Chambery, France by outsprinting Russian Dimitri Konyshev and Irishman Sean Kelly. The win makes LeMond only the fifth rider to win the Tour de France and the worlds in the same year. Before the race, LeMond had told *L'Équipe*, "I like cycling again."
- Ireland's Sean Kelly (PDM) wins the World Cup.
- France's Pascal Lino (RMO-Liberia) wins the Tour of the European Community.
- East Germany's Uwe Ampler wins his third consecutive Peace Race.
- Canada's Brian Walton (7-Eleven) wins the Milk Race.
- Great Britain's Robert Millar (Z-Peugeot) wins the Kellogg's Tour of Britain.
- Belgium's Eric Vanderaerden (Panasonic-Isostar) wins the Nissan International Classic.
- New Zealand's Graeme Miller wins the Kugler-Anderson Memorial Tour of Somerville.
- Susan Elias repeats as winner of the Mildred Kugler Women's Open.
- France's Jeannie Longo-Ciprelli again increases her own hour record, this time to 46.352 kilometers (28.803 miles) on October 1 in Mexico City.
- Longo-Ciprelli wins her third consecutive Tour de France Féminin. At one point, Longo-Ciprelli wins five consecutive stages (5, 6, 7, 8, and 9) during the race. Maria Canins is second for the third consecutive time.
- 7-Eleven's Andy Hampsten tests a prototype of Shimano's "STI" integrated brake/shift lever, which is introduced the following year. Judging from *Bicycling*'s description of the prototype levers, they would undergo further refinement before going into production: "Moving the right brake lever to the inside downshifts the rear derailleur. (The lever recenters automatically.) To upshift you push a small button atop the lever."[2]
- Cannondale specifies SRAM's CX Model Grip Shift on some of its mountain bikes.
- Rock Shox introduces its RS-1 suspension fork for mountain bikes.
- Due in large part to Hungary's attractive joint venture laws and tax breaks, Schwinn opens a bicycle production facility in an old Budapest factory. "We came to Hungary because we made a decision that we needed to be a more global company," said Steven M. Bina, director of Schwinn's European operations. "We wouldn't be here if there wasn't money to be made."[3]
- Saying that he'd received no help in the mountains from his ADR teammates during the Tour and that the team's management was consistently late with

his salary payments, Greg LeMond signs a three-year, $5.7 million dollar contract with Roger Zanner's "Z" team. The initial year of the contract makes the American the first cyclist to earn $2 million a year.

- *Sports Illustrated* selects Greg LeMond as its 1989 Sportsman of the Year.
- "We may soon be seeing the demise of Lycra cycling shorts as fashionable off-bike wear. According to the fashion magazine *W*, 'These shiny, second-skin numbers are by now tired even on the firmest of tushies, but when exposed to fat rolls, well, you get the picture. Jeans, ladies, think jeans when it's time to dress down.'"[4]

In the Tour de France:

- Greg LeMond's 8-second defeat of Laurent Fignon is the smallest margin of victory in Tour history. His speed of 54.545 km/h in the final time trial would be the fastest average speed for a Tour stage until 2005.
- LeMond (ADR-Agrigel) is only the third rider to take the overall lead on the Tour's final day. Neither of the other riders to do so, Jan Janssen (21 years earlier in 1968) and Jean Robic (21 years before Janssen in 1947), wore the yellow jersey during the race.
- Sean Kelly (PDM) wins his fourth green jersey, the last three of which he won without a stage win.
- Raul Alcala (PDM) is the first Mexican rider to win a stage of the Tour.
- Acacio Da Silva (Carrera Jeans-Vagabond) is the first Portuguese rider to wear the yellow jersey.
- Defending Tour winner Pedro Delgado (Reynolds-Banesto) loses 2:43 when he misses the start of the prologue.
- New Tour director general Jean-Marie Leblanc brings simplicity and stability to the race by getting rid of its "five-cent" sponsors.
- The '89 Tour marks the last appearances of the red "intermediate sprints" jersey (won by PDM's Sean Kelly) and patchwork "combination" jersey (won by the Netherlands' Steven Rooks, Kelly's teammate). It's the first Tour since 1967 not to include the white jersey (which would reappear in 2000).
- The team points category is also eliminated.
- The Tour starts in Luxembourg for the first time.
- LeMond's victory in the 21st stage is the last time that the race's final stage is a time trial.
- The Tour adopts the "modern format" of selecting 18 teams for the race based on UCI rankings plus four wild card teams.
- Fiat replaces Peugeot as the official car of the Tour de France.
- Greg LeMond and the American 7-Eleven team introduce aero bars to the Tour. LeMond's bike is equipped with MAVIC components, giving the company its only win in the event. The victory is the last one for a French component manufacturer.
- After the previous Tour, race director Jean-Marie Leblanc increases the winner's prize to 1.5 million francs. The race's previous first prize had consisted of 500,000 francs, an apartment, a car and a piece of art.
- "For the 1989 season, the small Belgian ADR squad was headed by Classics

specialist Eddy Planckaert, and toward the end of 1988 the team needed to sign one more rider with significant UCI points to qualify for the Tour. That rider was Planckaert's countryman [*sic*] Jannus Kuum [actually Planckaert is Belgian and Kuum, 1964–1999, was Norwegian]. Kuum, however, had an excellent season in '88 and was given a large offer from Stephen Roche's Carrera team. Planckaert was nearing the end of his career and desperately wanted to ride the Tour again before he retired. A tearful Planckaert called his friend Kuum and pleaded with him to join the team (only the top 16 [*sic*] teams on the UCI rankings automatically qualify for the Tour). Kuum relented and signed with ADR, thus giving the team enough points to qualify for the Tour de France....Without Kuum, [Greg] LeMond wouldn't have even started the tour [*sic*]."[5] Kuum would be eliminated from the '89 Tour following the 10th stage.

Chapter 10

1990–1999
The 'Mig' Dynasty

1990 • Kurt Stockton (American Commerce National Bank) wins the CoreStates US-PRO title in Philadelphia after finishing third behind Italy's Paolo Cimini (Gis-Benotto) and Laurent Jalabert (Toshiba) of France.

• Philippe Louviot (Toshiba) wins the French national road championship 56 years after his grandfather, Raymond Louviot (Genial-Lucifer).

• Switzerland's Daniel Wyder (Eurocar-Galli) wins the third Tour of the Americas by one second over Ireland's Malcom Elliot (Teka).

• On March 9, Manfred Nuscheler of Bern, Switzerland, pedals his trainer-mounted bike 271 rpm.

• "David Cornelsen set a record by cycling across the country, using only his hands and a specially built three-wheeler in 18 days 16 hours 52 minutes. He also raised about $25,000 for the American Paralysis Association for research. Three years ago, Dr. Cornelsen was injured in an automobile accident that left him paralyzed from the waist down. He completed his doctoral dissertation in social work in the hospital, then directed a program for victims of spinal-cord injuries at a Long Beach, Calif., hospital."[1]

• Mexico's Raul Alcala (PDM) wins the second (and last) Tour de Trump. Norway's Atle Kvolsvoll (Z) finishes second, 43 seconds back. Suffering from recent illnesses and undertraining, Greg LeMond (Z) finishes 78th, 1 hour 40 minutes 26 seconds back.

• Stanley Paul & Co. Ltd. publishes Paul Kimmage's cycling exposé, *Rough Ride*. The book would be reprinted in 1998.

• Italy's Marco Giovannetti (Seur-Deportes) wins the 45th Vuelta a España.

• Belgium's Rudy Dhaenens wins the world road championship race in Utsonomiya, Japan.

• Italian rider Gianni Bugno (Saloti-Chateau d'Ax) wins the 73rd Giro d'Italia, leading the race from start to finish.

• Bugno also wins the 1990 World Cup.

• 7-Eleven's Canadian star Steve Bauer finishes second in Paris–Roubaix, losing the sprint to Belgium's Eddy Planckaert (Panasonic-Sportlife) by less than a centimeter (½ inch).

- Scotland's Robert Millar (Z) wins the Dauphiné Libéré.
- 7-Eleven update: Ron Kiefel finishes seventh overall in the Tour of Sicily, Davis Phinney finishes third in Kuurne–Brussels–Kuurne, and Canada's Brian Walton finishes eighth in the Tour of the Mediterranean. Former 7-Eleven rider Chris Carmichael is appointed U.S. Cycling Federation's men's road coach.
- Motorola steps in as sponsor of the 7-Eleven team when Southland Corporation withdraws its support.
- Specialized Bicycle Components of Morgan Hill, Calif., and the Du Pont Company of Wilmington, Del., develop a three-bladed, carbon-fiber bicycle wheel that's said to cut 10 minutes off a 100-mile time trial. The new wheels, called Allez Epic, sell for $750 apiece.
- Shimano introduces its ST-7400 STI (Shimano Total Integration) brake/shift levers for road bikes, and SPD (Shimano Pedal Dynamics) mountain bike pedals.
- SunTour introduces Command dual-control shift levers for road bikes.
- Cool Tool of Chico, Calif, introduces the Cool Tool. The $19.95 tool weighs 200 grams (7 ounces) and includes allen wrenches, screwdrivers, a chain tool, adjustable wrench and 14-mm crank bolt socket. A 32-mm headset wrench and bottom bracket lockring tool can be added for $5 each.
- Citing one of the country's largest bicycle distributors, *Bicycling* reports that 95 percent of all bikes sold in California are mountain bikes. They account for 60 percent of bicycle sales in the central states and 70 percent in the east.
- The British Road Time Trial Council proposes an automatic 30-day suspension for racers who crash into parked cars.
- Former Coors Classic promoter Michael Aisner announces that International Classics Ltd. is bankrupt but says that he still expects to find a sponsor for a major American stage race.
- Belgium's Johan Bruyneel (Lotto) wins the Tour of the European Community.
- Czechoslovakia's Jan Svorada wins the Peace Race.
- Australia's Shane Sutton (Banana) wins the Milk Race.
- Ireland's Malcolm Elliot (Teka) wins the Kellogg's Tour of Britain.
- Holland's Erik Breukink (PDM-Ultima-Concorde) wins the Nissan International Classic.
- Matt Eaton wins the Kugler-Anderson Memorial Tour of Somerville.
- Jan Bolland of Quakertown, Ct., wins the Mildred Kugler Women's Open.
- The Tour de France Féminin is not held.
- Americans Ned Overend and Julie Furtado win the gold medals in the cross country events at the first UCI-sanctioned world mountain bike championships at Colorado's Purgatory Ski Area.
- The *Conseil du Cyclisme Professionnel* is formed to represent the interests of professional riders.

In the Tour de France:

- Greg LeMond (Z) joins Philippe Thys (1920) and Louison Bobet (1955) as a three-time Tour de France winner.
- LeMond is the fifth rider to win the race without winning any of its stages.

- The event's L'Alpe d'Huez stage is the first to be broadcast live on French television in its entirety.
- The 1990 Tour is the last in which riders on the leading team (Z) wear yellow caps.
- Canada's Steve Bauer (7-Eleven) wears the leader's yellow jersey for nine days.
- In the fall, a terse statement in *L'Équipe* announces that the 1987 "Levitan affair," which saw race co-director Félix Levitan fired for alleged financial mismanagement, has been settled.
- The Italian-registered Alfa Lum squad is the first "Russian" team in the Tour de France.
- Dimitri Konyshev (Alfa Lum) is the first Russian rider to win a stage in the race.
- Olaf Ludwig (Panasonic-Sportlife) is the first East German to win a Tour stage and to wear one of its leader's jerseys (the green jersey).
- Uzbekistan's Djamolidine Abdoujaparov and Latvia's Piotr Ugrumov (both with Alfa Lum) are the first riders from their countries to compete in the Tour.
- Alexandre Vladkin of *Sovietski Sport* is the first Russian reporter to cover the Tour.
- The Tour reverts to awarding only three jerseys: yellow, green and polka-dot.
- Protests by angry sheep farmers disrupt two of the race's early stages.
- The abbey at Mont-St-Michel (population 72) becomes the Tour's smallest stage "city."
- The race's 301-kilometer (187-mile) fifth leg from Avranches to Rouen is the last Tour de France stage of more than 300 kilometers.
- Second-place finisher Claudio Chiappucci (Carrera Jeans) is one of the first racers since Bic's Luis Ocaña (1973) to ride a titanium bike in the Tour. His bike is made by Carerra.

1991
- After 70 years as Shimano Iron Works, the Japanese company changes its name to Shimano, Incorporated.
- The American Tour de Trump becomes the Tour Du Pont when chemical company E.I. duPont de Nemours & Co., Inc., replaces the financially troubled real estate developer as the event's sponsor. Despite a wheel change during the stage, Holland's Erik Breukink (PDM) overcomes a 50-second deficit to Norway's Atle Kvalsvoll (Z) to win the event in the final 16-mile (26-kilometer) time trial. Breukink's final margin of victory is 12 seconds.
- For the fourth time in five years, Spain's Marino Lejarreta (ONCE) completes the Giro d'Italia, the Vuelta a España, and the Tour de France in the same year. By completing the '91 Tour, the Spaniard extends his streak of consecutive grand tour finishes (which had begun with the 1988 Tour de France) to ten.
- U.S. rider Jeff Evanshine wins the junior world road championship.
- Subaru-Motgomery's Lance Armstrong wins the national road championship over Steve Larsen in Salt Lake City.
- Riding for the U.S. national team in Europe, Armstrong also wins Italy's Settimana-Bergamasca.

- Davis Phinney (Coors Light) becomes the American champion at the CoreStates USPRO Championship in Philadelphia when he finishes second behind Tulip's Dutch sprinter Michel Zanoli.
- Italy's Gianni Bugno wins the world road championship in Stuttgart, Germany.
- Italian rider Franco Chioccioli (Del Tongo-MG Boys) wins the 74th Giro d'Italia.
- Spain's Melchor Mauri Prat (ONCE) wins the 46th Vuelta a España. Miguel Indurain finishes second—the closest he'll come to winning the Tour of Spain.
- In May Swiss journalist Manfred Nuscheler generates 1,020 watts (1.4 horsepower) for 60 seconds on a "Bike Generator"—creating enough electricity to power 100 electric razors.
- American mountain bike star John Tomac competes in Paris–Roubaix with the Motorola team.
- Following a rider protest during Paris–Nice, the FICP, the UCI, and the riders agree on March 25 that beginning on April 5 the pros can decide whether or not to wear hard-shell helmets depending on conditions.
- Italy's Maurizio Fondriest (Panasonic-Sportlife) wins the World Cup.
- Maryland's Brian Moroney wins the Kugler-Anderson Memorial Tour of Somerville.
- Pennsylvania's Karen Bliss wins the Mildred Kugler Women's Open.
- The Soviet Union's Viktor Rakshinsky wins the Peace Race.
- Chris Walker (Banana) wins the Milk Race.
- Australia's Phil Anderson (Motorola) wins the Kellogg's Tour of Britain.
- Ireland's Sean Kelly (PDM-Cidona) wins his fourth Nissan International Classic in seven years.
- The Tour of the European Community (Tour de l'Avenir) is not held.
- The Tour de France Féminin is not held.
- Campagnolo introduces an 8-speed cassette.
- 3Rensho's Yoshi Konno designs the Paris–Roubaix road fork. The steel fork gets its half-centimeter of travel from the use of "compressible balls."
- Schwinn closes its last large-scale American bike production plant located in Greenville, Miss., leaving the small Paramount division in Waterford, Wisc., as the company's sole remaining U.S. plant.
- Panaracer (National Tire Company) introduces the Smoke mountain bike tire. More than one million will be sold.
- SRAM settles its antitrust lawsuit against Shimano, which sold complete gruppos to bicycle manufacturers, for an estimated $3–5 million. Soon thereafter, Shimano lowers its complete gruppo discount from 10 percent to 2 percent. SRAM also opens a plant in Taiwan and begins selling its SRT 300 shifter to Trek and Specialized for use on their hybrid bikes.
- Following the death of Luis Puig, Hein Verbruggen is promoted from head of the FICP to president of the UCI, a position he would hold until 2005.
- According to the Insurance Institute for Highway Safety, cyclists are most likely to be involved in a fatal accident between 3 and 6 P.M. on Wednesdays in August. Sundays and Mondays from 3 to 6 A.M. in February are the safest times to ride.

- According to the Johns Hopkins Injury Prevention Center, nearly half the males who died in bicycle accidents between 1987 and 1991 were intoxicated.

In the Tour de France:
- Spain's Miguel Indurain (Banesto) wins the first of five consecutive Tours de France.
- Greg LeMond buys 18 Carbonframes Sapphires from Craig Calfee and 18 Tom Kellogg-designed titanium frames from Merlin for his Z team to use in the race.
- Race leader Rolf Sorensen (Ariostea) is unable to start the sixth stage following a crash near Valenciennes late in the previous stage.
- In an effort to "modernize," the organizers eliminate the mountain time trial, electing to run just two flat individual time trial stages (plus the prologue and a team time trial).
- The sixth-stage, 234-kilometer solo of Thierry Marie (Castorama) is the second-longest postwar breakaway in Tour history. In 1947 France's Albert Bourlon, a former POW on the Centre-Sud-Ouest regional team, rode alone for all of the 14th stage's 253 kilometers.
- Mauro Ribeiro (RMO-MAVIC) becomes the first Brazilian to win a Tour stage.
- Djamolidine Abdoujaparov (Carrera) becomes the first rider from Uzbekistan to win a Tour stage.
- More than 450 radio, print and television journalists keep as many as one billion people a day updated on the race. The race's television revenues are more than $5 million.
- Coca Cola, Fiat and Credit Lyonnais each pay Groupe Amaury $2 million a year in sponsorship fees. Twenty-five smaller sponsors pay as much as $1 million each.
- Fiat provides the race with 300 cars and 70 trucks which are seen by an estimated 10 million roadside fans.
- PMU (Pari Mutuel Urbain) off-track betting becomes the sponsor of the race's green jersey.
- France's Charly Mottet (RMO-MAVIC) wins the 246-kilometer 11th stage with an average speed of 47.23 km/h (29.35 mph), a record at the time for a road stage.
- The PDM team of third-place Erik Breukink is the first squad to withdraw from the Tour for medical reasons. Although team officials say that the illness is caused by a bad batch of the dietary supplement Intralipid, some of the first rumors of EPO use begin to circulate.
- Former Tour winner Stephen Roche (Tonton Tapis) is eliminated from the race after missing the start of the team time trial.
- In Pau, the riders stage a 40-minute protest calling for the reinstatement of Urs Zimmerman, who drove to Pau instead of flying, and to protest the UCI rule which fines them for not wearing hard-shell helmets. Most of the racers ride the stage bareheaded.
- The total of 158 finishers establishes a new mark for the most riders to complete the Tour de France.

- Vladimir Poulnikov (Carrera Jeans) is the first Ukrainian to take part in the Tour. He finishes 88th overall @ 1:50:50.
- Writer and journalist Antoine Blondin dies. Praising the writer, the Tour de France Society said that "Blondin recounted the Tour the way Victor Hugo might have done." He was 69.
- When his Seur team is not invited to the race, France's Ronan Pensec joins the Amaya Seguros squad because the race's 10th stage finishes in Quimper, only a few kilometers from his hometown of Douarnenez. He finishes 41st, 1:06:04 back.

1992 • Italy's Fabio Casartelli wins the men's road race at the XXVth Olympiad in Barcelona, Spain.
- After finishing 35 seconds back in 14th place at the Olympics, American rider Lance Armstrong signs a contract with the Motorola team. In his first professional race, Spain's San Sebastian Classic, Armstrong finishes 111th—dead last—11 minutes behind the 110th finisher.
- Riding the Mike Burrows-designed Lotus "Superbike," Great Britain's Chris Boardman wins the gold medal in the 4,000 meter individual pursuit with a time of 4:24.496, breaking the old record by more than seven seconds. The Lotus and Look KG 196 bikes begin the era of aerodynamic bicycles and spark a renewed interest in Francesco Moser's 1984 hour record.
- Campagnolo introduces its Ergopower integrated brake/shift levers.
- Shimano releases sealed-bearing cartridge bottom brackets which require a special 20-spline tool for installation and removal.
- Dia-Compe's threadless AheadSet headset begins to gain general acceptance.
- Shimano releases its 8-speed XTR gruppo for mountain bikes costing more than $1,500. The new gruppo weighs about a pound less than Deore XT, the company's former top-level off-road component set.
- It's only a paper bike. "Created by Yoshifumi Kato at the Japan Bicycle Technical Center in Inuyama, the prototype NFRB (natural fiber reinforced plastic) frame weighs slightly more than carbon fiber, and is 60 percent as strong. The designer says the paper frame's strength and 2.87-pound weight can be improved in future models, and that its further development could lead to bicycle recycling."[1] A thin plastic coating protects the frame in the rain.
- *Bicycling* staffer Don Cuerdon test drives the lumbering Worksman pizza delivery bike in New York City. At one point, while attempting a panic stop, Cuerdon reports that he "deftly locked the rear coaster brake, closed my eyes, and skidded the entire breadth of the Avenue of the Americas."[2] The 95-pound Worksman LGB (Low-Gravity, Boy's model) has a frame made of 16-gauge, one-inch steel tubing, a ⅜-inch chain, and optional Nev-R-Fail solid rubber tires (20-inch front, 26-inch rear). The bike, which comes equipped with a front cabinet big enough for five large pies, costs about $459. Worksman Trading Corporation of Ozone Park, N.Y., has been producing Worksman Business Cycles since 1898.
- *Bicycling* gives a thumbs-down "(t)o the Maine Department of Transportation,

which doubled—and in some cases nearly quadrupled—certain ferry rates for cyclists by lumping bikes into the fee classification for 'vehicles weighing less than 6,000 pounds.' Rates rose from $2.75 to $10, and from $20 to $40. Plus, cars transporting more than 4 bicycles will be charged an additional $14 per bike for a roundtrip [sic] ferry. We say they're all wet."[3]

- Specialized establishes its S-Works division whose goal is to produce the best bikes possible, regardless of cost. The new enterprise's motto is "Innovate or Die."
- SunTour introduces its XC-Pro MicroDrive mountain bike gruppo, which features Grease Guard hubs, a 20-32-42 tooth crankset and an 11-24 tooth 7-speed cassette with PowerFlo cogs.
- Bell Bicycle, Inc., and Reebok International collaborate on a helmet that uses an air-bladder fit system for the United States Cycling Team to use at the Olympics in Barcelona. The companies expect the helmet technology to trickle down to the consumer level soon.
- St. Louis-based 2 Bi 2 introduces a two-wheel-drive bicycle. The bike, which was invented by Bill Becoat, uses a cable running from the rear wheel to drive the front wheel. The machines come in a variety of children's and adult sizes, and cost between $140 and $1,300.
- Miguel Indurain (Banesto) wins the 75th Giro d'Italia. With his Tour victory, Indurain becomes the sixth rider and only Spaniard to win the Giro and the Tour in the same year.
- Swiss rider Tony Rominger (Clas-Cajastur) wins the 47th Vuelta a España.
- Italy's Gianni Bugno repeats as world road champion, winning in Benidorm, Spain.
- Gilbert Duclos-Lasalle (Z) attacks on the Ennevelin cobbles with 40 kilometers (25 miles) to go and solos to victory in Paris–Roubaix on a bike equipped with a custom Rock Shox fork. He would ride a similarly equipped bike to victory again the following year.
- American Bart Bowen (Subaru-Montgomery) wins the CoreStates USPRO title in Philadelphia by soloing away from his eight breakaway companions to win by 1:20.
- Thirty-year-old Greg LeMond (Z) wins the 1992 Tour Du Pont, defeating his teammate Atle Kvalsvoll, who finishes second for the second straight year, by 20 seconds. It's LeMond's first overall victory in an American race since the Coors Classic in 1985. It is his last professional victory.
- After abandoning the Tour and skipping the worlds, Greg LeMond signs a three-year deal to ride for GAN, which had taken over sponsorship of the former Z team.
- Two weeks after turning professional, 20-year-old Lance Armstrong wins his first race, stage 4A of Spain's Tour of Galega.
- Bridgestone charges "four bucks" for its 1992 Bicycle Catalog. In it the purchaser will find all sorts of information, such as the difference between melt-forging and cold-forging, quotes from Shakespeare and Gertrude Stein, and bicycle trading cards. The 48-page hand-illustrated catalog is printed with

soy-based inks on recycled stock made from 100 percent post-consumer waste paper.
- America's Andy Hampsten (Motorola) wins the Tour of Romandie.
- Germany's Olaf Ludwig (Panasonic) wins the World Cup.
- The Netherlands' Leontien Van Moorsel defeats France's Jeannie Longo-Ciprelli to win the renamed Tour Cycliste Féminin.
- France's Hervé Garel (RMO-Liberia) wins the 30th Tour de l'Avenir. From 1992 through 2006 the race is open to professional riders 25 and younger.
- Germany's Steffen Wesemann wins the Peace Race.
- New Jersey's Jonas Carney wins the Kugler-Anderson Memorial Tour of Somerville.
- California's Laura Charmeda wins the Mildred Kugler Women's Open.
- Ireland's Conor Henry wins the Milk Race.
- Italy's Max Sciandri (Motorola) wins the Kellogg's Tour of Britain. Sciandri holds dual citizenship and will race with a British license beginning in 1995.
- Australia's Phil Anderson (Motorola) wins the final edition of the Nissan International Classic.
- Thirty-five-year-old Nancy Raposo of Newport, R.I., sets the women's 24-hour record of 439.65 miles in Egg Harbor, N.J. Raposo's mark breaks the four-month-old record of 436.3 miles set by 28-year-old Anna Schwartz of Gainesville, Fla.
- When the Luxembourg-based FICP (*Fédération Internationale du Cyclisme Professionnel*) and the Rome-based FIAC (*Fédération Internationale Amateur de Cyclisme*) cycling organizations are reunited, Hein Verbruggen moves the headquarters of the UCI to Lausanne, Switzerland.

In the Tour de France:
- Miguel Indurain wins his second consecutive Tour de France.
- The Tour visits seven countries on the continent as a salute to the European Economic Community. To commemorate the event, the race holds a special Europe Without Borders sprint series which is won by Russia's Viatcheslav Ekimov (Panasonic-Sportlife).
- The race's speed of 39.5 km/h (24.5 mph) is the fastest Tour de France average at the time.
- French rider Philippe Luviot (ONCE) tests MAVIC's ZMS (Zap MAVIC System) 8000 "Zap" derailleur. Because of its wires, the micro processor-controlled rear derailleur of the $1,700 gruppo works poorly in the rain. It is marketed briefly beginning the following year before returning in the late '90s as the wireless "Mektronic" system.
- The Motorola team pioneers the use of two-way radios in the peloton.
- American Andy Hampsten (Motorola) wins on L'Alpe d'Huez.
- Claudio Chiappucci (Carrera Jeans-Tassoni) of Italy rides a brilliant breakaway to Sestriere 40 years after his countryman Fausto Coppi.
- Basque separatists fire-bomb the Channel 4 car of British journalist Phil Liggett; he is not in it at the time. In a letter dated Feb. 25, 2001, Liggett wrote that one of his worst memories of the Tour "was probably when the Basque

terrorists blew up my car in San Sebastian at the start of the 1992 event. The car contained all my Olympic accreditation as well as many treasured possessions and memorabilia of the Tour."

- During the 13th stage from St. Gervais to Sestriere, the Rhone-Alpes Regional Nature Protection Foundation protests the impact that the race and its spectators are having on the Parc de la Vanoise area. This is one of the few times that the Tour de France itself is the target of protesters.
- For the first time since 1910, the Tour de France skips the Pyrenees.
- Miguel Indurain rides the 64-kilometer final time trial at an average speed of 52.35 kph.
- The broom wagon's broom is moved to the inside of the van.
- Arunas Cepele (32nd) and Arturas Kasputis (71st), both with Postobon-Ryalcao, are the first Lithuanians to compete in the Tour.
- Of the 18 teams that had entered the '85 Tour, only Panasonic and Lotto are in the '92 event.

1993 • Miguel Indurain (Banesto) wins the 76th Giro d'Italia. With his third Tour de France victory, Indurain becomes the first rider to win both the Giro and the Tour de France in consecutive years.
- Switzerland's Tony Rominger (Clas) wins the 48th Vuelta a España. It's Rominger's second consecutive win in the event.
- Because of an incident in the Vuelta's second stage, the UCI institutes the "Abdoujaparov Rule" which requires sprinters to ride a straight line in the final 200 meters of a stage.
- The UCI and Vuelta organizer Unipublic agree to run the race in the fall beginning in 1995.
- Mexico's Raul Alcala (Wordperfect) passes Lance Armstrong (Motorola) twice in the final time trial (Alcala started behind the American and then passed him again after a puncture) to win the third Tour Du Pont by 2:26 over the American. "I'd better learn how to time trial," said Armstrong, "if I want to be the next Greg LeMond."
- Armstrong solos the last 17 miles to win the CoreStates USPRO race in Philadelphia by nearly two minutes.
- Armstrong also wins the Kmart Tour of West Virginia and Thrift Drug Classic in Pittsburgh to take the million-dollar Thrift Drug Triple Crown. He elects to take the $600,000 lump-sum payment from Lloyd's of London (with $210,000 of that going to the Internal Revenue Service) instead of 20 annuitized payments of $50,000.
- Armstrong becomes the third-youngest world professional road champion when he attacks with 10 kilometers to go on the rainy course in Oslo, Norway. He finishes the race 19 seconds ahead of a 10-man chase group. After Armstrong's victory, Italy Claudio Chiappucci says this about the American, "He is a strange one. One day it goes well with him, the other he won't even say 'hi.' I don't even want to predict about the future of his career. One thing is sure, he will never win a major tour."[1] Because there are no lugs on his "Eddy Merckx"

frame, there is much speculation that Armstrong's race winning bike is actually a re-painted titanium Litespeed.

- Davis Phinney, 34, the first American to win a road stage of the Tour de France, retires in mid November. "I am not retiring because of age or lack of abilities," he said. "But I don't have the singular focus you need to compete in professional cycling anymore." In his 18-year career, Phinney amassed 324 victories.
- Germany's Jan Ullrich, 19, wins the world road race championship for amateurs.
- After the UCI announces on January 1 that it will recognize only one hour record for both professional and amateur riders regardless of altitude or venue (indoor or outdoor tracks), two British riders break the record only days apart. On July 17, Graeme Obree rides 51.596 kilometers (32.062 miles) in Hamar, Norway, on a steel bike he built himself. Six days later Chris Boardman extends the mark to 52.270 kilometers (32.481 miles) in Bordeaux, France.
- The UCI also announces that it has approved the participation of professional riders in the Olympics beginning with the 1996 games in Atlanta, Georgia.
- Dutch climber Leontien Van Moorsel repeats as winner of the Tour Cycliste Féminin. France's Jeannie Longo-Ciprelli suffers a skull fracture during the event.
- France's Davy Thomas (Castorama) wins the 31st Tour de l'Avenir.
- The Czech Republic's Jaroslav Bilek wins the Peace Race.
- Pennsylvania's Gary Anderson wins the Kugler-Anderson Memorial Tour of Somerville.
- California's Marianne Berglund wins the Mildred Kugler Women's Open.
- Chris Lillywhite (Banana) wins the Milk Race.
- Phil Anderson (Motorola) wins the Kellogg's Tour of Britain.
- Italy's Maurizio Fondriest (Lampre-Polti) wins his second world cup in three years.
- The U.S. Rossin squad folds suddenly leaving Bobby Julich, among others, without a team.
- Greg LeMond announces his intention to retire following the 1994 world championships.
- Former Tour de France winners Laurent Fignon, Stephen Roche and Pedro Delgado all retire. Fignon's unusual retirement came suddenly in late August, when he pulled to the side of the road during the minor Grand Prix Ouest-France and abandoned.
- For the 10th anniversary of Tullio Campagnolo's death, the Italian company commissions leading Italian sports journalist Gianni Brera to write *The Giant and the File,* an in-house biography of its founder. By the company's 75th anniversary in 2008, the book, which is not meant for sale to the public, will be an "unfindable" collectable. Brera was killed in an automobile accident in December 1992, before the book was printed.
- After Schwinn goes bankrupt, its company and name are purchased by the Scott Sports Group and Zell/Chilmark Fund, LP, for $60 million and moved from Chicago to Boulder, Colo. "Explaining his desire to buy out the company,

Sam Zell said it was finally a chance to own a Schwinn. 'My parents wouldn't step up for the extra 50 bucks,' he recalled. 'They bought me a Huffy.'"[2]

• Richard Schwinn and Marc Muller purchase Schwinn's Paramount plant in Waterford, Wisc., and start Waterford Precision Cycles. For the first year and a half, the company continues to build Schwinn Paramounts.

• Swiss jeweler Volker Rhenisch creates a $1 million bicycle for the International Colored Gemstone Association's convention in Tel Aviv. "This rideable carbon fiber bike is studded with more than 1,188 grams of gold and platinum, and set with 13,000 carats of diamonds, emeralds, rubies, yellow sapphires, citrine, malachite, and onyx. The chain, gears, and pedals are gold."[3]

• The Viking 6AL/4V titanium chain weighs 239 grams (8.4 ounces)—72 grams (2.5 ounces) less than a Shimano Hyperglide chain of the same length—and costs $375. Because the pricey chain is almost half a millimeter wider than Shimano's chains, it hits the next larger cog, causing it to be noisy and shift poorly.

• Thanks to Shimano's successes with index shifting and mountain bike components, the Japanese giant's parts are specified on about 86 percent of all new bikes in the United States. SunTour has seven percent of the market, Campy six percent. About 85 percent of Shimano's $1.5 billion in sales comes from bicycle components, with most of the rest coming from fishing equipment. The company has 2,500 employees and $145 million in pretax profits.

In the Tour de France:

• Miguel Indurain (Banesto) follows Louison Bobet, Jacques Anquetil and Eddy Merckx as the fourth rider to win three consecutive Tours de France.

• Eleven of the 20 teams in the race use Shimano components, five use MAVIC, three use Campagnolo and one outfits its bikes with SunTour components.

• Belgian rider Johan Bruyneel (ONCE) wins what was then the Tour's fastest road stage, averaging 49.417 km/h (30.7 mph) for the 158 kilometers between Evreux and Amiens.

• Zenon Jaskula (GB-MG Maglificio) becomes the first Polish rider to win a Tour stage, and is the first Eastern-European rider to finish on the Tour's final podium.

• At 21, Lance Armstrong (Motorola) becomes one of the youngest riders ever to win a stage of the Tour.

• Tony Rominger (Clas-Cajastur) is the first Swiss rider to win the polka-dot jersey. He's also the first rider in three years to defeat Miguel Indurain in a Tour time trial.

• Germany's Didi Senft makes his first appearance as "El Diablo," the devil who chases the riders in the mountains. The first rider to be "animated" by Devil Didi is Colombia's Oliverio Rincon (Amaya) at the top of Andorra's Col d'Ordino.

• Pascal Lino (Festina) is the only French rider to win a stage (14) of the 1993 Tour de France. This marks the first time since World War II that the French haven't won at least two stages of the race.

• When the American Subaru-Montgomery team is invited to compete in the Tour as a combined team with the French Chazal squad, coach Eddie

Borysewicz turns down the offer saying he is determined to get his team into next year's race on its own. After the Spanish Kelme team also refuses to partner with the French squad, Chazal accepts the Tour's invitation and fields a full nine-man team.

- *La Société du Tour de France* becomes a subsidiary of ASO, the *Amaury Sport Organisation*, a holding company of the press group *Éditions Philippe Amaury*. The organization, which oversees sporting events, is presided over by former French skiing champion Jean Claude Killy.
- Kazakhstan's Oleg Kozlitine, Estonian Jan Kirsipuu (both with Chazal), and Slovakian Jan Svorada (Lampre-Polti) and are the first riders from their countries to compete in the Tour.

1994 • After riders from the Gewiss-Ballan squad take the first three places the Flèche Wallonne classic, a reporter asks team physician Michele Ferrari if the trio was using EPO. Ferrari responds by saying "EPO is not dangerous, it's the abuse that is. Even orange juice can be harmful if you drink ten liters of it."

- On the 19th of May, 1973 Tour de France winner Luis Ocaña of Spain commits suicide with a .38 caliber revolver in an outbuilding at his home in Caupenne d'Armagnac, in southwestern France. The only rider to seriously challenge Eddy Merckx in the Tour when the Belgian was in his prime, Ocaña crashed out during the 14th stage of the 1971 Tour while leading the Cannibal by more than seven minutes. His only Tour victory would come in the 1973 event, which Merckx had elected to skip. Ocaña had been experiencing financial problems at his vineyard as well as marital troubles and was reportedly suffering from hepatitis C and possibly cancer. He was 48.
- In June, the United States Cycling Federation acquires the United States Professional Cycling Federation, to become the sole governing body for the sport in the United States. "This announcement represents the completion of a long process to join forces," said U.S.C.F. president Mike Fraysse. "Everyone involved strongly believes the sport of bicycle racing will be better served under one governing body."
- Russia's Viatcheslav Ekimov (Wordperfect) wins the Tour Du Pont, beating second-place Lance Armstrong (Motorola) by 1:24.
- Steve Hegg (Chevrolet-L.A. Sheriff's) becomes the U.S. national champion at the USPRO race in Philadelphia. The race is won by 34-year-old Sean Yates (GBR) of Motorola.
- Getting even for Fred St. Onge's loss to Lee Welch in 1908, Hegg defeats in-line skater Tony Muse by two-tenths of a second in a 100-meter race. His elapsed time is 10.55 seconds. For his victory Hegg takes home $1,000.
- John Tomac (Tioga-Giant) wins the NORBA downhill title wearing a full-length rubberized Pearl Izumi "body condom" skinsuit.
- Evgeni Berzin (Gewiss-Ballan) becomes the first Russian rider to win a grand tour when he's victorious in the 77th Giro d'Italia over Marco Pantani. Miguel Indurain is third.
- By winning the Giro's sprinters' title, Polti's Djamolidine Abdoujaparov (UZB)

becomes the second rider, after Eddy Merckx, to win the points competition in all three grand tours.

- Swiss rider Tony Rominger (Mapei-Clas) wins the 49th Vuelta a España. Rominger's record third consecutive win in the event comes in the last springtime running of the race.
- The hour record falls four times in 1994. In late April Great Britain's Graeme Obree uses his radical "ski tuck" position to achieve a distance of 52.713 kilometers (32.756 miles)—the position is immediately banned by the UCI—before Tour winner Miguel Indurain (Banesto) increases the mark to 53.040 kilometers (32.959 miles) in early September. Vuelta winner Tony Rominger of Switzerland surpasses both marks by riding 53.832 kilometers (33.451 miles) on October 22. Two weeks later Rominger covers 55.291 kilometers (34.358 miles). All the records are set in Bordeaux, France.
- At the world championships Marty Nothstein becomes the first American rider to win the match sprint since Frank Kramer won it in Newark, N.J., in 1912. Later Nothstein wins a second gold in the keirin race.
- After four years of work, Frank Walburg completes the *Pedal Pusher Buyer's Guide*. In its 272 pages, the guide contains a stupefying amount of information about nearly every conceivable type of recent bicycle component and accessory. The book contains nearly 750,000 words, and thousands of color photos on glossy paper. The price is $8 cash, $10 check or money order, or $12 on a credit card. The author of this book sent cash, was notified by mail of a printing delay, and did receive his catalog—which he still has.
- Park Bicycle Tools sells six glueless GP-1 patches in a tiny plastic case for $2.95.
- In an effort to thwart the bike thieves of Manhattan, Kryptonite comes out with the New York Lock. The $75 U-lock has a hardened steel ⅝-inch (16-millimeter) diameter shackle, a 1⅜-inch (35-millimeter) crossbar, and weighs 3.4 pounds (1.5 kilograms). See 1988.
- Salomon Sports Group purchases French component company MAVIC. Salomon has annual revenues of $700 million.
- Union Frondenberg sells 36 6AL/4V titanium spokes for $89. At 4.2 grams each, the 14-gauge spokes, which are available in several lengths, are reportedly 56 percent lighter than stainless steel ones.
- Greg LeMond's GAN team rides titanium bikes made by Clark-Kent of Denver, Colo.
- Sachs introduces hydraulic disc brakes for mountain bikes.
- Three-time Tour winner Greg LeMond announces his retirement on December 3, at the Korbel Night of Champions, a fund raiser for the United States Cycling Federation Olympic team in Beverly Hills, California. The reason for his retirement, LeMond says, is that he has developed mitochondrial myopathy, a rare, degenerative muscle disease in which the mitochondria part of the cell is no longer able to provide his muscles with the oxygen needed to restore themselves. Most suspect that the disease is related to dozens of lead shotgun pellets that remain in LeMond's body from his 1987 hunting accident. He tells cycling correspondent Samuel Abt, "In the last seven years, I've had four

months that I felt good and in those four months I won two Tours de France and the world championships. But the rest of those years, I've just been struggling."[1] Veteran cycling commentator Phil Liggett remembers LeMond as one of his favorite riders, saying, "I did enjoy reporting Greg LeMond's wins because he always had plenty to say and was controversial too."

- A $33,000 beryllium mountain bike is stolen from the warehouse of American Bicycle Manufacturing in Minnesota.
- French rider Luc Leblanc wins the world professional road championship in Agrigento, Italy. Leblanc would later admit to using EPO throughout his career.[2] Great Britain's Chris Boardman wins the inaugural world time trial championship.
- America's Karen Kurreck wins the UCI's first women's time trial championship in Palermo, Italy.
- Australia's Deane Rogers wins the first junior men's time trial in Quito, Ecuador.
- Eighteen-year-old Christian Vande Velde wins the points race at the national senior track championships riding the same Schwinn Paramount his father, John, rode at the 1972 Olympics. Schwinn had provided bicycles to United States Olympic teams from 1956 through 1972.
- Italy's Gianluca Bortolami (Mapei-Clas) wins the World Cup.
- American Andy Hampsten signs with Miguel Indurain's Banesto team for 1995.
- Spain's Angel-Luis Casero (Banesto) wins the 32nd Tour de l'Avenir.
- Russia's Valentina Polkhanova wins the ninth Tour Cycliste Féminin.
- Maurizio Fondriest (Lampre) wins the Kellogg's Tour of Britain.
- Germany's Jens Voigt wins the Peace Race.
- Jamie Carney wins the Kugler-Anderson Memorial Tour of Somerville.
- Colorado's Jeanne Golay wins the Mildred Kugler Women's Open.
- The ABC Television Network buys the rights to broadcast the Tour de France in America through 1996.

In the Tour de France:
- Miguel Indurain (Banesto) follows Jacques Anquetil and Eddy Merckx as the third rider to win four consecutive Tours de France.
- Chris Boardman (GAN) and Sean Yates (Motorola) are the first British riders to wear the yellow jersey since Tom Simpson in 1962. Boardman's 55.152 km/h average in the prologue is the fastest speed ever recorded in a grand tour. Boardman's 15-second margin of victory is the largest in the prologue since Freddy Maertens' 17-second win in 1976.
- A picture-taking policeman causes a major crash at the finish of the first stage. The crash eliminates several prominent riders from the race, including France's Laurent Jalabert (ONCE).
- The Tour makes its first "Chunnel" transfer and pays its second visit to Great Britain 20 years. There, it runs stages from Dover to Brighton and in Portsmouth.
- A breakaway victory in the Lourdes–Luz-Ardiden stage helps France's Richard Virenque (Festina) win his first polka-dot jersey.

- Richard Virenque (Festina), who finishes fifth and wins the race's climbers' jersey, pledges his $47,000 in winnings to a relief agency helping Rwandan refugees. Virenque said he will also auction his bicycle and polka-dot jersey.
- A stomach ailment forces Switzerland's Tony Rominger (Mapei-Clas) to abandon while in second place.
- Eros Poli (Mercatone Uno), Italy's 187-pound (85-kilogram) "Giant of the Peloton," wins in Carpentras after a long breakaway which includes a climb of Mont Ventoux. He's named the Tour's most combative rider. During his ascent of Ventoux, Poli loses 20 minutes of a 24-minute lead.
- Piotr Ugrumov (Gewiss-Ballan) is the first Latvian to win a Tour stage.
- Jan Svorada (Lampre-Panaria) is the first rider from the Czech Republic to win a Tour stage.
- Longtime technical director Albert Bouvet supervises his last Tour de France.

1995 - Lance Armstrong (Motorola) wins the San Sebastian Classic, becoming the first American rider to win a World Cup event.
- In Duitama, Colombia, Abraham Olano becomes the first Spaniard to win the world professional road championship—with a little help from his countryman Miguel Indurain. Indurain wins the time trial. This year, the worlds are moved back to October from late August/early September.
- Italy's Linda Visentini wins the UCI's first junior women's time trial which is held in San Marino.
- Switzerland's Tony Rominger (Kelme-Avianca) wins the 78th Giro d'Italia. He wins all three time trials and holds the pink jersey from the second stage on.
- France's Laurent Jalabert (ONCE) wins the 50th Vuelta a España, the first since the UCI moved the race from its traditional springtime spot on the international event calendar to the fall. With the move, the Vuelta sees a dramatic increase in its stature when top pros use the event to garner late-season results and to prepare for the upcoming world championships.
- Norm Alvis (Saturn) solos the final six miles to take the United States champion's title at the CoreStates USPRO in Philadelphia.
- Also in Philadelphia, Canada's Clara Huges (Saturn) beats her teammate Jeanne Golay of Glenwood Springs, Colo., by five meters to win the Liberty Classic for women.
- The United States Cycling Federation changes its name to USA Cycling. The organization had been founded as the Amateur Bicycle League of America in 1920 and had become the USCF at the beginning of 1976.
- After having finished second for each of the past two years, Lance Armstrong wins the 1995 Tour Du Pont.
- Fred Rompelberg of Holland averages 166.944 mph (268.613 km/h) drafting a fuel-injected dragster at the Bonneville Salt Flats, breaking John Howard's 10-year-old bicycle land speed record by more than 14 mph (22 km/h).
- Huffy introduces Metaloids bicycles for 5 to 8-year-olds. The new bikes which are available at Kmart and Toys "R" Us, are made from recycled aluminum (each one contains the equivalent of about 120 soda cans) and sell for $149 to

$199. "[Aluminum] gives a softer ride than steel," said Timothy Dietz, Huffy's senior development engineer.

- Sachs' second-tier road gruppo, 7000, features crank arms, derailleur bodies, and brake levers and calipers that are painted red.
- Cannondale builds a "mountain bike/hybrid cross" with a 30-inch (76-centimeter) frame for 7-foot-1 Orlando Magic basketball star Shaquille O'Neal, The wall thickness of the frame's aluminum tubing is twice that used for Cannondale's regular bikes. Shaq has the bike painted maroon to match his car.
- French component and rim giant MAVIC enters the prebuilt wheel market with its Cosmic aerodynamic wheels. The price is about $850 per pair.
- On October 18, during a high-speed descent in the Milan–Turin classic, Marco Pantani crashes head-on into a car on the course, shattering both bones in his lower left leg. Following a three-hour operation, "a pneumatic external pin is bolted through his leg to keep it from shortening as it heals."[1] He would miss the 1996 season, spending most of it on crutches.
- On January 6, component maker SunTour announces its intention to withdraw from the United States market.
- The Tour de France Society announces that it will hold the Tour VTT (*Vélo Tout Terrain*) for mountain bikes during the last week of August.
- The official Tour de France web site (www.letour.fr) is launched with an English language version following in 1996. German and Spanish versions of the site soon follow.
- France's Emanuel Magnien (Castorama) wins the 33rd Tour de l'Avenir.
- Italy's Fabiana Luperini wins the Tour Cycliste Féminin.
- The Czech Republic's Pavel Padrnos wins the Peace Race.
- Massachusetts' Jason Snow wins the Kugler-Anderson Memorial Tour of Somerville.
- Pennsylvania's Jessica Grieco wins the Mildred Kugler Women's Open.
- On April 29 France's Catherine Marsal increases the women's hour record to 46.112 kilometers (28.654 miles) in Bordeaux, France.
- Seven weeks later, Great Britain's Yvonne McGregor bumps the women's hour mark to 47.411 kilometers (29.461 miles) in Manchester, England.
- In March, Switzerland's Manfred Nüscheler generates 2,378 watts (3.3 horsepower) for five seconds on his bicycle, enough to power 200 lamps.
- Belgium's Johan Museeuw (Mapei-GB) wins the World Cup.
- Nestor Mora, Augusto Triana Gonzalez and Hernan Patino of Manzana-Postobon are killed on February 21 when they're hit by a truck during a training ride in the Medellín, Colombia area.
- Keizo Shimano dies at the age of 62. He was the middle son of company founder Shozaburo Shimano and had headed the company's R&D department. John Neugent of Sachs USA said this about him: "I think Keizo's death is a landmark occasion to mourn the most powerful man in the bicycle industry ever....I think Keizo was the man responsible for the components that made the bicycle. Keizo Shimano had more influence than any other person in the history of the bicycle. A truly great and remarkable man."[2]

In the Tour de France:

- Miguel Indurain (Banesto) becomes the first rider to win five consecutive Tours de France. Eddy Merckx had won the race the first five times he entered between 1969 and 1974.
- The Tour's St. Brieuc prologue is held at night.
- 1992 Olympic gold medalist Fabio Casartelli (Motorola) of Italy dies after crashing on the descent of the Portet d'Aspet in the Pyrenees during the Tour's 15th stage. The 16th stage is ridden as a tribute to him.
- Canada's Steve Bauer (Motorola) starts his 11th Tour de France, the most of any North American so far. He finishes the race nine times.
- The Gewiss-Ballan team of Bjarne Riis rides the event's fastest team time trial until 2005, averaging 54.943 km/h (34.142 mph).
- French television covers 110 hours of the race live.
- The race organizers begin timing the riders' ascents of L'Alpe d'Huez.
- Italy's Marco Pantani climbs L'Alpe d'Huez in 38 minutes. He'll break his own record two years later.
- Serguëi Outschakov (Polti) becomes the first Ukrainian rider to win a Tour stage when he beats Lance Armstrong in the two-up sprint at the finish of the 13th stage in Revel.
- The weak Deutsche Telekom squad is invited to the Tour de France as a mixed nine-man team which is led by Germany's Rolf Aldag and includes three ZG Mobil-Selle Italia riders.

1996 • Lance Armstrong (Motorola) wins Flèche-Wallonne, becoming the first American—and the youngest rider—to claim a one-day Belgian classic.
- The Montgomery-Bell cycling team becomes United States Postal Service-Montgomery-Bell.
- Motorola announces that it's ending its sponsorship of the team at the end of the season. The efforts of the team's general manager Jim Ochowicz to find a new sponsor for the squad eventually fail. By the end of the year, Lance Armstrong signs a $2.5 million-dollar, two-year deal with the Cyrille Guimard-directed Cofidis team. Kevin Livingston also signs with the French squad, while George Hincapie goes with the new US Postal team, whose original jerseys feature a 32-cent stamp bearing the likeness of jazz great Louis Armstrong.
- Lance Armstrong takes five stage wins to claim the last Tour Du Pont by 3:15. The race dies late in the year when the chemical giant announces that it's ending its $2 million annual commitment to the event. Lamenting the situation in which American cycling suddenly finds itself, former national coach Eddie Borysewicz says, "We're going back to the '70s....No results, no sponsorship."[1]
- Russian rider Pavel Tonkov (Lampre-Vinavil) wins the 79th Giro d'Italia.
- Eddy Gragus (US Postal-Montgomery-Bell) attacks in the last turn to win the CoreStates USPRO race in Philadelphia.
- The XXVIth Olympiad in Atlanta is the first Olympic Games to allow professional riders to compete. The 222-kilometer road race is won by Swiss rider

Pascal Richard. Competing at the behest of Spain's King Juan Carlos and IOC president Juan Antonio Samaranch, Miguel Indurain wins the 52-kilometer individual time trial in a time of 1:04:05. After the Olympics, Indurain abandons the Vuelta and skips the world championships in Lugano.

- France's Jeannie Longo-Ciprelli wins the women's Olympic road race on her fourth try.
- Switzerland's Alex Zülle (ONCE) wins the 51st Vuelta a España.
- Mountain biking replaces the team time trial as an Olympic sport.
- Shimano introduces low-profile V brakes for mountain bikes.
- Bell Sports buys bike helmet maker Giro.
- In its Christmas catalogue, upscale retailer Neiman Marcus offers a circular, four-wheel "bicycle" for eight. The odd looking machine features motorcycle suspension and sells for a mere $50,000.
- Judith Crown and Glenn Coleman write *No Hands: The Rise and Fall of the Schwinn Bicycle Company, an American Institution* (illustrated, 350 pp. New York: Henry Holt & Company. $25).
- Using the stretched-out "Superman" position, and buoyed by a partisan crowd, Great Britain's Chris Boardman breaks Tony Rominger's two-year old hour record by covering 56.375 kilometers (35.031 miles) in Manchester, England on September 6.
- On October 26, France's Jeannie Longo-Ciprelli extends the women's hour record to 48.159 kilometers (29.926 miles) at the Olympic Velodrome in Mexico City.
- SRAM engineers John Cheever and Sam Patterson win the Intellectual Property Owners Association's Entrepreneurship Award for their patents (5,102,372, 5,197,927, and 5,476,019), which helped SRAM take 50 percent of the bicycle shifter market away from Japanese component giant Shimano. SRAM's sales have grown from $4 million in 1992 to $50 million in 1995.
- In honor of its 100th anniversary, Schwinn makes 4,000 replicas of its classic Black Phantom cruiser. The company says it expects to sell all of the $3,000 bikes.
- Belgium's Johan Museeuw wins the world championship in the newly-renamed elite men's road race in Lugano, Switzerland. Swiss rider Alex Zülle takes the rainbow jersey in the time trial. UCI president Hein Verbruggen uses the event to propose the "Charter of Lugano," which, effective January 1, 2000, would limit bikes used in international competition to those of the standard "double diamond" design with both wheels the same size.
- In Lugano, Italy's Giuliano Figueras wins the UCI's first under-23 world road championship and his countryman Luca Sironi wins the new under-23 men's time trial.
- At the end of the season, 34-year-old Andy Hampsten announces that he's retiring after a 12-year career as a professional.
- Italy's Fabiana Luperini repeats as winner of the Tour Cycliste Féminin. France's Jeannie Longo-Ciprelli is third, marking the eighth time she's finished on the final podium since 1985.
- David Etxebarria (ONCE) wins the Tour de l'Avenir.

- Germany's Steffen Wesemann (Telekom) wins the Peace Race, and 7 of the race's 10 stages.
- New Zealand's Julian Dean (Shaklee) wins the Kugler-Anderson Memorial Tour of Somerville.
- Pennsylvania's Jessica Grieco repeats as winner of the Mildred Kugler Women's Open.
- Belgium's Johan Museeuw (Mapei) wins the World Cup.
- Roger Lapébie, winner of the 1937 Tour de France, dies on October 12. He was 85.
- French Journalist Pierre Chany dies of pleurisy on June 18. "[Chany]…joined the Tour paper *L'Équipe* at the start of the 1950s, becoming head of cycling. The editor and Tour organiser [sic] Jacques Goddet called him 'a sacred animal of the profession.'"[2] Chany was the only correspondent to cover all 49 Tours held between 1947 and 1995. Shortly before his death, Chany had said that doping would be the death of cycle sport. He was 73.
- On October 8, Lance Armstrong holds a press conference in Austin, Texas to announce that he has cancer. Six days earlier he had been diagnosed with stage-three choriocarcinoma, a rare and particularly lethal form of blood-borne cancer. On October 3, the malignant testicle is removed, and on the 7th he begins chemotherapy treatment after it's discovered that the condition had spread, according to Armstrong, "into my abdomen." He fails to mention that he also has 10 to 12 golf-ball size tumors in his lungs. Near the end of his address, Lance Armstrong emphasized "that I intend to beat this disease, and further, I intend to ride again as a professional cyclist."[3]

In the Tour de France:
- Bjarne Riis (Telekom) is the first Danish rider to win the Tour de France. In 2007 he will admit to using EPO during this time period and will be temporarily stripped of his win. No new winner will be named since many of the other top finishers are eventually either found guilty of doping offenses or suspected of them. Riis will be reinstated as winner of the '96 Tour de France in July 2008.
- Evgeni Berzin (Gewiss) is the first Russian rider to wear the yellow jersey.
- Second-place finisher Jan Ullrich (Telekom) is the first German rider to finish on the podium since Kurt Stoepel in 1932.
- Germany's Erik Zabel (Telekom) wins the green jersey with 335 points. In 2007 he will admit to having tried EPO during the race and will be stripped of his win. Zabel's disqualification makes France's Frederic Moncassin (GAN) the presumptive winner of the 1996 green jersey with 274 points.
- Team Polti's Diasuke Imanaka, 33, is the first professional Japanese rider in the Tour, and the first rider from his country since Kisso Kawamuro competed in the 1926 and 1927 events. The Hiroshima native is testing Shimano's new 9-speed Dura Ace components on his Fausto Coppi bicycle. He is eliminated on time after the 15th stage.
- Race leader Stephen Heulot (GAN) abandons the race because of tendinitis in his knee.

- Third-place finisher Richard Virenque (Festina) is the first French rider on the podium since Laurent Fignon in 1989.
- The 190-kilometer (118-mile) ninth stage is shortened to 46 kilometers (29 miles) because of snow on the Galibier and Iseran Passes. It's the Tour's first weather-shortened stage since the race skipped the Col du Tourmalet in 1922.
- Chepe Gonzalez (Kelme) is the first Colombian rider to win a non-mountainous Tour stage.
- During the 11th stage, farmers protesting higher taxes block the route with trees and scatter nails on the road. Because the nails endanger the riders, the group (the *Confédération de Défense des Commerçants et des Artisans*) is one of the few to be sued by the race organizers.

1997
- Miguel Indurain announces his retirement on January 2, 1997. Tour director and former rider Jean-Marie Leblanc recalls, "There have been years in which I myself was stunned by the almost perfect performance of Miguel Indurain who, during the Tour de France never gave the impression of failing."
- Scott USA sells Schwinn Cycling and Fitness to Questor Partners Fund of Jay Alix and Dan Lufkin, which also owns the Ryder truck leasing company. The selling price is reportedly $43,000,000.
- SRAM acquires Sachs Bicycle Components from Mannesmann Sachs, AG, making SRAM the world's second-largest bicycle component company, after Shimano.
- Campagnolo and Shimano each introduce 9-speed cassettes.
- Trek introduces its Y-66 and Y-77 Y-Foil OCLV (Optimum Compaction/Low Void) bicycles at the Interbike show. The bicycles' beam-frame design reportedly makes them four percent faster than bikes with a similar conventional frame. Ultegra-equipped models retail for about $2,700.
- Swiss rider Alex Zülle (ONCE) repeats in the 52nd Vuelta a España.
- Italy's Ivan Gotti (Saeco) wins the 80th Giro d'Italia. During the event, a team from the NAS, Italy's narcotics squad, raids the hotel of the MG-Technogym team in Cavalese and discovers 20 boxes of anabolic steroids and 3 boxes of growth hormones. MG-Technogym immediately withdraws from the race.
- Italy's Michele Bartoli (MG-Technogym) wins the World Cup.
- Bart Bowen (Saturn) becomes the USPRO Champion in Philadelphia after Motorola's George Hincapie, who finished third, is disqualified for drafting his team car following a puncture. The race was won by Italy's Massimiliano Lelli of Saeco.
- Italy's Fabiana Luperini wins her third consecutive Tour Cycliste Féminin. Canada's Linda Jackson is third.
- France's Laurent Roux (TVM-Farm Frites) wins the Tour de l'Avenir.
- Steffen Wesemann (Deutsche Telekom) repeats as winner of the Peace Race, winning the prologue and three stages.
- Pennsylvania's Brett Aitken wins the Kugler-Anderson Memorial Tour of Somerville.
- Florida's Karen Bliss-Livingston wins the Mildred Kuger Women's Open.
- French rider Laurent Brochard wins the elite men's road race in San Sebastian,

Spain. France's Laurent Jalabert prevails in the time trial.
- The UCI sets the upper hematocrit level for most male riders at 50 percent.
- Adidas purchases ski maker Salomon, which also owns French rim company MAVIC, in September.
- Brunswick buys the Mongoose and Service Cycle brands.
- Communist Marie-George Buffet is elected France's Minister of Youth and Sport in May 1997 and immediately announces that she plans to get tough on doping in sports.
- Lance Armstrong begins training in January with his Cofidis team in Wasquehal, northern France. "I feel much better," he said. "The chemotherapy has been hard at times, but my doctors say everything's doing all right."[1]
- In August, Cofidis drops Lance Armstrong from its roster. At the Anaheim, Calif., trade show, the then-unemployed Armstrong said, "Basically, they've given up on me. They knew I wanted to race. They think I'm finished, which is great. I love that."[2] He is replaced on the team by Switzerland's Tony Rominger.
- On October 14, Lance Armstrong joins the United States Postal Service cycling team. After Armstrong's signing with US Postal, Trek comes on board as the team's bike sponsor, replacing GT.

In the Tour de France:
- Jan Ullrich (Deutsche Telekom) is the first German to win the Tour de France.
- The 50th postwar Tour de France begins in Rouen, near where Jean Robic launched his race-winning, last-stage attack in 1947.
- Marco Pantani (Mercatone Uno) breaks his own record by climbing L'Alpe d'Huez in 37:35.
- The Italian Saeco-Estro team of super sprinter Mario Cipollini switches to American-made Cannondale CAAD 3 aluminum bicycles. Cipollini wins the race's first two stages.
- The American US Postal team rides its first Tour on American-made Trek OCLV carbon fiber bikes. Several teams use American-made Spinergy Rev-X wheels in the race.
- The award for the race's best young rider becomes the Souvenir Fabio Casartelli.
- On the 30th anniversary of Tom Simpson's death, his daughters place a plaque at his memorial high on Mont Ventoux. It reads, "There is no mountain too high. Your daughters Jane and Joanne, July 13, 1997."
- France's Richard Virenque (Festina) becomes the first rider to win four consecutive polka-dot jerseys.
- The very popular French Tour commentator Robert Chapatte dies on January 20 at the age of 75. One of the major personalities of French cycling, Chapatte began his broadcasting career after having competed in the Tour from 1948 through 1952.
- François-René Duchâble plays Bach and Liszt piano pieces atop the Col du Tourmalet.
- Joona Laukka (Festina) is the first Finnish rider to compete in the Tour. He "finnishes" 35th.

1998 • First Union Bank buys CoreStates and retains sponsorship of Philadelphia's USPRO Championship race. The American title is won by George Hincapie (US Postal) in a sprint over Italy's Massimiliano Mori (Saeco). Hincapie's sprint had been set up by his Postal teammates Lance Armstrong, Tyler Hamilton and Frankie Andreu.
- After criticizing the Mercury and Navigators teams ("They just sit around and look at everybody"), Lance Armstrong wins the six-stage Cascade Cycling Classic by 15 seconds over Scott Moninger (Navigators).
- A week before a union contract at its Celina, Ohio, plant is due to expire, Huffy Corporation announces that it plans to close the 40-year-old facility and move its bike production to Mexico or another country.
- Citing safety concerns, the International Cycling Union bans Spinaci-style aero bars, such as those made by Cinelli, from mass-start events. Cinelli sues the UCI alleging that the ban is based on "conjecture rather than evidence."
- America's Bobby Julich (Cofidis) is awarded the victory in France's Criterium International after Frenchman Christophe Moreau (Festina) is disqualified "for doping offenses."
- Paul Kimmage's 1990 drug exposé *Rough Ride* is reprinted prior to the 1998 Tour de France.
- Marco Pantani (Mercatone Uno) wins the 81st Giro d'Italia. By winning the Tour de France weeks later, Pantani becomes the seventh rider (and only the second Italian after Fausto Coppi in 1952) to win both races in the same year. Mario Cipollini (Saeco) wins four stages of the Giro to bring his total in the race to 25, tying Eddy Merckx for third behind Costante Girardengo (30) and Alfredo Binda (41).
- Italy's Michele Bartoli (Asics-CGA) wins the World Cup.
- In August, organizers of the Tour of Spain announce a change to the 53rd Vuelta a España's 13th stage so it doesn't go into France. "Since it is impossible to predict how French judges will behave," said race director Alberto Gadea, "we cannot go." During the event, the racers establish an all-time stage record of 51.137 km/h (31.777 mph) for a grand tour during a short, largely downhill stage. The race is won by Spain's Abraham Olano (Banesto). Beginning with this year's running of the event, the race leader's jersey is gold, which it will remain through the 2009 Vuelta.
- France passes the Buffet Law, named after Mme Marie-George Buffet, France's Minister for Youth and Sport, in an effort to fight drug abuse in all sports.
- Stuart O'Grady (Credit Agricole) wins Great Britain's Pru Tour.
- Lithuania's Edita Pucinskaite wins the renamed Grande Boucle women's race in France.
- France's Christophe Rinero wins the Tour de l'Avenir.
- Germany's Uwe Ampler (Mroz) wins the Peace Race.
- New Jersey's Jonas Carney wins the Kugler-Anderson Memorial Tour of Somerville.
- Karen Bliss-Livingston repeats as winner of the Mildred Kugler Women's Open.

- In Valkenburg, the Netherlands, Oscar Camenzind becomes the first Swiss rider to win the elite men's road race since Ferdi Kübler in 1951. '95 road champion Abraham Olano of Spain wins the time trial.
- 1990 world champion Rudy Dhaenens of Belgium is killed in an automobile accident. He would have turned 37 that week.
- Following his admission of doping in 2013, the International Cycling Union will strip Lance Armstrong of all his professional results dating back to August 1, 1998.

In the Tour de France:

- Marco Pantani (Mercatone Uno) wins the 1998 Tour de France.
- The drug raids of the "Festina Affair" cause seven teams to leave the race.
- The Tour starts a week late because of World Cup soccer matches in France. The Dublin prologue marks the race's first visit to Ireland, where former Tour director Félix Levitan, who'd been fired in 1987 for financial mismanagement, returns as a guest of the race.
- Great Britain's Chris Boardman (GAN) crashes out of the race while wearing the yellow jersey.
- Festina becomes the first team to be kicked out of the Tour de France.
- Belgium's Tom Steels (Mapei) wins the strike-shortened (from 221 kilometers to 205.5) 12th stage with an average speed of 48.76 km/h (30.30 mph), making it the fastest stage over 200 kilometers (124 miles) until 2003.
- In Albertville, Daniel Mangeas celebrates his 500th stage with the Tour since becoming its official announcer in 1976.
- Following a strike by the riders, the race's 17th stage is canceled.
- Winner Marco Pantani establishes a then-record average speed for the race: 39.98 km/h (24.84 mph).
- Bobby Julich's (Cofidis) third-place finish makes him the second American to finish on the podium.
- Magnus Backstedt (GAN) becomes the first Swedish rider to win a stage in the Tour.
- Neither the winner of the polka-dot jersey nor the winner of the green jersey wins a stage.
- Axel Merckx (Polti), son of Belgian great Eddy Merckx, rides in his first Tour, finishing 10th.
- The Tour begins tracking the riders' positions by using GPS technology.
- The leader of the "most aggressive rider" category is distinguished by wearing a red number.
- French cartoonist Pellos (René Pellarin) dies at the age of 98. Once described as "[Antoine] Blondin with a pencil," Pellos drew caricatures of the Tour de France and its riders from 1931 through 1981.
- Of the Tour's estimated 250 million francs in revenues, 56 percent come from commercial sponsors, 30 percent from TV rights, and 14 percent from fees paid by host communities.
- After the Tour de France, sales of Festina wristwatches reach an all-time high.

1999 • Italy's Ivan Gotti (Polti) wins the 82nd Giro d'Italia after Marco Pantani is
kicked out of the race prior to its penultimate stage at Madonna di Campiglio
for having a hematocrit level above 50 percent. Prior to his ejection, Pantani
had held a six-minute lead with two stages remaining in the race. Mario Cipollini raises his Giro stage win total to 29.

- France's Laurent Jalabert (ONCE) wins the Giro's sprint title to become only
the third rider (after Eddy Merckx and Djamolidine Abdoujaparov) to win the
points competition of all three grand tours.

- Germany's Jan Ullrich (Deutsche Telekom) wins the 54th Vuelta a España.

- Ullrich also wins the elite men's time trial title in Verona, Italy. Spanish rider
Oscar Freire wins the elite men's road race.

- US Postal rider Marty Jemison finishes fifth to claim the FirstUnion USPRO
title. The race is won by Denmark's Jakob Piil (aka "Jakob Piil Storm"; Accept-
card Pro Cycling).

- The Consumer Product Safety Commission (CPSC) establishes a bicycle helmet safety standard that becomes law in the United States.

- The Huffy corporation announces it will close its last two American factories,
located in Farmington, Mo., and Southhaven, Miss. "Closing the plants will cut
costs and complete the company's transformation from single-brand manufacturer to a multibrand design, marketing, and distribution company, Huffy
said."[1] Between the two factories, 600 people will lose their jobs.

- The *New York Times* runs a brief article featuring the Pashley Delibike. Made
by Pashley Cycles of Stratford-on-Avon, England, (telephone 44-178-929-
2263, www.pashley.co.uk) for more than 70 years, the $1,100 delivery machine
features a low center of gravity thanks to the wicker basket mounted above its
small front wheel.

- In May, former Festina *soigneur* Willy Voet's drug exposé *Chain Massacre* is published in France (the English version is published as *Breaking the Chain*). The
book is ghostwritten by former *L'Équipe* cycling writer Pierre Ballester, who'll co-
author 2004's *LA Confidential: Les Secrets de Lance Armstrong* with David Walsh.

- The Outdoor Life Network (now Versus) signs a multi-year contract to broadcast the Tour de France in the United States.

- Thierry Claveyrolet, winner of the Tour's polka-dot jersey in 1990, "is found
dead at his home. It is believed he took his own life."[2]

- Lance Armstrong (US Postal) is the first cyclist to be featured on boxes of
Wheaties since the likeness of 1986 U.S. amateur road champion Doug Smith
graced 10 million boxes of the cereal in 1988.

- Campagnolo introduces a 10-speed cassette four years before Shimano.

- "Mavic introduces its wireless electronic derailleur system, Mektronic, which
the UCI rejects."[3]

- In February, former Chrysler Corporation chairman Lee Iacocca makes the
rounds at the National Automobile Dealers Association convention in San
Francisco trying to sell franchises for the electric bicycle that his Los Angeles-
based EV Global Motors Company will begin selling in the spring.

- Marc Wauters (Rabobank) wins Great Britain's Pru Tour.

- Naturalized Belgian Andre Tchmil (Lotto-Mobistar) wins the World Cup.
- Spain's Unai Osa (Banesto) wins the Tour de l'Avenir.
- Lithuania's Diana Ziliute wins the Grand Boucle.
- Germany's Steffen Wesemann (Telekom) wins the Peace Race.
- Eric Wohlberg of Toronto, Canada wins the Kugler-Anderson Memorial Tour of Somerville.
- Pennsylvania's Laura Van Gilder wins the Mildred Kugler Women's Open.
- France's Félicia Ballanger becomes the first woman to win five straight sprint titles at the World Track Cycling Championship when she wins in Berlin.
- Luke David Armstrong is born to Lance and Kristin Armstrong on October 12, 1999.
- American Jonathan Vaughters (US Postal) wins the Route du Sud.

In the Tour de France:
- Prior to being stripped of his victories, Lance Armstrong wins the Tour de France 954 days after his last chemotherapy session. He is the second American to win the race. He is also the first winner since Laurent Fignon to win four stages of the race, and only the fourth rider to win all three of the event's time trials.
- Armstrong is the first rider on an American team to win the Tour and the first winner to ride an American bike.
- Armstrong's "Trek" time trial bike is actually a repainted Litespeed Blade. The machine's front brake is a fifteen-year-old Dura-Ace AX model.
- Armstrong's average speed of 40.276 km/h (25.028 mph) is a new race record.
- For the first time since 1956, there are no former winners entered in the race.
- There are only two overall leaders of the race for the first time since 1977, when only Bernard Thevenet and Didi Thurau wore the *maillot jaune.*
- Jaan Kirsipuu is the first Estonian rider to win a Tour stage and to wear the yellow jersey.
- The American GT bicycle company replaces Vitus as the exclusive supplier of bikes to Team Lotto just prior to the Tour de France.
- Mario Cipollini is the first rider to win three consecutive Tour stages since Gino Bartali in 1948 (his 12 victories also ties him with Bartali for most Tour stage wins by an Italian rider).
- Cipollini is the first rider to win four consecutive Tour stages since Charles Pélissier in 1930 and René Pottier in 1906. (In 1909, Tour winner François Faber of Luxembourg won five consecutive stages.)
- Cipollini also wins the fastest road stage in Tour history, averaging 50.355 km/h.
- Erik Zabel is the first rider to win the event's green jersey four consecutive times.
- For the second consecutive year, neither the winner of the polka dot jersey nor the winner of the green jersey wins a stage.
- The start of the 17th stage is delayed by firemen who are protesting poor working conditions.
- For the first time since 1926, there are no French stage winners in the Tour de France.

- Shimano achieves its first overall Tour victory on the 25th anniversary of its top of-the-line Dura-Ace gruppo.
- The French National Assembly passes a law requiring professional bike racers to submit to testing in order to establish physiological baselines for future drug testing.

Chapter 11

2000–2009
Good Times, Bad Times

2000 • Two-time Tour de France winner Gino Bartali dies of a heart attack on May 5, 2000. His two Tour de France victories came 10 years apart in 1938 and 1948. Bartali was also a three-time winner of the Giro, winning that race both before and after the Second World War. In the great rider's obituary, John Wilcockson noted that Bartali had been one of the final links "to an era when cycling was a rougher, more rudimentary sport, and its heroes were giants."[1] Gino Bartali was 85.
  • On January 1, the UCI's rule requiring bicycles to be of the traditional double diamond frame design and have both wheels the same size goes into effect. "After January 2000," remarked one UCI official, "bikes will again look like bikes."
  • JKH Investments, majority owner of Litespeed, buys Merlin Metalworks from Saucony, Inc.
  • North Carolina-based Performance Bike Shop buys Bike Nashbar in April for an undisclosed amount. Performance president Garry Snook says he plans to keep the two bicycle mail-order giants separate. "The Nashbar brand means something to its customers," he said. "That was one of the things we felt had value and we paid for. We felt it was foolish for us not to continue it."[2]
  • American Tyler Hamilton (US Postal) wins the 52nd Dauphiné Libéré.
  • Italy's Stefano Garzelli wins the 83rd Giro d'Italia.
  • Italy passes law number 376, which calls for criminal penalties for doping in sports. The law, under which anyone caught using, supplying or administering banned substances faces up to three years in prison, makes Italy one of the few countries to impose criminal sanctions for doping offenses, on top of the normal sporting sanctions.
  • In June, three-time Tour de France winner Greg LeMond, 39, is inducted into the United States Bicycling Hall of Fame in Somerville, N.J.
  • Former Tour de France winner Stephen Roche and his wife Lydia open the 27-room Roche Marina Hotel on the French Riviera.
  • Mapei-Quick Step's Fred Rodriguez wins the FirstUnion USPRO Champion-

ship by outsprinting George Hincapie (US Postal) for second place. The race winner is Australia's Henk Vogels (Mercury).

- Lance Armstrong's inspirational autobiography *It's Not About the Bike* becomes a *New York Times* bestseller during the Tour de France. Armstrong co-wrote the book with Sally Jenkins.
- Specialized joins American bike companies Trek (US Postal), Cannondale (Saeco-Valli & Valli) and GT (Lotto-Adecco) in the European pro peloton when it begins supplying the French Festina team with S-Works M4 bicycles.
- Spanish rider Roberto Heras gives Kelme its first victory in a major tour when he wins the 55th Vuelta a España.
- Germany's Jan Ullrich wins the 239-kilometer (149-mile) road race over two Telekom teammates at the XXVIIth Olympiad in Sydney, Australia. Russia's Viatcheslav Ekimov wins the time trial over Ullrich, while Lance Armstrong takes the bronze medal a month after fracturing his C7 neck vertebra in a training crash. America's Mari Holden wins the silver medal in the women's time trial. Six weeks prior to the games, the IOC had approved the use of French- and Australian-developed urine and blood tests to detect the athletes' use of EPO.
- At the world championships in Plouay, France, Latvia's Romans Vainsteins becomes the first Eastern European rider to win the elite men's road race. The race's average speed is a record 42.963 km/h (26.697 mph). Serguei Gontchar of the Ukraine wins the elite men's time trial.
- Mari Holden wins the women's world championship in the time trial, covering the 25-kilometer (15.6-mile) course in 33:14. France's Jeannie Longo-Ciprelli is second, three seconds back.
- On September 8, the UCI announces that it is recognizing only hour records set on conventional track bikes. The UCI's decision results in the reinstatement of the Eddy Merckx's 1972 Mexico City mark of 49.431 kilometers (30.716 miles) while Chris Boardman's aero-aided 1996 ride of 56.375 kilometers (35.031 miles) will stand as the "world best performance." On October 27, Boardman covers 49.441 kilometers (30.723 miles) on a track in Manchester, England, breaking the Belgian's 28 year-old record by 10 meters (10.93 yards).
- Also riding a conventional track bike, Australia's Anna Wilson-Millward re-establishes the women's hour record at 43.501 kilometers (27.032 miles) on October 18 at the Vodafone Arena Velodrome in Melbourne, Australia, bettering Cornelia Van Oosten's 1978 mark of 43.082 kilometers (26.771 miles).
- On November 5, France's Jeannie Longo-Ciprelli resets the women's hour mark at 44.767 kilometers (27.818 miles) in Mexico City. A month later, she bumps the record to 45.094 kilometers (28.021 miles). Longo-Ciprelli's aero-aided 1996 mark of 48.159 kilometers (29.926 miles) would stand as the women's world best performance.
- Longo-Ciprelli breaks the year-old record of Canada's Genevieve Jeanson for the climb up the Mt. Washington Auto Road. Longo-Ciprelli makes the 7.6-mile (12.25-kilometer) climb in 58:14, bettering the old mark of 1:01:57. Jeanson finishes second in 1:00:14. The men's race is won by Tim Johnson of

Middleton, Mass., in a time of 55:46.

- On September 16, 44 year-old Manfred Nüscheler sets the roller speed record of 164.1 km/h (101.97 mph) in Berne, Switzerland. To establish the record, Nüscheler reportedly pedals a 54 x 11 gear at up to 284 rpm. He uses a Moser frame and Campagnolo components.
- On October 2, a judge in Ghent, Belgium finds 57-year-old former Festina team physician Eric Ryckaert guilty of trafficking Eprex for a three-year period prior to the Tour's 1998 "Festina Affair." Ryckaert is fined 600,000 Belgian francs (about $13,000).
- North Carolina's Jonas Carney wins the Kugler-Anderson Memorial Tour of Somerville.
- Georgia's Tina Mayolo wins the Mildred Kugler Women's Open.
- Germany's Erik Zabel (Deutsche Telekom) wins the World Cup.
- Spain's Joane Somarriba (Alfa Lum) wins the Grande Boucle.
- Poland's Piotr Wadecki wins the Peace Race.
- Spain's Iker Flores (Euskaltel-Euskadi) wins the Tour de l'Avenir.
- Big Mat-Aubervilliers 93 rider Thierry Bourguignon writes *Tours et Detours* (Paris, Botega Editions).
- The racing career of former La Française des Jeux rider Christophe Bassons (now with Jean Delatour) ends when *Positif*, his story of drugs in the peloton, is published.

In the Tour de France:

- Prior to being stripped of his victories, Lance Armstrong wins his second consecutive Tour de France.
- The white jersey, which is worn by the leader of the Tour's Souvenir Fabio Casartelli category, returns after an 11-year absence. It is awarded to the race's best rider 25 and under.
- For only the second time since its inception in 1967, no prologue is held at the start of the race. Defending champion Lance Armstrong does not start the event in the yellow jersey.
- Tour owner Philippe Amaury buys a controlling interest in the Futuroscope theme park. He will sell his stake in the park in 2002, after incurring a loss of €35 million.
- The team time trial returns to the event following a five-year absence. During the leg, protesters move some hay bales into the road, but fail to disrupt the stage.
- Italy's Alberto Elli (Deutsche Telekom), 36, is the oldest rider to wear the yellow jersey since World War II.
- The race's 12th leg is the first road stage to finish atop Mont Ventoux since 1972.
- Twelve-year-old Philippe Tardy is killed during the 13th stage when he's hit by one of the vehicles in the Tour's publicity caravan. Later, Tour director Jean-Marie Leblanc writes "that the Tour's success does not go on without excess, even when its organizers try hard to avoid it," but said that he would try to control the excess by reducing the number of vehicles in the publicity caravan from 700 to 250, planning an itinerary off the race route for vehicles with

orange accreditation, and by giving all drivers a *Tour de France Driving Regulations* brochure. Leblanc concluded by writing that "Sport is life, and Philippe must not have lost his in vain."

- During the 18th stage, Lance Armstrong wears the yellow jersey for the 22nd day in his career, surpassing fellow American Greg LeMond's 21 days in the *maillot jaune*.
- For the first time the Tour's history, its final stage is run completely within the city of Paris.
- German sprinter Erik Zabel wins his record fifth consecutive green jersey.
- US Postal's Frankie Andreu finishes his ninth Tour in nine starts, surpassing Andy Hampsten's American mark of eight. Canada's Steve Bauer started eleven Tours, completing nine.
- Santiago Botero is the second Colombian after Luis "Lucho" Herrera (1985 and 1987), to win the Tour's climbing category.
- Basque protesters dressed as racers join the leaders on the road at the end of the 15th stage.
- Philippe Chapuis, who dresses as Bibendum, the Michelin man in the race's publicity caravan, is awarded the Medal of the Tour de France for 20 years' service.
- The publicity caravan consists of 200 vehicles representing 40 companies. The organizers charge advertisers 130,000 francs ($18,000) for the first three vehicles and 30,000 francs ($4,200) for each additional vehicle.
- After he manages to secure press credentials, a fan named Scott Coady uses a hand-held video camera to film the race. His movie, *The Tour, Baby*, becomes a cult hit.
- Dr. Pierre Dumas dies in February. He had been a physician for the Tour de France from 1952 until 1977. Dr. Dumas was 78.
- Former race director Jean-François "Jacques" Goddet dies on December 15, 2000, at the age of 95. *La Societe du Tour de France* announces plans to honor him with a memorial on the Col du Tourmalet in the Pyrenees. Goddet directed the race for fifty-one years beginning in 1936, when he took over early in the race for an ailing Henri Desgrange. He was promoted to race director for the 1937 event. "I only knew him a little," said two-time Tour winner Laurent Fignon. "But what I remember of him is his personality. He had true moral values, and, even if sometimes he could appear hard, he was always just in his judgments."

2001 • US Postal rider George Hincapie becomes the first American rider in five years to win a classic when he edges Mercury-Viatel's Leon Van Bon to claim the 63rd edition of Belgium's Ghent–Wevelgem.
- The scene at the 84th Giro d'Italia is reminiscent of those during the '98 Tour when police searching for illegal drugs raid the riders' San Remo hotels on the evening of June 6. The following day, the racers refuse to ride and the event's 18th stage is canceled. The riders finish the Giro only after being threatened with harsh sanctions if they abandon. Belgium's Rik Verbrugghe wins the

event's flat, wind-aided 7.6-kilometer (4.7-mile) prologue with an average speed of 58.874 km/h (36.50 mph), fastest ever for a major tour. Forty-seven other riders also eclipsed the mark of 55.152 km/h (34.271 mph) that Chris Boardman had established in the prologue of the 1994 Tour de France. Italy's Gilberto Simoni (Lampre-Daikin) wins the race.

- The International Cycling Union moves into its futuristic, aluminum-clad, €70-million headquarters in Aigle, Switzerland.
- Effective January 1, 2001, UCI rule 1.3.019 mandates that bicycles used in sanctioned events can weigh no less than 14.99 pounds (6.8 kilograms).
- Fred Rodriguez (Domo-Farm Frites) repeats as the First Union USPRO champion in Philadelphia by beating George Hincapie (US Postal) and Trent Klasna (Saturn) to the line. The field included 164 riders from 23 nations.
- Former Festina *directeur sportif* Bruno Roussel publishes his version of the 1998 Festina Affair, *Tour of Vices.*
- Without winning a stage, Spain's Angel Casero (Festina) claims the 56th Vuelta a España on the last day over fellow Spaniard Oscar Sevilla. US Postal's Levi Leipheimer is third @ 2:59, becoming the first American to finish on the podium. The race is the fastest ever Vuelta with an average speed of 42.534 km/h (26.37 mph). Casero is riding an American-made Specialized bike.
- Cofidis' Guido Trenti, who holds dual American and Italian citizenship, becomes the first "American" to win a stage of the Vuelta (stage 19).
- In Lisbon, Portugal, Oscar Freire wins the elite men's road race at the world championships for the second time in three years. Jan Ullrich, 1999 winner in the time trial, again takes the race against the clock, this time by :06 over Britain's David Millar. America's Danny Pate wins the under-23 men's time trial.
- In early January, Brunswick Corporation of Lake Forest, Ill., sells its bike division (Mongoose, Mongoose Pro, and Roadmaster brands) to Madison, Wisc.-based Pacific Cycle, LLC, for $60 million. Brunswick says it plans to focus its efforts on boats and motors, fitness equipment, billiards, and bowling.
- Two months after striking a potential deal with Huffy, bankrupt Schwinn/GT is purchased at auction by a joint offer from Chris Hornung of Pacific Cycle and Nautilus' Kevin Lamar on September 11, 2001.
- Huffy introduces the Micro Monkey Bike, which is made of bicycle and scooter parts and sits on six-inch wheels. Sales of the $50 bike are reported as "brisk." "The goofier it looks," says Huffy VP of marking Bill Smith, "the more they like it."
- Shimano offers the Nexave Di2 (Digital Integrated Intelligence) system which uses a tiny computer to shift gears and adjust the suspension on "comfort bikes" costing upwards of $2,000. Di2 components are not currently available in the United States. Di2 would return on Shimano's electronic Dura-Ace components at the 2008 Interbike trade show.
- After years of having its bikes painted to look like those of other manufacturers in the European peloton, Litespeed signs a three-year deal to replace GT as supplier of bicycles to the Lotto-Adecco team. The Chattanooga, Tenn.-based company steps in after the bankruptcy of Schwinn/GT when the company's

new owners are uninterested in sponsoring the team.

- In October, the Professional Cyclist's Association guarantees an annual minimum wage of €15,000 ($13,700) for rookies and €23,000 ($21,000) for all other professional riders beginning in 2002.
- On November 20, Lance Armstrong's wife Kristin gives birth to twin girls: Grace Elizabeth and Isabelle Rose.
- The Swiss Army announces that the "world's last remaining bicycle-mounted combat regiment" will be abolished in 2003.[1]
- Spain's Joane Somarriba repeats as winner of the Grande Boucle.
- Russia's Denis Menchov (iBanesto.com) wins the Tour de l'Avenir.
- Canada's Eric Wohlberg wins the Kugler-Anderson Memorial Tour of Somerville.
- North Carolina's Christina Underwood wins the Mildred Kugler Women's Open.
- Denmark's Jacob Piil wins the Peace Race.
- The Netherland's Erik Dekker (Rabobank) wins the World Cup.
- Twenty-six-year-old Spanish rider Ricardo Otxoa is killed on February 15 when he and his twin brother and Kelme teammate Javier are hit by a car while on a training ride near Cartama, Spain. Javier, who won the 10th stage of the 2000 Tour de France to Lourdes-Hautacam, suffers serious injuries to his head, back, and possibly his spinal cord. He lapses into a lengthy coma from which he is slowly recovering.
- The Postmaster General says that anthrax incidents following the 9/11 terrorist attacks on the United States could end up costing the United States Postal Service up to $4 billion.[2] At the end of the year the U.S.P.S. announces that it is finishing the year with a $1.68 billion loss.

In the Tour de France:

- Prior to being stripped of his victories, Lance Armstrong (US Postal) becomes the fifth rider to win three consecutive Tours de France, following in the footsteps of Miguel Indurain, Eddy Merckx, Jacques Anquetil and Louison Bobet.
- German sprinter Erik Zabel (Telekom) wins his record sixth straight green jersey on the race's final day. Zabel would later be stripped of the first green jersey he won in 1996 after admitting to EPO use that year.
- France's Laurent Jalabert (CSC-Tiscali) becomes only the third rider—and the only non-winner—to win both the Tour's green points jersey (1995) and its King of the Mountains competition (2001). Jalabert would claim the climbing title again in 2002, his final year of racing.
- Jalabert becomes the third Frenchman to win two stages on Bastille Day, his other stage win coming in 1995. Jacques Anquetil won stages on France's national holiday in 1961 and 1964, Bernard Thévenet in 1970 and 1975.
- Until Lance Armstrong's disqualification, the Tour de France has its second "repeat podium," which also occurred in 1978-1979. The top three finishers that year were: Bernard Hinault, Joop Zoetemelk, and Joaquim Agostinho.
- Of the twenty-one teams in the race, a postwar record eight are French.

- In the wake of the previous year's death of a 12-year-old boy, only caravan vehicles with a "clear mission" are allowed on the on the Tour's route, the others must follow a secondary route until they near the day's finish. Everyone also receives a copy of the "rules of the road."
- *Le Journal du Dimanche* reports that the race's major sponsors, including Credit Lyonnais and Fiat, are ready to pull their support from the event because of a perceived lack of progress in its fight against doping. Coca Cola reportedly reduces its annual Tour budget from $4.35 million to $872,000.
- In late June, Outdoor Life Network (which would become Versus, and then NBC Sports) becomes the official English language partner of Letour.com, the Tour de France's official web site.
- The UCI begins using a urine test to detect the use of EPO. The test was developed by France's national anti-doping lab in Chatenay-Malabry.
- A disgruntled fan plows his car into a crowd on Bastille Day, injuring three people.
- A 14-man breakaway finishes almost 36 minutes up on the peloton during the eighth stage.
- French journalist and official race archivist Jacques Augendre covers his 50th Tour de France. After the race, he says that Lance Armstrong could break Miguel Indurain's record of five consecutive Tour victories.
- A plaque is placed at the Col d'Aubisque site where, 50 years earlier, race leader Wim Van Est had crashed out of the event, falling 20 meters (65 feet) into some trees. He wasn't seriously injured.

2002 • On July 1 the price of a first-class postage stamp increases from 34¢ to 37¢.
- US Postal's Chann McRae becomes the U.S. national champion when he finishes the First Union USPRO Championship behind Mark Walters (Navigators), who's the first Canadian to win the event.
- Former Belgian rider Marcel Kint dies on March 23. Known as the "Black Eagle," Kint became world champion in 1938, a title he held until the race resumed in 1946, when he finished second. In 1943, he won Paris–Roubaix and the first of three consecutive Flèche-Wallonnes. Kint was 87.
- Fred Rodriguez (Domo-Farm Frites) and George Hincapie (US Postal) finish behind Italy's Mario Cipollini (Acqua & Sapone) in Ghent–Wevelgem. It's the first time that two American riders have finished on the podium of a classic.
- Italy's Paolo Savoldelli (Index-Alexia) wins the 85th Giro d'Italia. After breaking his shoulder and bonking on the Passo Coe, the race's final climb, American rider Tyler Hamilton (CSC-Tiscali) wins the 14th stage individual time trial, and finishes second overall @ 1:41. During the race, former winners Stefano Garzelli and Gilberto Simoni (later exonerated) are kicked out for using banned substances, Mario Cipollini brings his Giro stage win total to 40, and Cadel Evans becomes the first Australian to wear the leader's pink jersey.
- American Levi Leipheimer (Rabobank) wins the third stage of the 26th Route du Sud, an uphill time trial, and finishes first overall.
- Lance Armstrong becomes the first American to win late May's Midi Libre. He

wins the 54th Dauphiné Libéré two weeks later with his Postal teammate Floyd Landis finishing second, 2:03 back.

- Sam Abt marks 25 years of covering the sport with the publication of his book *Off to the Races: 25 Years of Cycling Journalism.*
- US Postal's Roberto Heras (ESP) wins the Tour of Catalonia.
- An assistant to the Paris prosecutor announces that a 19-month doping probe against the US Postal team will conclude during the summer, adding, "There has been no positive test."[1]
- Saying that it's disappointed with the progress the sport is making against doping, industrial building products company Mapei announces that it will end its 10-year sponsorship of its Italian-based professional cycling team at the end of the season.
- Italy's Paolo Bettini (Mapei-Quick Step) wins the World Cup.
- Shortly before the start of the Tour de France, the Italian cycling federation announces that it's suspending 1998 Tour winner Marco Pantani for eight months for allegedly using insulin during the 2001 Giro d'Italia. The suspension is overturned on appeal.
- During the Giro's 15th stage, the German Cycling Federation announces that it's suspending 1997 Tour winner Jan Ullrich for six months after he was found positive for amphetamines in an out of competition test. Ullrich would have missed the Tour de France anyway, due to recent knee surgery.
- Aitor Gonzalez (Kelme-Costa Blanca) defeats fellow Spaniard Roberto Heras by 3:22 in the final day's time trial to win the 57th Vuelta a España by 2:14 over the US Postal rider. Heras wins two stages of the race. Italy's Mario Cipollini ends a three month "retirement" at the event by winning three stages in the first week before abandoning. "Cipo" says that he's using the race as preparation for the upcoming world championships in Belgium.
- Thirty-five-year-old Cipollini of Italy wins the 2002 elite men's world road championship in Zolder, Belgium aboard an American-made Specialized bicycle. Robbie McEwen finishes the 256-kilometer (159-mile) race two bike lengths back to become the first Australian to finish on the podium in the event. The race's average speed is a record 46.538 kph (28.919 mph). Colombia's Santiago Botero wins the time trial, completing the 40.4-kilometer (25.1-mile) event in 48:08.
- The worlds mark the final race of French star Laurent Jalabert. During his 14 years as a professional, "Jaja" won the Vuelta (1995), the world time trial championship (1997) and became only the third rider—after Eddy Merckx and Bernard Hinault—to win both the green jersey (1995) and the climbing competition (2001 and 2002) in the Tour de France.
- SRAM acquires Rock Shox in March for $5.6 million.
- "The Cat Eye GameBike attachments ($150) turn the stationary bicycle into a controller for Sony PlayStation games. Cyclists control the game by varying pedaling speed and turning the handlebars."[2]
- The Czech Republic's Ondrej Sosenka wins the Peace Race after his teammate Piotr Przydzial is disqualified.
- Belarus' Zinaida Stahurskaia wins the Grande Boucle.

- Russia's Evgeni Petrov (Mapei-Quick Step) wins the 40th Tour de l'Avenir.
- Cycling trainer Ed Burke, Ph.D., dies of a heart attack on November 7, 2002 while riding his bicycle. He was 53.
- Shimano president emeritus Shozo Shimano dies at the age of 74. He had served as the component company's president since the death of his father, Shozaburo, in 1958 until 1992, when he was replaced by his brother Yoshizo.
- Yozo Shimano replaces his uncle Yoshizo Shimano as president of Shimano, Inc. Yozo is the son of Shozo Shimano.
- *Sports Illustrated* chooses Lance Armstrong as its Sportsman of the Year.
- The Associated Press names Lance Armstrong its Male Athlete of the Year over baseball slugger Barry Bonds and golfer Tiger Woods.

In the Tour de France:

- Prior to being stripped of his victories, Lance Armstrong becomes the fourth rider to win four consecutive Tours de France. Armstrong's 15 stage victories are the most of any active rider, while his 46 days in the yellow jersey move him up to fifth in the all-time list behind five-time winners Eddy Merckx (96—or 111 if you count half stages), Bernard Hinault (77), Miguel Indurain (60) and Jacques Anquetil (51).
- During the race's 14th stage, Armstrong breaks Marco Pantani's two year-old record for the ascent of Mont Ventoux by 53 seconds.
- Armstrong chooses not to start the race's prologue in the yellow jersey.
- Armstrong's elapsed time of 82 hours 5 minutes 12 seconds is the lowest ever for the Tour de France. So is second-place Joseba Beloki's time of 82:12:29.
- Many experts call US Postal's 2002 Tour team one of the best of all time. Commentator Phil Liggett says that the squad is "the finest team ever assembled in the modern era of cycling." His TV sidekick Paul Sherwen concurs, calling Postal "the best team in the last 50 years."
- Saeco-Longoni Sports' invitation to the Tour de France is revoked after the team's leader, Gilberto Simoni, is kicked out of the Tour of Italy for doping violations.
- Raimondas Rumsas (Lampre-Daikin) becomes the first Lithuanian to finish on the podium—at age thirty-one. He is later accused of doping during the race, but keeps his third-place finish.
- King of the Mountains winner Laurent Jalabert (CSC-Tiscali) uses a 14-pound bicycle with 26-inch wheels for some ascents, but switches to a conventional racing bike for the descents.
- Robby McEwen (Lotto-Adecco) defeats seven-time points winner Eric Zabel by 19 points (280 to 261) to become the first Australian to win the green jersey.
- By capturing the stage nine time trial, Santiago Botero (Kelme-Costa Blanca) becomes the first Colombian to win a Tour de France time trial.
- All of the Tour's prize money is awarded in Euros instead of francs (in 2002, a Euro was roughly equivalent to one US dollar). Of the race's total purse of €2,664,035, €335,390 would go to the overall winner, while the best sprinter and the best climber would each receive €22,867, and the best young rider

would be awarded €18,294. Each daily stage winner would get €7,620, while the day's most aggressive rider and the winner of a *hors categorie* climb would earn €1,525 and €760 respectively.

- At 3,277.5 kilometers, the 2000 Tour de France is the shortest Tour since 1905.
- Seven-year-old Melvin Pompele is killed when he's hit by the caravan vehicle of the Haribo candy company near Retjons before the race's tenth stage.
- With his win of the race's second stage in Saarbrucken, Germany, Spain's Oscar Freire is the first reigning world champion to win a Tour stage since Bernard Hinault in 1981.
- Journalists Phil Liggett (Outdoor Life Network and *Cycle Sport*) and John Wilcockson (*VeloNews*) celebrate 30 years of covering the Tour de France. Liggett began covering the event in 1973 when he was a driver for the late David Saunders.
- Prior to Armstrong's being stripped of his title, the 2002 Tour de France marks the first time that riders on Shimano-equipped bikes have won all three of the event's major jerseys.

2003 • Kazakh rider Andrei Kivilev (Cofidis) dies in Saint-Etienne's Bellevue Hospital on March 12, the day after crashing during the second stage of Paris–Nice. His countryman Alexandre Vinokourov (Telekom) wins the race and dedicates the victory to his fallen friend.
- On April 4, the UCI says that a rule making helmet use mandatory for professional riders will go into effect by the start of the Giro d'Italia on May 10. Beginning then, the racers will be allowed to remove their helmets only during a stage-ending or race-ending climb of 5 kilometers (3.1 miles) or longer.
- Tyler Hamilton (Team CSC) wins Liège–Bastogne–Liège on May 27 after his teammates chase down Lance Armstrong on the Côte du Saint Nicolas, 6 kilometers from the finish. With his victory, Hamilton becomes the first American to win "La Doyenne," cycling's oldest classic, and the first American to win one of the classics' "Five Monuments": Milan–San Remo, the Tour of Flanders, Paris–Roubaix, the Tour of Lombardy and Liège–Bastogne–Liège.
- Tyler Hamilton (Team CSC) wins the Tour de Romandie.
- Lance Armstrong (US Postal) wins the 55th Dauphiné Libéré after winning the time trial, despite a 45-mph crash which costs him two stitches in his right elbow. Tyler Hamilton (Team CSC) drops out before the final stage because of a stomach bug.
- Chris Horner (Saturn-Timex) wins the inaugural, five-stage Dodge Tour de Georgia in late April.
- SRAM drops the Grip Shift name and enters the road bike market with chains and cassettes.
- Finishing fourth behind Italy's Stefano Zanini (Saeco Macchine Per Cafe), Mark McCormack (Saturn-Timex) becomes U.S. Professional Champion in the 19th Wachovia USPRO championship in Philadelphia.
- A second book by Lance Armstrong and co-author Sally Jenkins, *Every Second Counts*, is released in October.

- Denis Zanette (Fassa Bortolo) dies of a heart attack on January 10 while visiting his dentist in Pordenone. Zanette won the 18th stage of the 1995 Giro d'Italia. He was 32.
- In June, 23-year-old French racer Fabrice Salanson (Brioches la Boulangere) dies in his sleep.
- Italy's Gilberto Simoni (Saeco) wins the 86th Giro d'Italia.
- During the Giro, World Champion Mario Cipollini (Domina Vacanze-Elitron) wins his 41st and 42nd stages of the event to eclipse the 70-year-old mark of Italian great Alfredo Binda (Legnano) for total stage victories in a grand tour. "I would have been happy just to polish his shoes," 'Super Mario' once said of Binda, whose 41 stage wins had come in just his first eight Giri d'Italia and included victories in the mountains and a time trial. It had taken Cipollini, whose best overall finish was 89th in 1997, 13 trips to the Giro to rack up his 42 sprint wins. Binda had five overall victories in the race.
- Belgian great Rik Van Steenbergen dies on May 15, 2003. A professional from 1943 to 1966, he won 270 road races, 715 track events and 3 world professional road championships. Van Steenbergen was 78.
- Tyler Hamilton leaves the CSC team when he agrees to a two-year, $2.5-million deal to lead the Swiss Phonak squad.
- US Postal's 37-year-old Viatcheslav Ekimov (Russia) wins the six-stage Tour of the Netherlands.
- Cannondale Bicycle Corporation of Bethel, Conn., emerges from bankruptcy protection and is bought by Pegasus Capitol of Greenwich, Conn.
- Brunswick Corporation of Lake Forest, Ill., agrees to pay $1 million to settle claims connected with 31 serious incidents caused by defective forks on its Mongoose and Roadmaster bicycles. The company recalls more than 100,000 bicycles.
- Spain's Joane Somarriba wins her third Grande Boucle in four years.
- Italy's Paolo Bettini (Quick Step-Davitamon) wins the World Cup.
- Germany's Steffen Wesemann wins the Peace Race.
- Colorado's Jonas Carney wins the Kugler-Anderson Memorial Tour of Somerville.
- Pennsylvania's Sarah Uhl wins the Mildred Kugler Women's Open.
- Spain's Egoi Martinez (Euskaltel-Euskadi) wins the 41st Tour de l'Avenir.
- The Netherlands' Leontien Zijlaard-Van Moorsel increases the women's hour record to 46.065 kilometers (28.625 miles) in Mexico City.
- US Postal's Roberto Heras wins the 58th Vuelta a España, taking the lead from ONCE-Eroski's Isidro Nozal in the event's penultimate stage, a mountain time trial. With Heras' victory and Lance Armstrong's Tour win, US Postal becomes the first team since the '83 Renault-Elf squad (when Bernard Hinault won the Giro and Laurent Fignon won the Tour) to win two grand tours in the same year with different riders.
- Italy's Alessandro Petacchi (Fassa Bortolo) wins five stages of the Vuelta to become the first rider to win four or more stages in each grand tour in the same year.

- The world championship road and time trial events are held in Hamilton, Ontario. Spain's Igor Astarloa wins the 260-kilometer (162-mile) elite men's road race, which is held on a course designed by former Canadian great Steve Bauer, while Great Britain's David Millar takes the time trial, finishing 1:25 ahead of Australia's Michael Rogers. Millar would later be disqualified for a doping violation and the time trial title would be awarded to Rogers on September 8, 2004, 21 days before the 2004 world championships in Verona, Italy.

In the Tour de France:

- Prior to being stripped of his Tour de France victories, Lance Armstrong becomes the fifth rider to win the Tour de France five times, and only the second besides Miguel Indurain to win the race five consecutive times.
- The race's 13th stage marks Lance Armstrong's 52nd day in the leader's yellow jersey, moving him ahead of Jacques Anquetil and behind Eddy Merckx (96), Bernard Hinault (78) and Miguel Indurain (60). By the end of the 2003 Tour de France, Lance Armstrong had worn the *maillot jaune* for a total of 59 days.
- Armstrong's average speed for the three-week race is a record 40.94 km/h (25.44 mph).
- US Postal is the first American squad to prevail in the team time trial.
- The Tour de France celebrates its centenary by having the race's route pass through all six of the event's original stage cities. The Tour's centenary is also marked by a new logo, the publication of books, the issuance of a medal by Monnaie de Paris, a commemorative stamp from La Poste, the release of documentary films, and various "expositions."
- Along the route, the race pays tribute to the Tour's founding fathers and great riders: Henri Desgrange, Geo Lefèvre, Jacques Goddet, Fausto Coppi, and Louison Bobet.
- The initials of Tour founder Henri Desgrange return to the leader's yellow jersey for the first time since 1983. This time, they're located on the *maillot jaune*'s shoulders.
- During the race's tenth stage, the main pack is delayed for more than a minute by supporters of dissident farmer José Bové.
- The 90th Tour de France marks its first Paris start since the 50th anniversary event in 1963 as well as the first ever prologue in the City of Light.
- A special, "fine-gilt" centennial trophy by sculptor Milcko Stack is awarded to the overall winner with silver-plated replicas being awarded to the winners of the different Tour classifications.
- The organizers introduce a special *Centenaire* classification, the winner of which will be the rider with the best classification at each of the original Tour's six stage finishes. Riders receive €1,903 ($2,112) for a win in each of the six original stage cities, with the classification's overall winner—Australia's Stuart O'Grady (Credit Agricole)—receiving a prize of €100,000 ($112,000).
- Following the conclusion of the race, Tour organizers host a 30-kilometer ride through Paris with up to 10,000 participants, all of whom will receive a free "*La Randonée du Centenaire*" jersey. A centenary parade is also held in Paris.
- France's Richard Virenque wins his sixth climber's jersey in ten years, tying

him with Spain's Federico Bahamontes and Belgium's Lucien Van Impe.

- For the first time, the team time trial begins from a start ramp, which was borrowed from the organizers of the Vuelta.
- Despite riding the final 19 stages with a broken collarbone, American Tyler Hamilton (Team CSC) wins the mountainous 16th stage and finishes fourth overall.
- While the Tour's 14th stage is underway on July 20, Ag2r Prevoyance's Lauri Aus is killed in a training accident in his native Estonia. The race holds a moment of silence for him prior to the start of the 15th stage. Aus competed in the Tour de France in 1997, when he won the Tour du Limousin, and again in 2000 when he was Estonia's national champion in both the road race and the time trial. Lauri Aus was thirty-three.
- The 18th stage to St.-Maixent-L'Ecole, which was won by Spain's Pablo Lastras, is the Tour's second-fastest road stage at 49.938 km/h (31.031 mph).
- The 19th stage time trial to Nantes becomes the Tour's second-fastest long (non-prologue) time trial with winner David Millar of Scotland covering the 49-kilometer parcours in 54:05, for an average speed of 54.348 km/h (33.771 mph).
- Victor Hugo Peña (US Postal) becomes the first Colombian rider to wear the yellow jersey.
- Alexandre Vinokourov (Telekom) becomes the first Kazakh rider to finish on the podium.
- During the race, an IMAX film documentary about how a rider handles the stress of competing in the Tour de France is filmed. The subject of the movie is Tyler Hamilton.
- A record seven Australian riders take part in the race.
- 1950 Tour winner Ferdi Kübler of Switzerland celebrates a birthday on July 24, during the race's 17th stage. At 84 Kübler is the oldest surviving Tour de France winner.
- German-based director Pepe Danquart films *Hell on Wheels* (*Hollentour*, in German) at the Tour de France. The 123-minute documentary focuses on Team Telekom in general, and its riders Erik Zabel and Rolf Aldag in particular. In 1993, Danquart won an Academy Award for his live action short film, *Black Rider* (*Schwarzfahrer*).

2004 • Marco Pantani, who in 1998 became the seventh rider (and second Italian after Fausto Coppi) to win the Giro and the Tour in the same year, dies of "heart problems" (a probable overdose) on February 14. He was 34.
- Two-time world champion Alberic "Briek" Schotte dies in Flanders at the age of 84. During his professional cycling career, which ran from 1940 to 1959, Schotte finished second to Gino Bartali in the 1948 Tour de France and won the world road championship in 1948 and 1950.
- Lance Armstrong (US Postal-Berry Floor) wins the second annual Dodge Tour de Georgia. On April 22, Armstrong wins two stages of the race, a sprint finish of the third stage in Rome, Ga., and that evening's 18.5-mile (29.8-kilometer) individual time trial.

- On April 23 the United States Postal Service announces that it will be ending its sponsorship of its professional cycling team at the end of the year. The Postal Service had been the team's primary sponsor since 1996.
- In mid June, Discovery Communications announces a three-year, multimillion dollar deal to replace the United States Postal Service as the primary sponsor of Lance Armstrong's team.
- Jan Ullrich's autobiography, *All or Nothing*, is published in June.
- Also in June, La Martinière publishes *L.A. Confidential: les Secrets des Lance Armstrong*, in which authors David Walsh and Pierre Ballester report that former US Postal *soigneur* Emma O'Reilly claimed to have purchased drugs for Armstrong and disposed of syringes for him. Attempts by Armstrong's attorneys to have his denial of the charges printed on the book's dust jacket are rejected by a French judge.
- Tyler Hamilton (Phonak) wins his second consecutive Tour de Romandie.
- Floyd Landis (US Postal) wins the 30th running of the five-stage Tour of Algarve.
- Postal's George Hincapie wins the 28th Three Days of De Panne.
- Within the span of one week (April 18–April 25), 32-year-old Italian Davide Rebellin (Gerolsteiner) wins the 39th Amstel Gold Race in the Netherlands, the 68th Flèche Wallonne, and the 90th Liège–Bastogne–Liège events in Belgium.
- Fred Rodriguez (Acqua & Sapone) finishes fourth in the 20th Wachovia USPRO Championship to become America's national champion for the third time in five years. The race is won by Francisco Ventoso (Prodir-Saunier Duval), a 22 year-old Spaniard.
- Twenty-two-year-old Damiano Cunego (Saeco) wins the 87th Giro d'Italia, becoming the youngest winner of the event since 21-year-old Giuseppe Saronni in 1979. Fassa Bortolo's Alessandro Petacchi sets a postwar mark when he wins nine stages (Alfredo Binda of the Legnano team won 12 stages in the 1927 Giro, while three postwar riders have scored seven Giro stage wins: Roger de Vlaeminck in 1975, Freddy Maertens in 1977 and Saronni in 1980). American Freddy Rodriguez becomes the fifth U.S. rider to win a Giro d'Italia stage when he claims the race's ninth leg.
- The 2004 season marks the final year for the UCI's season-long World Cup, which began in 1989, and will become part of the more comprehensive UCI ProTour in 2005. The current UCI rankings will be replaced by rankings in the ProTour and five continental race calendars. The World Cup replaced the Super Prestige Pernod Trophy competition, which had existed, in one form or another, from 1958 through 1988. The SPPT replaced the Desgrange-Colombo Challenge, which had run from 1948 through 1958, and, unofficially, in 1959.
- Italy's Paolo Bettini (Quick Step-Davitamon) is the final winner of the World Cup.
- The UCI mandates that beginning January 1, helmets meeting European Community impact standards must be used for time trials as well as road stages.
- At the age of 45, France's Jeannie Longo-Ciprelli records her 850th win when she solos to victory in the hilly Trophée des Grimpeurs.

- Lance Armstrong (US Postal), Tyler Hamilton (Phonak), George Hincapie (US Postal), Bobby Julich (CSC) and Jason McCartney (Healthnet-Maxxis) are selected for the U.S. road team at the XXVIIIth Olympiad in Athens. Rabobank's Levi Leipheimer later replaces Armstrong, who declines the invitation. Hamilton and Julich are selected to compete in the individual time trial.
- Shimano introduces a 10-speed Dura-Ace gruppo which includes a crank with an integrated HollowTech2 bottom bracket spindle and external bearings.
- Italy's Paolo Bettini wins the 224.4-kilometer (139.4-mile) Olympic road race in 5:41:44, while American Tyler Hamilton wins the 48-kilometer (30-mile) individual time trial in a time of 57:31. Hamilton's result will be called into question after a test indicates he may have received an illegal blood transfusion. He's eventually allowed to keep the gold medal.
- Belgium's Axel Merckx betters his famous father by winning an Olympic medal—a bronze in the road race. Eddy Merckx crashed on the last lap of the road race in the 1964 Tokyo Olympics.
- Spain's Roberto Heras (Liberty Seguros) wins the 59th Vuelta a España, it's his third win in the event. Tyler Hamilton (Phonak) wins a time trial stage of the race, making him the first American to win a stage in all three major tours—until he's disqualified for homologous blood doping. US Postal's Floyd Landis becomes the first American rider to wear the race's gold leader's jersey, while his countryman and teammate David Zabriskie wins a road stage.
- Spain's Oscar Freire wins the 2004 world elite men's road race in Verona, Italy, covering the 265.5-kilometer (165-mile) course in 6:57:15. Australia's Michael Rogers wins the 46.75-kilometer (29-mile) individual time trial in 57:30 to defend the title he inherited three weeks earlier following the doping disqualification of 2003 winner David Millar (GBR).
- Italy's Michele Scarponi wins the Peace Race.
- Victor Repinski of Leicester, Mass., wins the Kugler-Anderson Memorial Tour of Somerville.
- Oregon's Melissa Sanbom wins the Mildred Kugler Women's Open.
- The women's Grande Boucle race is not held.
- France's Sylvain Calzati (RAGT-Semences) wins the 42nd Tour de l'Avenir.
- In February, 21-year-old Belgian racer Johan Sermon dies in his sleep.
- Dutch rider Gerrie Knetemann dies of a heart attack on November 2. During his professional career, Knetemann won 129 races including the 1978 world road championship and 10 stages of the Tour de France. He was 53.

In the Tour de France:

- Prior to being stripped of his results, Lance Armstrong wins an unprecedented sixth consecutive Tour de France, surpassing five-time winners Jacques Anquetil, Eddy Merckx, Bernard Hinault, and Miguel Indurain (with only Indurain's five victories being consecutive).
- Following his stage win in Villard-de-Lans, Armstrong begins his 61st day in the yellow jersey, surpassing Miguel Indurain. The American now trails only Eddy Merckx (96 days) and Bernard Hinault (75 days). Armstrong would finish the race with 66 days in yellow.

- Armstrong becomes the first rider in Tour history to win four consecutive mountain stages: stage 13 in the Pyrenees and stages 15, 16 and 17 in the Alps. Armstrong also wins an individual time trial and is a member of the team time trial-winning US Postal team.
- The King of the Mountains category features double climbers' points for the final second-category or harder ascent of each stage.
- Richard Virenque (Quick Step-Davitamon) wins a record seventh polka dot jersey.
- The finish of the team time trial marks the first time that American riders (Lance Armstrong, George Hincapie, and Floyd Landis) have held the Tour's top three spots in the general classification.
- The US Postal team wins the team time trial with the Tour's third-fastest t.t.t speed.
- The team time trial features a bonus system and a three-minute maximum time loss provision.
- Daniel Baal, the Tour's deputy director, resigns on January 31. Baal, who'd held the position since October 2001, is replaced by Christian Prudhomme, formerly the chief Tour de France commentator for France 2 Television.
- Skoda replaces Fiat as the official vehicle of the Tour de France. The Czech car company also replaces Nestle Aquarel as sponsor of white jersey.
- The invitation of Comunitat Valenciana-Kelme is retracted amid allegations of doping.
- The Tour salutes France's ever-popular Raymond Poulidor, "The Eternal Second."
- The race holds its first individual time trial up L'Alpe d'Huez, where the event salutes Marco Pantani. Lance Armstrong's winning time for the climbing portion of the stage is within one second of the late Italian's record.
- During the time trial up L'Alpe d'Huez, an unidentified 64-year-old fan from the Paris area dies after he falls 130 feet (40 meters).
- With the finish of the ninth stage in Gueret, the Tour pays its first visit France's La Creuse District.
- The Tour's third stage marks the first time since 1985 that the race has included cobblestone sections.
- American Levi Leipheimer (Rabobank) finishes ninth overall.
- Switzerland's Fabian Cancellara (Fassa Bortolo) rides the third-fastest prologue in Tour history. The two fastest prologues were ridden by Britain's Chris Boardman in 1994 and 1998.
- Cancellara (born March 18, 1981) becomes the first rider born in the 1980s to win a stage in the Tour de France.
- By earning a 12-second bonus for finishing second in the second stage, Norway's Thor Hushovd becomes the first rider from his country to wear the Tour de France's yellow jersey.
- Postal's George Hincapie competes in his ninth consecutive Tour de France, tying the mark set by Frankie Andreu in 2000 for the longest streak by an American.
- Lance Armstrong takes part in his tenth Tour de France ('93-'96 and '99-'04),

setting the mark for the most Tour appearances by an American rider.

• 2004 marks the final year for the American team's US Postal Service sponsorship. In 2011, documents obtained by ESPN through a Freedom of Information request would reveal that its final four years of sponsoring the team had cost the Postal Service $31.9 million.

2005 • American Bobby Julich wins the 63rd running of Paris–Nice. The race is the very first event of the new UCI Pro Tour.

• Julich also wins the Critérium International. He had also won the race in 1998 after France's Christophe Moreau (Festina-Lotus) was disqualified for a doping violation.

• American Tom Danielson (Team Discovery Channel) wins the third Dodge Tour de Georgia.

• Italy's Paolo Savoldelli (Team Discovery Channel) wins the 88th Giro d'Italia, finishing 28 seconds ahead of Lampre-Caffita's Gilberto Simoni. Australian Brett Lancaster (Panaria) wins the Giro's short prologue and his countryman Robbie McEwen wins an early stage and also spends a day in the race leader's pink jersey. American David Zabriskie (Team CSC) wins a time trial stage of the event while Team Discovery Channel is the first American team to take part in the race since the 1989 7-Eleven-Wamash squad. Lance Armstrong's later Tour de France victory makes Team Discovery the first squad since the 1983 Renault-Elf team to win the Giro and the Tour with two different riders. In 2003 US Postal's Armstrong and Heras claimed respective victories in the Tour and Vuelta.

• Italy's super sprinter Mario Cipollini retires prior to the Tour of Italy. The Lion King bows out by riding a ceremonial prologue wearing a pink skinsuit which lists his 42 Giro stage victories, a record for a rider in a grand tour.

• The Ukraine's Yaroslav Popovych (Team Discovery Channel) wins Tour of Catalonia.

• Chris Wherry (Health Net-Maxxis) wins the Wachovia USPRO Championship race in Philadelphia. The organizers announce that the race will include only American riders in 2006 and may not be held in Philadelphia.

• George Hincapie (Team Discovery Channel) wins the prologue of the 57th Critérium du Dauphiné Libéré. The American covers the 7.9-kilometer (4.9-mile) course in 9:55 for an average speed of 47.798 km/h (29.702 mph).

• Tier I Trade Teams become known as ProTour teams, Tier II Trade Teams become Professional Continental teams, and Tier III Trade Teams become Continental teams.

• The International Olympic Committee announces that BMX racing will replace the men's kilometer and women's 500 meter track events at the 2008 Beijing Olympic Games.

• The UCI institutes the 3-kilometer mercy rule for flat races and stages following a crash in the 2004 Tour de France.

• On July 19, 29-year-old Czech rider Ondrej Sosenka (Aqua & Sapone) rides 49.700 kilometers (30.884 miles) on a Moscow velodrome, bettering Chris

Boardman's five-year-old hour record by 259 meters (283 yards). Sosenka won the 2002 Peace Race after his teammate Piotr Przydzial was disqualified.

- On August 23, the same day he signed a lifetime personal services contract with Trek bicycles, Lance Armstrong again became the target of the French press. *L'Équipe* ran a four-page article under the headline "The Armstrong Lie," saying that six of the American's urine samples taken during his first Tour victory in 1999 had tested positive for traces of EPO. Tour director Jean-Marie Leblanc said, "...we were all fooled" by Armstrong. The Texan blasted back that it was "preposterous" that he'd "fooled" anyone, and reiterated, "I've never taken performance-enhancing drugs." He called the story a "witch hunt" and said that the paper was engaging in "tabloid journalism" since the findings were leaked to the press and couldn't be replicated. The bad press prompts the Texan to say that he was considering a return to competition. "It was fairly serious, but I didn't realize how much play it would get," Armstrong said of his plan to possibly unretire. "My fault. In hindsight I shouldn't have done it."
- While still awaiting the outcome of the appeal of his doping suspension, Tyler Hamilton wins the Volkswagen Mt. Washington Hillclimb, an annual, unsanctioned race held at Pinkham Notch, N.H. His winning time for the climb is 51:11, less than two minutes off the race record set in 2002 by Tom Danielson. It is Hamilton's first race in 11 months.
- Nordisk Film releases Thomas Gislason's *Overcoming*, a 105-minute documentary about the 2004 season of Bjarne Riis and his Team CSC.
- America's Bobby Julich (Team CSC) wins the first Benelux Tour, beating Erik Dekker by 21 seconds.
- America's Levi Leipheimer (Gerolsteiner) wins the 9-stage Tour of Germany, beating Jan Ullrich by 31 seconds.
- Ireland's Pat McQuaid succeeds Hein Verbruggen as president of the UCI.
- Spain's Roberto Heras (Liberty Seguros) wins the 60th Vuelta a España, collecting his fourth victory in his country's national tour. Heras is later stripped of the victory and fired by his team after testing positive for EPO. The Vuelta victory is then awarded to Russia's Denis Menchov (Rabobank), making him the second rider after Henri Cornet in the 1904 Tour de France to retroactively be awarded the victory in a grand tour.
- Spanish rider Ruben Plaza (Comunitat Valenciana) covers the Vuelta's supposed 38.9-kilometer (24.2-mile) stage 20 time trial in 41:31, which would give him an average speed of 56.218 km/h (34.93 mph) if the course is measured correctly. Results of the stage are suspect because Plaza eclipses the recent mark set by America's David Zabriskie in the flat, 19-kilometer opening stage of the Tour de France—by 1.542 km/h. Nine other riders also better Zabriskie's mark.
- Belgium's Tom Boonen wins the 273-kilometer (170-mile) elite men's road race at the 2005 world championships in Madrid, Spain. Boonen, who started his season with a victory in Paris–Roubaix, is the 25th Belgian to win the world professional road title. Australia's Michael Rogers wins the elite men's time

trial, covering the 44.1-kilometer (27.4-mile) course in 53:34. Roger's victory makes him the first professional rider to win three consecutive world time trial championships.

- Italy's Danilo Di Luca (Liquigas) wins the inaugural UCI ProTour championship.
- Idaho's Kyle Wamsley wins the Kugler-Anderson Memorial Tour of Somerville.
- Laura Van Gilder (Quark) wins the Mildred Kugler Women's Open.
- Switzerland's Priska Doppman wins the Grande Boucle.
- Denmark's Lars-Ytting Bak (Team CSC) wins the 43rd Tour de l'Avenir.
- Charly Gaul dies of a pulmonary embolism on December 6, ten days after a fall in his Itzig, Luxembourg home. A climber, who was known as the Angel of the Mountains, Gaul improved his time trial riding to the point where he won the Tour de France in 1958 and the Giro d'Italia in 1956 and 1959. He was 72.
- Lance Armstrong is voted the Associated Press Male Athlete of the Year for the fourth consecutive year. He's the only athlete to win the award four times since it was first given in 1931.

In the Tour de France:

- Lance Armstrong competes in his final race as a professional (until his comeback in 2008). Prior to being stripped of his results, Armstrong wins his record seventh consecutive Tour de France and wears the leader's yellow jersey for a total of 83 days during his career, placing him between Eddy Merckx (96 days) and Bernard Hinault (78 days). Armstrong wins the race's final time trial to bring his total number of Tour de France stage wins to 25, and is the oldest winner of the Tour de France since Gino Bartali, who won the 1948 event a week after his thirty-fourth birthday.

    "Winning was my biggest desire," the American said. "This year there was no question of making history. I just wanted people to remember me as someone who bowed out at the summit."

- American David Zabriskie (Team CSC) sets a new average speed mark for a non-prologue Tour stage. Zabriskie's speed of 54.68 km/h (33.98 mph) eclipses the mark of fellow American Greg LeMond, who averaged 54.54 km/h (33.89 mph) in the 1989 race's final stage.
- Zabriskie becomes only the third American rider after Greg LeMond and Lance Armstrong to wear the Tour's yellow leader's jersey.
- Zabriskie's Tour stage win makes him the first American to win a stage in each of the three grand tours.
- Race founder Henri Desgrange's initials move from the shoulders of the yellow jersey to its right breast.
- A record three Americans (Zabriskie, Hincapie, and Armstrong) win individual stages in the race.
- Besides Armstrong, four other Americans finish in the top 20: Levi Leipheimer (Gerolsteiner) 6th, Floyd Landis (Phonak) 9th, George Hincapie (Discovery Channel) 14th, and Bobby Julich (Team CSC) 17th.
- Scott becomes the tenth U.S.-based manufacturer (after Murray, Huffy/Serot-

ta, Clark-Kent, Merlin, Trek, Cannondale, GT, Litespeed, and Carbonframes) to have its bikes used in the Tour when the company's bikes are ridden by the Saunier Duval-Prodir team.

- Jean-Marie Leblanc, who directed the race for 17 years, announces that he'll retire following the 2006 event. Leblanc plans to follow the '06 Tour which will be run by assistant director Christian Prudhomme. Prudhomme "will take the helm" on his own in 2007.
- The route of the race's second stage between Challans and Les Essarts contains a record 45 roundabouts.
- With the cooperation of Konica-Minolta, the riders wear special *dossards* during the third stage to honor the 20th anniversary of *Reporters Sans Frontières*. Also, a book about the impact of journalism on the Tour de France is published to mark the occasion.
- Brandt begins sponsoring the combativity classification.
- Team Discovery Channel (and 14 other teams) breaks the team time trial record of 54.930 km/h (34.14 mph) set ten years earlier by Gewiss-Ballan.
- The route of the race takes the riders up the 1,171-meter (3,841-foot) Ballon d'Alsace, the very first mountain the Tour's racers tackled 100 years earlier.
- The race is shortened by 14 kilometers (8.7 miles) when the official start of the race's tenth stage is moved from Grenoble to Brignoud in order to allow for a demonstration by farmers protesting wolf attacks on their livestock.
- Many of the racers ride the Tour's 15th stage wearing white armbands to honor Fabio Casartelli, who died in a crash on the Col du Portet d'Aspet ten years earlier.
- America's George Hincapie (Team Discovery Channel) rides his tenth consecutive Tour de France while Lance Armstrong takes part in his eleventh Tour in 13 years.
- Hincapie is also the first Armstrong teammate to win an individual Tour stage during the Boss's seven-year reign. Two stages later, Paolo Savoldelli becomes the second Armstrong teammate to win a stage.
- Because of slippery conditions on the Champs-Élysées, the race's official time is taken the first time the riders cross the finish line in Paris. The remainder of the final leg's eight laps are ridden to determine a stage winner.
- Thor Hushovd (Credit Agricole) is the first Norwegian rider to win the green jersey.
- After both Jan Ullrich and Lance Armstrong are stripped of their results, T-Mobile's Alexandre Vinokourov (KAZ) becomes the winner of stage 20, a 55.5-kilometer (34.5-mile) individual time trial, in a time of 1:13:02.

2006 • A May doping investigation centering around Dr. Eufemiano Fuentes in Madrid results in the release of a lengthy list of suspected riders which includes the names of Jan Ullrich, Ivan Basso, Alberto Contador, Joseba Beloki, the recently-retired Francisco Mancebo and the suspended Tyler Hamilton. Contador would be cleared a week later.

- On July 21, T-Mobile announces that it is terminating Jan Ullrich's contract.

Sources at the team say they believed the German rider is guilty of associating with the Spanish doping ring and said he wouldn't be welcomed back even if proven innocent. Contributing to Ullrich's sacking are the facts that, under German law he could be suspended for only three weeks, and that he'd refused to submit to the team's request to undergo DNA testing. Four days later the unemployed rider vows to return to the Tour de France and win it. "I've always said that I'll finish my career with a victory in the Tour," Ullrich stated. "It couldn't happen this year and that's why I'll have to wait for another year. Jan Ullrich doesn't quit." Also canned that day is Ullrich's teammate Oscar Sevilla. Rudy Pevenage, the German's trainer and confidant at T-Mobile, had been released earlier in the month. The housecleaning at T-Mobile would continue with the departures of Ullrich's friends Andreas Klöden, Matthias Kessler and Steffen Wesemann and the Kaiser's support riders Serguei Gontchar and Eddy Mazzoleni.

- In mid-September, while Ullrich is away on his honeymoon, his home in Switzerland is raided by German authorities looking for evidence that will connect the former Tour winner to *Operación Puerto*. Investigators also search the headquarters of his former T-Mobile team in Bonn.
- On July 25, Levi Leipheimer announces that he'll leave Gerolsteiner at the end of the year and ride for Discovery Channel in 2007. "...Discovery made me an offer I could not refuse," said Leipheimer, who'd finished the Tour de France in 13th place, 19:22 back.
- On June 27, the Court of Arbitration for Sport rules that Tyler Hamilton can keep gold medal he received for the time trial in the 2004 Olympics.
- Ivan Basso (Team CSC) wins the 89th Giro d'Italia. He is later suspended by his team and does not start the Tour de France.
- Kazakhstan's Alexandre Vinokourov (Astana) wins the 61st Vuelta a España. America's Tom Danielson (Discovery Channel) wins the race's 17th stage.
- America's Floyd Landis (Phonak-iShares) has a banner spring, amassing victories in the inaugural Amgen Tour of California, the 64th Paris–Nice and the fourth Ford Tour de Georgia.
- On September 27, Floyd Landis has his hip replaced using the Smith & Nephew Birmingham Hip Resurfacing System.
- American Levi Leipheimer (Gerolsteiner) wins the 58th Critérium du Dauphiné Libéré by 1:48 over Christophe Moreau (Ag2r). Fellow American Dave Zabriskie wins the prologue and the third stage, which is also a time trial.
- Discovery Channel's Tom Danielson (USA) wins the seven-stage Tour of Austria.
- The United States' Christian Vande Velde (Team CSC) wins the Tour of Luxembourg.
- The USPRO road championship is moved from Philadelphia to Greenville, S.C. The race is also shifted from June to September and open only to American professionals. The race is won by George Hincapie.
- American Saul Raisin lapses into a coma following a crash in the first stage of the Circuit de la Sarthe. Eventually he returns to the United States to begin a lengthy recovery.

- Shimano announces in February that nine ProTour riders have been testing an electric version of its flagship Dura-Ace gruppo. If the electric version is put into production it would not be available until at least 2008 and would not replace the cable-actuated version.
- SRAM introduces a pair of complete 10-speed road gruppos called Force and the lower-priced Rival. Rival had been the name of a Sachs-Huret rear derailleur manufactured in the mid to late 1980s. Sachs had bought Huret in the '80s and SRAM bought Sachs in late 1997.
- "Karl T. Ulrich, a professor at the Wharton School of the University of Pennsylvania, has put forth a provocative theory. Traveling by bicycle, he argued in a recent paper, may cause more environmental harm than driving around in pollution-spewing, fossil-fuel-swallowing cars and sport utility vehicles. How can this be? Bicyclists are healthier, he wrote, so they live longer. Over their lifetimes, they consume more energy than they save."[1]
- In late May, Dutch investigator Emile Vrijman releases a UCI-initiated report clearing Lance Armstrong of earlier *L'Équipe* accusations that the American had been found to have used doping products during his first Tour de France victory in 1999. The report does nothing to settle the matter; World Anti-Doping Agency president Dick Pound quickly fires back saying that Vrijman's report is "so lacking in professionalism and objectivity that it borders on farcical."
- In February Armstrong wins an out-of-court victory over SCA Promotions for the $5 million plus interest he's owed for winning his sixth straight Tour de France in 2004. SCA had contended that it didn't have to pay since there were several "unresolved doping allegations." Armstrong is paid because the contract contains no clause regarding doping.
- Italy's Paolo Bettini wins the 265.9-kilometer (165.2-mile) elite men's road race in Salzburg, Austria. Switzerland's Fabian Cancellara wins the 50.83-kilometer (31.59-mile) individual time trial in 1:00:11.75.
- America's Kristin Armstrong wins the women's time trial title at the worlds.
- Spain's Alejandro Valverde (Caisse d'Espargne-Illes Ballears) wins the second annual UCI ProTour championship.
- Juan Haedo wins the Kugler-Anderson Memorial Tour of Somerville.
- Georgia's Tina Pic wins the Mildred Kugler Women's Open.
- Great Britain's Nicole Cook wins the Grande Boucle.
- Spain's Moises Duenas Nevado (Agritubel) wins the 44th Tour de l'Avenir.
- On July 3, former cycling trainer Freddy Sergant is sentenced to four years in prison for his role in a Belgian doping network. Prosecutors claimed that Sergant was a key figure in a ring that sold more than 2,000 doses of "Belgian cocktail"—a mixture of amphetamines, cocaine and heroin—in France and Belgium between 2002 and 2005. Former French rider Laurent Roux admits to the court in June that he had regularly used banned doping products—including the so-called *"Pot Belge"*—throughout his 10-year career, which ended in 2003. In July Roux is sentenced to 30 months in prison with 20 months suspended. He plans to appeal, saying "I have the impression that, despite what just happened in the Tour de France, that I'm the [scapegoat] for a totally corrupt system."

- The Vuelta loses its new main sponsor, which pulled out following the disqualification of the race's 2005 winner Roberto Heras and in the wake of the Tour's Landis affair.

In the Tour de France:
- Floyd Landis becomes the second Tour de France winner (after Maurice Garin in 1904) to be stripped of his victory and the first to lose it because of doping. Landis' disqualification makes Oscar Pereiro the winner of the 2006 Tour de France, and the second rider after Henri Cornet in 1904 to be awarded the Tour victory retroactively.
- Pereiro (Caisse D'Epargne-Illes Balears) becomes the sixth rider to win the Tour de France without winning one of its stages.
- The day before the race starts, a doping investigation in Spain causes several top riders to be suspended from their teams. Comunitat Valenciana's invitation to the race is withdrawn for the second time in three years. Failing to make the six-rider minimum, the Astana-Würth squad (Liberty Seguros had canceled its sponsorship) of Tour hopeful Alexander Vinokourov does not start the race after five of his teammates are suspended. Minus Ullrich and Sevilla, T-Mobile starts with seven riders. Without Ivan Basso and Francisco Mancebo, Team CSC and Ag2r-Prevoyance start with eight riders each. Of the originally-scheduled 22 teams and 198 riders, only 20 teams and 176 riders start the race. None of the top five riders from the previous Tour de France start the event.
- Serguëi Gontchar wins the first individual time trial to become the first Ukrainian rider to wear the yellow jersey.
- Jean-Marie Leblanc oversees his last Tour as the race's director. Beginning in 2007, the duties will fall to Christian Prudhomme.
- Riders on the leading team wear numbers on a yellow background. The new *dossards* are sponsored by Inter Sport.
- French bank Le Crédit Lyonnais unveils its new "LCL" logo in conjunction with its 25th year as sponsor of the Tour de France's yellow jersey.
- The race's fourth stage marks the first time in the Tour's history that reigning world champions hold the top two spots in the event's General Classification; Belgian race leader Tom Boonen (Quick Step-Innergetic) is the current world road champion while Australian world time trial champion Michael Rogers (T-Mobile) holds down the second spot, one second back. Boonen is also the first reigning world champion to lead the Tour since Greg LeMond in 1990.
- The Tour's 16th stage marks the first time that a leg of the race has finished at La Toussuire, a ski station in the Alps to which the ascent is longer than that of L'Alpe d'Huez.
- George Hincapie (Discovery) starts his 11th consecutive Tour de France. His 10th time finishing the race is also a record for an American rider.
- Hincapie becomes the fourth American rider to wear the Tour de France's yellow jersey.
- Floyd Landis (Phonak-iShares) becomes the fifth American rider to wear the yellow jersey.

- The 2006 Tour de France has a record 10 lead changes among seven riders.
- Before the start of the 11th stage, Tour directors Jean-Marie Leblanc and Christian Prudhomme present American cycling writer Sam Abt with the Tour's *Plateau d'Argent* silver plate in recognition of his covering the race for 30 consecutive years. Abt writes for the *Herald-Tribune*.
- In recognition of his 15th and final Tour, 40-year-old Viatcheslav Ekimov is given the honor of leading the first of the race's final eight laps on the *Avenue des Champs Élysées*. The Russian had competed in every Tour de France since 1990 except the 1999 and 2005 editions on the following teams: Panasonic-Sportlife, Novemail-Histor, Wordperfect, Novell, Rabobank and US Postal Service/Discovery Channel. Ekimov's 15-Tour mark leaves him one behind 1980 Tour winner Joop Zoetemelk (1970–1973 and 1975–1986) and ties him with Guy Nulens (1980–1994, did not finish in 1980 and 1983), and 1976 Tour winner Lucien Van Impe (1969–1981, 1983 and 1985).
- Because of Jan Ullrich's suspension for suspicion of doping, there are no former winners in the race.
- The night before the Tour's final time trial, ABC News selects Floyd Landis as its "Person of the Week," asking the rhetorical question, "Lance who?"
- Pereiro's 32-second margin of victory over Andreas Klöden is the race's second smallest until the following year when Alberto Contador defeats Cadel Evans by 23 seconds.
- Philippe Amaury, the French publishing tycoon who owns Tour de France organizer ASO, dies of cancer on May 23 at the age of 66. Amaury also owned Éditions Philippe Amaury, which publishes *L'Équipe, Le Parisien, Aujourd'hui en France, L'Echo Républicain, France Football,* and *Vélo* magazine. After his passing, his affairs are handled by his widow, Marie-Odile Amaury and son, Jean-Etienne.

2007 • On August 10, 2007, Tailwind Sports announces that Team Discovery Channel will cease operations after the 2007 season. "We couldn't in good conscience ask someone to spend the sort of money that it would require to sponsor the team in the current situation," said Tailwind GM Bill Stapleton. "It's not an environment conducive in our opinion to make an investment."
- American Levi Leipheimer (Discovery Channel) wins the 2nd Amgen Tour of California by 0:21 over Germany's Jens Voigt (Team CSC).
- Slovenia's Janez Brajkovic (Discovery Channel) wins the fifth Tour de Georgia, completing the 7-stage, 658-mile (1,059-kilometer) race 12 seconds ahead of America's Christian Vande Velde (Team CSC).
- Italy's Danilo DiLuca (Liquigas) wins the 90th Giro d'Italia by 1:55 over Luxembourg's Andy Schleck (CSC).
- Levi Leipheimer beats Discovery teammate George Hincapie by 1:11 to win the USA Cycling professional road championship in Greenville, S.C. Leipheimer completes the 177-kilometer (110-mile) course in 4:22:19. David Zabriskie covers the 30-kilometer (18.6-mile) time trial course in 39:34 to beat Danny Pate (Slipstream-Chipotle) by one second.
- Paolo Bettini of Italy repeats as world champion by winning the 267.4-kilome-

ter (166.2-mile) elite men's road race in Stuttgart, Germany. Fabian Cancellara (SUI) also repeats, winning the 44.9-kilometer (27.9-mile) individual time trial in 55:41.

- Belgium's Stijn Vandenbergh (unibet.com) wins the five-day Tour of Ireland, which returns after a 15-year absence.
- Russia's Denis Menchov (Rabobank) wins the 62nd Vuelta a España by 3:31 over Spain's Carlos Sastre (CSC).
- Jason McCarthy (USA) wins stage 14 of the Vuelta. It's the final grand tour stage win for the American Discovery Channel team.
- George Hincapie (USA) caps Discovery's run with a victory in the inaugural Tour of Missouri. His win in the week-long, UCI 2.1 stage race is the team's last overall race win.
- Dutch amateur Bauke Mollema wins the 45th Tour de l'Avenir. It is the first amateur version of the race (for national under-23 teams) to be held since 1980.
- Australia's Stuart O'Grady (CSC) becomes the first non-European winner of Paris–Roubaix.
- Australia's Cadel Evans (Predictor-Lotto) wins the third annual UCI ProTour championship.
- Joseph "Jef" Planckaert dies on May 22 at the age of 73. Planckaert had won Het Volk in 1958 and finished second to Jacques Anquetil in the 1962 Tour de France. He had also finished fifth in the 1960 Tour and won stage six of the 1961 race.
- France's Jean Stablinsky dies following a long illness. Born in Poland in 1932 as Edward Stablewski, "Stab" became a French citizen in 1948, and won the French national championship four times between 1960 and 1964 (he finished second to Raymond Poulidor in 1962). Stablinsky won the first televised world road championship—the 1962 event in Salo, Italy—by finishing on a spectator's bike after puncturing. He rode as a *domestique* for Jacques Anquetil for many years until the two had a falling out and then switched to the Mercier team of Anquetil's rival Poulidor, for his final season in 1968.
- Great Britain's Nicole Cooke repeats as winner of the Grande Boucle. Her compatriot Emma Pooley is third.
- Canada's Hilton Clarke wins the Kugler-Anderson Memorial Tour of Somerville.
- Philadelphia's Theresa Cliff-Ryan wins the Mildred Kugler Women's Open.
- Simon Spotlight Entertainment publishes *Positively False: The Real Story of How I Won the Tour de France*, by Floyd Landis with Loren Mooney.
- Ballantine Books publishes David Walsh's *From Lance to Landis: Inside the American Doping Controversy at the Tour de France*.
- Gates Corporation of Denver begins selling its CenterTrack belt system for commuter and urban bicycles. The polyurethane drive belts are reinforced with carbon fiber.
- American Continental team BMC registers the first team time trial victory in Europe by an all-American squad when it wins stage 2B of the UCI's 2.2 Giro del Friuli Venezia Giulia.

In the Tour de France:

- Spain's Alberto Contador (Discovery Channel) wins the 94th Tour de France, defeating Australia's Cadel Evans (Predictor-Lotto) by 23 seconds.
- Former Tour director Félix Levitan dies at the age of 95. Levitan had joined the race as Jacques Goddet's deputy in 1947 when Émilion Amaury's *Parisien Libéré*, for which Levitan worked, put on the race with newly-formed *L'Équipe*. Eventually Levitan rose to the position of co-organizer, but in 1987 he was fired by Amaury's son Philippe, who died of cancer in 2006, for reportedly supporting the ill-fated Tour of America with Tour de France funds—a charge Levitan denied. Years later, the Tour's owners tersely said that the Levitan matter had been settled, and he even started visiting the race as a guest of the organizers beginning in 1998.
- In May 2007, '96 Tour winner Bjarne Riis admits taking EPO for the five years he was a member of Team Telekom, including the year he won the Tour. Riis was soon stripped of his Tour de France victory but no new winner was named since many other top finishers from that year either later admitted doping or were suspected of it. Riis, director of Team CSC (which would become Saxo Bank in 2009), is banned from the 2007 Tour de France. He would be reinstated as the winner of the 1996 event one day before the start of the 2008 Tour de France.
- Milram's Erik Zabel admits to using EPO in the 1996 Tour de France (when he was with Telekom), and is stripped of that year's green jersey. He is allowed to compete in the 2007 Tour de France.
- All the riders in the race sign the UCI's one-page anti-doping pledge, which includes a two-year ban from racing and a fine of one year's salary for a positive result among its conditions.
- The race starts in London on the second anniversary of the terrorist bombings of the city's mass transit system.
- At the start of the race, the French newspaper *L'Équipe* runs its first ever English headline, "God Save le Tour."
- Before the race starts (and even by its finish), the matter of who actually won the 2006 Tour de France remains undecided pending Floyd Landis' appeal to the Court of Arbitration for Sport. Spain's Oscar Pereiro, who finished second in the '06 event, starts the 2007 Tour wearing number 11.
- For the second consecutive year, there are (technically) no former winners in the race. Floyd Landis wouldn't be stripped of his 2006 victory until September 20, 2007, and Oscar Pereiro wouldn't be awarded the victory until October 15.
- After a decade of the French media claiming that there are "two speeds" in cycle racing (clean French teams and everyone else), *L'Équipe* begins printing a general classification of French riders on the same page as the real GC.
- The wild card South African-sponsored, British-registered, Italian-run, Pro Continental Barloworld team is the first "British" Tour squad since ANC-Halfords in 1987.
- David Millar briefly wears the polka-dot jersey early in the race to become the first British rider to lead the climbing competition since Robert Millar won it in 1984.

- At the conclusion of the eighth stage, the race visits Tignes for the first time. During the 15th stage, the riders make their first climb up the recently-opened Col de Bales in the Pyrenees.
- Germany's National television networks ARD and ZDF end their coverage of the race prior to its tenth stage after learning that T-Mobile rider Patrik Sinkewitz had tested positive for elevated testosterone levels a month before the race. A spokesman for the stations told cyclingnews.com that "Our contract stated that we broadcast the Tour as a competition of clean riders, not of people using doping substances." Coverage of the Tour continues on two other German television stations.
- Robbie Hunter is the first South African rider to win a stage (11) in the Tour de France. He's the first rider from the African continent to win a leg of the race since Marcel Molines (Algeria) and Custodio Dos Reis (Morocco) won stages 13 and 14 of the 1950 race.
- By winning his 12th Tour stage, Australia's Robbie McEwen ties Germany's Erik Zabel for the most stage victories by an active rider.
- During the race's second rest day, the results of Alexander Vinokourov's post-time trial doping test come back positive for homologous blood doping. "Vino" pleads his innocence by saying that the abnormalities were caused by his earlier crash. He and his Astana team are asked to leave the race immediately, which they do.
- Several teams are slow to leave the starting line at the beginning of stage 16 to emphasize that they want a clean race.
- Following Michael Rasmussen's victory in stage 16, his Rabobank team pulls him out of the race while in the lead for violating team rules. Rasmussen becomes the first yellow jersey to be pulled from the race by his team because of suspicion of doping.
- Also following stage 16, Italy's Christian Moreni (Cofidis) tests positive for a banned substance. He and his team are expelled from the race.
- The 31 seconds separating first place from third gives the Tour its closest final podium in history.
- Saunier Duval-Prodir rides Scott bicycles equipped with Force components made by the American SRAM company. Team leader Iban Mayo tests the company's prototype Red components.
- Christian Prudhomme, 46, becomes the Tour de France's sole race director following the retirement of Jean-Marie Leblanc, who'd overseen the race since 1989.
- Discovery's George Hincapie extends his record American streak to 12 consecutive Tour starts.
- *Lanterne Rouge* Wim Vansevenant (Predictor-Lotto) is the fifth rider to twice finish last in the race and only the third rider to do it in consecutive Tours. He had finished next to last in 2005.
- Xavier Louy, who directed the Tour de France during 1988's "Delgado Affair," publishes *Sauvons le Tour* (*Save the Tour*), which contains several interesting theories about the impact that drugs and the UCI have had on the

race. One of the theories Louy puts forth in his book is that much of cycling's
drug problem originated with professional soccer since both the Festina Affair (1998) and Operación Puerto (2006) coincided with the start of soccer's
World Cup.

2008 • Floyd Landis loses what is probably his final attempt to reclaim victory in the
2006 Tour de France when a three-member panel at the Court of Arbitration
for Sport votes unanimously against him.

- American Levi Leipheimer (Astana) wins the third Amgen Tour of California.
Rock Racing's Tyler Hamilton, Oscar Sevilla, and Santiago Botero are not al-
lowed to start the race, reportedly because they are still under investigation by
Spanish authorities for *Operacion Puerto*. Forty-one-year-old sprinter Mario
Cipollini briefly ends his three-year retirement to ride for Rock Racing. He
finishes third in the second stage.

- In June Tour de France owner ASO and Tour of California owner AEG (An-
schutz Entertainment Group) announce the formation of a marketing partner-
ship "to develop and initiate comprehensive cross promotional platforms" for
both races.

- Tour de France owner ASO buys a 49 percent interest in Unipublic, the company that owns the Vuelta a España. Ownership of the other 51 percent is
retained by Spain's Grupo Antena 3 media company.

- Astana's Alberto Contador wins the 91st Giro d'Italia after his team is notified
of their acceptance into the race one week before the start. Contador defeats
Italy's Riccardo Riccò (Saunier Duval-Scott) by 1:57 to become the second
Spaniard (after Miguel Indurain) to win the event.

- American SRAM Red components are on the American Trek and Scott bikes
of the Giro's top two finishers.

- The fifth-place finish of Russia's Denis Menchov (Rabobank) gives him a top-
five finish in all three grand tours.

- The victory of Italy's Daniele Bennati (Liquigas) in the third stage gives him at
least one stage win in each of the grand tours.

- Christian Vande Velde (Slipstream-Chipotle, later Garmin-Chipotle) becomes
the second American rider after Andy Hampsten to wear the Giro's pink jersey.

- Stage 16 of the Giro becomes the slowest-ever stage of a grand tour when it
takes Italian winner Franco Pellizotti (Liquigas) 40:26 to complete the 12.9-ki-
lometer (8-mile) mountain time trial up the Plan de Corones (half of it on
gravel), for an average speed of 19.142 km/h (11.895 mph).

- Lance Armstrong completes the Boston Marathon in 2:50:58.

- Shimano buys Pearl Izumi from Nautilus for $70 million.

- Belarus rider Kanstantsin Sivtsov of Team High Road (later called Team Columbia) wins the sixth Tour de Georgia Presented by AT&T.

- Trek drops Greg LeMond's bicycles from its line and sues the three-time Tour
de France winner to end its 13-year licensing agreement with him. Trek president John Burke cites LeMond's recent remarks on doping, his decision to

offer a mass-market accessory line, and his "inconsistent" commitment to the bike line as reasons for the split.

- Eugene A. Sloane, author of *The Complete Book of Bicycling*, dies at 91. In the introduction to the 1980 edition of his book *The All New Complete Book of Bicycling*, he wrote, "People laughed when I sat down at this typewriter a few years ago and predicted gasoline would cost two dollars a gallon. Now I forecast either strict gas rationing or a price of five dollars per gallon." At the time this was written, gasoline was four dollars a gallon.
- Competitor Group, which is owned by New York-based private equity company Falconhead Capitol, purchases *VeloNews* owner Inside Communications.
- On July 8 France's Jeannie Longo-Ciprelli wins the national title in the individual pursuit with a 3:48.896. In June she won the French national time trial and road race titles, the two events in which she'll compete in her seventh Olympic games in August. Longo-Ciprelli will turn 50 in October.
- Shimano-sponsored teams test the new (7900) Dura-Ace components in the Tour de France. They also test an electronic version of the gruppo. Campagnolo-sponsored teams test prototypes of 11-speed Super Record, which the company unveils (along with 11-speed versions of Chorus and Record) for its 75th anniversary. Campagnolo had produced the original Super Record components from 1974 until 1987.
- Shimano unveils the electronic version (7970) of its flagship Dura-Ace gruppo, which uses Di2 (Digital Integrated Intelligence) technology.
- Team High Road (which becomes Team Columbia just before the Tour de France) becomes an American-registered team when owner Bob Stapleton bases the squad in San Luis Obispo, Calif. The sponsorship deal with Columbia comes about only after the executives of the company's European division in Geneva agree to place the logo for Omni-Shade, Columbia's new sun-protection apparel technology, beneath the company's logo on the jerseys.
- At the XXIXth Olympiad in Beijing Spain's Samuel Sanchez wins the 245-kilometer (152-mile) men's road race. Switzerland's Fabian Cancellara wins the men's individual time trial, America's Levi Leipheimer takes the bronze.
- America's Kristin Armstrong wins the gold medal in the women's Olympic time trial. Great Britain's Nicole Cooke wins the road race.
- France's Jeannie Longo-Ciprelli competes in her seventh Olympic games at the age of 49. She finishes fourth in the women's time trial.
- New Jersey's Lucas Haedo wins the Kugler-Anderson Memorial Tour of Somerville.
- Georgia's Tina Pic wins the Mildred Kugler Women's Open.
- Belgium's Jan Bakelants wins the 45th Tour de l'Avenir.
- Spain's Alberto Contador (Astana) wins the 63rd Vuelta a España by 46 seconds over Levi Leipheimer. If not for the time bonuses he'd earned during the race, Contador's margin of victory over his American teammate would have come down to his advantage in the event's time trials: 0.067 seconds.
- With his victory in the Vuelta, Contador becomes just the fifth rider (after Anquetil, Gimondi, Merckx, and Hinault) to win all three grand tours. All of

Contador's grand tour victories come in a 14-month period (July 2007–September 2008).

- Italy's Alessandro Ballan wins the 260-kilometer (162-mile) elite men's road race at the world championships in Varese, Italy. Germany's Bert Grabsch wins the individual time trial, with America's David Zabriskie finishing third in the 43.7-kilometer (27.2-mile) race of truth, behind Canadian Svein Tuft. Olympic champion Nicole Cooke of Great Britain wins the women's road race, while America's Amber Neben wins the time trial.

- On September 9, Lance Armstrong, who'll soon turn 37, announces that he plans to come out of retirement, and that he's going to try to win an eighth Tour de France, a feat that would make him the race's oldest winner. "I am happy to announce," he said, "that after talking with my children, my family, and my closest friends, I have decided to return to professional cycling in order to raise awareness of the global cancer burden." Five weeks later, he confirms that he also plans to compete in his first Tour of Italy during its 100th anniversary year. "I raced a long time professionally and I never did the Giro," he said. "It's one of the biggest regrets I ever had."

- Tyler Hamilton (Rock Racing) wins the U.S. professional championship in Greenville, S.C., nipping Blake Caldwell (Garmin-Chipotle) by less than a centimeter. Following a second positive drug test, this one at the Tour of California in early 2009, Hamilton retires, but is allowed to keep his American champion's title. According to *VeloNews*, "The only doping-related situation in which a national title would be revoked is if drug test results of an athlete collected before an event come back positive afterward."[1]

- Italy's Marco Pinotti (Team Columbia) wins the five-stage Tour of Ireland.

In the Tour de France:

- Spain's Carlos Sastre (CSC-Saxo Bank) is the seventh rider to win the Tour de France without winning a stage.

- In October, blood tests show that Bernhard Kohl and Germany's Stefan Schumacher (Gerolsteiner), who won both of the race's time trials, both tested positive for CERA. If Kohl is disqualified, third place overall would go to Russia's Denis Menchov (Rabobank) @ 2:10 and the polka-dot jersey would pass to race winner Carlos Sastre (CSC-Saxo Bank) with 80 points. Schumacher's victory in the stage four time trial would go to Luxembourg's Kim Kirchen (Team Columbia), and the win in stage 20 would pass to Switzerland's Fabian Cancellara (CSC-Saxo Bank). As of October 2009, the Tour's *Les Statistiques* lists third place overall and the climber's jersey to be "*non attribuée.*"

- The Astana team of 2007 winner Alberto Contador and third-place finisher Levi Leipheimer is not invited to the race because of the team's doping infractions under its previous management.

- For the third straight year, the previous winner does not start the race.

- For a record third consecutive year, Silence-Lotto's Wim Vansevenant (BEL) finishes last.

- Team Columbia's George Hincapie competes in his 13th consecutive Tour de France.

- The wild card entry Garmin-Chipotle makes the 2008 edition of the Tour de France the first to include two American teams.
- For the first time, two Norwegians—Thor Hushovd (Credit Agricole) and Kurt-Asle Arvesen (CSC-Saxo Bank)—win stages in the same Tour.
- Three months prior to the start of the race, the start of stage 15 is moved from Digne-les-Bains to Embrun because of the risk of rockslides on a 4-kilometer (2.5-mile) section of the Col de Larche. The new stage is about 30 kilometers (18.5 miles) shorter than the original one and will take the riders over the 2,744-meter (9,000-foot) Col d'Agnel on the Italian border.
- The region of Brittany sponsors the race's first three stages.
- During the third stage protesters from the communist-dominated la CGT (*Confédération Générale du Travail*) slow the race while calling on French President Sarkozy to protect their jobs. After the stage, race official Bernard Hinault gives a protester a hard shove off the awards podium.
- Eighty-year-old singer and actress Line Renaud waves the ceremonial start flag to begin the race. She had also had that honor when the race started in Belgium in 1958.
- Felt (Garmin-Chipotle) becomes the eleventh American bicycle to race in the Tour de France (after Huffy/Serotta, Carbonframes, Merlin, Clark-Kent, GT, Litespeed, Cannondale, Specialized, Trek, and Scott).
- Cervélo becomes the first Canadian-based bike company to win the Tour de France. Cervélo S.A. is based in Toronto, Canada and Neuchatel, Switzerland.
- For the first time since 1966 there is no prologue time trial to start the Tour de France. Technically there were no prologues for the 2000 and 2005 Tours either, but the first stages of both of those races were time trials of less than 20 kilometers (12.5 miles).
- No time bonuses are awarded for sprints or stage finishes.
- British sprinter Mark Cavendish (Team Columbia) wins four stages.
- Oscar Freire (Rabobank) becomes the first Spanish rider to win the green jersey.
- Bernhard Kohl (Gerolsteiner) becomes the first Austrian to win the polka-dot jersey, but later tests positive for CERA.
- Because of a feud between ASO and the UCI, the Tour de France is run under the auspices of the French Cycling Federation and doping control is handled by the French Anti-Doping Agency.
- The French referees complicate things for television announcers by not announcing the names of riders in breakaways until the gap has reached 30 seconds. The rule was reportedly implemented so team directors didn't know which riders were in a breakaway until it was established (unless they were watching the race on the televisions in their cars).
- American SRAM Red components have their first yellow jersey (France's Romain Feillu of Agritubel) after stage three. Stage 10 is won by Italy's Leonardo Piepoli of Saunier Duval-Scott on an American Bike (Scott) equipped with American components (SRAM).
- Versus signs a five-year, $27.5 million deal with ASO for American broadcast

rights to the Tour and other races. The cable channel airs virtually all of the mountainous 15th, 16th, and 17th stages live in America. Versus gets its live feed from France 2 television, while France 3 airs programming before and after each stage, and France 4 airs a Tour-related show later in the evening.

- Race announcer and Brittany resident Daniel Mangeas receives a plaque honoring his 35 years of service to the Tour before the start of the second stage.
- Also before the start of the second stage in Auray, the Tour honors Pierre Cogan, the race's oldest surviving rider at 94. Cogan competed in seven Tours de France between 1935 and 1951, completing six of them. He finished in the top 12 four times, with a best finish of seventh in 1950, when he rode for Helyett-Hutchinson.
- Spain's Manuel Beltran (Liquigas) is ejected from the race and suspended by his team after he tests positive for EPO following the first stage.

2009 • Lance Armstrong returns to racing in the Tour Down Under riding a custom-painted Trek Madone Red. Armstrong's stock frame is emblazoned with his foundation's LIVE**STRONG** logo, "1274," the number of days he was retired, and "27.5," the approximate number, in millions, of people who died from cancer during that time. The black and yellow airbrushed paint job takes 30 hours to do, not including curing time.

- The Katusha (Katiollia Russian Global Cycling Project) team of *directeur sportif* Andrei Tchmil becomes the first Russian-registered ProTour team. In 1990 the Italian-registered Alfa Lum squad had replaced most of its riders with those from the former Soviet Union.
- Former Professional Continental squad Garmin-Slipstream joins Columbia-Highroad as America's second UCI-registered ProTour team.
- Russia's Denis Menchov (Rabobank) wins the 100th anniversary Giro d'Italia. Still recovering from the broken collarbone he'd suffered during the Vuelta Ciclista Castilla y León in late March, American Lance Armstrong (Team Astana) finishes 12th overall.
- In May, American cycling standout Steve Larsen dies from a respiratory virus. Larsen was the only American cyclist to have competed in the world championships in all four cycling disciplines: road, track, cyclocross, and mountain bike. He was 39.
- In August Armstrong defeats six-time defending champion Dave Wiens in the Leadville, Colo., 100-mile mountain bike race. Making amends for his two-minute defeat the previous year, Armstrong beats Wiens by 28 minutes. "He's just off of the Tour," said Wiens of Armstrong after the race. "Last year he was just off of the couch."
- During the Tour de France Armstrong announces that he and Astana team director Johan Bruyneel are forming a ProTour team to be sponsored by Fort Worth, Texas-based electronics retailer RadioShack in 2010.
- Eighteen-year-old American Taylor Phinney (Trek-Livestrong) wins the under-23 edition of Paris–Roubaix.

- Officials in Boston announce that they are in talks with the Montreal-based Public Bike System Company to set up a system of 2,500 bikes and 290 rental stations by the summer of 2010. The largest existing bike rental system in the United States is in the District of Columbia, which has 12 rental stations and 100 bicycles.
- Look celebrates its 25th anniversary with the introduction of Kéo 2 Max, a refined version of its latest pedal, which features a wider platform, as well as a limited-edition (25 available worldwide) Mondrian-inspired version of its 596 time trial bike. The 1984 jersey design of the Look-sponsored La Vie Claire cycling team had been based on an abstract painting by Dutch artist Piet Mondrian (1872–1944).
- In June two-time Tour de France winner Laurent Fignon is diagnosed with advanced intestinal cancer. The Professor says the disease is probably not related to his drug use as a rider since cortisone, the riders' drug of choice before EPO, was injected and did not pass through the stomach. "If there was a direct link [to drugs] with my cancer," said Fignon, "I think there would be a lot of other cyclists that would also be suffering from the same cancer."[1]
- Also in June 196 French convicts take part in the 14-stage Tour de France Cycliste Pénitentiaire 2009, a 2,200-kilometer (1,367-mile) non-competitive ride from Villeneuve d'Ascq to Paris. Only six of the inmates are allowed to complete the entire course, with the others taking part in two legs of the ride before returning to prison. No breakaways are allowed.
- Lee Crider of Sacramento, California, is sentenced to three years in prison for stealing Lance Armstrong's time trial bike and two other bicycles after the prologue of the Tour of California. Dung Hoang Le, who cooperated with authorities, is sentenced to 90 days in jail after pleading no contest to buying Armstrong's $10,000 time trial bike for $200.
- Great Britain's Russell Downing (Candi TV) wins the 3-stage Tour of Ireland on his 31st birthday. During the race, Adrien Niyonshuti (MTN-Energade), who's coached by former American pro Jonathan Boyer, becomes the first Rwandan rider to compete in a major European race. Ireland's Malcolm Elliot, Downing's 48-year-old teammate, finishes 21st.
- Romain Sicard (France A) wins the 46th Tour de l'Avenir. America's Tejay van Garderen finishes second, one second back.
- The Netherlands' Edvald Boasson Hagen (Columbia-HTC) wins four consecutive stages on his way to the overall victory in the eight-stage Tour of Britain. He defeats Australian Chris Sutton (Garmin-Slipstream) by 23 seconds.
- George Hincapie (Columbia-HTC) wins the U.S. Professional road race in Greenville, S.C. It's his third national road championship and his first race since breaking his collarbone during the Tour de France. Garmin-Slipstream's David Zabriskie wins his fourth consecutive victory in the time trial, taking the 20.7-mile (33.3-kilometer) event in 39:37. He is the first rider to break the 40-minute mark on the course.
- Zabriskie also wins the Tour of Missouri. It's his first overall stage-race victory in his nine years as a professional.

- Spain's Alejandro Valverde (Caisse d'Epargne) wins the 64ᵗʰ Vuelta a España. The organizers announce that, beginning in 2010, the color of the race leader's jersey will be changed from gold to red (it had also been red in 1945). Forty-year-old Spaniard Iñigo Cuesta (Cervélo Test Team) competes in his 16ᵗʰ consecutive Vuelta, while his countryman José Vicente Garcia Acosta (Caisse d'Epargne) completes his 25ᵗʰ grand Tour (13 Vueltas and 12 Tours de France). The race was a good one for English-speaking riders, with Australia's Simon Gerrans (Cervélo Test Team) winning the 10ᵗʰ stage, America's Tyler Farrar (Garmin-Slipstream) winning the 11ᵗʰ stage, Canada's Ryder Hesjedal (Garmin) winning the mountainous 12ᵗʰ stage, Ireland's Philip Deignan (Cervélo) winning the 18ᵗʰ stage, and Great Britain's David Millar (Garmin) winning the 20ᵗʰ leg, an individual time trial. Gerrans' stage win makes him the first Australian to win a stage in each grand tour, and Hesjedal's victory makes him the first Canadian rider to win a Vuelta stage. Deignan's stage victory makes him the first Irishman to win a leg of a grand tour since Stephen Roche's victory in stage 16 of the 1992 Tour de France. By finishing the Vuelta, New Zealand's Julian Dean (Garmin-Slipstream) becomes the only rider to complete all three grand tours in 2009. Australia's Cadel Evans (Silence-Lotto) finishes in third place overall.
- France's Barbara Bautois achieves a speed of 72.5 mph (116.6 km/h) on a recumbent to beat the four-year-old women's record by 6 mph. Canada's Sam Whittingham pedals his recumbent 82.4 mph (132.6 km/h) to beat the year-old men's mark by 0.1 mph. The records, which were recorded on a 200-meter (219-yard) course after a flying start, were set on Nevada Route 305 near Battle Mountain.
- At the 76ᵗʰ world championships in Mendrisio, Switzerland, Cadel Evans solos to victory in the elite men's 262-kilometer (163-mile) road race in 6:56:26, becoming the first Australian to win the event. Switzerland's Fabian Cancellara claims his third title in the individual time trial, covering the 49.8-kilometer (31-mile) course in 57:55. Twenty-year-old Australian Jack Bobridge wins the Under 23 time trial, completing the 33.2-kilometer (20.6-mile) course in 40:45. On the women's side, Italy's Tatiana Guderzo wins the 124-kilometer (77-mile) road race in 3:33:25, and 36-year-old Kristin Armstrong (USA) takes the gold medal in the time trial—her last race before retiring—riding the 26.8-kilometer (16.6-mile) course in 35:26.
- In Mendrisio, the UCI management committee votes to phase out the use of two-way radios in all levels of road racing because their use "distorts the nature of cycle sport." A time table for the phase-out is to be determined later.
- In October, troubled former Belgian pro Frank Vandenbroucke dies of a pulmonary embolism at the age of 34.

In the Tour de France:

- Spain's Alberto Contador (Team Astana) wins the 96ᵗʰ Tour de France, the second consecutive Tour in which he's been allowed to compete. The organizers mistakenly play the Danish national anthem as Contador stands atop the final podium.

- The race unveils a new finish line structure and podium whose designs emphasize "extreme simplicity." At 6 meters (20 feet) in length, the new podium is 40 percent smaller than the old one, allowing it to be easily transported and "adapted to complex areas."
- After four years away from the race, Lance Armstrong (Team Astana) returns to the Tour to finish third. At 37 years 10 months 8 days he becomes the second-oldest rider to finish on the Tour's final podium after France's Raymond Poulidor (GAN-Mercier), who was 40 when he finished third in 1976. Portugal's Joaquim Agostinho (Flandria-Ca va Seul) was 37 years 3 months 15 days old when he finished third in 1979.
- Armstrong also ties Poulidor's record of eight finishes on the Tour's final podium. The American is the only rider in the 2009 Tour to have also competed in the 1993 event.
- Riders on bikes from North American-based companies take the top three spots overall and all of the race's jerseys. Contador and Armstrong ride 2010 prototype Trek 6 Series Madones and 2011 prototype Speed Concept time trial bikes equipped with American SRAM components, while Luxembourg's Andy Schleck (Team Saxo Bank), who finishes second and wins the white jersey, rides a Specialized Tarmac SL2 and S-Works Transition time trial bike outfitted with SRAM components. Green jersey winner Thor Hushovd (Cérvelo Test Team) of Norway rides a Cérvelo S3, and Italian king of the mountains, Franco Pellizotti (Team Liquigas), climbs aboard a Cannondale SuperSix.
- Bradley Wiggins (Columbia-HTC) finishes fourth overall, tying him with the 1984 finish of Robert Millar (Peugeot-Shell) for the best placing by a British rider.
- British sprinter Mark Cavendish (Columbia-HTC) takes six sprint victories, equaling the 1930 mark of France's Charles Pélissier—who outsprinted nine or more riders to win stages 3, 10, and 18–21. He also surpassed the 1976 and 1981 records of five sprint wins by Belgium's Freddy Maertens (Flandria-Velda and Boule d'Or-Sunair-Colnago respectively). In 1976 Maertens won eight Tour stages including the prologue and two individual time trials, and finished eighth overall. In just two Tours de France Cavendish, who now has a total of 10 stage wins, betters the British mark for stage wins held by Yorkshire sprinter Barry Hoban, who collected his eight victories between 1967 and 1975 while riding for Mercier-BP and GAN-Mercier.
- Fumiyuki Beppi (Skil-Shimano), who finished 112th and Yukiya Arashito (BBox Bouygues Telecom), who finished 129th, are the third and fourth Japanese riders to compete in the Tour, and the first to complete the event.
- American George Hincapie (Columbia-HTC) competes in his 14th Tour de France.
- Laura Antoine of St. Louis, Mo., is one of the Tour's "podium girls."
- The team time trial is part of the Tour for the first time since 2005. No time bonuses are awarded for the stage with each team receiving the time of its fifth finisher.
- The race includes just 55 kilometers (34.2 miles) of individual time trials.

- Carrefour Supermarkets replace Champion Supermarkets as sponsor of the polka dot jersey.
- At the conclusion of the second stage, Jussi Veikkanen (Française des Jeux) becomes the first Finnish rider to wear the polka dot jersey.
- Just before the team time trial, actor Ben Stiller rides Lance Armstrong's bike and bends a link in the chain, which has to be hastily replaced before the start of the stage.
- During the rainy sixth stage, which Versus announcer Phil Liggett calls "a day for the swimmers," a record 21 riders are listed as crash victims in the race's medical report.
- France's Brice Feillu (Agritubel) wins the Tour's third highest stage finish in Arcalis, Andorra, at 2,240 meters (7,349 feet). The race's highest stage finish was at the end of the 17th leg of the 1986 Tour on the 2,413-meter (7,915-foot) Col du Granon, where Spain's Eduardo Chozas (Teka) was the winner. The Tour's second-highest finish was at the end of the 1994 race's 17th stage to 2,275-meter (7,464-foot) Val-Thorens, which was won by Colombia's Nelson Rodriguez (ZG-Mobili). Germany's Jan Ullrich (Deutsche Telekom) won in Arcalis in 1997.
- The race's 10th stage is run without radio communication between the riders and their team cars. The average speed of the stage is unusually slow, and plans for another radio ban during the 13th stage are dropped.
- *VeloNews* Editorial Director John Wilcockson covers his 40th Tour de France, and is honored for his achievement before the start of the race's 10th stage in Limoges.
- Just 26.5 kilometers (16.5 miles) into the 11th stage, the race is briefly neutralized when a banner deflates across the road, blocking some of the riders.
- During the 12th stage to Vittel, Nestle Waters extends its contract as a race sponsor through 2013.
- Spanish champion Oscar Freire (Rabobank) and New Zealand's Julian Dean (Garmin) are shot with a pellet gun during the 13th stage near the end of the descent of the Col du Platzerwasel. Both riders continue in the race. Freire had a pellet removed from his thigh, Dean was hit in the right index finger.
- A 61-year-old woman is killed during the Tour's 14th stage when she steps into the path of a police motorcycle in Wittelsheim, about 40 kilometers (25 miles) from the start of the stage in Colmar.
- During the race's 20th stage, which finishes atop Mont Ventoux, the riders encounter oncoming traffic in the form of fire engines which are battling a forest fire in the area.
- Lance Armstrong's third book, *Comeback 2.0: Up Close and Personal*, is published on December 1. In the book, the Texan narrates photos of his comeback taken by Elizabeth Kreutz.

Chapter 12

2010–2015
Bike Tech Advancement Carries On

2010 • In May Floyd Landis publicly accuses Lance Armstrong and several of his teammates of using performance-enhancing drugs and blood transfusions to gain an unfair advantage. By August federal prosecutors have questioned many of his former teammates and associates.

• In the Tour of the Basque Country, 38-year old Chris Horner (RadioShack) defeats Spain's Alejandro Valverde (Caisse d'Epargne) by 7 seconds.

• The ProTour comes to North America for the first time, making stops in Quebec City and Montreal, Canada, where the races were won by Thomas Voeckler (Bbox-Bouygues Télécom) and Robert Gesink (Rabobank).

• Italy's Ivan Basso (Liquigas) wins the 93rd Giro d'Italia.

• After finishing second the previous year, America's Mara Abbott (PB&Co-TWENTY 12) wins the *Giro Donne*.

• Twenty-one-year-old Ben King (Trek-Livestrong) becomes the youngest winner of the men's road race at the USA Cycling professional championships. The next day his 20-year-old teammate Taylor Phinney nips Levi Leipheimer (RadioShack) by two-tenths of a second in the time trial. Mara Abbott (PB&Co) wins the women's road race, and the time trial is taken by Evelyn Stevens (HTC-Highroad).

• Greg LeMond and Trek Bicycle Corporation settle the once-bitter licensing agreement over the use of the three-time Tour de France champion's name on a line of bicycles. Trek ended the 13-year licensing agreement in 2008, after the company said that LeMond's allegations of drug use by Lance Armstrong were bad for business.

• Engineers at the Korean Institute of Industrial Technology have developed a carbon-fiber folding bicycle that weighs seven kilograms. The bike, which is between three and six kilos lighter than an aluminum folding bike, is expected to sell for about $2,600.

• London-based Green Endings offers a bicycle hearse for funerals. The service costs about £2,250, and includes a biodegradable cardboard coffin.

• *The Evening Standard* reports that suburban London train stops are the city's worst locations for bike thefts. Worst of all is Croyden, at which 2,145 bikes were stolen between 2008 and 2010.

- Canadian-born Oxford student Chris Graham "stole" his own bike nine times using bolt cutters to see if anyone would challenge him, reports the *London Times*. The 27-year-old student says that he was challenged by just one man who took no action.
- In the Netherlands, a 58-year-old man, whose Parkinson's disease had progressed to the point where he could take only a few steps before falling, is able to remain symptom free while riding his bicycle several miles. When his doctor asks twenty other severely affected patients about cycling, all can do it, probably, said one doctor, because cycling uses a different part of the brain than walking does.
- A French court convicts a dozen winemakers in Southern France of passing off 18 million bottles of Red Bicyclette wine as "pinot noir" to U.S. giant E&J Gallo when they actually contained a mixture of less expensive merlot and syrah. Gallo had purchased the bogus bottles between 2006 and 2008.
- Officials in Paris vote to double the number of bicycle trips made in the City of Light by the year 2020. The plan calls for adding 162 miles of bikes lanes, including one in each direction on the Champs-Élysées.
- China's Fuku Li (RadioShack) tests positive for trace amounts of clenbuterol four days after returning to Europe from China. Fuku would later say that the chemical came from something he had eaten back home, but at the time of his positive result Chinese authorities tell him to keep quiet and accept his two-year ban.
- Late in the year, fifty-year-old Alexi Grewal attempts a return to the professional peloton after 17 years away. He hopes to land on a team by 2012, but abandons his comeback after problems with transportation and having his bicycle stolen.
- At its October 1st management meeting in Melbourne, Australia, the UCI attempts to simplify professional cycling by the "complete merger" of the its Pro-Tour calendar with Historical calendars.
- After he steals a $1,000 bait mountain bike, 52-year-old Anthony Collins of Daytona Beach is sentenced to seven years after being designated a habitual felony offender.
- Nairo Quintana (Colombia) wins the 47th Tour de l'Avenir.
- Norway's Thor Hushovd wins the men's road race at the world championships held in Geelong, Australia, while Switzerland's Fabian Cancellara repeats in the time trial. The women's races are taken by Italy's Giorgia Bronzini on the road, while Emma Pooley (Great Britain) prevails in the race of truth.
- Australia's Michael Rogers (HTC-Columbia) wins 5th Tour of California.
- Ben Kersten (Australia) wins the Kugler-Anderson Memorial Tour of Somerville. The Mildred Kugler Women's Open is won by American Theresa Cliff-Ryan.
- Italy's Vincenzo Nibali (Liquigas-Doimo) wins the 65th Vuelta a España.
- Switzerland's Michael Albasini (HTC-Columbia) wins the Tour of Britain.

In the Tour de France:
- The 39-second margin of victory of Spain's Alberto Contador (Astana) is the

race's fifth closest until he is stripped of his victory 566 days later, making Luxembourg's Andy Schleck (Saxo Bank) the winner of the 97th Tour de France.

- Five weeks after the conclusion of the race, two-time Tour de France winner Laurent Fignon dies of cancer at age 50.
- A record 170 riders finish the race.
- The Tour de France marks the 100th anniversary of the "invention" of the race's first high-mountain stages in the Pyrenees by including all four "Circle of Death" climbs (Peyresourde, Aspin, Tourmalet, and Aubisque) in the race's 16th stage.
- The 97th Tour marks the 90th anniversary of Belgium's Philippe Thys becoming the first rider to win three Tours de France.
- Great Britain's Mark Cavendish (HTC-Columbia) wins five stages, but still loses the green jersey to Italy's Alessandro Petacchi (Lampre-Farnese).
- Petacchi becomes the first Italian since 1968 to win the green jersey (it was actually red that year at the request of its sponsor) when it was won by Franco Bitossi.
- By winning the Tour's green jersey, Petacchi becomes only the fourth rider to win the sprinting competition in each of the three grand tours. The others were: Eddy Merckx, Djamolidine Abdoujaparov, and Laurent Jalabert.
- Cavendish's leadout man, Mark Renshaw, is ejected from the race after interfering with Garmin-Transitions riders Julian Dean and Tyler Farrar in the sprint at the end of the 11th stage.
- The Tour de France organizers challenge farmers along the race's route "to decorate the fields in a hexagonal shape, representing the outline of France on a map. Each regional federation also needs to come up with a sentence, slogan, or motto for their display."
- The race's third stage includes 13.2 kilometers (8.2 miles) of cobblestones: 2.2 kilometers. (1.4 miles) over three sectors in Belgium, and 11 kilometers. (6.8 miles) over four sectors in France. This is the longest distance of cobblestone stretches to be included in the race since the 1983 event, which had a total of 28.4 kilometers (17.6 miles) of *pavé*.
- Frenchwoman Claire Pedrono is the race's first female *ardosier*. While an *ardosier* is actually a worker in a slate quarry, the term also applies to Mademoiselle Pedrono, whose job it is to ride on the back of a motorbike and show the riders their time intervals on a blackboard.
- As it had done in 1974, the race has the riders climb the Col du Tourmalet on consecutive stages.
- The race's 17th stage is only the second to finish atop the Tourmalet. The last time was the 17th leg of the 1974 Tour. In 1970 and 2002 stages had finished lower down the mountain in La Mongie.
- The race makes its 80th visit to Bordeaux, which is the most-visited stage city after Paris.
- The Tour visits 11 new stage towns.
- For the second consecutive year, the route of the Tour de France skips the regions of Normandy and Brittany.

- In May, American Floyd Landis, who'd been stripped of victory in the 2006 Tour de France for suspected doping, admits that he had used performance-enhancing drugs for most of his career as a professional road cyclist, including during the '06 Tour.
- Lance Armstrong (RadioShack) finishes his final Tour de France in 23rd place, 39:20 back. He'll go into "Retirement 2.0" the following February, after finishing 67th in the Santos Tour Down Under, and amid new doping allegations published in *Sports Illustrated*. In early February 2012, four days before Alberto Contador is stripped of his 2010 Tour win, the doping investigation into Armstrong is dropped.
- In October 2012, the UCI will strip lance Armstrong of all of his professional results based upon findings of the US Anti-Doping Agency that he and members of his teams engaged in what the UCI called "the most sophisticated, professional, and successful doping program that sport has ever seen."
- In late June the World Anti-Doping Agency signs an agreement to monitor drug testing at the Tour de France. The agreement allows WADA representatives "to observe all phases of the UCI's anti-doping controls," including selection of riders, handling of results, and reviewing related documents.
- Officials begin checking the bicycles for small electric motors to prevent "mechanical doping." Riders can get a spare bike only from a teammate, or team car.
- America's George Hincapie (BMC), and Frenchman Christophe Moreau (Caisse d'Epargne) compete in their 15th Tours. Saxo Bank's Stuart O'Grady rides his 14th Tour de France, the most for an Australian rider.
- One-hundred-ninety-seven riders on 22 teams start the race. Spain's Xavier Florencio (Cervélo Test Team) did not start after it was learned that he had used a cream containing ephedrine.
- In a protest organized by Fabian Cancellara, the main group crosses the finish line 3:56 behind stage winner Sylvain Chavanel to protest the slippery descent of the Stockeau on stage two. Each sprinter is awarded two points toward the green jersey.
- Teams in the Tour include the first truly British team (Sky) since 1987, and four American squads: HTC-Columbia, Radio Shack, Garmin-Transitions, and BMC.
- After the third stage, Sky's Geraint Thomas becomes the first British rider to wear the white jersey of the race's best young rider.
- There are 62 first-time riders in the race, including all 9 members of the Foot-on-Servetto team which includes Fabio Felline (ITA), the 2010 Tour's youngest rider at 19.
- For the prologue, the team managers can determine the placement of their riders in the team's allotted starting spots.
- The Tour Village, from where the race departs each morning, is revamped to increase "the number of allusions made to the race's outstanding champions." One feature honoring these champions is the *Allée des Heros* (Path of Heroes), which is made up of banners featuring larger-than-life likenesses of past Tour winners.

2011 • Beginning with its August issue, the print edition of *VeloNews* becomes *Velo* (the website continues as velonews.com). During the year, longtime staffers John Wilcockson, Ben Delaney, Charles Pelkey, Steve Frothingham, and Patrick O'Grady leave the magazine. Felix Magowan had left the publication in July 2009.

• University of Wisconsin-La Crosse student Wyatt Hrudka starts his own bicycle company. The 22-year-old senior, who founded Wyatt Bicycles with the help of a $32,000 loan from his father, sells his Thumbike-made single speeds for $350.

• Though Hong Kong has more than 1 million cyclists, the city has just 41,000 bicycle parking spaces. Illegally parked bikes are confiscated by authorities, and their owners have no way of reclaiming their machines before they're sent to the city's "bicycle graveyard" and eventually sold for scrap.

• Daimler AG's Smart Car division announces plans to manufacture an electric bike. The machine features electric pedal assist, and can't be driven on electricity alone.

• Thieves in Dublin, Ireland, perfect the technique of stealing iPhones (because they're easy to spot) from women (because they're unlikely to chase) while riding past them at high speed.

• Police in Ft. Lauderdale, Fla., say that 67-year-old Harry Gray was probably drunk when he allegedly chased a female cyclist around a parking lot in his electric wheelchair. When he caught her, Gray reportedly slammed the bicycle on the ground, causing the front wheel to come off.

• In England pet store employees refuse to sell a live catfish to retired photographer Brian Booth after he told them he'd be taking it home on his bike. Booth countered the staff's safety concerns by telling them that the fish was better off going by bike than in a car "because you don't get the jolts."

• After his 15,000 bikes and 90,000 spare parts take over his home and several garages, Pittsburgh's Craig Morrow moves his collection to a warehouse where he creates Bicycle Heaven, a sort-of museum and vintage parts shop.

• German scientists at Saarland University develop a wireless bicycle brake that fails only three times per one trillion uses—reliability so good, they say, that the technology could be used in aircraft systems.

• Power to the pedals. The new $1,500 Garmin Vector and $2,000 Look KeO Power pedals make moving your power meter from one bike to another a breeze. Look's pedals communicate with its Polar head, while the Garmin system is ANT+ compatible.

• Scientists in Bristol, England, have created a complete bike—including pedals, gears, and wheels—using a 3-D printer. The resulting plastic bike, called the Airbike, is said to be as strong as steel, but weigh 65 percent less.

• Spain's Juan José Cobo (Geox-TMC) wins the 66th Vuelta, finishing 13 seconds ahead of Great Britain's Chris Froome (Sky).

• Chris Horner (RadioShack) wins the 6th Amgen Tour of California.

• After Alberto Contador's decisive win is taken away from him, Italy's Michele Scarponi (Lampre) is awarded the victory in the 94th Giro d'Italia. The road for the race's 14th-stage ascent of the Zoncolan is so narrow that the teams are forced to put mechanics with spare bikes on the backs of motorcycles. During the race's third stage, 26-year-old Belgian sprinter Wouter Weylandt (Leopard-Trek) dies in a crash on the descent of the Passo del Bocco.

- The Tour of Britain is won by the Netherlands' Lars Boom (Rabobank).
- At the U.S. Professional Championships, Matthew Busche (RadioShack) prevails in the road race, and David Zabriskie (Garmin-Cervélo) wins the time trial. Robin Farina (NOW-Novartis) wins the women's road race, and Evelyn Stevens (HTC-Columbia) repeats in the time trial.
- The 48th Tour de l'Avenir is won by Esteban Chaves of Colombia.
- Mark Cavendish (GBR) wins the world championship road race in Copenhagen, and Germany's Tony Martin takes the time trial. Italy's Giorgia Bronzini repeats in the women's road race, and Judith Arndt of Germany wins the time trial.
- American Levi Leipheimer (RadioShack) wins the U.S.A. Pro Cycling Challenge in Colorado.
- Timothy Gudsell (New Zealand) wins the Kugler-Anderson Memorial Tour of Somerville. The Mildred Kugler Women's Open is claimed by Theresa Cliff-Ryan for the second straight year.
- When Lance Armstrong's former US Postal teammate Tyler Hamilton appears on the CBS news magazine *60 Minutes* and tells the nation, "I saw Lance inject EPO," Armstrong's attorney, Mark Fabiani, accuses the network of trying "to smear" his client.

In the Tour de France:

- Cadel Evans (Team BMC) is the first Australian, and first rider from the southern hemisphere, to win the Tour de France.
- At thirty-four, Evans is the third-oldest winner of the Tour de France after thirty-six-year-old Firmin Lambot in 1922, and Henri Pélissier (who was about three weeks older when he won in 1923).
- America's George Hincapie (BMC) starts his 16th consecutive Tour de France.
- At 2,645 meters (8,678 feet), the finish of stage 18 atop the Col du Galibier becomes the race's highest-ever stage finish. The previous highest finish for a stage of the Tour had been the Col du Granon at 2,413 meters (7,915 feet) in 1986.
- New rules for the green jersey competition place more emphasis on the finishing sprint, with the winner being awarded more points in comparison to the runner-up. Points are awarded to the first fifteen riders, with the winner receiving 45 points for a flat stage, 30 points for a medium-mountain stage, and 20 for a high-mountain stage. There is also now just one intermediate sprint during each stage, with 20 points going to the winner, and a declining number of points being awarded to the next 14 riders.
- The organizers introduce a "green flame" kite for the intermediate sprints.
- New rules for the climbing competition place more emphasis on summit finishes, where double points will be awarded to the winner. On *hors categorie* or first-category climbs, only the first six riders will score points (instead of the first eight), with the first rider receiving 20 points. Points are also awarded to

the first six riders on first-category climbs (first rider gets 10 points), to the first four riders on second-category climbs (first rider gets 5 points), to the first two riders on third-category climbs (first rider gets 2 points), and to the first rider on fourth-category climbs (1 point).

- Ten Americans take part in the Tour, tying the 2011 race with the 1986 event which included race winner Greg LeMond (ADR-Agrigel), and nine members of the 7Eleven-Hoonved squad.
- France's Yohann Gene (Europcar) is the first black rider to compete in the Tour de France since three Algerians and a Moroccan competed in the event between 1936 and 1950. Gene is from the French overseas department of Guadeloupe in the West Indies.
- No time bonuses are awarded to daily stage winners or podium finishers.
- For only the second time since the introduction of the prologue in 1967, the Tour de France starts with a road stage. The race also started without a prologue in 2008, when the first stage was also a road stage. In 2000, 2005, and 2009 an individual time trial replaced the prologue. In 1988 the race had started with a 6-kilometer "preface."
- Garmin-Cervélo sets a new record in the team time trial when the American squad covers the 23-km (14.3-mile) course in 24:48, for an average speed of 55.6 km/h (34.6 mph).
- After being hit by a press car during the ninth stage, both Johnny Hoogerland (Vacansoleil-DCM) and Juan Antonio Flecha (Sky) ride the tenth stage with red numbers to signify that they were the most courageous riders of the previous stage.
- All nine members of the Katusha team are Russian.
- Alexandr Kolobnev (Katusha) abandons the race prior to the tenth stage after an earlier drug test came back positive for Hydrochlorothiazide, a diuretic that can also be used as a masking agent.
- Andrey Amador (Movistar) is the first Costa Rican rider in the Tour.
- The Movistar team tests Campagnolo's electronic eleven-speed Super Record components.
- The race celebrates a century since it first ventured into the Alps in 1911.
- Just as it had done in 1974, the race's course takes the riders up the Col du Galibier on consecutive days.
- LCL Banque (formerly Le Credit Lyonnais) celebrates thirty years as sponsor of the Tour's yellow jersey.
- Sprinter Tyler Farrar (Garmin-Cervélo) wins the race's third stage on the Fourth of July to become just the second American (after his teammate Dave Zabriskie) to win a stage in all three grand tours. After crossing the finish line, Farrar held up his thumbs and index fingers in the form of a "W" to honor the memory of his friend, Wouter Weylandt, who'd died during the Giro.
- Tejay Van Garderen (HTC-Highroad) is the first American rider to wear the Tour's polka dot jersey. Greg LeMond had led the climbing competition during the 1986 Tour, but was wearing the yellow jersey at the time.
- Finishing second and third overall, Andy and Frank Schleck become the first

brothers to stand together on the Tour's final podium.

- British sprinter Mark Cavendish wins five stages, bringing his total number of stage victories to twenty in his last four Tours de France. The record for most stage wins by a sprinter is twenty-two, which has been held by France's André Darrigade since 1964.
- Andy Schleck becomes the first rider to finish second overall three times in a row at the Tour de France—until he's retroactively awarded first place in the 2010 event.
- Electronic components score their first overall victory in the Tour de France when Cadel Evans' bikes are equipped with Shimano's Dura-Ace Di2 (Digital Integrated Intelligence) derailleur system.

2012 • It's tough going for Lance Armstrong in 2012. During the last three months of the year alone, the Tour de France announces it will have no winner between 1999 and 2005 if he's stripped of his victories by the UCI; he is dropped by nearly all of his sponsors; he is officially banned from UCI competition for life; the UCI says that Armstrong and his teammates should return their prize money; he cuts ties with his Livestrong foundation; and London's *Sunday Times* sues him for nearly $1.5 million after it had settled with him in 2006 for reprinting claims that he had doped.

- In December the Copake (NY) Auction Company sells several bicycles that formerly belonged to the Pedaling History Bicycle Museum outside of Buffalo. Top sellers at the auction are an 1892 American Telegram bike ($26,450), and an 1887 Gormully & Jeffery "American Safety" bike ($24,150).
- As many as 600 fixed-gear riders are expected for Shanghai's second annual Alleycat Race. During the race, which is sponsored by Boxing Cat Brewery, the racers must pass twelve checkpoints in any order while riding in regular city traffic.
- Officials with the Colorado National Monument refuse to let a stage of next year's USA Pro Challenge pass through the park even though it allows access to a marathon and had been used for part of a stage by the Coors Classic in the 1980s.
- British bicycle designer Alex Moulton, whose small-wheeled machines became a part of pop culture in the 1960s, dies in Bath, England, at the age of 92.
- Edwin Pesek dies at the age of 93. One year after he'd parachuted into France on D-Day, Pesek and fellow American Tino Reboli won the six-day race in Chicago. After riding his last race at Madison Square Garden in 1961, Pesek went to work at Schwinn, were he stayed until he retired in 1992.
- To foil opportunistic bike thieves, police in Doncaster, England, are leaving unlocked "trap bikes" around the city. GPS systems hidden in the bikes make tracking the scofflaws a breeze.
- Police in New York City begin tracking accidents involving bicycles the same way as those involving cars. Previously cops had filled out a card for cycling mishaps, not a complete accident report.
- For around $6,000, cyclists in Great Britain can purchase the Hornster bicycle,

which features a horn from an American locomotive. The bike's 178-decibel horn runs on compressed air from a scuba tank.

- At the XXXth Olympiad in London, Alexander Vinokourov (KAZ) wins the men's road race, and Great Britain's Bradley Wiggins prevails in the individual time trial. Holland's Marianne Vos takes the women's road race while Kristin Armstrong (USA) captures the race against the clock.

- Several major American cities begin installing bicycle-specific traffic signals. Benefits of the lights, many of which feature a bike-shaped signal, include allowing cyclists to safely cross an intersection when the regular traffic signal turns yellow, and preventing collisions with turning motorists.

- The Tour of Britain is won by Australia's Nathan Hass (Garmin-Sharp).

- Tim Duggan (Liquigas-Cannondale) wins the U.S. Professional road race. David Zabriskie (Garmin-Barracuda) repeats in time trial. Amber Neben (Specialized-Lululemon) wins the women's time trial, and Megan Guarnier (TIBCO) captures the road race.

- France's Warren Barguil wins the Tour de l'Avenir.

- Philippe Gilbert (BEL) wins the world road championship in Valkenburg, the Netherlands, and Germany's Tony Martin repeats in the time trial. Marianne Vos (NED) wins the women's road race, and Germany's Judith Arndt repeats in the time trial.

- Luke Keough (USA) wins the Kugler-Anderson Memorial Tour of Somerville. Ruth Winder (USA) wins the Mildred Kugler Women's Open.

- Holland's Robert Gesink (Rabobank) wins the Amgen Tour of California.

- With his 16-second victory over Joaquin Rodriguez in the 95th Giro d'Italia, Ryder Hesjedal (Garmin-Barracuda) becomes the first Canadian rider to win a grand tour. Hesjedal is also the first racer from his country to wear the leader's jersey in a grand tour since Steve Bauer wore the yellow jersey during the 1990 Tour de France.

- America's Christian Vande Velde (Garmin-Sharp) wins the U.S.A. Pro Cycling Challenge.

- Adding to the success of North Americans in Italy is 21-year-old American Joe Dombrowski (Trek-Livestrong), who wins the under-23 *Giro Bio* (Baby Giro), riding in Italy for the U.S. National Team.

- After serving a backdated two-year suspension that amounts to eight months, Alberto Contador (Saxo-Tinkoff) returns to win the 67th Vuelta a España.

In the Tour de France:

- Sky's Bradley Wiggins becomes the first British rider and the first Olympic track champion to win the Tour de France. His Sky teammate, Christopher Froome, finishes second to mark the first time British riders have stood on the event's final podium.

- Because of its riders' success in the race, Team Sky earns a record $997,858.72 (U.S. dollars) in prize money. Last-place Vacansoleil took home a mere $11,758.87.

- Wiggins wears the Tour's yellow jersey for 14 consecutive days, a record for a British rider, and becomes the first rider since Bernard Hinault (1981) to wear the leader's jersey from stage seven all the way to Paris.

- At the conclusion of the race's 11th stage, Wiggins' Sky teammate Christopher Froome moves into second place overall, marking the first time that two British riders have held the top two spots in the Tour's general classification.
- The winner of the prologue is presented with a trophy created by glassmaker Louis Leloup.
- Le Coq Sportif returns to the Tour as the manufacturer of the jerseys for the race's special classifications. The company, which is celebrating its 130th anniversary, had previously been the supplier of the race's official jerseys from 1951 through 1988.
- The race is covered by a six-person Young Reporters Editing Team for the bi-daily publication *A Notre Tour* (*Now For Our Tour*). The team, which is comprised of two high school students from each of three countries, includes: Fiona Quimbre and Robin Wattraint of France, (who are associated with *L'Equipe*); Gabrielle Legourd and Joy Mentgen of Luxembourg (sportspress.lu); and Tom Duterme and Louis Bocher of Belgium (*La Dernière Heure*).
- Fabian Cancellara's (RadioShack-Nissan) fifth prologue victory ties him for Tour-opening wins with Frenchmen Bernard Hinault (who won the prologue in 1980, '81, '82, '84, and '85) and André Darrigade (who won the race's first stage in 1956, '57, '58, '59, and '61). Cancellara's win also ties him with Tour winners Laurent Fignon, Greg LeMond, and Joop Zoetemelk with twenty-two days in the race leader's yellow jersey. All five of his prologue victories have come outside of France (his other prologue wins were in Liège, London, Monaco, and Rotterdam).
- Cancellara wears the yellow jersey for eight days during the 2012 Tour, bringing his total number of days in the leader's jersey to twenty-eight, the most of any non-winner of the event. Cancellara's mark eclipses that of France's René Vietto, who had worn the *maillot jaune* for a total of 26 days in 1939 and 1947. Technically, Vietto led the race for 31 "stages," since the '39 Tour included several 2- and 3-part stages.
- During the Tour's tenth stage, the race makes its first visit to the 1,501-meter (4,925-foot) Col du Grand Colombier, the highest road pass in France's Jura Mountains.
- Didi Senft misses the Tour de France because he's recovering from brain surgery in his native Germany. Senft dresses as the devil who chases and inspires the riders in the Tour's high mountains.
- The Province of Liège is the only region to have hosted all three grand tours (it hosted the *Giro d'Italia* in 2006 and the *Vuelta a España* in 2009).
- Working for NBC Sports, commentator Phil Liggett covers his fortieth Tour de France. Versus owner Comcast had recently purchased NBC.
- Four British riders win a total of seven stages of the 2012 Tour: Bradley Wiggins (2), Chris Froome (1), and Mark Cavendish (3)—all Sky—and David Millar (1) of Garmin-Sharp.
- Sky's Mark Cavendish three stage wins bring his total to 23, surpassing French sprinter André Darrigade and American Lance Armstrong, who have 22 each.

Cavendish now trails just André Leducq (25), Bernard Hinault (28), and Eddy Merckx (34) for total number of stage victories.

- Cav's victory in Paris not only gives him a record four consecutive wins on the Champs Élysées, it also makes him the first wearer of the rainbow jersey to win there.
- When RadioShack's Jens Voigt (GER) and Chris Horner (USA) start the 99th Tour de France, it is the first time since 1928 that two forty-year-olds have started the race. Their arrival in Paris marks the first time since 1926 that two riders over forty have finished the Tour. It is the first time in the race's history that both forty-year-olds have been on the same team.
- Orica-GreenEDGE is the first full Australian team to compete in the Tour de France.
- America's George Hincapie (BMC) sets a new record when he starts his 17th consecutive (and final) Tour de France. As the racers enter Paris, Hincapie is given the honor of leading the race onto the Champs-Élysées.
- Australia's Stuart O'Grady starts his 16th Tour de France.
- Juan Jose "JJ" Haedo (Saxo Bank-Tinkoff Bank) is the first Argentine rider to take part in the Tour de France.
- Riders on the squad leading the team category wear yellow helmets as well as yellow-backed numbers.
- During the first rest day, Frenchman Remy Di Gregorio (Cofidis) is kicked out of the race on suspicion of doping, and eventually fired. After the alleged doping products turn out to be vitamins, a French court clears Di Gregorio to return to competition the following April. Six months later he wins his court case against Cofidis for "a substantial amount of money."
- A record 12 Australian riders take part in the 2012 Tour de France.
- The day before the race starts, a panel at the United States Anti-Doping Agency recommends moving forward with formal doping charges against Lance Armstrong. If he's found guilty of the charges, Armstrong could forfeit all seven of this Tour wins. See the addendum following this year's information.
- RadioShack-Nissan's team director, Johan Bruyneel skips the race because he has been named in an alleged doping conspiracy and doesn't want to be a distraction to the team.
- The organizers continue to tweak the points for the polka dot jersey competition. To increase the significance of the race's hardest (beyond-category) climbs, the first ten riders to the summit will be awarded points (up from six riders in 2011) with the first rider to the top receiving 25 points this year instead of 20. Double points continue to be on offer for summit finishes.
- With his victory in the first stage, twenty-two-year-old Peter Sagan (Liquigas-Cannondale) of Slovakia becomes the first Tour debutant to win the race's opening stage since Italy's Fabio Baldato in 1995, the first rider born during the 1990s to win a stage of the race, and the event's youngest stage winner since Lance Armstrong in 1993.
- With his victory in the eighth stage, the 2012 race's youngest rider, Thibaut Pinot (FDJ-Big Mat), becomes the first French stage winner of this year's Tour.

Pinot, who had turned twenty-two about a month before the race's prologue, also becomes the youngest French rider to complete the Tour de France since twenty-year-old René Vietto in 1934.

Addendum

One month after the finish of the 99th Tour de France, the United States Anti-Doping Agency announces that it has found Lance Armstrong guilty of using performance-enhancing drugs during his racing career, and is stripping him of all of his professional cycling results dating back to August 1, 1998.

This means that the Texan would lose all seven of his Tour de France victories from 1999 through 2005, as well as his later third-place finish, and possibly his bronze medal in the time trial from the 2000 Sydney Olympics—but not his 1993 world championship.

Just prior to the USADA's announcement, Armstrong decides to give up the fight—without admitting guilt—after his attempt to block the case is thrown out of court a few days earlier by an Austin, Texas, judge. Armstrong would continue his denials of doping until finally coming clean during the Oprah Winfrey interview, which aired on her OWN channel the evenings of January 17 and 18, 2013.

Armstrong also questions the USADA's authority to strip him of his results, but Travis Tygart, the agency's chief executive, says that the International Cycling Union, the sport's governing body, is bound by the decision to strip the Texan of his racing achievements. The UCI says that, since Armstrong has given up his right to a hearing, it would have to examine the agency's findings before rendering a final decision in the matter.

Calling USADA's investigation an "unconstitutional witch hunt," Armstrong says, "There comes a point in every man's life when he has to say 'Enough is enough.' For me that time is now."

On October 22, 2012, the UCI agrees with the USADA's decision to strip the Texan of his results, saying, "Lance Armstrong has no place in cycling, and he deserves to be forgotten...." Four days later, cycling's governing body "decided not to award [Armstrong's] victories to any other rider or upgrade other placings in any of the affected events."

2013 • In January the *New York Times* reports that Lance Armstrong is considering admitting that he used performance-enhancing drugs. On the 17th and 18th of the month, he admits to doping during his seven Tour de France victories in a nationally televised interview with Oprah Winfrey. Armstrong denied that he doped during his later comeback, but skeptics accuse him of lying because the statute of limitations hadn't run out on his more recent transgressions.

• American Mara Abbott (Exergy-TWENTY 16) wins the *Giro Rosa*.

• A Wisconsin newspaper runs a 75-year-old editorial from the *Wisconsin State Journal* that advocates for the licensing of cyclists and the construction of bike paths, supposedly for the safety of the riders.

• In Georgia, three Republican lawmakers introduce Bill BH 689, which would require cyclists to obtain a $15 bicycle license and to ride single file, in groups no larger than four with at least four feet between them. The bill would also allow communities to ban cyclists from certain roads. It is not expected to pass.

- Aston Martin introduces its $38,500 One-77 bicycle. The machine, of which only 77 will be produced, is built by Formula 1 supplier Bf1 Systems.

- After learning that bicycles are banned from its high school and middle school, officials in Tamaqua, Penn., consider revising the policy and adding at least one bike rack.

- Designer Jesse Stephenson of Port City, N.C., introduces the prototype of his E-Fox hybrid bike/electric car. The creation, which is said to look like a VW Beetle atop a tricycle, will have a starting price of $2,850.

- Al Fritz, the man behind Schwinn's popular Sting Ray bicycle, dies at the age of 88. Fritz was also instrumental in the development of the company's Airdyne exercise bike.

- New York Mayor Michael Bloomberg kicks off the city's bike share program, which is said to feature more than 6,000 bikes at 330 stations. The annual cost for Citi Bike is $95, or riders can pay $25 a week or $10 a day. Already 15,000 people are said to have signed up.

- Despite claims of having 6,000 bikes for the Citi Bike program, there are seldom more than 4,500 available—even in the middle of rainy nights—according to the program's own computer system, write *Wall Street Journal* reporters Tedd Mann and Josh Barbanel. Department of Transportation spokesman Seth Solomonow replies that the system map is a "customer service tool," not "a complete system inventory."

- Montreal-based Dorel Industries sees its stock sink as much as 15 percent. The decline, says the company, is due largely to slow sales of its Cannondale, Schwinn, Mongoose, and GT brands because of poor spring weather in the United States and Europe.

- Sherwoon Ross, who started Ross Bicycles, dies at the age of 92. Produced by the Chain Bike Corporation, Ross Bicycles once trailed only Schwinn and Huffy in U.S. sales. The company went bankrupt in 1989, and its name was sold to Rand Cycle.

- After nearly two years away from professional cycling, 39-year-old "Fast Freddie" Rodriguez (Jelly Belly) nips Brent Bookwalter (BMC) to win the U.S. professional road race in Chattanooga, Tenn., where Tom Zirbel (Optum-Kelly Benefit Strategies) prevails in the time trial. On the women's side, Jade Wilcoxson (Optum-Kelly Benefit Strategies) takes the road race, and Carmen Small (Specialized-Lululemon) wins the time trial.

- The 96th Giro d'Italia is won by Italy's Vincenzo Nibali (Astana).

- America's Chris Horner (RadioShack) wins the 68th Vuelta a España. At 41 Horner is the oldest rider to win a grand tour.

- BMC's Tejay Van Garderen (USA) wins Colorado's U.S.A. Pro Cycling Challenge.

- American Tejay Van Garderen (BMC) wins the Amgen Tour of California.

- Rui Costa (POR) wins the world road championship in Florence, Italy, and Tony Martin (GER) takes his third consecutive time trial title. On the women's

side Marianne Vos repeats in the road race, and her Dutch compatriot Ellen van Dijk wins the time trial.
- Team Sky's Bradley Wiggins (GBR) wins the Tour of Britain.
- Hilton Clarke (AUS) wins the Kugler-Anderson Memorial Tour of Somerville. In the Mildred Kugler Women's Open, American Kimberly Wells prevails.
- Spain's Rubén Fernández wins the 50th Tour de l'Avenir.

In the Tour de France:
- Great Britain's Chris Froome (Team Sky) wins the 100th Tour de France.
- NBC puts reporter Steve Purino on a motorcycle (driven by sixty-two-year-old Patrick Diablo) so he can provide live updates from the back of the race.
- The first three stages of the 100th Tour are run on the French island of Corsica, which pays the organizers $4 million for the three days of racing, plus another $2.6 million in expenses. It takes seven ships to get to Tour and its equipment to the island.
- The roads in the island's cities are so narrow that new stretch of road is built for the finish of the first stage, and the finishes of the next two legs are held outside of the finish towns.
- Because of Corsica's small roads and lack of space, large ferries are used as a pressroom, and to move the Tour's trucks around the island.
- The race includes 54 first-time riders.
- After missing the previous Tour de France due to illness, "Devil Didi" Senft returns to chase the riders on the race's steepest climbs, this time wearing a yellow outfit in honor of the event's 100th running.
- Germany's forty-one-year-old Jens Voigt (RadioShack-Leopard) competes in his sixteenth Tour de France.
- Nineteen-year-old Dutchman Danny Van Poppel (Vacansoleil-DCM) is the youngest rider to take part in the Tour de France since the Second World War.
- Great Britain's Mark Cavendish (Omega Pharma-Quick Step) wins his 25th stage, tying him at third place on the Tour's list of stage winners with France's André Leducq. The Brit now trails just Bernard Hinault (with 28 victories), and Eddy Merckx (34) on the race's all-time list of stage winners. The mark also ties Cavendish with Leducq for the most road-stage wins of any Tour de France rider (15 of Merckx's stage wins were time trials, as were 20 of Hinault's).
- Two weeks prior to the start of the race, Los Angeles-based Belkin electronics becomes the sponsor of the unsponsored Blanco squad, which had previously been sponsored by Rabobank.
- By winning the ninth stage to Bagneres-de-Bigorre, Garmin-Sharp's Dan Martin becomes the first Irish rider to win a stage of the Tour since 1992, when his uncle, Stephen Roche (Carrera Jeans-Tassoni), prevailed in the race's foggy 16th stage to La Bourboule.
- Australian rider Stuart O'Grady starts his record 17th Tour de France. O'Grady has the record because America's George Hincapie was stripped of one of his participations because he had admitted to doping.
- The Orica-GreenEDGE team bus arrives at the finish after the framework holding the finish-line banner has been lowered, and gets stuck under the structure.

The riders, who were only a few minutes away, were told that the finish will be moved out to the three-kilometer-to-go banner only to have it moved back to its original location once the bus was freed. Because of the confusion, all the riders are given the same time for the stage.

- Orica-GreenEDGE sets a new record in the team time trial with an average speed of 57.8 km/h (35.9 mph).
- Thirty-six-year-old Canadian Svein Tuft (Orica-GreenEDGE) is one of the Tour's oldest rookies. He is also the race's *lanterne rouge*.
- The route of the 2013 Tour de France includes ten UNESCO World Heritage sites.
- Only twice before the 2013 event (in 1948 and 1975) has the Tour held four road stages after the final time trial.
- The race concludes on the Champs Élysées at dusk, with the final podium awards being given at night in front of a brilliant light show on the Arc de Triomphe.
- Riders receive €22,500 for a stage win.

2014
- By finishing the 2014 Vuelta, Australia's Adam Hansen (Lotto-Belisol) completes his 10th consecutive grand tour, a streak that had started with the 2011 Vuelta. Hansen's latest finish ties the mark set by Spain's Marino Lejarreta (ONCE) in 1991, and puts him two back of Spaniard Bernardo Ruiz (Faema), who completed his 12th consecutive grand tour in 1958. Hansen says he plans to ride all three grand tours again in 2015.
- Because it's being sanctioned by USA Cycling, Lance Armstrong is banned from participating in a non-competitive South Carolina bike ride that includes George Hincapie and several of the pair's former US Postal teammates.
- Assaf Biderman's Cambridge, Mass., company Superpedestrian introduces the Copenhagen Wheel, which functions like a hybrid car by powering the bicycle with an electric motor and storing braking energy in a rechargeable battery.
- In her "15 worst Internet hoaxes" of 2014, *Washington Post* writer Caitlin Dewey lists "Bikers did not 'surrender' the Brooklyn Bridge to pedestrians" as number four. Despite the claims made by those at a parody Twitter account called @BicycleLobby, it turned out that the bleached American flags that flew briefly over the bridge had actually been the work of two German artists.
- In May the UCI announces that it will allow the use of track-legal pursuit bikes in hour record attempts. Fan favorite Jens Voigt breaks the nine-year-old hour record by riding 51.11 kilometers (31.76 miles) in Grenchen, Switzerland. Afterward, the 43-year-old German retires from the sport, saying "I'm in so much pain…but what a way to retire." Shut up, legs.
- Six weeks after Voigt set his hour mark, Germany's Matthias Brandle rides 51.352 kilometers (31.910 miles) on the UCI track in Aigle, Switzerland.
- In December, University of California, Berkeley, law professor Molly Shaffer Van Houweling sets the United States women's hour record by riding 44.173 kilometers (27.449 miles) in Carson, Calif.
- The European Patent Office reports that it has more than 96,000 bicycle-related

patents, including twenty that allow cyclists to exercise a dog while riding.

- Silca introduces its $450, seven-pound, SuperPista Ultimate floor pump. Designed to last a lifetime, the pump includes features such as: rosewood handles, a hose used for aircraft brake lines, and a heavy-duty aluminum barrel and base.
- "Pedal Power: From Wacky to Workhorse," an exhibit at the Los Altos (Calif.) History Museum includes the first bicycle ridden by Greg LeMond, and an early Tom Ritchey bike, as well as Schwinn Sting Rays, a wooden bike, and even a police bike.
- In Boulder, Colo., 38-year-old John Samson III is suspected of stealing 43 high-end bicycles between May and September. The value of the machines ranged from $700 to $9,000, for a total of $147,000.
- In September the Knesset approves the use of electric bicycles in Jerusalem as long as their maximum speed is 25 km/h, above which the motor must stop operating.
- Mexico City's public bicycle system has 180,000 users this year who make 13.5 million two-wheel trips, according to Mayor Miguel Angel Mancera.
- The Spokes Group of Eastern North Carolina teams up with the Salvation Army to raise $21,000 so they can give 300 local underprivileged children bikes and helmets for Christmas.
- In July Jen Graham writes a letter to the editor of the *Hull* (UK) *Daily Mail* to say that she and a friend, who were pushing babies in strollers, were not allowed to board a train because two cyclists were also boarding the train. "Apparently policy states," wrote Ms. Graham, "that the bicycles were more important than our babies. So we were left at the train station to find another train."
- Looking for a new high-wheeler? Al Sneller and Diane Blake of Orlando make ones that are based on the 1885 Victor. The bikes can be built with wheels ranging from 46–60 inches.
- Jack Hairston of West Palm Beach, Fla., still needs 100 bikes and 400 helmets to reach his goal of 1,000 bikes to give away to local kids. The previous year the 73-year-old gave away 900 bikes.
- In May, AAA of Colorado expands its roadside assistance program to include members whose bicycles break down by picking them up and transporting them to the destination of their choice.
- Spain's Alberto Contador (Tinkoff-Saxo) wins the 69th Vuelta a España.
- Nairo Quintana (Movistar) becomes the first Colombian to win the Giro d'Italia.
- Chiropractor Eric Marcott (SmartStop) wins the U.S. Professional road race, while Taylor Phinney (BMC) takes the time trial. Alison Powers (United Healthcare) wins both the women's road race and time trial. Powers, who had also won the national criterium championship in 2013, will announce her retirement on October 23, 2014.
- Sky's Bradley Wiggins (GBR) wins the Amgen Tour of California.
- America's Tejay Van Garderen (BMC) repeats as winner of the U.S.A. Pro Cycling Challenge.

- Michael Kwiatkowski of Poland prevails in the road race at the world championships in Ponferrada, Spain, while Bradley Wiggins (GBR) wins the time trial. Pauline Ferrand-Prévot (FRA) wins the women's road race, and Germany's Lisa Brennauer wins the time trial.
- Miguel Ángel López (COL) wins the 51st Tour de l'Avenir.
- Adam Alexander (USA) wins the Kugler-Anderson Memorial Tour of Somerville. America's Erica Allar wins the Mildred Kugler Women's Open.
- Dutchman Dylan van Baarle (Garmin-Sharp) wins the Tour of Britain.

In the Tour de France:

- By winning the 101st Tour de France, Vincenzo Nibali (Astana) becomes the sixth rider to win all three grand tours, following Jacques Anquetil, Felice Gimondi, Eddy Merckx, Bernard Hinault, and Alberto Contador.
- Nibali gives one of his 19 yellow jerseys to the mother of the late Marco Pantani, the last Italian rider to win the Tour.
- All three former winners in the tour, Chris Froome, Alberto Contador, and Andy Schleck, crash out of the race before its first rest day.
- Markings on the race leader's yellow jersey include the white rose of Yorkshire.
- Race announcer Daniel Mangeas calls his final Tour de France. Mangeas had been delighting race fans with his encyclopedic knowledge of the riders since 1976.
- The race starts in England for the second time, marking its fourth visit to Great Britain since 1974.
- The wild-card Net App-Endura squad is made up completely of Tour rookies.
- Germany's 42-year-old Jens Voigt (Trek Factory Racing) starts—and finishes—his record-tying 17th Tour de France.
- After the first stage, Voigt becomes the oldest rider to wear the race's polka dot jersey.
- Ji Cheng (Giant-Shimano) is the first Chinese rider to take part in the Tour de France. He is also the race's *lanterne rouge.*
- Race organizers allow some of the riders to mount small front- and rear-facing cameras to their bicycles. Video recorded by the cameras is shown the next day.
- Before the start of the 13th stage the race observes a moment of silence for the 298 people who died when Malaysian Airlines flight MH17 was shot down over Ukraine.
- During the 13th stage French rider Thomas Voeckler stops to yell back at some hecklers who'd asked him if he'd forgotten how to ride a bike.
- French favorite Raymond Poulidor attends his 52nd Tour de France.
- The appearances of Jean-Christophe Peraud and Thibaut Pinot on the final podium mark the first time a French rider has finished there since Richard Virenque (Festina) finished third in 1997. The last time two French riders had finished on the podium was in 1984, when Laurent Fignon (Renault) won and Bernard Hinault (La Vie Claire) finished second.
- The start of the race's fourteenth stage is slightly delayed by firefighters protesting long work hours.

- Spain's José Rojas (Movistar) is kicked out of the race for holding onto a car during the 18th stage.
- By winning the race's 19th leg, Ramunas Navardauskas (Garmin-Sharp) becomes the first Lithuanian to win an individual Tour stage.
- For the first time since 1953 the Tour includes just one long time trial.
- On the Tour's final day, 120 female riders on 20 teams take part in La Course by Le Tour de France, a 13-lap, 91-kilometer (56.5-mile) race on the Champs-Élysées. The race, which is won by world champion Marianne Vos (Rabobank-Liv) in 2:00:41, features podium boys, an all-female jury, and a first prize of €22,500—the same amount as a male stage winner receives.
- Some of the teams equip their *domestiques* with backpacks that hold five water bottles.
- The Tour de France recognizes the beginnings a century ago of World War I, passing through some of its great battle sites, including: Arras, Chemin des Dames, Verdun, and Douaumont.
- Propane and natural gas company Antargaz replaces Brandt as the sponsor of the Tour's combativity award.
- RAGT Semences sponsors the team award and the yellow numbers worn by riders of the leading team.
- Krys Opticians sponsors the *dossards* (numbers) worn by the riders.

2015 • Campagnolo's Chorus, Record, and Super Record gruppos are overhauled and include new 4-arm cranksets.
- Shimano introduces XTR Di2 M9050. *Bicycling* calls the new electronic gruppo, which can be integrated with Fox's iRD electronically controlled suspension, "the next natural step in the incremental evolution of mountain bike drivetrains."
- American actor Dustin Hoffman has a cameo in the Lance Armstrong biopic *The Program*. In 1984 Hoffman had followed the Tour de France for two days to prepare for his role in movie version of Ralph Hurne's 1973 novel, *The Yellow Jersey*. The movie would never be made.
- American Secretary of State John Kerry hits a curb and breaks his right femur while cycling in Scionzier, France. The crash happened early during his ride to the Col de la Colombiere.
- New regulations in the District of Columbia require landlords of buildings with at least eight units to provide one secure bicycle parking space for every three residential units, or enough spaces to meet requested demand. Assisted-living facilities are exempt from the regulation.
- Called "Everesting," a new challenge has serious riders attempting to climb 29,029 feet on their bicycles. The ascent must be accomplished by doing repeated climbs in a single ride on a single stretch of road with only short breaks and no sleep. The results must be uploaded and verified on Strava.
- Professional cyclist Krystain Herba rides his bike up the 3,139 steps of Taiwan's Taipei 101 tower in 2 hours 13 minutes, to break his own record of 2,919 steps set in Melbourne in 2014.

- Scientists in London studied 120 male and female subjects between the ages of 55 and 79 and failed to find any expected signs of aging for the age group. The catch? All the male members of the study had to be able to bicycle 100 kilometers (62 miles) in less than six and a half hours, while the women had to be able to cover 60 kilometers (37 miles) in less than five and a half hours.
- Inventor Nick Zamora begins raising KickStarter funds to develop the CydeKick, an add-on bicycle generator and power storage system that provides electricity for lights and cell-phone charging. The CydeKick is said to add no mechanical drag to the bicycle.
- The demand for bicycles in Mexico has seen imports of the machines skyrocket. Between 2010 and 2014 the country went from importing 76,000 bicycles to importing 318,000—that's an increase from $6.2 million to $39.2 million US dollars. Ninety percent of the bicycles come from China.
- Spain's Alberto Contador (Tinkoff-Saxo) wins the 98th Giro d'Italia.
- Italy's Fabio Aru (Astana Pro Team) wins the 70th Vuelta a Espana.
- Australian Adam Hansen (Lotto-Soudal) finishes 55th in the Vuelta to complete his record-breaking 13th consecutive grand tour.
- Cannondale-Garmin's Joe Dombrowski (USA) wins the 2015 Larry H. Miller Tour of Utah.
- Tinkoff-Saxo's Peter Sagan (SVK) wins the 10th Amgen Tour of California.
- Australia's Rohan Dennis (Team BMC) becomes the first foreigner to win the USA Pro Challenge.
- Slovakia's Peter Sagan wins the men's elite road race at the 2015 world championships held in Richmond, Virginia. Great Britain's Elizabeth Armitstead wins the women's road race. Vasil Kiryienka (BLR) wins the men's individual time trial. New Zealand's Linda Melanie Villumsen wins the women's individual time trial. Team BMC (USA) repeats as winner of the men's team time trial, while Germany's Velocio-Sram squad captures the women's ttt.

In the Tour de France:

- Team Sky's Chris Froome (GBR) wins his second Tour de France in three years.
- In an effort to emphasize winning, the race increases the green jersey points for the first three finishers of a flat road stage to 50, 30, and 20 points, as opposed to the previous Tour's 45, 35, and 30 points.
- The race features only 14 kilometers (8.7 miles) of individual time trial distance, the least, according to organizers, since 1947.
- In honor of the 40th anniversary of the Tour's finishing on the Champs-Élysées, the leader's yellow jersey features a filigree of the Arc de Triomphe, and the racers ride past the Eiffel Tower.
- The first three finishers of the race's second through eighth stages receive time bonuses of 10, 6, and 4 seconds.
- The riders have to contend with seven sections of cobblestones totaling 13.3 km (8.3 miles).
- The race's Pra Loup stage commemorates the battle that took place there be-

tween Eddy Merckx and Bernard Thévenet in 1975.

- The race's team time trial honors Bernard Hinault, who, in 1985, was the last Frenchman to win the Tour de France.
- The race also pays tribute to Fabio Casartelli, who lost his life in a crash during the 1995 Tour de France.
- The race's 20th stage between Modane and L'Alpe d'Huez, skips the Col du Galibier due to the closure of the Chambon Tunnel because of a landslide in April. During the 110.7-kilometer (68.8-mile) leg, the riders ascend the Col de la Croix-de-Fer instead.
- Team BMC's Rohan Dennis completes the race's opening 13.8-kilometer (8.6-mile) time trial in 14:56. His average speed of 55.3 km/h (34.4 mph) surpasses the 55.15 km/h mark set by Great Britain's Chris Boardman (GAN) during the prologue of the 1994 Tour.
- Part of the race's third stage from Antwerp to Huy is neutralized for a time following a large high-speed crash on a straight stretch of road.
- German broadcaster ARD resumes its live coverage of the Tour de France following a three-year absence to protest the race's doping scandals.
- After testing positive for cocaine, Katusha's Luca Paolini is kicked out of the race.
- Great Britain's Mark Cavendish (Etixx-Quick Step) wins the event's seventh leg to collect his 26th Tour de France stage win.
- MTN-Qhubeka's Daniel Teklehaimanot (ERI) and Merhawi Kudus (ERI) are the first black African riders to compete in the Tour on an African team. Teklehaimanot becomes the first African rider to wear a Tour leader's jersey when he wears the polka dot jersey after stages six through nine.
- MTN-Qhubeka's Stephen Cummings (GBR) wins the race's 14th leg to give the South African squad its first Tour stage win, on Nelson Mandela Day.
- Halfway through the Tour, Lance Armstrong arrives in France to take part in a two-day charity ride for the organization Cure Leukemia. The fundraiser, which was organized by former footballer Geoff Thomas and is called Le Tour One Day Ahead, includes two stages of the race a day before the riders cover them.
- During the Tour's first rest day Italy's Ivan Basso (Tinkoff-Saxo) announces that he has testicular cancer and withdraws from the race.
- During the 14th stage a spectator throws urine on race leader Chris Froome while yelling, "Doper!"
- Police close a three-kilometer (two-mile) stretch of the event's 18th stage to fans when they deem the narrow cliffside hairpin bends of the Montvernier Laces (les Lacets de Montvernier) to be too narrow for spectator safety.

Endnotes

Year

1869 1. *Bicycling*, Sept./Oct. 1993, p. 81.

  2. Herlihey, David V., *Bicycle*, p. 136.

1870 1. Magowan, Robin, *Tour de France: The Historic 1978 Event*, p. 4.

1877 1. "Startling Changes Made in Bicycles," *New York Times*, 4 Apr. 1915, sec. 4, p. 3.

1880 1. "Wheelmen in Council," *New York Times*, Sept. 19, 1880, p. 9.

1883 1. "Startling Changes …"

1884 1. Ibid.

1886 1. Ibid.

1889 1. "Death of Bicyclist Freatman," *New York Times*, 16 Nov. 1889, p. 1.

1890 1. "To Chicago on a Bicycle," *New York Times*, 25 Aug. 1890, p. 5.

1891 1. "Bishop Coxe on Women Cyclers," *New York Times*, 7 July1891, p. 9.

  2. "The Ladies' Cycling Club." *New York Times*, 25 Sept. 1891, p.9.

1893 1. Nye, Peter, *Hearts of Lions: The Story of American Bicycle Racing*, p. 47–48.

  2. Fife, Graeme, *Tour de France: The History, the Legend, the Riders*, p. 21.

  3. Herlihey, pp. 268–9.

1895 1. Seray, Jacques, *1904; The Tour de France which was to be the last*, pp. 99–104.

  2. "Silver-Plated Bicycles," *New York Times*, 22 Dec. 1895, p. 7.

1896 1. Sergent, Pascal, "19th April 1896; The Legend Begins," *A Century of Paris-Roubaix*.

  2. *New York World*, 2 Feb. 1896.

1897 1. "One Half a Rider," *New York Times*, 9 Sept. 1897, p. 4.

  2. "Solid Lubricant for Bearings," Ibid.

  3. "News For the Wheelmen," *New York Times*, 24 Jan. 1898.

1898 1. Wilcockson, John, "Tales of the Unexpected," *VeloNews*, 6 Jan. 2003, p. 17.

1899 1. "Recalls Bike Ride at Mile a Minute," *New York Times*, 27 June 1934, p. 21.

1900 1. Nye, Peter, *Hearts of Lions*, p. 30.

1901 1. Ibid., p. 62.

1902 1. Nye, Peter, *The Cyclist's Sourcebook*, p. 100.

1904 1. Nye, Peter, *Hearts of Lions*, pp. 72–3.

  2. Ibid., pp. 221–2.

1908 1. "Looking Back; 100 Years Ago, 1908," *Lewiston Sun Journal*, 27 Aug. 2008.

1909 1. "Motor Cycle Afire; 4 Killed," *New York Times*, 18 July 1909, p. 1.

1910 1. "Cyclist Hurled into Beehive," *New York Times*, 10 April 1910, p. 7.

  2. Nye, Peter, *Hearts of Lions*, p. 98.

  3. "World's Bicycle Record," *New York Times*, 27 June 1910, p. 8.

1912 1. Nye, Peter, *Hearts of Lions*, p. 85.

  2. Herlihy, David V., *Bicycle: the History*, p. 381.

  3. Ibid., p. 322.

  4. Fisher, Louis M., letter to the editor, *New York Times*, 11 March 1912, p. 12.

1913 1. Herlihy, p.322.

  2. "Police to Arrest Motor Cyclists," *New York Times*, 18 July 1913, p. 7.

  3. Novrup, Svend, *A Moustache, Poison, and Blue Glasses!*, p. 97.

  4. Woodland, Les, *The Unknown Tour de France*, p. 69.

1914 1. "New Bicycle Adds Speed and Danger," *New York Times*, 30 Aug. 1914, sec. 3, p. 3.

1915 1. "Motor Cycles At Garden," *New York Times*, 12 Oct. 1915, p. 8.

1918 1. "Blue Devils Ride In Race," *New York Times*, 17 June 1918, p. 14.

1919 1. Sergent, Pascal, *A Century of Paris–Roubaix*, "1919."

    2. "Crossed Continent on Bicycle," *New York Times*, 31 Oct. 1919, p. 32.

1921 1. "May Hit Chicago Bikers," *New York Times*, 22 Jan. 1921, p. 13.

    2. Nye, Peter, *The Cyclist's Sourcebook*, pp. 100, 101.

    3. Hemingway, Ernest, *A Moveable Feast*, p. 65.

    4. "Aims Legal Threat At Six-Day Races," *New York Times*, 17 Feb. 1921, p. 12.

1922 1. "Makes New Record For Riding Bicycle Across Continent," *New York Times*, 15 July 1922, p. 7.

    2. "Foresees a Revival of Bicycle Vogue," *New York Times*, 14 Sept. 1922, p. 35.

1923 1. "Cycling Show Opens," *New York Times*, 13 Feb. 1923, p. 28.

    2. "Italian Cyclist Honored," *New York Times*, 2 Sept. 1923, p. 20.

1924 1. Nye, Peter, *Hearts of Lions*, p. 151.

    2. "Italian Rider Finishes First In Bike Race Around France," *New York Times*, 22 July 1924, p. 13.

1925 1. Sergent, "1925."

1926 1. "Tax Men Get 6-Day Riders," *New York Times*, 18 March 1926, p. 16.

    2. "Weight-Reducing Wheel for Women," *New York Times*, 25 July 1926, p. 2.

1927 1. "Bicycling, Never Quite Dead, Now Enjoys a Small Revival," *New York Times*, 10 April, 1927, sec. 2, p. 16.

1928 1. "Freed As a Beggar," *New York Times*, 1 Feb. 1918, p. 6.

1929 1. Nye, Peter, *Hearts of Lions*, p. 149.

    2. Ibid., pp. 128, 129.

1930 1. "Bicycles' Return to Favor is Laid to Slump and Workers' Lack of Funds to Buy New Cars," *New York Times*, 5 Sept. 1930, p. 30.

1931 1. "Pedals Into Quebec From Panama," *New York Times*, (from the *Canadian Press*), 11 June 1931, p. 9.

    2. "Bicycle Races of Olympics To Be Held in the Rose Bowl," *New York Times*, 23 July 1931, p. 19.

1933 1. "Rode One Bicycle 26 Years," *New York Times*, 8 Jan. 1933, p. E6.

    2. The journalists and correspondents of *L'Auto* and *L'Équipe*, (Matt Rendell, ed.) *The Official Tour de France Centennial, 1903–2003*. p. 112.

1934 1. Nye, Peter, *Hearts of Lions*, p. 137.

    2. "Sets World's Cycling Record," *New York Times* (from the *Canadian Press*), 6 Oct. 1934, p. 10.

1935 1. "Curb on British Cyclists laid to Big Fatality Rise," *New York Times*, 1 March 1935, p. 12.

    2. "Random Notes For Travelers," *New York Times*, 21 July 1935, p. X6.

1936 1. Yates, Richard, "Joseph Magnani in Europe," *On the Wheel, No. 10*, Aug.–Sept. 1999, p. 17.

    2. "Bicycle Course Revived," *New York Times*, 27 March 1936, p. 23.

    3. "Rides Bicycle 60,000 Miles," *New York Times*, 27 July 1936, p. 22.

    4. "Bicycles and Trains," Geist, Dr. Roland C., *New York Times*, 11 May 1969, p. XX3

1938 1. "Sees Record Bicycle Tire Sales," *New York Times*, 7 Jan. 1938, p. 26.

    2. "1,130,736 Bicycles Built in 1937," New York Times, 19 Oct. 1938, p. 21.

    3. Champ, Robert Cordon, "The Derny 'Bordeaux–Paris,'" *On the Wheel*, No. 10, Aug-Sept. 1999, pp. 8, 9.

1939 1. Brunel, Philippe, *An Intimate Portrait of the Tour de France*, p. 31.

    2. The journalist and correspondents of *L'Auto* and *L'Équipe*, *The Official Tour de France Centennial; 1903–2003*, p. 138.

    3. "Scout Wins 'Bike' Plate No. 1," *New York Times*, 8 April 1939, p. 19.

1940 1. Cannell, Kathleen, "Parisians Returf Air Raid Trenches," *New York Times*, 14 July 1940, p. 18.

   2. "Italians Use Bicycles Built for Two," *New York Times* (UP), 31 Oct. 1940, p. 4.

   3. Yates, Richard, translator's note in Pascal Sergent, *A Century of Paris–Roubaix*, "1930."

1942 1. Yates, Richard, "Nineteen-Forty-Two," *Bikelore 2: The World of Wheels*, p. 19.

   2. Yates, Richard, "Les Quatre Jours de la Route," *Bikelore 2: The World of Wheels*, p. 62.

   3. Woodland, Les, ed., *The Yellow Jersey Companion to the Tour de France*, p. 387.

   4. Curtis, Michael, *Verdict on Vichy: Power and Prejudice in the Vichy Regime*, p.1.

   5. "Henderson Rides New 'Victory' Bicycle; 750,000 Planned for '42 and for Adults Only," *New York Times* (AP), 15 Jan. 1942, p. 12.

   6. "Order Trebles Adult Bicycles," *New York Times*, 13 March 1942, p. 38.

1943 1. "New Bicycle for the Waacs," *New York Times* (UP), 20 Feb. 1943, p. 16.

   2. Nye, Peter Joffre, "Joseph Magnani: Illinois Rider Challenged Coppi and Bartali in Giro," www.bikeraceinfo.com/riderhistories/JosephMagnani.html, p. 5 of 10.

   3. Yates, Richard, "Dante Gianello," *Bikelore: Some History and Heroes of Cycling*, p. 40.

1944 1. "Stump Pine Yields Substitute For Shellac, Patent List Shows," *New York Times*, 14 Oct. 1944, p. 19.

   2. Denny, Harold, "Normandy Battle Is Hedge to Hedge," *New York Times*, 6 July 1944, p. 5.

   3. Daniell, Raymond, "Parisians Endure Troubles Bravely," *New York Times*, 1 Sept. 1944, p. 4.

1945 1. "Biggest Contingent of Fighters To Return Since V-E Day Is Here," *New York Times*, 23 May 1945, p. 21.

   2. Yates, "Dante Gianello," p. 41.

   3. Sergent, "1938," *A Century of Paris–Roubaix*.

1946 1. Nye, Peter, *The Cyclist's Sourcebook*, p. 102.

1947 1. *100 Years of Bicycle Component and Accessory Design: Authentic Reprint Edition of the Data Book*, Van der Plas Publications, pp. 77, 81.

   2. "Will Distribute French Bikes," *New York Times*, 28 Jan. 1947, p. 39.

   3. "Yankee Bike For Douglas," *New York Times*, 18 April 1947, p. 23.

1948 1. *100 Years of Bicycle Component and Accessory Design: Authentic Reprint Edition of the Data Book*, p. 83.

   2. Nye, "Joseph Magnani," p. 7 of 10.

   3. "Business World; Bicycles From Japan Arrive," *New York Times*, 24 Dec. 1948, p. 22.

   4. Startt, James, *Tour de France/Tour de Force: A Visual History of the World's Greatest Bicycle Race*, p. 151.

1949 1. Maso, Benjo, *The Sweat of the Gods*, p. 101.

1950 1. Sergent, Pascal, *A Century of Paris–Roubaix*, "1950."

   2. Nye, Peter, *Hearts of Lions*, pp. 166–7.

1951 1. Berto, Frank; Shepherd, Ron and Henry, Raymond, *The Dancing Chain: History and Development of the Derailleur Bicycle*, p. 179.

   2. Berto, et al, p. 216.

   3. "Monopoly Broken in Bicycle Trade," *New York Times*, 15 Feb. 1951, p. 39.

   4. "U. S. First for British 'Cycles," *New York Times*, 10 Oct. 1951, p. 32.

1952 1. Jones, Stacy V., "Device to Immobilize Tail of Cow Could Make Bossy Belle of the Barn," *New York Times*, 6 Dec. 1952, p. 29.

1953 1. "Bicycling Handbook Outlines Group Play," *New York Times*, 8 Jan. 1953, p. 24.

   2. "Sidelights on the Financial and Business Developments of the Day; Bicycles for Two Million," *New York Times*, 11 Feb. 1953, p. 43.

1954 1. *100 Years of Bicycle Component and Accessory Design: Authentic Reprint Edition of the Data Book*, p. 83.

2. Brunel, Philippe, *An Intimate Portrait of the Tour de France: Masters and Slaves of the Road*, p. 5.

1955 1. Egan, Charles E., "President Raises Bicycle Duty 50%; Prices Will Go Up," *New York Times*, 20 Aug. 1955, p. 1.

1956 1. "Ockers Wins 5-Day Cycle Race," *New York Times*," 30 April 1956, p. 28.

2. "City Men Advised to Cycle to Work," *New York Times*, 22 Feb. 1956, p. 18.

3. Nye, Peter, *Hearts of Lions: The Story of American Bicycle Racing*, pp. 189–90.

1957 1. Woodland, Les, *The Unknown Tour de France: The Many Faces of the World's Biggest Bicycle Race*, pp. 11, 12.

2. "Mailmen on Bikes Run the Gauntlet," *New York Times*, 8 Sept. 1957, p. 126.

1958 1. Fotheringham, William, *Put Me Back On My Bike: In Search of Tom Simpson*, p. 142.

2. "White and Schwinn Sued," *New York Times*, 1 July 1958, p. 45.

3. "Jet Bicycle Rider Blasted Off," *New York Times* (Reuters), 11 May 1958, p. 29.

1959 1. "Pope Receives Cyclists," *New York Times*, 25 Jan. 1959, p. S4.

1960 1. Ollivier, Jean-Paul, *Fausto Coppi: The True Story*, p. 60.

2. Jew, Brian, "Coppi Murdered?" *VeloNews*, pp. 7, 74.

3. Daley, Robert, "Survival of the Fastest," *New York Times*, 30 Aug. 1960, p. 33.

4. Nye, Peter, *Hearts of Lions: The Story of American Bicycle Racing*, p. 216.

1961 1. Vanwalleghem, Rik, *Eddy Merckx: The Greatest Cyclist of the 20th Century*, p. 91.

1962 1. Berto, Frank; Henry, Raymond; Shepherd, Ron; *The Dancing Chain: History and Development of the Derailleur Bicycle*, pp. 178, 200.

2. Farnsworth, Clyde H., "Big Wheels Pedaling Little Wheels on Bicycle Built for Agility," *New York Times*, 30 Aug. 1964, p. 25.

1963 1. Watiez, Laurent, "Rik Van Looy; Anthology 1963–1970," *Day of Glory or Day of Pain: The Choice of Twenty Great Champions*, pp. 25, 26.

1964 1. Berto, Frank; Henry, Raymond; Shepherd, Ron, *The Dancing Chain: History and Development of the Derailleur Bicycle*, p. 190.

2. Devlin, John C., "150 Cycle to Fair in Rules Protest," *New York Times*, 18 May 1964, p. 32.

1965 1. Farnsworth, Clyde H., "Sales of Small-Wheel Bicycles Gain in Britain," *New York Times*, 4 Oct. 1965, p. supplement 7-2.

1966 1. "Tour de France to Become International Cycling Event," *New York Times*, 18 Aug. 1966, p. 42.

2. "Bicycle Rentals Soar As Result of the Strike," *New York Times*, 2 Jan. 1966, p. 58.

1967 1. Shanahan, Eileen, "High Court Cites Dealership Curbs," *New York Times*, 13 June 1967, p. 84.

2. "Summary of Actions Taken by the Supreme Court," *New York Times*, 13 June 1967, p. 32.

3. Salisbury, Harrison E., "North Vietnam Runs on Bicycles," *New York Times*, 7 Jan. 1967, p. 1.

4. Woodland, Les, ed., *The Yellow Jersey Companion to the Tour de France*, p. 360.

1968 1. "Officers to Be Given Bicycles to Patrol the Decks of a Supertanker," *New York Times*, 16 June 1968, p. 70.

1969 1. Vanwalleghem, Rik, *Eddy Merckx: The Greatest Cyclist of the 20th Century*, pp. 77, 112–13.

1970 1. "Vietcong Attack Delays Bicycle Race for Three Hours." *New York Times*, 22 Jan. 1970, p. 4.

1971 1. Vanwalleghem, p. 176.

2. Nye, Peter, *Hearts of Lions: The Story of American Bicycle Racing*, p. 244.

1972 1. Berto, Frank; Henry, Raymond; Shepherd, Ron; *The Dancing Chain: History and Development of the Derailleur Bicycle*, p. 194.
  2. "Deere Returns to Bikes," *New York Times* (AP), 16 Aug. 1972, p. 49.
  3. "Bicycle Lock Foils Thieves," *New York Times* (UPI), 2 May 1972, p. 24.
  4. Vanwalleghem, p. 127.
  5. Ayres, Martin, *VeloNews*, Vol. 29, No. 20, 11 Dec. 2000, p. 35.
1973 1. Maertens, Freddy, *Fall From Grace*, pp. 41, 42.
  2. Nye, Peter, *The Cyclist's Sourcebook*, p. 165.
  3. Grubb, Jake, "World's Fastest Bicycle," *Popular Mechanics*, May 1974, p. 147.
  4. McWhirter, Norris, *Guinness Book of Sports Records, Winners & Champions* (Bantam, 1981), p. 81.
  5. Derven, John, "Teledyne Titan," *Bicycle Guide*, Dec. 1989, pp. 54–59. Also see, Sloane, Eugene A., "Exotic Materials Make Easy-Going, Superlight Bike Frames," *Popular Mechanics*, March, 1975, pp. 107, 152.
1975 1. Hand, A.J., "Super Strong Graphite," *Popular Science*, April 1975, pp. 73–74.
  2. "Bike Enthusiasts Get Lift," *New York Times* (AP), 6 Sept. 1975, p. 22.
  3. Gerheart, Bob, "16 Years Ago in Bicycling," *Bicycling*, Dec. 1991, p. 23.
1976 1. Nye, Peter, *Hearts of Lions: The Story of American Bicycle Racing*, p. 243.
  2. McWhirter, p. 81.
  3. Berto, Frank, *The Birth of Dirt: Origins of Mountain Biking*, p. 41.
1977 1. Nye, Peter, *Hearts of Lions*, p. 251.
1978 1. Vanwalleghem, Rik, *Eddy Merckx: The Greatest Cyclist of the 20th Century*, p. 201.
  2. Vanwalleghem, p. 176.
  3. Abt, Samuel, *Breakaway: On the Road with the Tour de France*, p. 106.
  4. Vanwalleghem, p. 113.
  5. Brunel, Philippe, *An Intimate Portrait of the Tour de France*, p. 109.
  6. "James Tuite's Notebook; Werblin's Eye Lingers on Garden State Track," *New York Times*, 10 Jan. 1978, p. 41.
  7. Berto, Frank; e-mail to author, April 28, 2004.
1979 1. Attley, Marilee, "Vive le Greg." *Bicycle Racing in the Modern Era*, p. 54.
  2. Berto, Frank; Henry, Raymond; Shepherd, Ron; *The Dancing Chain: History and Development of the Derailleur Bicycle*, p. 240.
1980 1. Blumenthal, Tim, "A Time of Innocence," *Bicycling*, Feb. 1995, p. 112.
  2. Corrigan, Ed, "No Gold for Heiden in Bike Race," *New York Times*, 26 May 1980, p. C8.
1981 1. Berto, et. al., *The Dancing Chain*, p. 252.
  2. Amdur, Neil, "Legacy of Bob Cook, Cyclist: There Are Mountains to Move," *New York Times*, 23 Mar. 1981, p. C1.
1982 1. LeMond, Greg and Gordis, Kent, *Greg LeMond's Complete Book of Bicycling*, p. 29.
  2. Maso, Benjo, *The Sweat of the Gods*, p.119.
  3. Maertens, Freddy with Adrians, Manu, *Fall From Grace*, p. 130.
  4. "Sports People; Breaking Away," *New York Times*, 15 Aug. 1982, p. S6.
  5. DeCrosta, Tracy, ed., "The Open Road: The Comeback Kid," *Bicycling*, May 1982, p. 13.
  6. "The Open Road: High Crime," *Bicycling*, Aug. 1982, p. 144.
1983 1. LeMond, Greg, and Gordis, Kent, *Greg LeMond's Complete Book of Bicycling*, p. 32.
1984 1. Abt, Samuel, *Breakaway: On the Road With the Tour de France*, p. 68.
  2. Abt, Samuel, *Off to the Races*, pp. 28, 29.
  3. Wilcockson, John, "Between Extremes," *VeloNews*, 7 Apr. 2008, p. 96.
  4. "US Skil Team Canceled," *Winning: Bicycle Racing Illustrated*, March 1985, p. 67.

1985 1. "Cycle Group Bans Use of Blood Doping," *New York Times* (AP), 19 Jan. 1985, p. 29.

2. Abt, Samuel, *Breakaway: On the Road with the Tour de France*, p. 160.

3. "People and Places: Klein Frames Win Patent After Ten-year Fight," *Bicycling*, June 1985, p. 13.

1987 1. Brunel, Philippe, *An Intimate Portrait of the Tour de France*, p. 71.

2. "Tour Winners: Lucien Aimar," *Cycle Sport*, October 2003, p. 76.

3. "Dropouts," *Bicycling*, Feb. 1988, p. 20.

1988 1. Abt, Samuel, *In High Gear: The World of Professional Bicycle Racing*, p. 133.

1989 1. Abt, Samuel, *A Season in Turmoil*, p. 151.

2. Martin, Scott (ed.), "Paceline," *Bicycling*, July 1989, p. 22.

3. Greenhouse, Steven, "Schwinn Is Building Bikes The U.S. Way in Hungary," *New York Times*, 22 Mar. 1990, p. D1.

4. "Dropouts," *Bicycling*, Dec. 1989, p. 21.

5. "The Tour Win That Almost Wasn't," *Bicyclist*, July 1998, p. 10.

1990 1. Anderson, Susan Heller, "Chronicle," *New York Times*, 15 Sept. 1990, p. 24.

1992 1. Strickland, Bill, ed., "Paceline; Paper Dreams," *Bicycling*, Apr. 1992, p. 21.

2. Cuerdon, Don, "Worksman Pizza Bike," *Bicycling*, Dec. 1992, p. 79.

3. Strickland, Bill, ed., "Paceline," *Bicycling*, Nov. 1992, p. 22.

1993 1. *VeloNews* 26 Mar. 2007, p. 10.

2. Stead, Deborah, "Off the Shelf; Why the Wheels Stopped Turning," *New York Times*, 6 Oct. 1996, p. F8.

3. Strickland, Bill, ed., "Paceline," *Bicycling*, Jan, 1994, p. 16.

1994 1. Abt, p. 163.

2. Pelkey, Charles, "Festina Trial." *VeloNews*, 11 December 2000, p. 78.

1995 1. Zukowski, Stan, "Bike Shorts," *Bicycling*, June 1996, p. 36.

2. Neugent, John, quoted in Frank Berto, *The Dancing Chain*, 2nd ed., p. 318.

1996 1. Brice, Arthur, "Bike Shorts," *Bicycling*, March 1997, p. 25.

2. Woodland, Les, ed., *The Yellow Jersey Companion to the Tour de France*, p. 81.

3. http://www.acor.org/TCRC/16.html

1997 1. "Sports People; Armstrong is Training," *New York Times* (AP), 11 Jan. 1997, p. 36.

2. "Sports People; Ready for Comeback, Armstrong Seeks Team," *New York Times*, 5 Sept. 1997, p. B14.

1999 1. "Company News; Huffy to Stop Making Bicycles in United States," *New York Times*, 28 Sept. 1999, p. C4.

2. *Cyclesport*, November 1999, pp. 10, 11.

3. "1999," *VeloNews* 26 Mar 2007, p. 70.

2000 1. Wilcockson, John, "Gino Bartali (1914–2000); The Man of Iron," *VeloNews*, 29 May 2000, p.6.

2. "Velonotes; Performance Buys Nashbar," *VeloNews*, 29 May 2000, pp.88-9.

2001 1. VeloNotes, *VeloNews*, 7 May 2001, p. 7.

2. CNN, 8 November 2001.

2002 1. Associated Press, 18 June 2002.

2. "The Active Life, With a Digital Assist," *New York Times*, 21 Nov. 2002, p. G3.

2006 1. Mitchell, Dan, "Are Cyclists Destroying the Earth?" *New York Times*, 22 July 2006, p. C5

2009 1. Startt, James, "Fignon Wonders if Drug Use Caused Cancer," www.bicycling.com, 14 June 2009.